Bedford Cultural Editions

WILLIAM WELLS BROWN

Clotel;
or,
The President's Daughter:
A Narrative of Slave Life
in the United States

D0711852

Bedford Cultural Editions

SERIES EDITORS: J. Paul Hunter, *University of Virginia*, and William E. Cain, *Wellesley College*

Aphra Behn, *Oroonoko*
EDITED BY Catherine Gallagher, University of California, Berkeley

William Wells Brown, *Clotel*, Second Edition
EDITED BY Robert S. Levine, University of Maryland

Frances Burney, *Evelina*
EDITED BY Kristina Straub, Carnegie Mellon University

Charles Chesnutt, *The Marrow of Tradition*
EDITED BY Nancy Bentley, University of Pennsylvania,
and Sandra Gunning, University of Michigan

The Commerce of Everyday Life: Selections from The Tatler *and*
The Spectator
EDITED BY Erin Mackie, Princeton University

Stephen Crane, *Maggie, a Girl of the Streets*
EDITED BY Kevin J. Hayes, University of Central Oklahoma

Rebecca Harding Davis, *Life in the Iron-Mills*
EDITED BY Cecelia Tichi, Vanderbilt University

Charlotte Perkins Gilman, *The Yellow Wallpaper*
EDITED BY Dale M. Bauer, University of Illinois at Urbana-Champaign

Nathaniel Hawthorne, *The Blithedale Romance*
EDITED BY William E. Cain, Wellesley College

Alexander Pope, *The Rape of the Lock*
EDITED BY Cynthia Wall, University of Virginia

Reading the West: An Anthology of Dime Westerns
EDITED BY Bill Brown, University of Chicago

Bedford Cultural Editions

WILLIAM WELLS BROWN

Clotel;
or,
The President's Daughter:
A Narrative of Slave Life
in the United States

SECOND EDITION

EDITED BY

Robert S. Levine
University of Maryland

BEDFORD/ST. MARTIN'S   BOSTON • NEW YORK

For Bedford/St. Martin's

Senior Executive Editor: Stephen A. Scipione
Editorial Assistant: Kate Mayhew
Production Associate: Ashley Chalmers
Marketing Manager: Adrienne Petsick
Cover Art: Detail from *The Death of Clotel*, an original illustration from the 1853 edition of the novel.
Cover Design: Andrea M. Corbin
Project Management: DeMasi Design and Publishing Services
Composition: Jeff Miller Book Design
Printing and Binding: Haddon Craftsmen, Inc., an RR Donnelley & Sons Company

President: Joan E. Feinberg
Editorial Director: Denise B. Wydra
Editor in Chief: Karen S. Henry
Director of Marketing: Karen R. Soeltz
Director of Production: Susan W. Brown
Associate Director, Editorial Production: Elise S. Kaiser
Manager, Publishing Services: Andrea Cava

Library of Congress Control Number: 2010934492

Manufactured in the United States of America.

For information, write: Bedford/St. Martin's, 75 Arlington Street, Boston, MA 02116   (617-399-4000)

ISBN-13: 978-0-312-62107-0

Published and distributed outside North America by:
PALGRAVE MACMILLAN
Houndmills, Basingstoke, Hampshire RG21 6XS
Companies and representatives throughout the world.
ISBN-13: 978-0-230-33364-2
ISBN-10: 978-230-33364-8

A catalogue record for this book is available from the British Library.

About the Series

The need to "historicize" literary texts — and even more to analyze the historical and cultural issues all texts embody — is now embraced by almost all teachers, scholars, critics, and theoreticians. But the question of how to teach such issues in the undergraduate classroom is still a difficult one. Teachers do not always have the historical information they need for a given text, and contextual documents and sources are not always readily available in the library — even if the teacher has the expertise (and students have the energy) to ferret them out. The Bedford Cultural Editions represent an effort to make available for the classroom the kinds of facts and documents that will enable teachers to use the latest historical approaches to textual analysis and cultural criticism. The best scholarly and theoretical work has for many years gone well beyond the "new critical" practices of formalist analysis and close reading, and we offer here a practical classroom model of the ways that many different kinds of issues can be engaged when texts are not thought of as islands unto themselves.

The impetus for the recent cultural and historical emphasis has come from many directions: the so-called new historicism of the late 1980s, the dominant historical versions of both feminism and Marxism, the cultural studies movement, and a sharply changed focus in older movements such as reader response, structuralism, deconstruction, and psychoanalytic theory. Emphases differ, of course, among schools and individuals, but what these movements and approaches have in common is a commitment to explore — and to have students in the classroom study interactively — texts in their full historical and cultural dimensions. The aim is to discover how older texts (and those from other traditions) differ from our own assumptions and expectations, and thus the focus in teaching falls on cultural and historical difference rather than on similarity or continuity.

The most striking feature of the Bedford Cultural Editions — and the one most likely to promote creative classroom discussion — is the inclusion of a generous selection of historical documents that contextualize the main text in a variety of ways. Each volume contains works (or passages from works) that are contemporary with the main text: legal and social documents, journalistic and autobiographical accounts, histories, sections from conduct books, travel books, poems, novels, and other historical sources. These materials have several uses. Often they provide information beyond what the main text offers. They provide, too, different perspectives on a particular theme, issue, or event central to the text, suggesting the range of opinions contemporary readers would have brought to their reading and allowing students to experience for themselves the details of cultural disagreement and debate. The documents are organized in thematic units — each with an introduction by the volume editor that historicizes a particular issue and suggests the ways in which individual selections work to contextualize the main text.

Each volume also contains a general introduction that provides students with information concerning the political, social, and intellectual context for the work as well as information concerning the material aspects of the text's creation, production, and distribution. There are also relevant illustrations, a chronology of important events, and, when helpful, an account of the reception history of the text. Finally, both the main work and its accompanying documents are carefully annotated in order to enable students to grasp the significance of historical references, literary allusions, and unfamiliar terms. Everywhere we have tried to keep the special needs of the modern student — especially the culturally conscious student of the turn of the millennium — in mind.

For each title, the volume editor has chosen the best teaching text of the main work and explained his or her choice. Old spellings and capitalizations have been preserved (except that the long "s" has been regularized to the modern "s") — the overwhelming preference of the two hundred teacher-scholars we surveyed in preparing the series. Original habits of punctuation have also been kept, except for occasional places where the unusual usage would obscure the syntax for modern readers. Whenever possible, the supplementary texts and documents are reprinted from the first edition or the one most relevant to the issue at hand. We have thus meant to preserve — rather than counter — for modern students the sense of "strangeness" in older texts, expecting that the oddness will help students to see where older texts are not like modern ones, and expecting too that today's historically informed teachers will find their own creative ways to make something of such historical and cultural differences.

In developing this series, our goal has been to foreground the kinds of issues that typically engage teachers and students of literature and history now. We have not tried to move readers toward a particular ideological, political, or social position or to be exhaustive in our choice of contextual materials. Rather, our aim has been to be provocative — to enable teachers and students of literature to raise the most pressing political, economic, social, religious, intellectual, and artistic issues on a larger field than any single text can offer.

J. Paul Hunter, University of Virginia
William E. Cain, Wellesley College
Series Editors

About This Volume

Over the last several decades, William Wells Brown's *Clotel; or, The President's Daughter* has come to achieve canonical status as the first published novel by an African American. Although there is little dispute about *Clotel*'s importance to African American and U.S. literary history, the novel remains a difficult, elusive work for many readers. One problem is that Brown assumes an antebellum readership immersed in debates on slavery and race. He does not simply allude to influential texts on these subjects; at times he quotes from them verbatim and at great length. Is Brown a plagiarist? Or are there more complex ways of understanding his authorial strategies and perspectives? This edition is grounded on the assumptions that *Clotel* is an immensely important literary achievement, and that to appreciate Brown's artistry in the novel it is essential to have some knowledge of the cultural issues and texts that he engages. A principal aim of this Cultural Edition, then, is to help readers become conversant with a wide range of those issues and texts.

At the same time, this edition aspires to help readers think about *Clotel* not just in relation to its specific antebellum cultural moment but also in relation to the nation's ongoing conversations on race and slavery. Specifically, it situates the novel in relation to these larger issues by providing materials on the "President" and his "daughter." *Clotel* was inspired in part by rumors, in circulation since 1802, that Thomas Jefferson had had sexual relations and children with at least one of his slaves. As elaborated more fully in the Introduction, these rumors had a basis in Jefferson's actual behavior. As Brown well knew, Jefferson the slaveholder was the very embodiment of the contradictory fact that a nation ideologically committed to principles of freedom and equality was also a nation in which slavery was the law of the land. Jefferson's actions as a slaveholder continue to engage the attention of professional historian and layperson alike, for much remains at stake in assessing the legacy of the principal author of the Declaration of Independence. *Clotel*'s bold confrontation with that legacy is one of many aspects of the novel that helps to give it a continued power and relevance in African American and U.S. literary and cultural studies.

The documents and annotations in this edition are intended to help readers situate *Clotel* in its time, the decade of the 1850s, and also to think about the novel's continued pertinence to debates in the United States on race, gender, and slavery's myriad legacies. Brown's novel emerged in response to historically specific cultural problems and literary challenges, but it remains a vital and even prophetic meditation on Jefferson's contradictory legacy of slavery and freedom and on African Americans' heroic efforts to challenge and revise that legacy.

NEW TO THE SECOND EDITION

The last decade has seen an upsurge of scholarly interest in William Wells Brown, along with important new work on Thomas Jefferson and Sally Hemings. This revised edition of *Clotel* draws on that recent scholarship and offers an enhanced focus on matters both historical and aesthetic. The introduction has been updated, and a number of documents are new to Part Two, which has now been reorganized into four sections. The first two sections focus on Thomas Jefferson, both as the author of the Declaration of Independence and as the father of slaves. The third provides eleven of the principal "source" materials of the novel, thus allowing readers to address the fascinating issue of Brown's use of those sources. The materials in the final section help to illuminate how Brown wrote and then revised his first novel.

ACKNOWLEDGMENTS

I did the bulk of my research on the first edition at the Library of Congress and am pleased to acknowledge the assistance of its expert staff. I am also grateful to librarians at the Boston Athenæum, the

Schomburg Center for Research in Black Culture at the New York Public Library, and the University of Maryland's Interlibrary Loan Office.

My continued thanks go to William Cain for initially entertaining my proposal to do a Cultural Edition of *Clotel* and for remaining a hands-on and committed editor during the several years that I worked on the first edition. At Bedford/St. Martin's, I am pleased to thank Chuck Christensen, Joan Feinberg, and Steve Scipione for their continued support and encouragement over the years. For their work producing the first edition, I remain grateful to Emily Berleth at Bedford/St. Martin's and Leslie Connor and the staff at Stratford Publishing Services; for the production of the second edition, I thank Elise Kaiser at Bedford, and Linda DeMasi of DeMasi Design and Publishing Services. Thanks to Katherine Gilbert and Nicole Simonsen, who assisted with numerous details on the first edition, and to Kate Mayhew, who provided invaluable assistance on the second.

I was particularly fortunate in Bedford's choice of project referees on the first edition. For their cogent readings of the draft of the manuscript, I am indebted to Leonard Cassuto, Russ Castronovo, John Ernest, Dana Nelson, and Karen Sánchez-Eppler. I owe a special debt of thanks to John Ernest for having led me to William C. Nell's 1851 *Services of Colored Americans*, and to Leonard Cassuto for his careful line-by-line editorial suggestions. For their help along the way with various aspects of the first edition, I wish also to thank Jonathan Auerbach, Allan Austin, Vincent Carretta, Neil Fraistat, Ivy Goodman, Ezra Greenspan, Patricia Herron, Carla Peterson, Kenneth Price, and Martha Nell Smith.

For their helpful suggestions on the second edition, I am indebted to Brown scholar Ezra Greenspan, and, yet again, to John Ernest. I also profited from the insights of Dawn Coleman, Kenneth Florey, Ivy Goodman, Kirsten Gruesz, Kenneth Price, Beth Lueck, Eliza Richards, Xiomara Santamarina, and Edlie Wong.

Above all, I remain grateful for the work my indefatigable and brilliant editor, Kathy Retan, performed on the first edition. Kathy is the sort of editor who supposedly vanished from the publishing landscape long ago. She still has my sincere thanks for helping me to shape the first edition into as good and as useful a volume as possible. This second edition would be unimaginable without her stellar contributions to the first.

Robert S. Levine
University of Maryland

Contents

Illustrations

Part One

Clotel;
or,
The President's Daughter
The Complete Text

Introduction:
Cultural and
Historical Background

I know that upon the 4th of July, our 4th of July orators talk of Liberty, Democracy, and Republicanism. They talk of liberty, while three millions of their own countrymen are groaning in abject Slavery. This is called the "land of the free, and the home of the brave;" it is called the "Asylum of the oppressed;" and some have been foolish enough to call it the "Cradle of Liberty." If it is the "cradle of liberty," they have rocked the child to death.

—William Wells Brown, *A Lecture Delivered before the Female Anti-Slavery Society of Salem* (1847)

William Wells Brown's *Clotel; or, The President's Daughter: A Narrative of Slave Life in the United States* is a landmark work, the first novel by an African American. Published in 1853 in London, *Clotel* appeared at a time when Brown, an escaped slave, was still legally regarded as property within the borders of the United States. (His British admirers would purchase his free papers in 1854.) Purporting to tell the stories of Thomas Jefferson's slave mistress, daughters, and granddaughters, *Clotel* "talks back" to U.S. culture, providing a brilliantly ironic challenge to the nation's patriotic narratives, particularly those that celebrate Thomas Jefferson's America as a nation of freedom and equality for all. Brown accomplishes his goals of social critique not only by providing his readers with what he suggests is a secret history of Jefferson's black paramour and descendants but also by appropriating and working transformations on numerous texts published

3

between 1780 and 1853. Those texts include a short story by Lydia Maria Child, factual accounts from abolitionist books and journals, a speech by Andrew Jackson, debates in Congress, slave narratives, earlier writings by Brown, and poems and essays on Jefferson's alleged sexual relationship with his slave Sally Hemings. The critic John Ernest has usefully termed Brown's authorial work in *Clotel* as that of a "cultural editor" (23)—a writer and compiler who presses his readers to rethink their assumptions about race, gender, and slavery by teaching them how they might better read cultural texts and scripts. And yet, as Ernest allows, there are limits to the effectiveness of Brown's narrative strategies, for the fact is that most of his readers, both then and now, "have never seen the sources themselves" (24). This Cultural Edition of *Clotel* seeks to rectify that situation, providing readers with Brown's most important acknowledged sources along with a number of cultural texts that help to put those sources, and the novel itself, into a fuller political, ideological, and literary context.

In the final chapter of *Clotel*, Brown declares that he created his novel by drawing on his personal experiences and wide reading, which he then "combined" into the narrative that "made up my story" (p. 226 in this volume). Brown's comments on his sources suggest the importance of considering his textual appropriations in relation to his career as a former slave who had risen to become a noted abolitionist, reformer, and man of letters. His comments also suggest that he liked to make up stories; in fact, he liked storytelling so much that he told different stories about his own life history in his various autobiographical writings, asserting in some places that he was the grandson of Daniel Boone, describing in others how he unwittingly participated in the power structure of slavery, and detailing in still others his subversive relation to the slave owners. A deadly serious moralist, Brown was also something of a confidence man and trickster whose views on such explosive subjects as race and gender can be difficult to pin down. An artist who challenges the culture's "official" stories, Brown can seem to be suspicious of any kind of coherent or definitive narrative.

But there are certain facts we can state about Brown's life history with relative assurance. The author of over fifteen books and one of the most renowned antislavery lecturers and reformers of the time, Brown was born a slave on a plantation near Lexington, Kentucky, most likely in 1814, the son of a white man and a slave named Elizabeth. As a boy he spent several years in the Missouri territory, and by 1827 he was living in St. Louis with his master, Dr. John Young. After working a variety of jobs, ranging from house servant to assistant to a slave trader, Brown, accompanied by his mother, attempted to escape from slavery in 1833. Captured in Illinois, he was returned to Young and eventually sold to Enoch Price, a St. Louis merchant and steamboat owner. In 1834 Brown made a second escape attempt, this time by himself, and with the help of the Quaker Wells Brown, whose name he subsequently adopted, he successfully made his way to Cleveland, Ohio. Shortly thereafter, he married the free black Elizabeth Schooner, and over the next nine years worked on a steamboat in Lake Erie, regularly helping slaves to escape on the underground railroad. In 1836, after moving to Buffalo, New York, he initiated his career as a reformer, organizing and later serving as president of a black temperance society while continuing his antislavery activities.

Brown began lecturing for the Western New York Anti-Slavery Society in 1843; his reputation as a speaker and reformer grew, and he lectured for several other organizations as well. In 1847 he moved to Boston and commenced working as a paid lecturer for William Lloyd Garrison's Massachusetts Anti-Slavery Society. That same year he published his *Narrative of William W. Brown*, which rivaled Frederick Douglass's 1845 *Narrative* for popularity and consequently made him, as had been true for Douglass, vulnerable to fugitive-slave catchers. Estranged from his wife, Brown traveled to Paris to attend the 1849 International Peace Congress, and after touring Great Britain as an antislavery lecturer, he decided to remain in England when he learned that the U.S. Congress had passed the Fugitive Slave Law in 1850. Thus, when Brown published the first African American novel in 1853, it appeared not in the United States but in England.

Though *Clotel* was Brown's first novel, by 1853 he had published, in addition to his *Narrative*, *A Lecture Delivered before the Female Anti-Slavery Society of Salem* (1847), an edition of antislavery songs (1848), a catalogue description of antislavery drawings (1850), and a travel book, *Three Years in Europe* (1852). He would go on to publish three significantly revised versions of *Clotel*, two major histories of blacks in the United States, a play, several memoirs, and some of his most famous speeches. Like Frederick Douglass, who had escaped from slavery in 1838, Brown regarded social reform and writing as significant ways of forwarding the cause of antislavery and antiracism in the United States. He presented himself, as Douglass did (and as Benjamin Banneker did in his famous letter to Thomas Jefferson; see pp. 252–55), as living proof, against the claims of proslavery and racist ideology, of an African American's ability to become a learned man of letters.

KIDNAPPING TEXTS

Central to Brown's authorial labors, indeed to his emergence as a man of letters, was his practice of using and reusing textual materials (including his own) that were already circulating in the culture. *Clotel*'s prefatory third-person "Narrative of the Life and Escape of William Wells Brown," for example, draws abundantly from Brown's first-person *Narrative* (1847). But what are we to make of the fact that in *Clotel* itself Brown takes whole passages, sometimes pages and pages of other peoples' writings, and uses those words and paragraphs and pages in his own novel? Some readers (perhaps students asked to write essays on *Clotel*) might well wonder whether Brown was simply a plagiarist. Although it would be anachronistic to accuse Brown of plagiarism in our sense of the term (the nineteenth century had very different notions of copyright and literary ownership, though the modern notion of individual rights to literary property was beginning to emerge), it nonetheless *is* useful to think of Brown as a kind of plagiarist. Stephen Rachman notes that plagiarism can be regarded as a form of literary trickery that "has its roots in *plagiarus*, Latin for 'a kidnapper, a seducer,' as well as a literary thief" (52). According to the *Oxford English Dictionary*, "plagiary" also refers to "one who abducts the child or slave of another." By that definition, the abolitionists who attempted to help the slaves escape from the slave catchers unleashed by the Fugitive Slave Law of 1850 (which legally required all U.S. citizens to return escaped slaves to their masters) could be understood metaphorically as types of plagiarists. And yet if we were to put the interpretive emphasis on theft and kidnapping, we could regard the slave masters themselves as "plagiarists," and Brown's taking of texts as a kind of kidnapping and trickery characteristic of a liberator; he steals the texts of a culture that steals black bodies. Writing *Clotel* in the wake of the Fugitive Slave Law's edict to return escaped blacks to their "proper" place on the southern plantation, Brown attempts to liberate a variety of texts by placing them in "improper" relation within his revisionary narrative. In doing so, Brown presses his readers to raise questions about the arbitrariness and morality of the existing arrangements of the social order.

According to a scholar of nineteenth-century debates on plagiarism, "the plagiarist disrupts the field of significations that the law sets in place, disrupting claims of legitimacy and natural authority" (Weinauer 700). Such disruption can occur when marginalized subjects, who have little access to the power structure, show how easy it is to appropriate, manipulate, and parody the language of the oppressors. Rather than simply using that language to uphold the power structure, the plagiarist in effect inhabits that language, getting inside it, so to speak, in order to explore and ultimately to reveal its cultural uses and abuses. A black author's intelligent mimicry of the proslavery rhetoric that insists upon blacks' lack of intelligence, for example, works quite powerfully to reveal the bankruptcy of such rhetoric, and thus the ways in which that rhetoric serves the ends of racist white enslavers. In *Clotel*, Brown again and again artfully inhabits and arranges various discourses and texts so as to suggest the limits of their truth-telling capacities, thereby undermining the narratives and texts of the dominant culture. At times the various "stolen" cultural texts seem to converse with one another; at other times, such as when we move from descriptions of black victimization to images of violent black rebellion, they seem to challenge or deconstruct one another. Parody, fragmentation, and oddly disruptive juxtapositions of ofttimes incompatible cultural discourses characterize Brown's narrative method in *Clotel*.

Ironically inhabiting and mimicking a hodgepodge of discourses (political, sentimental, reformist, and so on), *Clotel* can be read as a stunning example of literary pastiche—a technique of creating a literary work by borrowing from or imitating other works and styles. Unlike the plagiarist, the author of pastiche tends to be fairly open in acknowledging his or her textual sources, for without some acknowledgment, the point of the pastiche would be lost. In Brown's case, writing as he does from a marginalized minority position in U.S. culture, there is a powerful sociocritical dimension to his use of pastiche, for he generally wishes to subvert and transform the very discourses that he imports into his novel. By drawing on a variety of cultural discourses and texts, Brown also makes use of the (post)modernistic technique of bricolage, a close cousin to pastiche, which involves taking bits and pieces of writings (sometimes long pieces) and (re)assembling those "found" cultural materials into something new. The critic Ann duCille nicely describes the new fictive world created by Brown's techniques of pastiche and bricolage in *Clotel* as "an 'unreal estate,' a fictive realm of the fantastic and coincidental . . . an ideologically charged space, created by drawing together a variety of discursive fields—including 'the real' and 'the romantic,' the simple and the sensational, the allegorical and the historical" (18). Within the "unreal estate" of *Clotel*, Brown points to the gaps and blindnesses of much of the materials that he appropriates, with the large aim of helping his readers to see the culture more clearly.

As "cultural editor," Ernest writes, "Brown gathers the documents that reveal the national disunity—not the meaninglessness of the national text but its meaningful incoherence—and he constructs or reshapes his various narrative lines to instruct his readers to read beyond the text" (34; see also Loughran). The "meaningful incoherence" that Brown's work reveals is the paradoxical space of an antebellum culture that celebrates democratic freedom while upholding slavery. Brown's narrative method, then, in addressing large questions of slavery and freedom, presses the reader to "read beyond" the nation's founding documents, and thus to rethink the politics and deeds of the nation's Founding Fathers. In fact, among the cultural sources that find their way into *Clotel* are the Declaration of Independence and the histories and counterhistories of Thomas Jefferson's relationship with his slaves at Monticello, his estate in central Virginia, particularly the rumors circulated by abolitionists during the 1830s and 1840s about Jefferson's sexual relationship with his slave Sally Hemings (see Part Two, Chapter 2). Brown took from these abolitionist counterhistories in particular the informing donnée of his novel: that the Father of American Freedom was also the father of slaves. And he asks his readers to wrestle with the large question of what happens to U.S. narratives of progress and freedom when they are disrupted by such a historical contradiction.

AMERICAN GENEALOGIES: THOMAS JEFFERSON AND SALLY HEMINGS

In a lecture delivered at an August 1854 antislavery meeting in Manchester, England, Brown proclaimed: "No one can read . . . the declaration of the American independence, and compare that document with the history of the legislation of the federal government in the United States, without being struck with the marked inconsistency of the theory of the people and their acts; the one declaring that all men are created equally, endowed by their Creator with certain inalienable rights, among which are life, liberty, and the pursuit of happiness, and the other is the history of the encroachment of slavery upon liberty, or legislation in favour of slavery in that country against the cause of freedom" (Ripley I:399). To a significant extent, that "inconsistency" first manifested itself at the 1787 Constitutional Convention, where the delegates entrusted with establishing the new government agreed to approve three key provisions on slavery: Article 1, section 2, which allowed the slave states to count slaves as three-fifths of a person when assessing taxation and congressional representation; Article 1, section 9, which stated that Congress could not interfere with the importation of slaves until 1808; and Article 4, section 2, which called for the return of fugitive slaves and thus set the groundwork for Congress's passage of the Fugitive Slave Law of 1793 and the later passage of the Compromise of 1850's infamous Fugitive Slave Law. What remains debatable is whether the delegates of the Constitutional Convention, in search of sectional compromise, had in fact violated the spirit of Jefferson's Declaration of Independence and the American Revolution itself. Northerners opposed to the compromises believed that there had been a violation, and it is no coincidence that nineteenth-century abolitionists would regularly point to that violation and its attendant contradictions by invoking the Revolutionary ideals encapsulated in the Declaration (see, for example, Frederick Douglass's famous speech, "What to the Slave Is the Fourth of July?" [pp. 267–72], and from Brown's *Lecture* [pp. 365–68] the passage that serves as the epigraph to this Introduction).

But given the racism of Jefferson and other Revolutionary leaders, an argument can be made that there had been no violation at all, and that in the emergent United States, slavery and freedom, as Brown and other antislavery writers would lament, went hand in hand. The historian David Brion Davis remarks, for example, that "the American Revolution freed southern slaveholders from various imperial restraints, opening the way for Indian removal and for a westward expansion of slavery that met no serious opposition until the rise of the Republican party in response to the Kansas-Nebraska Act of 1854" (273). And in his magisterial study of the first two centuries of slavery in North America, Ira Berlin comments on the perverse ways in which the Declaration worked to strengthen slaveholders' convictions of the moral soundness of the "peculiar institution," and thus to legitimate their efforts to make slavery the law of the land: "If indeed all men were created equal and some men were slaves—the argument ran—then, perhaps, those who remained in the degraded condition of slaves were not fully men after all. The implications of this twisted reading of the Declaration of Independence . . . would have a powerful influence on Americans, black and white" (224). But how "twisted" was this reading of the Declaration of Independence? That is one of the large questions that Brown addresses head-on in his novel about the president's daughters and granddaughters.

By deciding to use the most famous propositions of the Declaration of Independence as the epigraph to *Clotel*, Brown immediately calls attention to the disturbing fact that the nation of freedom, equality, and the pursuit of happiness is also the home of slavery. To Jefferson's credit, the epigraph also suggests why blacks and whites opposed to slavery and racial hierarchies in the United States would turn to the Declaration to justify both their quest for equality and their resistance to authoritarian power. In *Clotel*, the "heroic young slave" (p. 211) George Green proclaims that he participated in Nat Turner's bloody slave conspiracy of 1831 because he was inspired when he heard his "master read in the Declaration of Independence 'that all men are created free and equal'" (p. 212). Like the patriotic abolitionists whom Brown celebrates in his 1847 *Lecture* as occupying "a higher position, than those who put forth their Declaration in 1776, in behalf of American liberty" (96), George is a patriot in the Jeffersonian tradition who outshines even Jefferson. For as Brown reminds his readers in *Clotel*, the Founding Father who helped to give such powerful expression to American ideals of freedom was also a slaveholder who apparently saw no contradiction between his commitment to political equality and his status as a plantation master. Any effort to understand American genealogies of slavery and freedom, Brown suggests, must begin with that basic fact.

As is well known, among the nation's founders Jefferson was not alone in holding slaves. George Washington purchased and traded slaves while running his Mount Vernon estate in Virginia, and during the 1790s owned upwards of three hundred slaves, most of whom he freed at his death. James Madison and other notable Southern political leaders also owned slaves and had important roles in developing the constitutional compromises ensuring that slavery would remain part of the social and legal fabric of the new nation. Jefferson, however, stands as a particularly interesting case, for his views on slavery and on blacks appear to have wavered. In his draft version of the Declaration, Jefferson blamed the British for introducing the practice of slavery to America, and he called for its eventual abolition (pp. 235–42). During the 1780s, he proposed a gradual abolition program that would have ended the slave trade and prohibited slavery in the western territories, and he set a date around the year 1800 after which all children born of slaves would be regarded as free. In 1806, during his second term as president, he signed legislation ending the importation of slaves; and he regularly voiced his hopes that the spread of slavery would lead to its diffusion and demise. But despite views that in their time and place could be regarded as antislavery, Jefferson ran a fairly extensive slave plantation at Monticello, with approximately two hundred slaves, and from the 1790s until his death in 1826 blamed his substantial financial debts for making it impossible for him to end slavery at his own estate. Moreover, in response to the 1819–21 debates on the Missouri Compromise, which ultimately set territorial limits on the spread of slavery (until these limits were repealed by the 1854 Kansas-Nebraska Act), Jefferson's views on slavery hardened. Outraged by Congress's efforts to exclude slavery from Missouri and the unsettled territories to its west and north, Jefferson vociferously defended Southerners' rights to decide when and how to bring about the end of slavery on their own. The Compromise of 1820, which admitted Missouri as a slave state and Maine as a free state, while banning slavery from the remaining unorganized territory north of latitude 36° 30′, did little to assuage his discomfort with what he regarded as a Federalist conspiracy to limit the power of the Southern slave states.

Jefferson's *Notes on the State of Virginia* (1787) can be taken as a key to his contradictory thinking on slavery and race. In *Notes*'s chapters on slavery (pp. 242–51), Jefferson expresses an overall abhorrence of the institution, focusing in particular on how slavery corrupts the masters. His implicit argument is that slavery goes against the grain of the Enlightenment political philosophy that encouraged the colonists to challenge England's authoritarianism in the first place. In an eerie and prescient anticipation of Herman Melville's novella of slave revolt, "Benito Cereno" (1855), he imagines the slaves as so angry about their mistreatment, and so hateful toward their white enslavers, that their primary desire is to wage an apocalyptic war of vengeance against the masters. And yet even as Jefferson's imaginings of a bloody race war imply that he understands blacks' all too human resistance to their degradation, he presents the specter of such a war as evidence not for blacks' humanity but rather for the political "fact" that blacks and whites can never live together in the United States. By the 1820s he would come to support the efforts of the American Colonization Society to ship the free blacks to Africa.

Repressing his cross-racial identification with vengeful black rebels, Jefferson in *Notes* presents blacks as physically, morally, and mentally inferior to whites. In this way he anticipated, and even helped to give rise to, the "scientific" racialist writings of the 1840s and 1850s, by Samuel Morton and many others, that insisted on the "objective" fact of black inferiority and difference (see Nelson); those writings served as an intellectual foundation for white supremacist thinking and emerged

as a crucial discursive and ideological force in the culture against which
Brown and other antebellum black writers had to do battle. Though
Jefferson was aware that it was difficult for free blacks to acquire an
education, and virtually impossible for slaves to do so, he proclaimed
in an 1814 letter to his friend Edward Coles that blacks are "as incapable as children of taking care of themselves, and are extinguished
promptly wherever industry is necessary for raising young. In the mean
time they are pests in a society by their idleness, and the depredations
to which this leads them" (*Writings* 1345). According to Jefferson,
blacks' apparent inability to rise in white society revealed not their
lack of training or experience (or the barriers erected by white racists)
but their essential inferiority. In his letter to Coles he worries over the
possibility of "black" blood contaminating "white" blood, asserting
that blacks' "amalgamation with the other color produces a degradation to which no lover of his country, no lover of excellence in the human
character can innocently consent" (*Writings* 1345). Quite understand-
ably, one historian refers to Jefferson as "the intellectual godfather of
the racist pseudo-science of the American school of anthropology"
(Finkelman 186).

But even as Jefferson was going on record in *Notes* with his statements on blacks' mental and physical inferiority, he apparently was
struck by the beauty (and intelligence) of one of his slaves, Sally Hemings, and arguably was himself guilty of the very "crimes" against
race and the nation that he later anxiously contemplated in his letter
to Coles. Hemings accompanied Jefferson's nine-year-old daughter
Mary to Paris in 1787, where Jefferson was serving as U.S. minister to
France. Jefferson had assumed that position in 1785, three years after
the death of his wife, Martha, and he had summoned Mary and Sally
to Paris shortly after his daughter Lucy had died at Monticello. At the
time, Jefferson was forty-four and Hemings was fourteen. To a significant extent, the light-skinned Sally was somewhat like family, for in
1773, shortly before he began working on his draft of the Declaration,
Jefferson had inherited her mother, Betty Hemings, and ten of Betty's
twelve children, from his father-in-law, John Wayles, who was in all
likelihood the father of six of those children. Sally Hemings would
therefore have been the half sister of Jefferson's wife and may have
borne a physical resemblance to her. Hemings remained with Jefferson
in Paris for twenty-six months, returning with him to Monticello in
1789 and giving birth to their first child in 1790. The evidence suggests Jefferson and Hemings had seven children together, four of whom
survived into adulthood (see Gordon-Reed, *Hemingses*). All were so

light-complected that they were often mistaken for whites. Most in the area assumed that the father was someone other than Jefferson, perhaps Samuel or Peter Carr, the rakish sons of Jefferson's sister, though the evidence showed that Jefferson, who traveled frequently, was at Monticello nine months before each of the births.

"Amalgamation" thus had an important place in the Jefferson-Wayles family history, and there was ample evidence in the bodies of the light-skinned Hemings slaves at Monticello that amalgamation remained part of the family history. Rumors about Jefferson's possible sexual relationship with Sally Hemings were first publicly circulated in 1802 by James Callender, an alcoholic journalist angered by Jefferson's refusal to appoint him postmaster of Richmond, Virginia. Callender attempted to damage Jefferson's reputation in crudely racist fashion, fully aware that perhaps the worst thing he could say about a white leader was that he had had sexual relations with a black slave woman. Callender declared in the 1 September 1802 issue of the Richmond *Recorder*: "It is well known that the man, *whom it delighteth the people to honor*, keeps, and for many years has kept, as his concubine, one of his own slaves. Her name is SALLY . . . By this wench Sally, our president has had several children" (pp. 276–77). Following up on his accusations in the 22 September 1802 issue of the *Recorder*, Callender charged Jefferson not only with sexual immorality but also with having committed egregious crimes against the state and the nation: "Put the case that every white man in Virginia had done as much as Thomas Jefferson has done towards the utter destruction of its happiness, that eighty thousand white men had; each of them, been the father of five mulatto children. Thus you have FOUR HUNDRED THOUSAND MULATTOES in addition to the present swarm. The country would be no longer habitable, till after a civil war, and a series of massacres" (2). The controversy over Jefferson's possible relationship with Hemings continued for several months, but abruptly came to an end when Callender drowned in the James River, apparently when attempting to bathe while drunk. Jefferson won his 1804 reelection by a landslide.

Because Callender's charges emerged from a highly partisan perspective, they were not taken very seriously in their own time (and were dismissed, until recently, by most twentieth-century historians). But rumors persisted about Jefferson's sexual relationships with one or more of his female slaves, and during the 1830s the charges were revived and echoed not by other proslavery and racist writers like Callender, but by antislavery British and American writers (see the examples in Part Two, Chapter 2). With the upsurge of abolitionist activity and writings during the 1830s, spawned in part by William Lloyd Garrison's 1831 founding of the abolitionist newspaper the *Liberator*, there was suddenly such a proliferation of texts asserting Jefferson's paternity of slave children that the popular British writer Captain Frederick Marryat could declaim with full authority in his widely read *A Diary in America: With Remarks on Its Institutions* (1839): "It is a well-known fact that a considerable portion of Mr. Jefferson's slaves were his own children. If any of them absconded, he would smile, thereby implying that he should not be very particular in looking after them; and yet this man, this great and GOOD man, . . . who asserted that slavery of the Negro was a violation of the most sacred rights of life and liberty, permitted these his slaves and his children, the issue of his own loins, to be sold at auction after his demise, not even emancipating them, as he might have done, before his death" (281).

Although Jefferson did leave instructions for emancipating the Hemings slaves after his death, William Wells Brown takes as his point of departure in *Clotel* the possibility that two of Jefferson's slave daughters, and his slave mistress, remained enslaved and were sold at auction. By setting *Clotel* after Jefferson's death, Brown chooses to keep Jefferson offstage and to explore the fate of Currer's children by Jefferson rather than the president's relationship with Currer (the Hemings character). Thus, rather than presenting a fictionalized version of the Jefferson-Hemings relationship, Brown develops a more metaphorical and clearly fictional account of the travails of Jefferson's black "descendants"—the daughters (and sons) of a failed (or unfinished) American Revolution. That said, Brown, like many abolitionists of the time, probably regarded the rumors about Jefferson and Hemings as literal truth. Near the conclusion of Chapter 1 of *Clotel*, he writes with little irony or ambiguity: "Thus closed a negro sale, at which two daughters of Thomas Jefferson, the writer of the Declaration of American Independence, and one of the presidents of the great republic, were disposed of to the highest bidder!" (p. 88). Brown may be telling a fictionalized story but, as with his histories of the 1860s and 1870s, he is also writing an alternative history, one that deauthorizes the heroic founding narrative that has Jefferson at its untroubled center as the "father" of American freedom.

Encouraging its readers to develop a skeptical relationship to glorified stories of the national past, *Clotel* can be regarded as what Lee Quinby terms a "genealogical fiction," a text that "breaks the hold of official truth and the metaphysics of memory, putting in their place the truth of countermemory" (xviii; see also Castronovo 31–66). As a genealogical fiction, *Clotel* shares a good deal with two other novels of the period that also pose challenges to cultural memory by raising questions about the fathers: Nathaniel Hawthorne's *The House of the Seven Gables* (1851) and Herman Melville's *Pierre* (1852). Both novels depict what appears on the surface to be a thriving, prosperous, democratic America, and both ultimately show that beneath that happy surface lies an ambiguous history of violation and deceit. Pierre fears that the woman he is attracted to may be his sister, for he learns that his father may have had a daughter out of wedlock who may well be "black," just as his father before him, a Revolutionary hero, may have had sexual relations with his slaves (see Levine); and in Hawthorne's *House*, the main characters and the reader learn that the esteemed Judge Pyncheon, in the tradition of his esteemed forefather Colonel Pyncheon, is a thief. Both novels develop contrasts between official and unofficial history, locating the truth in the margins and shadows. Like Brown, Hawthorne and Melville encourage the reader to rethink national genealogies and dominant cultural narratives. In contesting those narratives, the genealogical fictionalist takes seriously the "unofficial," marginalized perspectives of cultural outsiders. Access to sites of exclusion and repression, to the truth of conflict and power, Hawthorne remarks in *House*, may best be available from "private, diurnal gossip" (122).

Until recently, most historians have rejected the "gossip" that Jefferson could have had sexual relations and fathered children with Sally Hemings (but see Fawn Brodie's *Thomas Jefferson: An Intimate History* [1974] and Barbara Chase-Riboud's best-selling historical novel *Sally Hemings* [1979], both of which chronicle Jefferson's sexual relationship with Hemings). In his prize-winning *American Sphinx: The Character of Thomas Jefferson* (1997), for example, the historian Joseph J. Ellis comments only briefly on Jefferson and his slaves at Monticello, exploring other broad intellectual movements before concluding with an appendix, "A Note on the Sally Hemings Scandal," that by its very placement at the end of the volume ensures that the overall study will remain uncontaminated by the "scandal." While conceding that there is suggestive evidence of a relationship between Hemings and Jefferson, and that at "the purely metaphoric level, then, the story of an enduring sexual connection between Jefferson and Sally Hemings conveys an elemental truth about the hidden history of race relations in America" (306), Ellis nonetheless takes the high historiographic road of dismissing the allegations: "Within the scholarly world, especially within the community of Jefferson specialists, there seems to be a clear consensus that the story is almost certainly not true. Within the much murkier world of popular opinion, especially within the black community, the story appears to have achieved the status of a self-evident truth" (305). Unlike Hawthorne, who locates the truth of Judge Pyncheon precisely in the world of popular opinion, Ellis rejects the "murky" world of black popular opinion and places his faith in the "experts."

But as Annette Gordon-Reed argues in *Thomas Jefferson and Sally Hemings: An American Controversy* (1997), for nearly two hundred years that "murky" black world has based its opinion on less traditional but perhaps more valid sources than rational and "disinterested" scholarly argument—specifically, on an oral and written tradition among the black descendants of Sally Hemings. While the Jefferson family has asserted that one of the Carrs was in all probability the father of Sally's children, some of the Hemings children (and their friends) have talked of their knowledge that Jefferson was the father of some or all of Sally Hemings's children. As Gordon-Reed shows, Madison Hemings, in an interview published in the 13 March 1873 *Pike County (Ohio) Republican*, made a particularly compelling case for claiming Thomas Jefferson as his father (pp. 287–90). This account was corroborated by Israel Jefferson, another former slave at Monticello, and by such indirect evidence as the fact that Jefferson freed only the Hemings slaves at his death (Gordon-Reed 7–58).

Further corroboration came in 1998 in the form of evidence based on DNA testing. In a study appearing in the highly regarded scientific journal *Nature*, Eugene A. Foster, a pathologist and geneticist, reported that a DNA analysis demonstrated all but conclusively that Thomas Jefferson was the father of Hemings's youngest son, Eston (1808–1852), and thus could have been the father of some of her other children as well. In a series of genetic tests researchers traced the Y chromosome of male descendants of Eston Hemings against the Y chromosome of male descendants of Thomas Jefferson's uncle on his father's side, with whom he shared genetic material, and found a match. This testing also eliminated Peter Carr and Samuel Carr as possible fathers of Eston Hemings, for no match was found among the male descendants of the Carr family (see Foster et al.). Because Jefferson was known to have been at Monticello at the various times of conception, the genetic evidence suggests rather strongly that Jefferson was the father of at least this one slave. Formerly skeptical historians, such as Joseph Ellis, who coauthored an accompanying article in *Nature* with biomedicist Eric S. Lander, quickly concurred with the conclusions of the testing, though questions remain about what the scientific revelations say about Jefferson. Ellis and Lander offer a rather bland conclusion to their essay: "Our heroes—and especially presidents—are not gods or saints, but flesh-and-blood humans, with all of the frailties and imperfections that this entails" (14).

One of the disturbing aspects of Ellis's and other historians' quick capitulation to the scientific "facts" is that the historical evidence that helped to support the findings of the scientists had for a long time been readily available. The difference now is that respected white scientists are finally saying what the Hemings descendants have said all along. What has not changed are the hierarchies of knowledge that dictate social truths. A full consideration of the Jefferson-Hemings relationship should prompt much more than a pious concession of human frailty: It should instead lead to a rethinking of the history of blacks and whites in America, of connections between slavery and freedom, of the dynamics of race in American history, and of the relationship of the politics of gender to the politics of slavery. It should also inspire a rethinking of how those histories traditionally have been told in the United States and how they might now be more truthfully revised. Such a reconceptualization would commence approximately one hundred fifty years after William Wells Brown began the process in his phantasmagorical, fragmented, *un*writing of American history in *Clotel*.

RACE, GENDER, AND THE PROBLEM OF THE TRAGIC MULATTA

Brown's assumed knowledge of Jefferson's sexual consortings with at least one of his slave women was certainly taken seriously by the abolitionist press. In the 3 February 1854 *Liberator*, an anonymous reviewer of *Clotel* refers to the "warmest commendations" that the novel has received in England and expresses the hope that the book "might be reprinted in this country, believing it would find many readers." The reviewer then turns to the heart of the matter:

> While the Declaration of Independence is preserved, the memory of Thomas Jefferson, its author, will be cherished, for the clear recognition it makes of the natural equality of mankind, and the inalienable right of every human being to freedom and the pursuit of happiness. But it will also be to his eternal disgrace that he lived and died a slave-holder, emancipating none of his slaves at his death, and, it is well understood, leaving some of his own children to be sold to the slave speculators, and thus to drag out a miserable life of servitude. Of the last, 'Clotel' was one—beautiful, intelligent, captivating (pp. 385–86).

Reviewers in England similarly took for granted that Jefferson had children by at least one of his female slaves, and thus praised Brown for chronicling in the form of a novel what they took to be the historical facts of the lives of those light-complected children (see, for example, the review reprinted from the *Hereford Times* in the 20 January 1854 issue of the *Liberator*, pp. 382–83).

The Jefferson-Hemings relationship had a particularly resonant connection to Brown's own life history (which has to be taken as an important "source" of the novel) and the life histories of many other black abolitionists. As a "mulatto" (a word used loosely in antebellum culture to refer to blacks who showed evidence of having "white" blood in their genealogical lines), Brown could regard himself metaphorically, in James Callender's terms, as part of the "swarm" of Jefferson's "FOUR HUNDRED THOUSAND MULATTOES." Brown's light-complected skin insistently told the story that he owed his very existence to the sexual violation of his mother by a slave owner. In her biography of her father, Josephine Brown proclaimed: "If there is one evil connected with the abominable system of slavery which should be loathed more than another, it is taking from woman the right of self-defence, and making her subject to the control of any licentious villain who may be able to purchase her person" (11). As Brown himself would write in *Three Years in Europe*, the whiteness of the slaves "is attributable, solely to the unlimited power which the slave owner exercises over his victim," and "there seems to be no limits to the system of amalgamation carried on between master and slave" (274). Though Brown is obviously critical of the masters' power, and is concerned in particular about the vulnerability and victimization of slave women, the fact remains that had there been no such violations, neither Brown nor his daughter (nor, for that matter, Frederick Douglass and many other black abolitionists) would have been alive to offer their condemnation of the patriarchal institution. *Clotel* can be read, in part, as a meditation on the history of such violations—one that is informed by a complex mix of Brown's guilt and anger at the violation that brought about his existence (see Chaney 49–79). Arguably, it is precisely because of his own personal history that Brown makes an effort to find something redemptive and transformative in the relationship between white men and black women. Although Brown implicitly discounts the possibility that there had been an emotional bond between Jefferson and Currer by focusing on the slave mother's abandonment by her master, the novel, both in the account of the initial attraction between Horatio and Clotel and in the later story of Morton and Althesa, suggests that interracial love is possible and that individuals have the potential to see their way past culturally inscribed racial boundaries and hierarchies. Nevertheless, Brown realistically emphasizes how such individuals are eventually destroyed by these hierarchies.

For his representations of cross-racial sexuality and love, Brown may have been inspired by rumors of the Jefferson-Hemings relationship and by his meditations on his own genealogy, but his specific literary source for the stories of Clotel and Althesa, Jefferson's fictional daughters, was Lydia Maria Child's "The Quadroons," first published in an antislavery journal in 1842 and slightly revised for book publication in 1846. (The story is reprinted on pp. 319–29.) Briefly, the antislavery tale, set in Georgia, tells of Edward's attraction to Rosalie, whom he cannot legally marry because she has black blood. They have a daughter, Xarifa, but after a number of years in which he treats Rosalie as a mistress, the socially ambitious Edward marries Charlotte, the daughter of a wealthy man in the community. Distraught at the marriage, Rosalie eventually dies of grief, and an equally distraught Edward takes up drinking and dies when he falls from a horse. Their daughter Xarifa is sold into slavery, and when her white lover attempts to rescue her, he is shot and killed. In response, Xarifa goes mad and dies of a broken heart.

Despite having nothing much to do with Jefferson, Child's "The Quadroons" spoke to Brown's interest in genealogy and racial politics. Though he changed the names and settings, he used much of Child's language verbatim. In doing so, he risked more than simply being accused of plagiarism; he also risked giving his apparent assent to the notion that stories of whites (or people who look white to the eye) were more important than stories of blacks. It is worth recalling that the reviewer of *Clotel* in the *Liberator* emphasized that Clotel is "beautiful, intelligent, captivating." As Brown makes clear in the opening chapter of the novel, Clotel's conventional attractiveness gives rise to a bidding war among the young white men who compete to possess her. Later in the novel we are told the story of Salome, a free white woman who is mistaken for a mulatto and taken into slavery, and Brown would seem to be suggesting that her tragedy is more worthy of our attention (and even more tragic) than that of a dark-skinned black born into slavery. We are also told how Morton's romantic attraction to Althesa has its origins in his conviction that it is unfair for a woman as white and attractive as Althesa to suffer the life of a slave.

In focusing on the fate of the white-complected daughters and granddaughters of Jefferson, Brown was particularly responsive to

Child's use of the figure of the "tragic mulatta"—the woman who looks white to the eye but nonetheless suffers the fate of the black slave. Like Child, Brown in his writings sought to expose the sexual vulnerability and exploitation of black women in Southern slave culture, and in *Clotel* he strategically deploys the trope of the tragic mulatta in an effort to heighten his white readers' concerns about the plight of the slaves by showing how women's vulnerability crosses racial divides; the titles to chapters fourteen and fifteen, "A Free Woman Reduced to Slavery" and "To-day a Mistress, To-morrow a Slave," underscore this important point. In this respect, Brown was influenced not only by Child's story but also by Harriet Beecher Stowe's enormously popular *Uncle Tom's Cabin* (1852). Like Stowe, who presents a number of "tragic mulattas" (Eliza and Cassy being the most prominent), Brown linked himself with literary sentimentalism's project of attempting to make readers feel the plight of the marginalized other by depicting black slaves as not all that different from the whites who were reading about them. This was a literary and political strategy, as duCille argues, which "attempt[ed] to insinuate into the consciousness of white readers the humanity of a people they otherwise constructed as subhuman—beyond the pale of white comprehension" (8). In *Clotel*, the white liberator Georgiana can be taken as an idealized version of such a reader, for as a result of her encounters with Northern antislavery sentiment and her rereading of the Bible, she "had learned to feel deeply for the injured negro" (p. 109).

And yet even as Child and Brown boldly address the immorality of slavery through the figure of the tragic mulatta, their light-complected black characters can seem perhaps too enamored of the white culture that denies them their rights and humanity. In Child's "The Quadroons," the slave women have no clear relation to the world of the slaves or of blackness; in focusing on the main characters' attraction to white men, the story can appear to uphold racial hierarchies and even to support Jefferson's notion, as expressed in *Notes*, of the physical unattractiveness of blacks. But though Child and Brown can be accused of a certain complicity in the dominant culture's racial valuations, there are important differences between Child's story and Brown's revision that need to be emphasized. It is crucial to note, for example, that in an effort to put Child's story into conversation with other cultural discourses of the time, Brown breaks it into three sections (see chapters IV, VIII, and XXIII), and at the end of each section moves away from the original narrative to explore other concerns, characters, and generic modes. For example, the sentimental account of Clotel's failed "marriage" to Horatio Green is preceded and immediately followed by more realistic scenes of slave trading. Even more strikingly, in the later account of the deaths of Althesa's daughters, Brown draws on the tragic conclusion of Child's story, yet narrates these deaths in a chapter that begins with descriptions of a yellow fever epidemic and is immediately followed by descriptions of Nat Turner's slave rebellion. Through such juxtapositions, Brown reminds his readers that the daughters' sad story takes place within a larger context of suffering and rebellion.

Presenting his readers with a fractured and somewhat altered version of Child's story, Brown, through his method of literary pastiche and bricolage, suggests the limitations of this "kidnapped" text. Within the larger narrative framework of *Clotel*, Child's story (as reimagined and recontextualized by Brown) emerges as a much less stable story, one that is overly dependent on conventional notions of race, gender, and sentiment. Unlike Child, Brown points to the possibilities of black rebellion, particularly among the female slaves, presenting most of the black women characters derived from "The Quadroons" as active agents who claim their rights to watch out for themselves and those they love, and who uphold those rights as markers of their freedom and humanity. Because the Child story is included in this Cultural Edition, it can be left to readers of *Clotel* and "The Quadroons" to make their own determinations about the effectiveness of Brown's appropriation and revisions. But a few additional words should be said about race, genealogy, and sentimentalism in *Clotel* and other writings of the period.

In *Uncle Tom's Cabin*, Augustine St. Clare imagines the possibility of a racial war of extermination (similar to that which haunted Jefferson's *Notes*) and proclaims to his racist brother Alfred: "If ever the San Domingo hour comes, Anglo Saxon blood will lead on the day. Sons of white fathers, with all our haughty feelings burning in their veins, will not always be bought and sold and traded. They will rise, and raise with them their mother's race" (234). Alluding to the massive slave rebellion of the 1790s in San Domingo, which led to the loss of over 60,000 lives, St. Clare's comments are informed by racialist notions of the time that conceived of blacks and whites as essentially different, with the differences penetrating to the very blood. Though most scientists today regard "race" as an unworkable biological category dependent upon absurd (and insidious) notions of essential differences between "white" and "black" blood, the fact is that many of the most prestigious biologists and ethnologists of the nineteenth century thought quite differently on this matter, arguing that humankind consisted of a variety of discrete races.

The historian George M. Fredrickson has coined the term "Romantic Racialism" (97) to describe Harriet Beecher Stowe's and other liberal whites' paternalistic views of blacks' supposed racial differences from whites. Influenced by Alexander Kinmont's *Twelve Lectures on the Natural History of Man* (1839), Stowe celebrates blacks for what she believes are their more naturally Christian ways—domestic, noncompetitive, relatively passive. The aggressive feelings that may lead to a violent rebellion, she suggests, are more characteristic of white males, whose drive toward mastery has important sources in their blood. At times in *Clotel* Brown can seem to share a similar racialist perspective on blood differences. For example, the reader is informed during a discussion of the 1831 Nat Turner rebellion and its aftermath: "The infusion of Anglo-Saxon with African blood has created an insurrectionary feeling among the slaves of America hitherto unknown. Aware of their blood connection with their owners, these mulattoes labour under the sense of their personal and social injuries" (p. 201). Like Stowe, Brown in this passage would appear to be promoting the idea that peoples of different skin colors have different blood that ultimately generates different patterns of behavior. And yet his use of the word "aware" links blacks' anger to their political awareness that intertangled black and white genealogies give the lie to the essentialist claims of racial difference regularly invoked to defend the practice of slavery. Moreover, his positive presentation of the black rebels Nat Turner, Picquilo, and William all argue for Brown's desire to challenge and revise the romantic racialism of the liberal North. In subsequent revisions of *Clotel*, Brown would even make the lightly complected rebel George Green into a full-blooded, prideful black (see the selection from *Clotelle: A Tale of the Southern States* in Part Two, Chapter 4, p. 388–95).

With respect to the variously complected blacks of *Clotel*, Brown's approach to the problem of race might more usefully be termed "colorist" than "racialist," which is to say that he ultimately rejects the notion of biological or blood differences and emphasizes instead the inevitable cultural differences among light- and dark-complected slaves (and former slaves)—differences that have almost everything to do with the deleterious influences of white supremacist slave culture. The problem of color, then, emerges as one of the large subjects of *Clotel* (and of at least two important later novels by African American writers who were influenced by *Clotel*, Frances Harper's *Iola Leroy* [1892] and Pauline Hopkins's *Hagar's Daughter* [1901]). The plantation slave Sam, who is described as "one of the blackest of his race" (p. 135), appears virtually pathological in his denial of his blackness. Rather than accept the reality of his physical appearance, he makes pathetic efforts to pass himself off as a mulatto, smearing grease on his hair in an ultimately doomed attempt to straighten it, and pompously asserting his distance from "pure" blacks: "I don't like to see dis malgemation of blacks and mulattoes" (p. 136). Like the typical white in blackface performing on Northeast minstrel stages of the period, Sam initially comports himself in ways that appear contemptible and little short of laughable, including the way he speaks in dialect. But the surprise is that Sam, like all of the slaves of *Clotel*, is presented as possessing a communal political consciousness: soon after his "minstrel" performance as a black who harbors an impossible desire to be white, he learns of the death of his owner, and, along with other slaves of the plantation, eschews dialect and sings songs expressing his loathing of slavery and the master. Sam's performance as a loyal black slave who actually hates slavery thus works to undermine the racist ideology that proclaimed blacks were happiest in a subordinate, enslaved position.

As his portrayal of Sam's subversive use of minstrelsy suggests, Brown, unlike Stowe and other racialists of the period, regarded race as anything but a stable biological category. Instead, he portrays race as something that is "performed" within racist culture (see Gilmore 37–66). A similar perspective on race and performance informs the novel's accounts of several of the slaves' escape attempts. Inspired by the escape of William and Ellen Craft (see pp. 368–70), Brown presents characters who manage to escape by cleverly performing the roles of lordly white master and subordinate black slave. The cross-dressed and racially "passing" George and Mary, for example, like black Sam who metaphorically puts on blackface, destabilize notions of essential racial difference between whites and blacks that had come to inform the ethnographic racial science and cultural formations of the period. Exposing the limits of such racialism, Brown implicitly calls on his readers to reevaluate the place of African Americans in U.S. culture. As he would remark in his 1863 *The Black Man*: "There is nothing in race or blood, in color or features, that imparts susceptibility of improvement to one race over another. The mind left to itself from infancy, without culture, remains a blank. Knowledge is not innate. Development makes the man" (35–36).

PARALLEL LINES

Development made William Wells Brown. Having successfully fashioned his own escape from bondage, Brown presents himself in *Clotel*'s prefatory "Narrative of the Life and Escape of William Wells Brown" as "most assiduous in his studies" (p. 78), staying up to the wee hours of the morning "to read when others are asleep" (p. 79). Brown was not alone among antebellum African Americans in presenting himself to his readers as exemplary of blacks' ability to overcome what Frederick Douglass in *My Bondage and My Freedom* (1855) referred to as the "brutification" (152) of slavery. The period between 1845 and 1861 saw a flourishing of African American writing, as authors such as Douglass, Brown, Wilson, and Jacobs depicted blacks' struggles to rise in racist U.S. culture. This "Afro-American Literary Renaissance," as William L. Andrews has termed it, came at a time when blacks were experiencing an increasing despair at their prospects in the United States. The emergence of such powerful texts as Martin R. Delany's *The Condition, Elevation, Emigration, and Destiny of the Colored People of the United States* (1852), Solomon Northup's *Twelve Years a Slave* (1853), James Whitfield's *America and Other Poems* (1853), Frances Harper's *Poems* (1854), Douglass's *My Bondage and My Freedom* (1855), Harriet Wilson's *Our Nig* (1859), and Harriet A. Jacobs's *Incidents in the Life of a Slave Girl* (1861) attests to African Americans' high regard for literature as an expressive and political vehicle for addressing white racism and the dire political developments of the 1850s.

When *Clotel* appeared in England in 1853, the situation in the United States looked particularly grim. Following the acquisition of the vast territories gained from the war with Mexico (1846–48), Congress had approved the Compromise of 1850, which allowed California to enter the Union as a free state, left the Utah and New Mexico territories open to the possibility of becoming slave states, abolished the slave trade in the District of Columbia, and, as mentioned, imposed a more stringent Fugitive Slave Law that required all U.S. citizens to return escaped slaves to their masters. Rather than putting an end to antislavery activity, the Fugitive Slave Law outraged black and white abolitionists (and even less politically inclined Northerners with heretofore moderate antislavery sentiments), who regarded the new law as a clear sign that the Southern "slave power" had control of the federal government and that slavery would remain absolutely central to Northern and Southern U.S. culture. (For the text of the Fugitive Slave

Law, see the selection from Martin Delany printed in Part Two, Chapter 3, pp. 348–53.) As Brown remarked in an 1854 speech to the Pennsylvania Anti-Slavery Society on the pervasive ills of slavery: "We need not go out of the free States to see its cruelties. . . . Look at the coloured people of the free States, thrown out of your schools, your churches and your social circles, deprived of their political rights and debarred from those avenues of employment that are necessary to a proper maintenance of themselves and their families. We find the degrading influences of slavery all about us" (Ripley IV: 248).

Those "influences" became only more apparent in the mid to late 1850s. The passage of the 1854 Kansas-Nebraska Act, which repealed the territorial limits on slavery established by the Missouri Compromise, meant that slavery could continue its spread west. A central provision of this bill, which was drafted by the influential senator from Illinois, Stephen A. Douglas, was its support for popular sovereignty— the idea that settlers of future states would have full power to vote on whether to legalize slavery in their state constitutions. Unsurprisingly, the Kansas-Nebraska Act destroyed the sectional "peace" that had supposedly been established by the Compromise of 1850. During the mid-1850s, proslavery and antislavery forces clashed violently in what came to be termed "Bleeding Kansas." For black abolitionists, perhaps the most distressing development of the 1850s was the Supreme Court's 1857 ruling on *Dred Scott v. Sanford*, which asserted that African Americans had no legal rights in the United States and could never become citizens. The ruling also addressed the territorial issues raised by the Kansas-Nebraska Act, asserting in the broadest and most unambiguous terms that it was unconstitutional for the federal government to exclude slavery from the territories. The *Dred Scott* decision thus worked to further radicalize antislavery opinion in the North and midwest, and became a point of contention in the increasingly heated (and nationally prominent) political debates between Stephen Douglas and the Republican prairie lawyer Abraham Lincoln, who challenged Douglas for his senate seat in the election of 1858. Following the *Dred Scott* decision a number of African Americans, including Brown, began to champion black emigration to Haiti or Africa.

Brown's attraction to Haiti was short lived. Like many black abolitionists, he came to see the Civil War as a war against slavery, and he embraced the Union cause. Committed to a war that he hoped would reform the United States, he wrote three new versions of *Clotel* (1860–61, 1864, 1867), the final version of which, *Clotelle; or, The Colored Heroine*, portrays blacks playing a crucial role in the cultural politics of Reconstruction (for selections from his revisions, see pp. 388–406). Brown himself sought to play a central role in the reconstruction of the nation, as he was initially optimistic about the federal government's post–Civil War efforts to reorder the social and economic structure of the South (and North) by granting African Americans their civil and political rights. He worked as a black temperance leader and antiracist reformer, and authored black histories that he hoped would contribute to black pride and further inform whites about African Americans' crucial contributions to the nation. However, in his last published volume, *My Southern Home* (1880), Brown conveyed his despair at the failure of Reconstruction—which effectively ended in 1877 when President Hayes withdrew federal troops from the South— and urged Southern blacks to consider migrating north. But even with the persistence of antiblack racism and the restoration of segregationist Jim Crow practices in the South, Brown retained a hopeful belief that racial harmony could be achieved in the United States at some future historical moment (see Part Two, Chapter 4, pp. 410–14).

The bases of Brown's idealistic hopes that the United States could one day live up to its (Jeffersonian) ideals as a nation of freedom and opportunity can be found in an especially resonant passage in *Clotel*. At the opening of chapter XXI, the narrator offers a mythic account of the birth of slavery and freedom in the Northern and Southern colonies. On a particular day in 1620, the narrator writes, the Puritans' "May-flower brought the seed-wheat of states and empire.... This ship had the embryo elements of all that is useful, great, and grand in Northern institutions; it was the great type of goodness and wisdom, illustrated in two and a quarter centuries gone by; it was the good genius of America" (p. 180). On that same day in the South "a low rakish ship hastening from the tropics" carried "the first cargo of slaves on their way to Jamestown, Virginia" (p. 181). In the examples of these two ships Brown presents a rather clear allegory (albeit an artful one, as the Puritans did have slaves) of the struggle between slavery and freedom in the nascent republic:

> Behold the May-flower anchored at Plymouth Rock, the slave-ship in James River. Each a parent, one of the prosperous, labour-honouring, law-sustaining institutions of the North; the other the mother of slavery, idleness, lynch-law, ignorance, unpaid labour, poverty, and duelling, despotism, the ceaseless swing of the whip, and the peculiar institutions of the South. These ships are the representation of good and evil in the New World, even to our day. When shall one of those parallel lines come to an end? (p. 181)

By rhetorically asking when the evils spawned by slavery will come to an end, Brown, even in this highly polarized formulation, signals his belief that a reformative social transformation can occur, and that the very spirit needed to bring about that transformation is the spirit that initially brought the nation into being. At the same time, with its demythologizing of Jefferson and its ultimate revelation that the idea of "parallel lines" is a fiction, *Clotel* provides no easy solutions and, particularly with its jaded view of Northern racism, no easy choices between "good" and "evil." Instead, Brown challenges his readers to rethink historical narratives and imperatives, and in this way begin the process of reimagining and reconceiving New World possibilities.

William Wells Brown, circa 1855. Frontispiece to Brown's *The American Fugitive in Europe* (1855).

Chronology of
Brown's Life and Times

1814

William Wells Brown born on a plantation near Lexington, Kentucky, the son of a slave woman named Elizabeth and a white man, most likely a relative of her owner, Dr. John Young. William is one of Elizabeth's seven children; the evidence suggests that there were several different fathers of her six sons and one daughter.

1816

December: Founding of the American Colonization Society, which sought to transport free blacks to Africa.

Dr. Young moves to the Missouri Territory, taking William and his other slaves with him. Sometime in the next few years, Young adopts into his family a nephew named William Moore and decides to change his slave William's name to Sandford.

1818

Birth of Frederick Douglass in Tuckahoe, Maryland.

1819

Washington Irving (1783–1859), *The Sketch Book.*

1820

Enactment of the Missouri Compromise: Missouri admitted as a slave state, Maine as a free state, and slavery excluded in the Louisiana Territory north of latitude 36°30′.

1821

William Cullen Bryant (1794–1878), *Poems*; James Fenimore Cooper (1789–1851), *The Spy.*

1822

Denmark Vesey's slave conspiracy in Charleston, South Carolina, is betrayed by a house slave; over thirty blacks are executed.

1824

Lydia Maria Child (1802–1880), *Hobomok.*

1826

July 4: Deaths of Thomas Jefferson and John Adams.

Cooper, *The Last of the Mohicans.*

1827

Young moves to St. Louis and buys a farm outside of the city. Pressed by financial circumstances, he sells Brown's mother, sister, and three brothers (two brothers had died), and begins to hire out his remaining slaves. Over the next few years Brown works at a tavern, at a St. Louis hotel, and on a steamboat, the *Missouri.*

New York State abolishes slavery.

First African American newspaper, *Freedom's Journal*, begins publication in New York City.

Catharine Sedgwick (1789–1867), *Hope Leslie.*

1829

David Walker (c.1790–1830) publishes his militant *Appeal* in Boston; Southern whites attempt to prevent its dissemination.

Antiblack riots in Cincinnati; several hundred blacks emigrate to Upper Canada.

William Apess (1798–?), *A Son of the Forest.*

1830

Brown is employed in the printing office of the Reverend Elijah P. Lovejoy, editor of the *Saint Louis Times.* During 1830 and 1831 he is also hired out to the steward's department of the steamboat *Enterprise*, where he first encounters the slave trader James Walker. He also works as an assistant to Dr. Young.

First national black convention convenes in Philadelphia.

1831

January 1: William Lloyd Garrison (1805–1879) publishes the first issue of his abolitionist newspaper the *Liberator*.

August: Nat Turner leads a slave rebellion in Southampton County, Virginia. Approximately sixty whites and two hundred blacks are killed. Turner is captured in October and executed in November. That same month Thomas Gray publishes *The Confessions of Nat Turner*.

1832

Brown is hired out for a year to the slave trader James Walker.

Founding of the New England Anti-Slavery Society in Boston.

Nullification Crisis: After a special convention in South Carolina nullifies the federal government's new protective tariff and affirms the state's willingness to secede from the Union, President Jackson issues a proclamation of condemnation. The following year Congress lowers tariffs and passes the Force Bill, which authorizes Jackson to use U.S. troops to uphold federal law.

Garrison, *Thoughts on African Colonization*.

1833

Brown returns to Young's plantation and finds his sister has again been sold and is to be taken to Natchez, Mississippi. He attempts to escape from slavery with his mother but is captured in Illinois and returned to Young. Young sells him to Samuel Willi, a St. Louis merchant, for $500. His mother is sold and taken to New Orleans. Later that year Willi sells Brown for approximately $650 to the St. Louis merchant and steamboat owner Enoch Price, who initially employs Brown as a coachman.

Founding of the American Anti-Slavery Society in Philadelphia.

Child (1802–1880), *An Appeal in Favor of That Class of Americans Called Africans*.

1834

January: Brown escapes from slavery, traveling at night from Cincinnati to Cleveland, and receiving much valued help from the Ohio Quakers Wells Brown and his wife. Brown reassumes his name of William and in gratitude also assumes the name of his male benefactor. By the spring Brown has a job on the Lake Erie steamer *Detroit*, and by the end of the summer he has married the free black Elizabeth Schooner. Over the next nine years he works as a steamboatsman on Lake Erie, regularly helping fugitive slaves escape to Canada.

August: Great Britain abolishes slavery in the West Indies; in 1835 African Americans begin annually to celebrate West Indies emancipation on August 1.

Antiblack riots in Philadelphia and New York.

Founding of the *Southern Literary Messenger.*

1835

The Browns' first daughter dies in infancy.

President Jackson calls for the suppression of antislavery writings, thus supporting the bans set in place by most of the Southern states.

William Gilmore Simms (1806–1870), *The Yemassee.*

1836

Birth of Clarissa Brown. Near the end of the year Brown moves his family to Buffalo, New York, where he continues his work as a steamboatsman and conductor on the Underground Railroad, and also organizes and eventually becomes the president of a temperance society.

Abolitionists present to Congress the first of hundreds of petitions to end slavery in the District of Columbia.

Texas proclaims independence from Mexico.

Ralph Waldo Emerson (1803–1882), *Nature;* Richard Hildreth (1807–1865), *The Slave;* Jarena Lee (1783–?), *The Life and Religious Experiences of Jarena Lee, A Coloured Lady.*

1837

Passage of a gag rule prohibiting the reception of antislavery petitions in Congress and restricting congressional debate.

The antislavery newspaper editor Elijah Lovejoy is murdered by a mob in Alton, Illinois.

The Colored American, the second major African American newspaper, begins publication in New York City.

Financial panic: Failures of numerous banks lead to severe unemployment, which persists into the early 1840s.

Catharine Beecher (1800–1878), *An Essay on Slavery and Abolitionism.*

1838

Trail of Tears: Thousands of Native American Cherokees die during a federally mandated march from their native home in Georgia to the Indian Territory in Oklahoma.

Edgar Allan Poe (1809–1849), *The Narrative of Arthur Gordon Pym.*

1839

Birth of Josephine Brown.

Black rebellion on the Spanish slaver *Amistad*; the U.S. Supreme Court grants the rebels their freedom in 1841.

Theodore Dwight Weld (1803–1895), *American Slavery as It Is.*

1840

May: Formation of the antislavery Liberty Party in Albany, New York.

June: Leaders of the World's Antislavery Convention in London vote to ban women from public participation.

According to his later writings, Brown visits Haiti, Cuba, and islands of the West Indies. Upon his return, he resumes his antislavery activities, continuing to help fugitive slaves escape to Canada.

A schism in the American Anti-Slavery Society on key principles and tactics (including whether women, as Garrison argued, should have an important role in antislavery organizations) leads to the formation of the anti-Garrisonian group, the American and Foreign Anti-Slavery Society.

Founding of the Washingtonian Temperance Society, which quickly leads to the emergence of temperance as one of the most popular social reforms of the period.

Richard Henry Dana (1815–1882), *Two Years Before the Mast.*

1841

Slave rebellion on the slaver *Creole* bound from Virginia to New Orleans; the slaves are freed after taking the ship to the British colony of Nassau.

1843

August: Brown meets Frederick Douglass at antislavery meetings in Buffalo. Attending the National Convention of Colored Citizens of the United States in Buffalo, he joins Douglass in voting against the adoption of Henry Highland Garnet's militant "Address to the Slaves of the United States of America," which called on slaves to use violence against their masters.

October: Brown publishes a letter attacking Garnet in the October *National Anti-Slavery Standard*; this is his first known published writing. Around this time Brown becomes a lecturing agent for the Western New York Anti-Slavery Society.

Timothy Shay Arthur (1809–1885), *Temperance Tales*; William Prescott (1796–1859), *History of the Conquest of Mexico.*

1844

May: In New York, Brown attends the tenth anniversary meeting of the American Anti-Slavery Society, which condemns the U.S. Constitution as a proslavery document. He makes his first speech at this convention, which William Lloyd Garrison also attends. When he returns to Buffalo, Brown (according to his account) finds that his wife is involved with another man. This begins a period of public marital discord.

1845

July: The *United States Magazine and Democratic Review* proclaims that it is the United States' "manifest destiny to overspread the continent."

December: Texas is admitted to the Union as a slave state.

Brown moves his family to Farmington, New York, where there are integrated schools for his daughters.

Frederick Douglass (1818–1895), *Narrative of the Life of Frederick Douglass, An American Slave*; Margaret Fuller (1810–1850), *Woman in the Nineteenth Century.*

1846

May: The United States declares war on Mexico.

June: Brown attends a meeting of the Liberty Party, where he hears the Reverend Mr. Peck of Rochester scoff at the notion that blacks have natural, inalienable rights.

August: David Wilmot, a congressman from Pennsylvania, proposes that slavery should be banned in any territories acquired from the Mexican war. His proviso is defeated.

December: Attending the annual meeting of the Western New York Anti-Slavery Society in Rochester, Brown gives a speech supporting African Americans' rights to vote.

Herman Melville (1819–1891), *Typee.*

1847

Brown becomes a lecturing agent for the Massachusetts Anti-Slavery Society. After separating from his wife, he takes custody of their two daughters and moves to Boston. During the summer he publishes *Narrative of William W. Brown, A Fugitive Slave*, which is brought out by the Boston Anti-Slavery Office. The *Narrative* goes through four American editions and sells approximately ten thousand copies; it eventually goes through five British editions. Later that year he debates Garnet on moral suasion at the National Convention of Colored

People in Troy, New York, and in November he addresses the Female Anti-Slavery Society of Salem. His speech is published as a pamphlet, *A Lecture Delivered Before the Female Anti-Slavery Society of Salem*.

1848

February: The Mexican War ends with the Treaty of Guadalupe Hidalgo; the United States gains one-half-million square miles of new territory in the southwest for $15 million.

July: Brown publishes *The Anti-Slavery Harp: A Collection of Songs for Anti-Slavery Meetings*, which includes "Jefferson's Daughter." That same month Elizabeth Schooner Brown appears in Boston with a baby and demands financial support from Brown. After a mediating committee for the Massachusetts Anti-Slavery Society exonerates Brown, Elizabeth returns to Buffalo. She reportedly dies in 1851.

The first women's rights convention is held in Seneca Falls, New York, led by Lucretia Mott (1793–1880) and Elizabeth Cady Stanton (1815–1902).

1849

January: Brown meets the escaped slaves William and Ellen Craft and lectures with them over the next four months.

July–August: Elected as a delegate to the International Peace Congress in Paris, Brown sails from Boston to Liverpool, arriving on July 28. He attends the Peace Congress in August, and upon his return to London gives the first of hundreds of antislavery lectures delivered in Great Britain over the next five years.

Henry Bibb (1815–1854), *Narrative of the Life and Adventures of Henry Bibb*; Josiah Henson (1789–1883), *The Life of Josiah Henson*; James W. C. Pennington (1807–1870), *The Fugitive Blacksmith*; Henry David Thoreau (1817–1862), *A Week on the Concord and Merrimack Rivers* and "Resistance to Civil Government."

1850

September: Congress approves an omnibus of compromise measures intended to quell sectional discord on slavery. Among the approved bills is the Fugitive Slave Law, which mandates that all U.S. citizens are required to return fugitive slaves to their owners. Brown decides to remain in England after the passage of the Fugitive Slave Law; later that year he once again lectures with the Crafts.

Brown publishes *A Description of William Wells Brown's Original Panoramic Views*, a catalogue accompanying an exhibition of antislavery drawings.

Nathaniel Hawthorne (1804–1864), *The Scarlet Letter*, Emerson, *Representative Men*; Olive Gilbert, ed., *The Narrative of Sojourner Truth*; Susan Warner (1819–1885), *The Wide, Wide World*.

1851

July: Brown's daughters arrive in England, and in August he enrolls them in a seminary in Calais, France, where they remain for a year before enrolling in the Home and Colonial School in London, a teacher training school.

The "Maine Law" bans the manufacture and distribution of alcoholic beverages; over the next several years thirteen states adopt versions of this law.

Henry Box Brown (1815–?), *Narrative of the Life of Henry Box Brown*; John C. Calhoun (1782–1850), *A Disquisition on Government*; Hawthorne, *The House of the Seven Gables*; Melville, *Moby-Dick*.

1852

March: Harriet Beecher Stowe (1811–1896), *Uncle Tom's Cabin*. Stowe's tremendously popular antislavery novel sells upwards of one million copies in the United States and abroad during the 1850s, and further polarizes the North and South.

Brown writes for pay for London newspapers, travels to France, and publishes a travel narrative, *Three Years in Europe; or, Places I Have Seen and People I Have Met*. His "A True Story of Slave Life" appears in the December *Anti-Slavery Advocate*.

Martin R. Delany (1812–1885), *The Condition, Elevation, Emigration and Destiny of the Colored People of the United States*; Melville, *Pierre*.

1853

May: At the anniversary meeting of the British and Foreign Anti-Slavery Society at Exeter Hall, Brown sees Harriet Beecher Stowe for the first time.

November: Brown publishes *Clotel; or, The President's Daughter: A Narrative of Slave Life in the United States* with the London house of Partridge and Oakey.

Formation of the American, or Know-Nothing, Party, which campaigns for repeal of naturalization laws and greater privileges for native-born whites; the party's activities culminate in an upsurge of political nativism.

Douglass, "The Heroic Slave"; Sarah Hale (1788–1879), *Liberia*; Solomon Northup (1808–1863?), *Twelve Years a Slave*; James M. Whitfield (1822–1871), *America and Other Poems*.

1854

May: Sponsored by Senator Stephen A. Douglas (1813–1861) of Illinois, the Kansas-Nebraska Act is approved by Congress; the act repeals the Missouri Compromise, making it legal for the white voting residents of a territory to determine whether it should be admitted as a slave or free state. The passage of the act leads to increased violence in the territories.

July: Ellen Richardson, who had helped to purchase Frederick Douglass's freedom in 1846, purchases Brown's manumission from Enoch Price for $300.

Formation of the Republican Party, which is opposed to the extension of slavery into the territories.

September–October: Brown returns to the United States, arriving in Philadelphia in late September and in Boston in October. On October 13 a public meeting is held in Boston in Brown's honor.

December: Brown publishes two works, both with 1855 imprints: *The American Fugitive in Europe: Sketches of Places and People Abroad* (an expanded version of *Three Years in Europe*), and *St. Domingo: Its Revolution and Its Patriots*.

After passing their qualifying examinations, Brown's daughters accept teaching positions in England.

Arthur, *Ten Nights in a Bar-room*; Caroline Lee Hentz (1800–1856), *The Planter's Northern Bride*; Thoreau, *Walden*; Frances Ellen Watkins [Harper] (1824–1911), *Poems on Miscellaneous Subjects*.

1855

August: Josephine Brown joins her father in Boston. In December she publishes a life of her father, *Biography of an American Bondman, by His Daughter*, which has an 1856 imprint.

Brown lectures for the American Anti-Slavery Society and the Massachusetts Anti-Slavery Society, and would lecture hundreds of times on the antislavery circuit the next five years.

Douglass, *My Bondage and My Freedom*; Fanny Fern [Sara Payson Willis] (1812–1889), *Ruth Hall*; Henry Wadsworth Longfellow (1807–1882), *Song of Hiawatha*; Melville, "Benito Cereno" and *Israel Potter*; William C. Nell (1816–1874), *Colored Patriots of the American*

Revolution; Samuel Ringgold Ward (1817–1866), *Autobiography of a Fugitive Negro*; Walt Whitman (1819–1892), *Leaves of Grass*.

1856

May: In the midst of an acrimonious debate on Kansas, South Carolina Congressman Preston Brooks (1819–1857) canes and severely injures Massachusetts Senator Charles Sumner (1811–1874) two days after Sumner delivers an antislavery speech on Kansas.

Brown writes his first play, "Experience, or, How to Give a Northern Man a Backbone," which satirizes the proslavery writings of the Northern minister Nehemiah Adams. Over the next two years, Brown delivers a number of public performances of his unpublished drama.

Josephine Brown returns to England.

Emerson, *English Traits*; Stowe, *Dred: A Tale of the Great Dismal Swamp*.

1857

March: The Supreme Court rules on *Dred Scott* v. *Sandford*, asserting that African Americans cannot become U.S. citizens and thus have no legal rights.

May: At the annual meeting of the New England Anti-Slavery Convention in Boston, Brown offers a resolution asserting the slaves' right to use revolutionary violence to obtain their freedom.

During the summer, Brown lectures with Frances Ellen Watkins [Harper], and at a fall "disunion convention" he supports the proposition that the Northern states should consider breaking from the Southern states.

Banking failures lead to a severe financial panic in the United States.

Edited by James Russell Lowell (1819–1891), *The Atlantic Magazine* begins publication.

Melville, *The Confidence-Man*; Sedgwick, *Married or Single?*

1858

Brown publishes *The Escape; or, A Leap for Freedom. A Drama in Five Acts*, which he has been publicly performing with "Experience" since the summer of 1857.

Stephen Douglas and Abraham Lincoln engage in widely reported debates during the campaign for the U.S. Senate seat from Illinois; Douglas is reelected.

Henry Highland Garnet founds the African Civilization Society, which promotes black emigration to Africa.

1859

August: At a black convention, Brown attacks black emigration and colonization.

October: Hoping to spark a slave insurrection, John Brown leads a small group of blacks and whites in an unsuccessful raid on the federal arsenal at Harper's Ferry, Virginia. He is hanged for treason on December 2.

Brown publishes *Memoir of William Wells Brown*.

Dion Boucicault (1822?–1890), *The Octoroon*; Dana, *To Cuba and Back*; Delany, *Blake* (1859–62); E. D. E. N. Southworth (1819–1899), *The Hidden Hand*; Stowe, *The Minister's Wooing*; Harriet Wilson (1825–1900), *Our Nig*.

1860

April 12: Brown marries Anna Elizabeth Gray of Cambridgeport.

November: Abraham Lincoln elected president of the United States.

December: South Carolina secedes from the Union.

Brown begins serialized publication of *Miralda; or, The Beautiful Quadroon*, which appears in sixteen installments in the weekly *Anglo-African*, running from 1 December 1860 to 16 March 1861.

William Craft (1824–1900), *Running a Thousand Miles for Freedom; or, The Escape of William and Ellen Craft from Slavery*; Hawthorne, *The Marble Faun*.

1861

February: Birth of William Wells Brown Jr., who dies in infancy.

March: Lincoln inaugurated.

April 1: Civil War begins with Confederate troops attacking and seizing Fort Sumter in South Carolina.

April: At a meeting of African American leaders, Brown votes against an approved resolution calling on blacks to fight for the Union cause.

Brown lectures in support of black emigration to Haiti and is listed as one of the "Special Contributors" to the *Pine and Palm*, a newspaper that promotes Haitian emigration. During the late summer and fall, he tours the black communities of Canada; his report on his travels appears over eight issues of *Pine and Palm*.

Rebecca Harding Davis (1831–1910), *Life in the Iron Mills*; Harriet A. Jacobs (1813–1897), *Incidents in the Life of a Slave Girl, Written by Herself*; Frederick Law Olmsted (1822–1903), *The Cotton Kingdom*.

1862

May: Birth of Clotelle Brown.

December: Brown publishes *The Black Man, His Antecedents, His Genius, and His Achievements*; the book has an 1863 imprint and copyright.

Abandoning his support for black emigration to Haiti, Brown chooses to support the Union's effort in the Civil War; on numerous occasions he speaks on the future of blacks in the United States.

Congress abolishes slavery in the District of Columbia.

1863

January: Lincoln's Emancipation Proclamation frees the slaves in the Confederate states.

July: New York City draft riots. Hundreds of blacks are killed or wounded when white workers riot over four days to protest the draft.

A black regiment, the Fifty-Fourth Massachusetts Volunteers, attacks Fort Wagner in Charleston, South Carolina.

Joining Frederick Douglass, Martin Delany, Henry Highland Garnet, and other African American leaders, Brown helps to recruit black soldiers for the Union army.

1864

Brown publishes *Clotelle: A Tale of the Southern States* in James Redpath's "Books for the Camp Fire" series for Union soldiers.

After reading and apprenticing in medicine for two years, Brown, though not formally trained, begins to work as a doctor and sign his name as an "M.D." He practices medicine for the next nineteen years.

Congress authorizes equal pay and treatment for the African American Union troops.

Augusta Jane Evans (1835–1909), *Macaria; or, Altars of Sacrifice*.

1865

April 9: Confederate General Robert E. Lee surrenders to the Union General Ulysses S. Grant at Appomattox Courthouse, Virginia, formally ending the Civil War.

April 15: Lincoln assassinated.

December: Ratification of the Thirteenth Amendment to the Constitution, which abolishes slavery in the United States.

Whitman, *Drum-Taps*.

1866

April: Congress approves the Civil Rights Act, which grants citizenship and legal protections to African Americans.

Brown resumes active work in temperance reform. Over the next seventeen years he participates in the Order of the Sons of Temperance, the John Brown Division of the Sons of Temperance, and the Independent Order of Good Templars.

Melville, *Battle-Pieces*.

1867

January: Congress overrides the veto of President Andrew Johnson and grants voting rights to African American citizens of the District of Columbia.

March: Congress passes the Reconstruction Acts, which are intended to help the former Southern slaves achieve their full rights as citizens. These acts are enforced by the presence of federal troops in the South.

Brown publishes *The Negro in the American Rebellion* and *Clotelle; or, The Colored Heroine*.

Henry Ward Beecher (1813–1887), *Norwood*; Child, *A Romance of the Republic*; John William De Forest (1826–1906), *Miss Ravenel's Conversion*; Augusta Jane Evans Wilson (1835–1909), *St. Elmo*.

1868

July: Ratification of the Fourteenth Amendment, granting citizenship and equal protection under the law to all individuals born or naturalized in the United States.

Brown helps to found the National Association for the Organization of Night Schools and the Spread of Temperance Among the Freed People of the South.

Louisa May Alcott (1832–1888), *Little Women*; Elizabeth Stuart Phelps (1844–1911), *The Gates Ajar*.

1870

March: Ratification of the Fifteenth Amendment, guaranteeing African Americans the right to vote.

Clotelle Brown dies of typhoid fever.

Thomas Wentworth Higginson (1823–1911), *Army Life in a Black Regiment*.

1871

During a visit to Kentucky, Brown (according to his testimony) is abducted by members of the Ku Klux Klan; he escapes, he says, by using a hypodermic needle to inject a drug into the group's leader while the others lie in a drunken stupor.

1873

Brown publishes *The Rising Son; or, The Antecedents and Advancement* of the Colored Race, with an imprint of 1874.

Widespread financial panic and depression.

Alcott, *Work*.

1874

Founding of the Women's Christian Temperance Union.

1875

Congress approves a Civil Rights Act, guaranteeing African Americans equal rights to public facilities and accommodations, and equal rights to serve on juries.

1877

Brown travels to Glasgow to attend a meeting of the Right Worthy Grand Lodge of the World of the Independent Order of Good Templars.

The end of Reconstruction: A compromise decides the close presidential election between the Republican Rutherford B. Hayes and the Democrat Samuel Tilden. Southern democrats grant Hayes the victory in exchange for the withdrawal of federal troops from the South. As a result of the withdrawal, African Americans suffer a precipitous loss of their civil rights and become subject to new Jim Crow laws and a wave of violence.

Henry James (1843–1916), *The American*; Sidney Lanier (1842–1881), *Poems*.

1879

May: Death of William Lloyd Garrison.

Albion Tourgée (1838–1905), *A Fool's Errand*.

1880

After touring several Southern states during the winter of 1879–80, Brown publishes *My Southern Home: Or, The South and Its People*.

Henry Adams (1838–1918), *Democracy*; George Washington Cable (1844–1925), *The Grandissimes*.

1883

The Supreme Court invalidates the 1875 Civil Rights Act.

Frances Willard (1839–1898), *Women and Temperance.*

1884

November 6: Brown dies from a tumor of the bladder. His wife, Anna Brown, who shares her husband's passion for temperance reform, subsequently serves for several years as president of a local branch of the Women's Christian Temperance Union. On 2 September 1902 she dies from burns suffered in a house fire.

Helen Hunt Jackson (1830–1885), *Ramona*; Mark Twain (1835–1910), *The Adventures of Huckleberry Finn.*

A Note on the Text
and Annotations

This volume reprints the 1853 first edition of the text of *Clotel; or, The President's Daughter: A Narrative of Slave Life in the United States*, published in London by Partridge & Oakey. Obvious printer's errors have been silently corrected; otherwise, this edition preserves mid-nineteenth-century usages and spellings, as well as Brown's sometimes peculiar style and syntax. The novel's original four illustrations have also been reprinted.

Wherever possible, the text of the documents in Part Two is that of the original edition or of an edition that would have been available to Brown and his contemporaries. As with the text of *Clotel*, only obvious printer's errors have been corrected.

In *Clotel*, Brown quotes widely from popular poetry, antislavery songbooks, political writings, classic literature, newspapers, the Bible, and many other sources. It was not always possible to track down a particular reference, but the annotations in this edition make a start at identifying his myriad sources. It should be noted that Brown's primary source for Biblical quotations was Noah Webster's idiosyncratic *The Holy Bible, Containing the Old and New Testaments, in the Common Version, with Amendments of the Language* (New Haven: Durrie & Peck, 1833).

CLOTEL;

OR,

THE PRESIDENT'S DAUGHTER:

A Narrative of Slave Life

IN

THE UNITED STATES.

BY

WILLIAM WELLS BROWN,

A FUGITIVE SLAVE, AUTHOR OF "THREE YEARS IN EUROPE."

With a Sketch of the Author's Life.

"We hold these truths to be self-evident: that all men are created equal; that they are endowed by their Creator with certain inalienable rights, and that among these are LIFE, LIBERTY, and the PURSUIT OF HAPPINESS." — *Declaration of American Independence.*

PREFACE.

More than two hundred years have elapsed since the first cargo of slaves was landed on the banks of the James River, in the colony of Virginia, from the West coast of Africa. From the introduction of slaves in 1620,[1] down to the period of the separation of the Colonies from the British Crown, the number had increased to five hundred thousand; now there are nearly four million. In fifteen of the thirty-one States, Slavery is made lawful by the Constitution, which binds the several States into one confederacy.

On every foot of soil, over which *Stars* and *Stripes* wave, the negro is considered common property, on which any white man may lay his hand with perfect impunity. The entire white population of the United States, North and South, are bound by their oath to the constitution, and their adhesion to the Fugitive Slave Law,[2] to hunt down the runaway slave and return him to his claimant, and to suppress any effort that may be made by the slaves to gain their freedom by physical force. Twenty-five millions of whites have banded themselves in solemn conclave to keep four millions of blacks in their chains. In all grades of society are to be found men who either hold, buy, or sell slaves, from the statesmen and doctors of divinity, who can own their hundreds, down to the person who can purchase but one.

Were it not for persons in high places owning slaves, and thereby giving the system a reputation, and especially professed Christians, Slavery would long since have been abolished. The influence of the great "honours the corruption, and chastisement doth therefore hide his head."[3] The great aim of the true friends of the slave should be to lay bare the institution, so that the gaze of the world may be upon it, and cause the wise, the prudent, and the pious to withdraw their support from it, and leave it to its own fate. It does the cause of emancipation but little good to cry out in tones of execration against the traders, the kidnappers, the hireling overseers, and brutal drivers, so long as nothing is said to fasten the guilt on those who move in a higher circle.

---

[1] *1620*: Dutch traders brought slaves to the colonial settlement at Jamestown, Virginia, as early as 1619; many of these slaves had already spent time in the New World.

[2] *Fugitive Slave Law*: One of the bills making up the Compromise of 1850, the Fugitive Slave Law imposed fines on anyone who helped a runaway slave, and ordered state and federal authorities to aid in the pursuit of runaways. For the text of the law, see Martin R. Delany, *The Condition, Elevation, Emigration and Destiny of the Colored People of the United States*, pp. 348–53 in this volume.

[3] *"honours . . . head"*: Shakespeare, *Julius Caesar* IV. iii, 13–14.

The fact that slavery was introduced into the American colonies, while they were under the control of the British Crown, is a sufficient reason why Englishmen should feel a lively interest in its abolition; and now that the genius of mechanical invention has brought the two countries so near together, and both having one language and one literature, the influence of British public opinion is very great on the people of the New World.

If the incidents set forth in the following pages should add anything new to the information already given to the Public through similar publications, and should thereby aid in bringing British influence to bear upon American slavery, the main object for which this work was written will have been accomplished.

W. Wells Brown.

22, Cecil Street, Strand, London.

CONTENTS.

Narrative of the Life
and Escape
of William Wells Brown

"Shall tongues be mute when deeds are wrought
Which well might shame extremest Hell?
Shall freemen lack th' indignant thought?
Shall Mercy's bosom cease to swell?
Shall Honour bleed?—shall Truth succumb?
Shall pen, and press, and *soul* be dumb?"[1]
— *Whittier.*

William Wells Brown, the subject of this narrative,[2] was born a slave in Lexington, Kentucky, not far from the residence of the late Hon. Henry Clay.[3] His mother was the slave of Doctor John Young. His father was a slaveholder, and, besides being a near relation of his master, was connected with the Wicklief family, one of the oldest, wealthiest, and most aristocratic of the Kentucky planters. Dr. Young was the owner of forty or fifty slaves, whose chief employment was in cultivating tobacco, hemp, corn, and flax. The Doctor removed from Lexington, when William was five or six years old, to the state of Missouri, and commenced farming in a beautiful and fertile valley, within a mile of the Missouri river.

Here the slaves were put to work under a harsh and cruel overseer named Cook. A finer situation for a farm could not have been selected in the state. With climate favourable to agriculture, and soil rich, the products came in abundance. At an early age William was separated from his mother, she being worked in the field, and he as a servant in his master's medical department. When about ten years of age, the young slave's feelings were much hurt at hearing the cries of his mother, while being flogged by the negro driver for being a few minutes behind the other hands in reaching the field. He heard her cry, "Oh, pray! oh, pray! oh, pray!" These are the words which slaves generally utter when

---

[1] *"Shall tongues . . . be dumb?"*: From John Greenleaf Whittier (1807–1892), "Stanzas for the Times" (1835).

[2] *William Wells Brown, the subject of this narrative*: Brown authored this third-person narrative of his life and escape. In doing so, he challenged the convention of the time that had white abolitionists writing such prefaces as a way of "legitimating" the efforts of the black author.

[3] *Henry Clay*: Kentucky congressman and nationalist, Henry Clay (1777–1852) championed the American Colonization Society's efforts to ship free blacks to Africa and was one of the principal architects of the Compromise of 1850.

imploring mercy at the hands of their oppressors. The son heard it, though he was some way off. He heard the crack of the whip and the groans of his poor mother. The cold chill ran over him, and he wept aloud; but he was a slave like his mother, and could render her no assistance. He was taught by the most bitter experience, that nothing could be more heart-rending than to see a dear and beloved mother or sister tortured by unfeeling men, and to hear her cries, and not be able to render the least aid. When William was twelve years of age, his master left his farm and took up residence near St. Louis. The Doctor having more hands than he wanted for his own use, William was let out to a Mr. Freeland, an innkeeper. Here the young slave found himself in the hands of a most cruel and heartless master. Freeland was one of the real chivalry of the South; besides being himself a slaveholder, he was a horse-racer, cock-fighter, gambler, and, to crown the whole, an inveterate drunkard. What else but bad treatment could be expected from such a character? After enduring the tyrannical and inhuman usage of this man for five or six months, William resolved to stand it no longer, and therefore ran away, like other slaves who leave their masters, owing to severe treatment; and not knowing where to flee, the young fugitive went into the forest, a few miles from St. Louis. He had been in the woods but a short time, when he heard the barking and howling of dogs, and was soon satisfied that he was pursued by the negro dogs; and, aware of their ferocious nature, the fugitive climbed a tree, to save himself from being torn to pieces. The hounds were soon at the trunk of the tree, and remained there, howling and barking, until those in whose charge they were came up. The slave was ordered down, tied, and taken home. Immediately on his arrival there, he was, as he expected, tied up in the smoke-house, and whipped till Freeland was satisfied, and then smoked with tobacco stems. This the slaveholder called *"Virginia play."* After being well whipped and smoked, he was again set to work. William remained with this monster a few months longer, and was then let out to Elijah P. Lovejoy,[4] who years after became the editor of an abolition newspaper, and was murdered at Alton, Illinois, by a mob of slaveholders from the adjoining state of Missouri. The system of letting out slaves is one among the worst of the evils of slavery. The man who hires a slave, looks upon him in the same light as does the man who hires a horse for a limited period; he feels no interest in him, only to get the worth of his money. Not so

---

[4] *Elijah P. Lovejoy*: The abolitionist editor of the Alton (Illinois) *Observer*, Lovejoy (1802–1837) was killed by a mob that was attempting to destroy his press.

with the man who owns the slave; he regards him as so much property, of which care should be taken. After being let out to a steamer as an under-steward, William was hired by James Walker, a slave-trader. Here the subject of our memoir was made superintendent of the gangs of slaves that were taken to the New Orleans market. In this capacity, William had opportunities, far greater than most slaves, of acquiring knowledge of the different phases of the *"peculiar institution."* Walker was a negro speculator, who was amassing a fortune by trading in the bones, blood, and nerves, of God's children. The thoughts of such a traffic causes us to exclaim with the poet,

> "———Is there not some chosen curse,
> Some hidden thunder in the stores of heaven,
> Red with uncommon wrath, to blast the man
> Who gains his fortune from the blood of souls?"[5]

Between fifty and sixty slaves were chained together, put on board a steam-boat bound for New Orleans, and started on the voyage. New and strange scenes began to inspire the young slave with the hope of escaping to a land of freedom. There was in the boat a large room on the lower deck in which the slaves were kept, men and women promiscuously, all chained two and two together, not even leaving the poor slaves the privilege of choosing their partners. A strict watch was kept over them, so that they had no chance of escape. Cases had occurred in which slaves had got off their chains and made their escape at the landing-places, while the boat stopped to take in wood. But with all their care they lost one woman who had been taken from her husband and children, and having no desire to live without them, in the agony of her soul jumped overboard and drowned herself. Her sorrows were greater than she could bear; slavery and its cruel inflictions had broken her heart. She, like William, sighed for freedom, but not the freedom which even British soil confers and inspires, but freedom from torturing pangs, and overwhelming grief.

At the end of the week they arrived at New Orleans, the place of their destination. Here the slaves were placed in a negro pen, where those who wished to purchase could call and examine them. The negro pen is a small yard surrounded by buildings, from fifteen to twenty feet wide, with the exception of a large gate with iron bars. The slaves

---

[5] "———*Is there . . . blood of souls?"*: From Joseph Addison (1672–1719), *Cato* (1716) I.1.21–24. Brown significantly revises the final line, which in the original reads, "Who owes his greatness to his country's ruin?"

are kept in the buildings during the night, and turned into the pen during the day. After the best of the gang were sold off, the balance was taken to the Exchange coffee-house auction-rooms, and sold at public auction. After the sale of the last slave, William and Mr. Walker left New Orleans for St. Louis.

After they had been at St. Louis a few weeks another cargo of human flesh was made up. There were amongst the lot several old men and women, some of whom had grey locks. On their way down to New Orleans William had to prepare the old slaves for market. He was ordered to shave off the old men's whiskers, and to pluck out the grey hairs where they were not too numerous; where they were, he coloured them with a preparation of blacking with a blacking brush. After having gone through the blacking process, they looked ten or fifteen years younger. William, though not well skilled in the use of scissors and razor, performed the office of the barber tolerably. After the sale of this gang of negroes they returned to St. Louis, and a second cargo was made up. In this lot was a woman who had a child at the breast, yet was compelled to travel through the interior of the country on foot with the other slaves. In a published memoir of his life,[6] William says, "The child cried during the most of the day, which displeased Mr. Walker, and he told the mother that if her child did not stop crying, he would stop its mouth. After a long and weary journey under a burning sun, we put up for the night at a country inn. The following morning, just as they were about to start, the child again commenced crying. Walker stepped up to her and told her to give the child to him. The mother tremblingly obeyed. He took the child by one arm, as any one would a cat by the leg, and walked into the house where they had been staying, and said to the lady, 'Madam, I will make you a present of this little nigger; it keeps making such a noise that I can't bear it.' 'Thank you, sir,' said the lady. The mother, as soon as she saw that her child was to be left, ran up to Mr. Walker, and falling on her knees, begged of him in an agony of despair, to let her have her child. She clung round his legs so closely, that for some time he could not kick her off; and she cried, 'O my child, my child. Master, do let me have my dear, dear child. Oh! do, do. I will stop its crying, and love you for ever if you will only let me have my child again.' But her prayers were not heeded, they passed on, and the mother was separated from her child for ever.

[6] *published memoir of his life*: A reference to William Wells Brown's *Narrative of William W. Brown* (1847), from which he occasionally quotes in this prefatory "Narrative."

"After the woman's child had been given away, Mr. Walker rudely commanded her to retire into the ranks with the other slaves. Women who had children were not chained, but those who had none were. As soon as her child was taken she was chained to the gang."

Some time after this, Walker bought a woman who had a blind child; it being considered worthless, it was given to the trader by the former owner of the woman on the score of humanity, he saying that he wished to keep mother and child together. At first Walker declined taking the child, saying that it would be too much trouble, but the mother wishing to have her boy with her, begged him to take it, promising to carry it the whole distance in her arms. Consequently he took the child, and the gang started on their route to the nearest steamboat landing, which was above one hundred miles. As might have been expected, the woman was unable to carry the boy and keep up with the rest of the gang. They put up at night at a small town, and the next morning, when about to start, Walker took the little boy from its mother and sold it to the innkeeper for the small sum of *one dollar.* The poor woman was so frantic at the idea of being separated from her only child, that it seemed impossible to get her to leave it. Not until the chains were put upon her limbs, and she fastened to the other slaves, could they get her to leave the spot. By main force this slave mother was compelled to go on and leave her child behind. Some days after, a lady from one of the free states was travelling the same road and put up at the same inn: she saw the child the morning after her arrival, and heard its history from one of the slaves, which was confirmed by the innkeeper's wife. A few days after, the following poem appeared in one of the newspapers, from the pen of the lady who had seen the blind child: —

"Come back to me, mother! why linger away
From thy poor little blind boy, the long weary day!
I mark every footstep, I list to each tone,
And wonder my mother should leave me alone!
There are voices of sorrow and voices of glee,
But there's no one to joy or to sorrow with me;
For each hath of pleasure and trouble his share,
And none for the poor little blind boy will care.

"My mother, come back to me! close to thy breast
Once more let thy poor little blind one be pressed;
Once more let me feel thy warm branch on my cheek,
And hear thee in accents of tenderness speak!
O mother! I've no one to love me — no heart

Can bear like thy own in my sorrows a part;
No hand is so gentle, no voice is so kind!
Oh! none like a mother can cherish the blind!

"Poor blind one! no mother thy wailing can hear,
No mother can hasten to banish thy fear;
For the slave-owner drives her, o'er mountain and wild,
And for one paltry dollar hath sold thee, poor child!
Ah! who can in language of mortals reveal
The anguish that none but a mother can feel,
When man in his vile lust of mammon hath trod
On her child, who is stricken and smitten of God?

"Blind, helpless, forsaken, with strangers alone,
She hears in her anguish his piteous moan,
As he eagerly listens—but listens in vain,
To catch the loved tones of his mother again!
The curse of the broken in spirit shall fall
On the wretch who hath mingled this wormwood and gall,
And his gain like a mildew shall blight and destroy,
Who hath torn from his mother the little blind boy."[7]

The thought that man can so debase himself as to treat a fellow-creature as here represented, is enough to cause one to blush at the idea that such men are members of a civilised and Christian nation.

Nothing was more grievous to the sensitive feelings of William, than seeing the separation of families by the slave-trader: husbands taken from their wives, and mothers from their children, without the least appearance of feeling on the part of those who separated them. While at New Orleans, on one occasion, William saw a slave murdered. The circumstances were as follows:—In the evening, between seven and eight o'clock, a slave came running down the levee, followed by several men and boys. The whites were crying out, "Stop that nigger! stop that nigger!" while the poor panting slave, in almost breathless accents, was repeating, "I did not steal the meat—I did not steal the meat." The poor man at last took refuge in the river. The whites who were in pursuit of him, ran on board of one of the boats to see if they could discover him. They finally espied him under the bow of the steamboat "Trenton." They got a pike-pole, and tried to drive him from his hiding-place. When they struck at him he would dive under

[7] *"Come back . . . little blind boy"*: Brown's source for this poem by Margaret Baily (1807–1859) is *The Liberty Minstrel*, ed. George W. Clark (New York, 1845); he reprinted the poem in *The Anti-Slavery Harp*, ed. Brown (Boston, 1848).

the water. The water was so cold, that it soon became evident that he must come out or be drowned.

While they were trying to drive him from under the boat or drown him, he in broken and imploring accents said, "I did not steal the meat; I did not steal the meat. My master lives up the river. I want to see my master. I did not steal the meat. Do let me go home to master." After punching and striking him over the head for some time, he at last sunk in the water, to rise no more alive.

On the end of the pike-pole with which they had been striking him was a hook, which caught in his clothing, and they hauled him up on the bow of the boat. Some said he was dead; others said he was "playing 'possum;" while others kicked him to make him get up; but it was of no use—he was dead.

As soon as they became satisfied of this they commenced leaving one after another. One of the hands on the boat informed the captain that they had killed the man, and that the dead body was lying on the deck. The captain, whose name was Hart, came on deck, and said to those who were remaining, "You have killed this nigger; now take him off my boat." The dead body was dragged on shore and left there. William went on board of the boat where the gang of slaves were, and during the whole night his mind was occupied with what he had seen. Early in the morning he went on shore to see if the dead body remained there. He found it in the same position that it was left the night before. He watched to see what they would do with it. It was left there until between eight and nine o'clock, when a cart, which took up the trash from the streets, came along, and the body was thrown in, and in a few minutes more was covered over with dirt, which they were removing from the streets.

At the expiration of the period of his hiring with Walker, William returned to his master, rejoiced to have escaped an employment as much against his own feelings as it was repugnant to human nature. But this joy was of short duration. The Doctor wanted money, and resolved to sell William's sister and two brothers. The mother had been previously sold to a gentleman residing in the city of St. Louis. William's master now informed him that he intended to sell him, and, as he was his own nephew, he gave him the privilege of finding some one to purchase him, who would treat him better than if he was sold on the auction block. William tried to make some arrangement by which he could purchase his own freedom, but the old Doctor would hear nothing of the kind. If there is one thing more revolting in the trade of human flesh than another, it is the selling of one's own blood relations.

He accordingly set out for the city in search of a new master. When he arrived there, he proceeded to the gaol[8] with the hope of seeing his sister, but was again disappointed. On the following morning he made another attempt, and was allowed to see her once, for the last time. When he entered the room where she was seated in one corner, alone and disconsolate, there were four other women in the room, belonging to the same man, who were bought, the gaoler said, for the master's own use.

William's sister was seated with her face towards the door when he entered, but her gaze was transfixed on nothingness, and she did not look up when he walked up to her; but as soon as she observed him she sprang up, threw her arms around his neck, leaned her head upon his breast, and without uttering a word, in silent, indescribable sorrow, burst into tears. She remained so for some minutes, but when she recovered herself sufficiently to speak, she urged him to take his mother immediately, and try to get to the land of freedom. She said there was no hope for herself, she must live and die a slave. After giving her some advice, and taking a ring from his finger, he bade her farewell for ever. Reader, did ever a fair sister of thine go down to the grave prematurely, if so, perchance, thou hast drank deeply from the cup of sorrow? But how infinitely better is it for a sister to "go into the silent land"[9] with her honour untarnished, but with bright hopes, than for her to be sold to sensual slave-holders.

William had been in the city now two days, and as he was to be absent for only a week, it was well that he should make the best use of his time if he intended to escape. In conversing with his mother, he found her unwilling to make the attempt to reach the land of liberty, but she advised him by all means to get there himself if he possibly could. She said, as all her children were in slavery, she did not wish to leave them; but he loved his mother so intensely, that he could not think of leaving without her. He consequently used all his simple eloquence to induce her to fly with him, and at last he prevailed. They consequently fixed upon the next night as the time for their departure. The time at length arrived, and they left the city just as the clock struck nine. Having found a boat, they crossed the river in it. Whose boat it was he did not know; neither did he care: when it had served his purpose, he turned it adrift, and when he saw it last, it was going at a

---

[8] *gaol*: Jail.

[9] *"go into the silent land"*: From Henry Wadsworth Longfellow (1807–1882), "Song of the Silent Land" (1839), a translation of a poem by the German poet J. G. Von Salis-Seewis (1762–1834).

good speed down the river. After walking in the main road as fast as they could all night, when the morning came they made for the woods, and remained there during the day, but when night came again, they proceeded on their journey with nothing but the North Star to guide them. They continued to travel by night, and to bury themselves in the silent solitudes of the forest by day. Hunger and fatigue could not stop them, for the prospect of freedom at the end of the journey nerved them up. The very thought of leaving slavery, with its democratic whips, republican chains, and bloodhounds, caused the hearts of the weary fugitives to leap with joy. After travelling ten nights and hiding in the woods during the day for fear of being arrested and taken back, they thought they might with safety go the rest of their way by day-light. In nearly all the free states there are men who make a business of catching runaway slaves and returning them to their owners for the reward that may be offered; some of these were on the alert for William and his mother, for they had already seen the runaways advertised in the St. Louis newspapers.

All at once they heard the click of a horse's hoof, and looking back saw three men on horseback galloping towards them. They soon came up, and demanded them to stop. The three men dismounted, arrested them on a warrant, and showed them a handbill, offering two hundred dollars for their apprehension and delivery to Dr. Young and Isaac Mansfield in St. Louis.

While they were reading the handbill, William's mother looked him in the face, and burst into tears. "A cold chill ran over me," says he, "and such a sensation I never experienced before, and I trust I never shall again." They took out a rope and tied him, and they were taken back to the house of the individual who appeared to be the leader. They then had something given them to eat, and were separated. Each of them was watched over by two men during the night. The religious characteristic of the American slaveholder soon manifested itself, as before the family retired to rest they were all called together to attend prayers; and the very man who, but a few hours before, had arrested poor panting, fugitive slaves, now read a chapter from the Bible and offered a prayer to God; as if that benignant and omnipotent One con-secrated the infernal act he had just committed.

The next morning they were chained and hand-cuffed, and started back to St. Louis. A journey of three days brought the fugitives again to the place they had left twelve days previously with the hope that they would never return. They were put in prison to await the orders of their owners. When a slave attempts to escape and fails, he feels sure of either being severely punished, or sold to the negro traders and taken to the far south, there to be worked up on a cotton, sugar, or rice plantation. This William and his mother dreaded. While they were in suspense as to what would be their fate, news came to them that the mother had been sold to a slave speculator. William was soon sold to a merchant residing in the city, and removed to his new owner's dwelling. In a few days the gang of slaves, of which William's mother was one, were taken on board a steamer to be carried to the New Orleans market. The young slave obtained permission from his new owner to go and take a last farewell of his mother. He went to the boat, and found her there, chained to another woman, and the whole number of slaves, amounting to some fifty or sixty, chained in the same manner. As the son approached his mother she moved not, neither did she weep; her emotions were too deep for tears. William approached her, threw his arms around her neck, kissed her, fell upon his knees begging her forgiveness, for he thought he was to blame for her sad condition, and if he had not persuaded her to accompany him she might not have been in chains then.

She remained for some time apparently unimpressionable, tearless, sighless, but in the innermost depths of her heart moved mighty passions. William says, "She finally raised her head, looked me in the face, and such a look none but an angel can give, and said, 'My dear son, you are not to blame for my being here. You have done nothing more nor less than your duty. Do not, I pray you, weep for me; I cannot last long upon a cotton plantation. I feel that my heavenly Master will soon call me home, and then I shall be out of the hands of the slaveholders.' I could hear no more—my heart struggled to free itself from the human form. In a moment she saw Mr. Mansfield, her master, coming toward that part of the boat, and she whispered in my ear, 'My child, we must soon part to meet no more on this side of the grave. You have ever said that you would not die a slave; that you would be a freeman. Now try to get your liberty! You will soon have no one to look after but yourself!' and just as she whispered the last sentence into my ear, Mansfield came up to me, and with an oath said, 'Leave here this instant; you have been the means of my losing one hundred dollars to get this wench back'—at the same time kicking me with a heavy pair of boots. As I left her she gave one shriek, saying, 'God be with you!' It was the last time that I saw her, and the last word I heard her utter.

"I walked on shore. The bell was tolling. The boat was about to start. I stood with a heavy heart, waiting to see her leave the wharf. As I thought of my mother, I could but feel that I had lost

'The glory of my life,
My blessing and my pride!
I half forgot the name of slave,
When she was by my side.'[10]

"The love of liberty that had been burning in my bosom had well-nigh gone out. I felt as though I was ready to die. The boat moved gently from the wharf, and while she glided down the river, I realised that my mother was indeed

'Gone — gone — sold and gone,
To the rice swamp, dark and lone!'[11]

"After the boat was out of sight I returned home; but my thoughts were so absorbed in what I had witnessed, that I knew not what I was about. Night came, but it brought no sleep to my eyes." When once the love of freedom is born in the slave's mind, it always increases and brightens, and William having heard so much about Canada, where a number of his acquaintances had found a refuge and a home, he heartily desired to join them. Building castles in the air in the daytime; incessantly thinking of freedom, he would dream of the land of liberty, but on waking in the morning would weep to find it but a dream.

"He would dream of Victoria's domain,
And in a moment he seemed to be there;
But the fear of being taken again,
Soon hurried him back to despair."[12]

Having been for some time employed as a servant in an hotel, and being of a very active turn, William's new owner resolved to let him out on board a steamboat. Consequently the young slave was hired out to the steamer St. Louis, and soon after sold to Captain Enoch Price, the owner of that boat. Here he was destined to remain but a short period, as Mrs. Price wanted a carriage-driver, and had set her heart upon William for that purpose.

Scarcely three months had elapsed from the time that William became the property of Captain Price, ere that gentleman's family took

---

[10] 'The glory ... side': From Elizabeth Margaret Chandler (1807–1834), "The Bereaved Father," in The Poetical Works of Elizabeth Margaret Chandler; with a Memoir of Her Life and Character, by Benjamin Lundy (Philadelphia, 1836).

[11] 'Gone ... and lone!': From John Greenleaf Whittier, "The Farewell of a Virginia Slave Mother to Her Daughters Sold into Southern Bondage" (1838).

[12] "He would ... despair": Brown wrote poetry and he may well have been the author of this and several other of the unattributable quotations; see the Note on the Text and Annotations (p. 44).

a pleasure trip to New Orleans, and William accompanied them. From New Orleans the family proceeded to Louisville. The hope of escape again dawned upon the slave's mind, and the trials of the past were lost in hopes for the future. The love of liberty, which had been burning in his bosom for years, and which at times had been well nigh extinguished, was now resuscitated. Hopes nurtured in childhood, and strengthened as manhood dawned, now spread their sails to the gales of his imagination. At night, when all around was peaceful, and in the mystic presence of the everlasting starlight, he would walk the steamer's decks, meditating on his happy prospects, and summoning up gloomy reminiscences of the dear hearts he was leaving behind him. When not thinking of the future his mind would dwell on the past. The love of a dear mother, a dear and affectionate sister, and three brothers yet living, caused him to shed many tears. If he could only be assured of their being dead, he would have been comparatively happy; but he saw in imagination his mother in the cotton-field, followed by a monster task-master, and no one to speak a consoling word to her. He beheld his sister in the hands of the slave-driver, compelled to submit to his cruelty, or, what was unutterably worse, his lust; but still he was far away from them, and could not do anything for them if he remained in slavery; consequently he resolved, and consecrated the resolve with a prayer, that he would start on the first opportunity.

That opportunity soon presented itself. When the boat got to the wharf[13] where it had to stay for some time, at the first convenient moment Brown made towards the woods, where he remained until night-time. He dared not walk during the day, even in the state of Ohio; he had seen so much of the perfidy of white men, and resolved, if possible, not to get into their hands. After darkness covered the world, he emerged from his hiding-place; but he did not know east from west, or north from south; clouds hid the North Star from his view. In this desolate condition he remained for some hours, when the clouds rolled away, and his friend, with its shining face—the North Star—welcomed his sight. True as the needle to the pole he obeyed its attractive beauty, and walked on till daylight dawned.

It was winter-time; the day on which he started was the 1st of January, and, as it might be expected, it was intensely cold; he had no overcoat, no food, no friend, save the North Star, and the God which made it. How ardently must the love of freedom burn in the poor slave's bosom, when he will pass through so many difficulties, and even look

---

[13]*wharf:* The wharf is in Cincinnati, and Ohio was a free state.

death in the face, in winning his birth-right, freedom. But what crushed the poor slave's heart in his flight most was, not the want of food or clothing, but the thought that every white man was his deadly enemy. Even in the free states the prejudice against color is so strong, that there appears to exist a deadly antagonism between the white and coloured races.

William in his flight carried a tinder-box with him, and when he got very cold he would gather together dry leaves and stubble and make a fire, or certainly he would have perished. He was determined to enter into no house, fearing that he might meet a betrayer.

It must have been a picture which would have inspired an artist, to see the fugitive roasting the ears of corn that he found or took from barns during the night, at solitary fires in the deep solitudes of woods.

The suffering of the fugitive was greatly increased by the cold, from the fact of his having just come from the warm climate of New Orleans. Slaves seldom have more than one name, and William was not an exception to this, and the fugitive began to think of an additional name. A heavy rain of three days, in which it froze as fast as it fell, and by which the poor fugitive was completely drenched, and still more chilled, added to the depression of his spirits already created by his weary journey. Nothing but the fire of hope burning within his breast could have sustained him under such overwhelming trials,

> "Behind he left the whip and chains,
> Before him were sweet Freedom's plains."[14]

Through cold and hunger, William was now ill, and he could go no further. The poor fugitive resolved to seek protection, and accordingly hid himself in the woods near the road, until some one should pass. Soon a traveller came along, but the slave dared not speak. A few moments more and a second passed, the fugitive attempted to speak, but fear deprived him of voice. A third made his appearance. He wore a broad-brimmed hat and a long coat, and was evidently walking only for exercise. William scanned him well, and though not much skilled in physiognomy, he concluded he was the man. William approached him, and asked him if he knew any one who would help him, as he was sick? The gentleman asked whether he was not a slave. The poor slave hesitated; but, on being told that he had nothing to fear, he answered, "Yes." The gentleman told him he was in a pro-slaving

---

[14] *"Behind . . . Freedom's plains"*: From anon., "The Flying Slave," in *The Anti-Slavery Harp*, ed. Brown.

neighbourhood, but, if he would wait a little, he would go and get a covered waggon, and convey him to his house. After he had gone, the fugitive meditated whether he should stay or not, being apprehensive that the broad-brimmed gentleman had gone for some one to assist him: he however concluded to remain.

After waiting about an hour — an hour big with fate to him — he saw the covered waggon making its appearance, and no one on it but the person he before accosted. Trembling with hope and fear, he entered the waggon, and was carried to the person's house. When he got there, he still halted between two opinions, whether he should enter or take to his heels; but he soon decided after seeing the glowing face of the wife. He saw something in her that bid him welcome, something that told him he would not be betrayed.

He soon found that he was under the shed of a Quaker, and a Quaker of the George Fox stamp.[15] He had heard of Quakers and their kindness; but was not prepared to meet with such hospitality as now greeted him. He saw nothing but kind looks, and heard nothing but tender words. He began to feel the pulsations of a new existence. White men always scorned him, but now a white benevolent woman felt glad to wait on him; it was a revolution in his experience. The table was loaded with good things, but he could not eat. If he were allowed the privilege of sitting in the kitchen, he thought he could do justice to the viands. The surprise being over his appetite soon returned.

"I have frequently been asked," says William, "how I felt upon finding myself regarded as a man by a white family; especially having just run away from one. I cannot say that I have ever answered the question yet. The fact that I was, in all probability, a freeman, sounded in my ears like a charm. I am satisfied that none but a slave could place such an appreciation upon liberty as I did at that time. I wanted to see my mother and sister, that I might tell them that 'I was free!' I wanted to see my fellow-slaves in St. Louis, and let them know that the chains were no longer upon my limbs. I wanted to see Captain Price, and let him learn from my own lips that I was no more a chattel, but a MAN. I was anxious, too, thus to inform Mrs. Price that she must get another coachman, and I wanted to see Eliza[16] more than I did Mr. Price or Mrs. Price. The fact that I was a freeman — could walk, talk, eat, and

---

[15] *Quaker of the George Fox stamp*: George Fox (1624–1691) was the founder of the Quakers, or Society of Friends, a Christian sect known for its commitment to non-violence and abolitionism.

[16] *Eliza*: According to Brown's 1847 *Narrative*, Eliza was a maid belonging to the Price family; Mrs. Price hoped to secure Brown's loyalty by marrying him to Eliza.

sleep as a man, and no one to stand over me with the blood-clotted cow-hide—all this made me feel that I was not myself."

The kind Quaker, who so hospitably entertained William, was called Wells Brown. He remained with him about a fortnight, during which time he was well fed and clothed. Before leaving, the Quaker asked him what was his name besides William? The fugitive told him he had no other. "Well," said he, "thee must have another name. Since thee has got out of slavery, thee has become a man, and men always have two names."

William told him that as he was the first man to extend the hand of friendship to him, he would give him the privilege of naming him.

"If I name thee," said he, "I shall call thee Wells Brown, like myself."

"But," said he, "I am not willing to lose my name of William. It was taken from me once against my will,[17] and I am not willing to part with it on any terms."

"Then," said the benevolent man, "I will call thee William Wells Brown."

"So be it," said William Wells Brown, and he has been known by this name ever since.

After giving the newly-christened freeman "a name," the Quaker gave him something to aid him to get "a local habitation." So, after giving him some money, Brown again started for Canada. In four days he reached a public-house, and went in to warm himself. He soon found that he was not out of the reach of his enemies. While warming himself, he heard some men in an adjoining bar-room talking about some runaway slaves. He thought it was time to be off, and, suiting the action to the thought, he was soon in the woods out of sight. When night came, he returned to the road and walked on; and so, for two days and two nights, till he was faint and ready to perish of hunger.

In this condition he arrived in the town of Cleveland, Ohio, on the banks of Lake Erie, where he determined to remain until the spring of the year, and then to try and reach Canada. Here he was compelled to work merely for his food. "Having lived in that way," said he in a speech at a public meeting in Exeter Hall,[18] "for some weeks, I obtained a job, for which I received a shilling. This was not only the

[17] *It was taken . . . against my will*: The name "William" had been taken from Brown during his boyhood when his owner at the time, Dr. John Young, adopted a nephew named William Moore.

[18] *Exeter Hall*: Opened in 1831 in London, Exeter Hall, with a seating capacity of five thousand, was regularly used for antislavery rallies. For Brown's description of a meeting at Exeter Hall, see his 17 May 1853 letter to William Lloyd Garrison (pp. 377–80).

only shilling I had, but it was the first I had received after obtaining my freedom, and that shilling made me feel, indeed, as if I had a considerable stock in hand. What to do with my shilling I did not know. I would not put it into the bankers' hands, because, if they would have received it, I would not trust them. I would not lend it out, because I was afraid I should not get it back again. I carried the shilling in my pocket for some time, and finally resolved to lay it out; and after considerable thinking upon the subject, I laid out 6*d.*[19] for a spelling-book, and the other 6*d.* for sugar candy or barley sugar. Well, now, you will all say that the one 6*d.* for the spelling-book was well laid out; and I am of opinion that the other was well laid out too; for the family in which I worked for my bread had two little boys, who attended the school every day, and I wanted to convert them into teachers; so I thought that nothing would act like a charm so much as a little barley sugar. The first day I got my book and stock in trade, I put the book into my bosom, and went to saw wood in the wood-house on a very cold day. One of the boys, a little after four o'clock, passed through the wood-house with a bag of books. I called to him, and I said to him, 'Johnny, do you see this?' taking a stick of barley sugar from my pocket and showing it to him. Says he, 'Yes; give me a taste of it.' Said I, 'I have got a spelling-book too,' and I showed that to him. 'Now,' said I, 'if you come to me in my room, and teach me my A, B, C, I will give you a whole stick.' 'Very well,' said he, 'I will; but let me taste it.' 'No; I can't.' 'Let me have it now.' Well, I thought I had better give him a little taste, until the right time came; and I marked the barley sugar about a quarter of an inch down, and told him to bite that far and no farther. He made a grab, and bit half the stick, and ran off laughing. I put the other piece in my pocket, and after a little while the other boy, little David, came through the wood-house with his books. I said nothing about the barley sugar, or my wish to get education. I knew the other lad would communicate the news to him. In a little while he returned, and said, 'Bill, John says you have got some barley sugar.' 'Well,' I said, 'what of that?' 'He said you gave him some; give me a little taste.' 'Well, if you come to-night and help me to learn my letters, I will give you a whole stick.' 'Yes; but let me taste it.' 'Ah! but you want to bite it.' 'No, I don't, but just let me taste it.' Well, I thought I had better show it to him. 'Now,' said he, 'let me touch my tongue

---

[19] 6*d.*: Six pence; *d.* is an abbreviation for the British pence. There were twelve pence in the shilling, which was approximately equivalent to the U.S. dime. Brown uses British terms as a way of clarifying U.S. currency for his British readers.

against it.' I thought then that I had better give him a taste, but I would not trust him so far as I trusted John; so I called him to me, and got his head under my arm, and took him by the chin, and told him to hold out his tongue; and as he did so, I drew the barley sugar over very lightly. He said, 'That's very nice; just draw it over again. I could stand here and let you draw it across my tongue all day.' The night came on; the two boys came out of their room up into the attic where I was lodging, and there they commenced teaching me the letters of the alphabet. We all laid down upon the floor, covered with the same blanket; and first one would teach me a letter, and then the other, and I would pass the barley sugar from one side to the other. I kept those two boys on my sixpenny worth of barley sugar for about three weeks. Of course I did not let them know how much I had. I first dealt it out to them a quarter of a stick at a time. I worked along in that way, and before I left that place where I was working for my bread, I got so that I could spell. I had a book that had the word *baker* in it, and the boys used to think that when they got so far as that, they were getting on pretty well. I had often passed by the school-house, and stood and listened at the window to hear them spell, and I knew that when they could spell *baker* they thought something of themselves; and I was glad when I got that far. Before I left that place I could read. Finally, from that I went on until I could write. How do you suppose I first commenced writing? for you will understand that up to the present time I never spent a day in school in my life, for I had no money to pay for schooling, so that I had to get my learning first from one and then from another. I carried a piece of chalk in my pocket, and whenever I met a boy I would stop him and take out my chalk and get at a board fence and then commence. First I made some flourishes with no meaning, and called a boy up, and said, 'Do you see that? Can you beat that writing?' Said he, 'That's not writing.' Well, I wanted to get so as to write my own name. I had got out of slavery with only one name. While escaping, I received the hospitality of a very good man, who had spared part of his name to me, and finally my name got pretty long, and I wanted to be able to write it. 'Now, what do you call that?' said the boy, looking at my flourishes. I said, 'Is not that *William Wells Brown?*' 'Give me the chalk,' says he, and he wrote out in large letters *'William Wells Brown,'* and I marked up the fence for nearly a quarter of a mile, trying to copy, till I got so that I could write my name. Then I went on with my chalking, and, in fact, all board fences within half a mile of where I lived were marked over with some kind of figures I had made, in trying to learn how to write. I next obtained an arithmetic, and then a grammar, and I stand here to-night, without having had a day's schooling in my life." Such were some of the efforts made by a fugitive slave to obtain himself an education. Soon after his escape, Brown was married to a free coloured woman, by whom he has had three daughters, one of whom died in infancy. Having tasted the sweets of freedom himself, his great desire was to extend its blessing to his race, and in the language of the poet he would ask himself,

> "Is true freedom but to break
> Fetters for our own dear sake
> And with leathern hearts forget
> That we owe mankind a debt?

> "No! true freedom is to share
> All the chains our brothers wear,
> And with heart and hand to be
> Earnest to make others free."[20]

While acting as a servant to one of the steamers on Lake Erie, Brown often took fugitives from Cleveland and other ports to Buffalo, or Detroit, from either of which places they could cross to Canada in an hour. During the season of 1842, this fugitive slave conveyed no less than *sixty-nine* runaway slaves across Lake Erie, and placed them safe on the soil of Canada. The following interesting account of Brown's first going into business for himself, which we transcribe from his "Three Years In Europe,"[21] will show the energy of the man. He says, "In the autumn of 1835, having been cheated out of the previous summer's earnings by the captain of the steamer in which I had been employed running away with the money, I was, like the rest of the men, left without any means of support during the winter, and therefore had to seek employment in the neighbouring towns. I went to the town of Monroe in the state of Michigan, and while going through the principal streets looking for work, I passed the door of the only barber in town, whose shop appeared to be filled with persons waiting to be shaved. As there was but one man at work, and as I had, while employed in the steamer, occasionally shaved a gentleman who could not perform that office himself, it occurred to me that I might get employment here as a journeyman[22] barber. I therefore made immediate application for work, but the barber told me he did not need a

---

[20] *Is true . . . others free"*: From James Russell Lowell (1819–1891), "Stanzas on Freedom" (1844).
[21] *"Three Years in Europe"*: A reference to Brown's *Three Years in Europe; or, Places I Have Seen and People I Have Met* (London, 1852).
[22] *journeyman*: An apprentice or hired help.

hand. But I was not to be put off so easily, and after making several offers to work cheap, I frankly told him, that if he would not employ me, I would get a room near him, and set up an opposition establishment. This threat, however, made no impression on the barber; and as I was leaving, one of the men, who were waiting to be shaved, said, 'If you want a room in which to commence business, I have one on the opposite side of the street.' This man followed me out; we went over, and I looked at the room. He strongly urged me to set up, at the same time promising to give me his influence. I took the room, purchased an old table, two chairs, got a pole with a red stripe painted around it, and the next day opened, with a sign over the door, 'Fashionable Hairdresser from New York, Emperor of the West.' I need not add that my enterprise was very annoying to the 'shop over the way,' especially my sign, which happened to be the most extensive part of the concern. Of course I had to tell all who came in, that my neighbour on the opposite side did not keep clean towels, that his razors were dull, and, above all, he never had been to New York to see the fashions. Neither had I. In a few weeks I had the entire business of the town, to the great discomfiture of the other barber. At this time, money matters in the Western States were in a sad condition. Any person who could raise a small amount of money was permitted to establish a bank, and allowed to issue notes for four times the sum raised. This being the case, many persons borrowed money merely long enough to exhibit to the bank inspectors, and the borrowed money was returned, and the bank left without a dollar in its vaults, if, indeed, it had a vault about its premises. The result was, that banks were started all over the Western States, and the country flooded with worthless paper. These were known as the 'Wild Cat Banks.'[23] Silver coin being very scarce, and the banks not being allowed to issue notes for a smaller amount than one dollar, several persons put out notes of from 6 to 75 cents in value; these were called 'Shinplasters.'[24] The Shinplaster was in the shape of a promissory note, made payable on demand. I have often seen persons with large rolls of these bills, the whole not amounting to more than five dollars. Some weeks after I had commenced business on my

---

[23] *Wild Cat Banks*: Prior to the creation of the national banking system in 1854, wildcat banks (and other institutions and individuals) were known to issue banknotes without adequate financial backing. Their proliferation contributed to the Panic of 1837.

[24] *Shinplasters*: During the antebellum period, the term referred to paper money in denominations of less than one dollar that was issued by institutions or individuals not connected to the Bank of the United States. Reforms of such practices were instituted in the wake of the Panic of 1837.

'own hook,' I was one evening very much crowded with customers; and while they were talking over the events of the day, one of them said to me, 'Emperor, you seem to be doing a thriving business. You should do as other business men, issue your Shinplasters.' This of course, as it was intended, created a laugh; but with me it was no laughing matter, for from that moment I began to think seriously of becoming a banker. I accordingly went a few days after to a printer, and he, wishing to get the job of printing, urged me to put out my notes, and showed me some specimens of engravings that he had just received from Detroit. My head being already filled with the idea of the bank, I needed but little persuasion to set the thing finally afloat. Before I left the printer the notes were partly in type, and I studying how I should keep the public from counterfeiting them. The next day, my Shinplasters were handed to me, the whole amount being twenty dollars; and, after being duly signed, were ready for circulation. The first night I had my money, my head was so turned and dizzy, that I could not sleep. In fact, I slept but little for weeks after the issuing of my bills. This fact satisfied me, that people of wealth pass many sleepless hours. At first my notes did not take well; they were too new, and viewed with a suspicious eye. But through the assistance of my customers, and a good deal of exertion on my part, my bills were soon in circulation; and nearly all the money received in return for my notes was spent in fitting up and decorating my shop. Few bankers get through this world without their difficulties, and I was not to be an exception. A short time after my money had been out, a party of young men, either wishing to pull down my vanity, or to try the soundness of my bank, determined to give it 'a run.'[25] After collecting together a number of my bills, they came one at a time to demand other money for them; and I, not being aware of what was going on, was taken by surprise. One day as I was sitting at my table, stropping some new razors I had just purchased with the avails of my Shinplasters, one of the men entered and said, 'Emperor, you will oblige me if you will give me some other money for these notes of yours.' I immediately cashed the notes with the most worthless of the Wild Cat money that I had on hand, but which was a lawful tender. The young man had scarcely left, when a second appeared with a similar amount, and demanded payment. These were cashed, and soon a third came with his roll of notes. I paid these with an air of triumph, although I had but half a dollar left. I began now to think seriously what I should do, or how to act,

---

[25] *'a run'*: A banking crisis that occurs when many depositors attempt to withdraw their funds.

provided another demand should be made. While I was thus engaged in thought, I saw the fourth man crossing the street, with a handful of notes, evidently my Shinplasters. I instantaneously shut the door, and looking out of the window said, 'I have closed business for to-day: come to-morrow and I will see you.' In looking across the street, I saw my rival standing at his shopdoor, grinning and clapping his hands at my apparent downfall. I was completely 'done *Brown*'[26] for the day. However, I was not to be 'used up' in this way; so I escaped by the back door, and went in search of my friend, who had first suggested to me the idea of issuing my notes. I found him, told him of the difficulty I was in, and wished him to point out a way by which I might extricate myself. He laughed heartily at my sad position, and then said, 'You must act as all bankers do in this part of the country.' I inquired how they did; and he said, 'when your notes are brought to you, you must redeem them, and then send them out and get other money for them; and, with the latter, you can keep cashing your own Shinplasters.' This was, indeed, a new idea for me. I immediately commenced putting in circulation the notes which I had just redeemed, and my efforts were crowned with such success, that, together with the aid of my friend, who, like a philanthropist and Western Christian as he was, before I slept that night, my Shinplasters were again in circulation, and my bank once more on a sound basis."

In proportion as his mind expanded under the more favourable circumstances in which Brown was placed, he became anxious, not merely for the redemption of his race from personal slavery, but for the moral and religious elevation of those who were free. Finding that habits of intoxication were too prevalent among his coloured brethren, he, in conjunction with others, commenced a temperance reformation in their body. Such was the success of their efforts that, in three years, in the city of Buffalo alone, a society of upwards of 500 members was raised out of a coloured population of less than 700. Of that society Mr. Brown was thrice elected president. The intellectual powers of our author, coupled with his intimate acquaintance with the workings of the slave system, early recommended him to the Abolitionists, as a man eminently qualified to arouse the attention of the people of the Northern States to the great national sin of America. In 1843, he was engaged by the Western New York Anti-Slavery Society[27] as a lecturing agent. From 1844 to 1847, he laboured in the Anti-Slavery

[26] '*done* Brown': Swindled (slang), with a pun on Brown's name (and "race").
[27] *Western New York Anti-Slavery Society*: An affiliate of the American Anti-Slavery Society.

cause in connection with the American Anti-Slavery Society;[28] and from that period up to the time of his departure for Europe, in 1849, he was an agent of the Massachusetts Anti-Slavery Society.[29] The records of these societies furnish abundant evidence of the success of his labours. From the Massachusetts Anti-Slavery Society he early received the following testimonial. "Since Mr. Brown became an agent of this society, he has lectured in very many of the towns of this commonwealth, and gained for himself, the respect and esteem of all whom he met. Himself a fugitive slave, he can experimentally describe the situation of those in bonds as bound with them; and he powerfully illustrates the diabolism of that system which keeps in chains and darkness a host of minds, which, if free and enlightened, would shine among men like stars in the firmament." Another member of that society speaks thus of him: — "I need not attempt any description of the ability and efficiency which characterised the speeches of William Wells Brown throughout the meeting. To you who know him so well, it is enough to say that his lectures were worthy of himself. He has left an impression on the minds of the people, that few could have done. Cold indeed must be the hearts that could resist the appeals of so noble a specimen of humanity, in behalf of a crushed and despised race."

In 1847, Mr. Brown wrote a narrative of his life and escape from slavery, which rapidly ran through several editions. A copy of this he forwarded to his old master, from whom he had escaped, and soon after a friend of Mr. Brown's received the following letter:

"St. Louis, Jan. 10*th,* 1848.

"Sir, — I received a pamphlet, or a narrative, so called on the title-page, of the Life of William W. Brown, a fugitive slave, purporting to have been written by himself; and in his book I see a letter from you to the said William W. Brown. This said Brown is named William; he is a slave belonging to me, and ran away from me the first day of January, 1834.

"I purchased him of Mr. S. Willi, the last of September, 1833. I paid six hundred and fifty dollars for him. If I had wanted to speculate on him, I could have sold him for three times as much as I paid for him. I was offered two thousand dollars for him in New Orleans at one time,

---

[28] *American Anti-Slavery Society*: A national abolitionist organization founded in Philadelphia in 1833.

[29] *Massachusetts Anti-Slavery Society*: Founded in 1835 by William Lloyd Garrison (1805–1879), the Massachusetts Anti-Slavery Society was one of the most influential abolitionist organizations, enjoying particularly strong support in New England. It was affiliated with the American Anti-Slavery Society.

and fifteen hundred dollars for him at another time, in Louisville, Kentucky. But I would not sell him. I was told that he was going to run away, but I did not believe the man, for I had so much confidence in William. I want you to see him, and see if what I say is not the truth. I do not want him as a slave, but I think that his friends, who sustain him and give him the right hand of fellowship, or he himself, could afford to pay my agent in Boston three hundred and twenty five dollars, and I will give him free papers, so that he may go wherever he wishes to. Then he can visit St. Louis, or any other place he may wish.

"This amount is just half what I paid for him. Now, if this offer suits Mr. Brown, and the Anti-Slavery Society of Boston, or Massachusetts, let me know, and I will give you the name of my agent in Boston, and forward the papers, to be given to William W. Brown as soon as the money is paid.

"Yours respectfully,
"ENOCH PRICE."

"To Edmund Quincy,[30] Esq."

While Mr. Brown would most gladly have accepted manumission papers, relieving him from all future claim of the slaveholder, and thereby making his freedom more secure, he yet felt that he could not conscientiously purchase his liberty, because, by so doing, he would be putting money into the pockets of the manstealer which did not justly belong to him. He therefore refused the offer of Mr. Price. Notwithstanding the celebrity he had acquired in the North, as a man of genius and talent, and the general respect his high character had gained him, the slave spirit of America denied him the rights of a citizen. By the constitution of the United States he was every moment liable to be arrested, and returned to the slavery from which he had fled. His only protection from such a fate was the anomaly of the ascendancy of the public opinion over the law of the country.

It has been for years thought desirable and advantageous to the cause of Negro emancipation in America, to have some talented man of color always in Great Britain, who should be a living refutation of the doctrine of the inferiority of the African race; and it was moreover felt that none could so powerfully advocate the cause of "those in bonds" as one who had actually been "bound with them." Mr. Brown having received repeated invitations from distinguished English

---

[30] *Edmund Quincy*: The Boston reformer and writer Edmund Quincy (1808–1877) served as the corresponding secretary of the Massachusetts Anti-Slavery Society from 1844 to 1853.

Abolitionists to visit Great Britain, and being chosen a delegate to the Paris Peace Congress of 1849 by the American Peace Society,[31] and also by a convention of the coloured people of Boston, he resolved to acquiesce in the wishes of his numerous friends, and accordingly sailed from the United States on the 18th of July, 1849.

On leaving America he bore with him the following testimony from the Board of Managers of the Massachusetts Anti-Slavery Society:—

"In consequence of the departure for England of their esteemed friend and faithful co-labourer in the cause of the American slave, William W. Brown, the Board of Management of the Massachusetts Anti-Slavery Society would commend him to the confidence, respect, esteem, and hospitality of the friends of emancipation wherever he may travel:—

"1. Because he is a fugitive slave from the American house of bondage, and on the soil which gave him birth can find no spot on which he can stand in safety from his pursuers, protected by law.

"2. Because he is a man, and not a chattel; and while as the latter, he may at any time be sold at public vendue[32] under the American star-spangled banner, we rejoice to know that he will be recognised and protected as the former under the flag of England.

"3. Because, for several years past, he has nobly consecrated his time and talents, at great personal hazard, and under the most adverse circumstances, to the uncompromising advocacy of the cause of his enslaved countrymen.

"4. Because he visits England for the purpose of increasing, consolidating, and directing British humanity and piety against that horrible system of slavery in America, by which three millions of human beings, by creation the children of God, are ranked with four-footed beasts, and treated as marketable commodities.

"5. Because he has long been in their employment as a lecturing agent in Massachusetts, and has laboured with great acceptance and success; and from the acquaintance thus formed, they are enabled to

---

[31] *Paris... Society*: Convened in August 1849, the Paris Peace Congress drew approximately 800 delegates, including the black abolitionists Brown, Alexander Crummell (1819–1898), and J. W. C. Pennington (1807–1870). The Congress supported developing an international peacekeeping Congress of Nations. A league of nations was also one of the large goals of the American Peace Society, founded in 1828 by William Ladd (1778–1841) and then absorbed by the League of Universal Brotherhood, which was founded in 1846 by Elihu Burritt (1810–1879). Burritt was the guiding spirit of the Paris Peace Congress.

[32] *vendue*: auction.

certify that he has invariably conducted himself with great circumspection, and won for himself the sympathy, respect, and friendship of a very large circle of acquaintance."

The Coloured convention unanimously passed the following resolution:

"*Resolved,* — That we bid our brother, William Wells Brown, God speed in his mission to Europe, and commend him to the hospitality and encouragement of all true friends of humanity."[33]

In a letter to an American journal,[34] announcing his arrival at Liverpool, he speaks as follows: —

"No person of my complexion can visit this country without being struck with the marked difference between the English and the Americans. The prejudice which I have experienced on all and every occasion in the United States, and to some degree on board the *Canada*, vanished as soon as I set foot on the soil of Britain. In America I had been bought and sold as a slave, in the Southern States. In the so-called Free States I had been treated as one born to occupy an inferior position; in steamers, compelled to take my fare on the deck; in hotels, to take my meals in the kitchen; in coaches, to ride on the outside; in railways, to ride in the 'Negro car;' and in churches, to sit in the 'Negro pew.' But no sooner was I on British soil than I was recognised as a man and an equal. The very dogs in the streets appeared conscious of my manhood. Such is the difference, and such is the change that is brought about by a trip of nine days in an Atlantic steamer. * * * For the first time in my life, I can say 'I am truly free.' My old master may make his appearance here, with the constitution of the United States in his pocket, the fugitive slave law in one hand and the chains in the other, and claim me as his property; but all will avail him nothing. I can here stand and look the tyrant in the face, and tell him that I am his equal! England is, indeed, the 'land of the free, and the home of the brave.'"

The reception of Mr. Brown at the Peace Congress in Paris was most flattering. He admirably maintained his reputation as a public speaker. His brief address upon that "war spirit of America which holds in

[33] *. . . humanity"*: For accounts of the 16 July 1849 farewell gathering in Boston, see the *Liberator*, 20 July 1849 and 27 July 1849.

[34] *American journal*: Brown wrote regularly to the *Liberator* about his travels in Great Britain; see, for example, the issue of 2 November 1849 for a letter that bears some resemblance to the letter that follows.

bondage nearly four millions of his brethren," produced a profound sensation. At its conclusion the speaker was warmly greeted by Victor Hugo, the Abbé Duguerry, Emile de Girardin, Richard Cobden,[35] and every man of note in the assembly. At the soirée given by M. de Tocquerelle, the Minister for Foreign Affairs, and the other fêtes given to the members of the Congress, Mr. Brown was received with marked attention.

Having finished his Peace Mission in France, he returned to England, where he was received with a hearty welcome by some of the most influential abolitionists of this country. Most of the fugitive slaves, and in fact nearly all of the coloured men who have visited Great Britain from the United States, have come upon begging missions, either for some society or for themselves. Mr. Brown has been almost the only exception. With that independence of feeling, which those who are acquainted with him know to be one of his chief characteristics, he determined to maintain himself and family by his own exertions — by his literary labours, and the honourable profession of a public lecturer. From nearly all the cities and large provincial towns he received invitations to lecture or address public meetings. The mayors, or other citizens of note, presided over many of these meetings. At Newcastle-upon-Tyne[36] a soirée was given him, and an address presented by the citizens. A large and influential meeting was held at Bolton, Lancashire,[37] which was addressed by Mr. Brown, and at its close the ladies presented to him the following address: —

"An address, presented to Mr. William Wells Brown, the fugitive slave from America, by the ladies of Bolton, March 22nd, 1850: —

"Dear friend and brother, — We cannot permit you to depart from among us without giving expression to the feelings which we entertain towards yourself personally, and to the sympathy which you have awakened in our breasts for the three millions of our sisters and brothers who still suffer and groan in the prison-house of American bondage. You came among us an entire stranger; we received you for the sake of your mission; and having heard the story of your personal

---

[35] *Victor Hugo ... Richard Cobden*: Vicomte Victor Marie Hugo (1802–1885), French poet and novelist, who would become best known for *Les Misérables* (1862); Abbé Duguerry (?–1871), curé of the Parish of La Madeleine; Emile de Girardin (1806–1881), prominent journalist and editor of *La Presse*; Richard Cobden (1804–1865), British politician known for his advocacy of free trade.

[36] *Newcastle-upon-Tyne*: A city in northern England on the River Tyne.

[37] *Bolton, Lancashire*: A town in a northwest county of England which at the time was a cotton-textile center.

wrongs, and gazed with horror on the atrocities of slavery as seen through the medium of your touching descriptions, we are resolved, henceforward, in reliance on divine assistance, to render what aid we can to the cause which you have so eloquently pleaded in our presence.

"We have no words to express our detestation of the crimes which, in the name of liberty, are committed in the country which gave you birth. Language fails to tell our deep abhorrence of the impiety of those who, in the still more sacred name of religion, rob immortal beings not only of an earthly citizenship, but do much to prevent them from obtaining a heavenly one; and, as mothers and daughters, we embrace this opportunity of giving utterance to our utmost indignation at the cruelties perpetrated upon our sex, by a people professedly acknowledging the equality of all mankind. Carry with you, on your return to the land of your nativity, this our solemn protest against the wicked institution which, like a dark and baleful cloud, hangs over it; and ask the unfeeling enslavers, as best you can, to open the prison doors to them that are bound, and let the oppressed go free.

"Allow us to assure you that your brief sojourn in our town has been to ourselves, and to vast multitudes, of a character long to be remembered; and when you are far removed from us, and toiling, as we hope you may be long spared to do, in this righteous enterprise, it may be some solace to your mind to know that your name is cherished with affectionate regard, and that the blessing of the Most High is earnestly supplicated in behalf of yourself, your family, and the cause to which you have consecrated your distinguished talents."

A most respectable and enthusiastic public meeting was held at Sheffield,[38] to welcome Mr. Brown, and the next day he was invited to inspect several of the large establishments there. While going through the manufactory of Messrs. Broadhead and Atkin, silver and electro-platers, &c., in Love-street, and whilst he was being shown through the works, a subscription was hastily set on foot on his behalf, by the workmen and women of the establishment, which was presented to Mr. Brown in the counting-house by a deputation of the subscribers. The spokesman (the designer to Messrs. Broadhead and Atkin) addressing Mr. Brown on behalf of the workpeople, begged his acceptance of the present as a token of esteem, as well as an expression of their sympathy in the cause he advocates, viz. that of the American slave. Mr. Brown briefly thanked the parties for their spontaneous free

[38] *Sheffield*: A factory town and industrial center in northern England.

will offering, accompanied as it was by a generous expression of sympathy for his afflicted brethren and sisters in bondage.

Mr. Brown has been in England nearly four years, and since his arrival he has travelled above twenty thousand miles through Great Britain, addressed one hundred and thirty public meetings, lectured in twenty-three mechanics and literary institutions, and given his services to many of the benevolent and religious societies on the occasion of their anniversary meetings. After a lecture, which he delivered before the Whittington Club, he received from the managers of that institution the following testimonial:

"*Whittington Club and Metropolitan Athenæum,*[39]
"189, *Strand*, June 21, 1850.

"My dear sir,

I have much pleasure in conveying to you the best thanks of the Managing Committee of this institution for the excellent lecture you gave here last evening, and also in presenting you in their names with an honorary membership of the club. It is hoped that you will often avail yourself of its privileges by coming amongst us. You will then see, by the cordial welcome of the members, that they protest against the odious distinctions made between man and man, and the abominable traffic of which you have been the victim.

"For my own part, I shall be happy to be serviceable to you in any way, and at all times be glad to place the advantages of the institution at your disposal.

"I am, my dear sir,
"Yours truly,
"WILLIAM STRUDWICKE,
"Secretary."

"Mr. W. Wells Brown."

On the 1st of August, 1851, a meeting of the most novel character was held at the Hall of Commerce, London, the chief actors being American fugitive slaves. That meeting was most ably presided over by Mr. Brown, and the speeches made on the occasion by fugitive slaves were of the most interesting and creditable description. Although a residence in Canada is infinitely preferable to slavery in America, yet

[39] *Whittington Club and Metropolitan Athenæum*: At the time a prestigious London club with over two thousand members, including Charles Dickens and several members of Parliament.

the climate of that country is uncongenial to the constitutions of the Negroes, and their lack of education is an almost insuperable barrier to their social progress. The latter evil Mr. Brown attempted to remedy by the establishment of Manual Labour Schools in Canada for fugitive slaves. A public meeting, attended by between 3,000 and 4,000 persons, was held on the 6th of January 1851, in the City Hall, Glasgow, which was presided over by Alexander Hastie, Esq., M.P., at which resolutions were unanimously passed, approving of Mr. Brown's scheme; which scheme, however, never received that amount of support which would have enabled him to bring it into practice; and the plan at present only remains as an evidence of its author's ingenuity and desire for the elevation of his oppressed and injured race. Mr. Brown subsequently made, through the columns of the *Times*, a proposition for the emigration of American fugitive slaves, under fair and honourable terms, from Canada to the West Indies, where there is a great lack of that labour which they are so capable of undertaking.[40] These efforts all show the willingness of this fugitive slave to aid those of his race. Last year Mr. Brown published his "Three Years in Europe; or, Places I have seen and People I have met." And his literary abilities may be partly judged of from the following commendations of that ably written work:—

"The extraordinary excitement produced by 'Uncle Tom's Cabin'[41] will, we hope, prepare the public of Great Britain and America for this lively book of travels by a real fugitive slave. Though he never had a day's schooling in his life, he has produced a literary work not unworthy of a highly educated gentleman. Our readers will find in these letters much instruction, not a little entertainment, and the beatings of a manly heart, on behalf of a down-trodden race, with which they will not fail to sympathise." — *The Eclectic.*

"When he writes on the wrongs of his race, or the events of his own career, he is always interesting or amusing." — *The Athenæum*

"The appearance of this book is too remarkable a literary event to pass without a notice. At the moment when attention in this country is directed to the state of the coloured people in America, the book appears with additional advantage; if nothing else were attained by its

---

[40] *Mr. Brown . . . undertaking*: Brown's letter on West Indies emigration can be found in the (London) *Times*, 4 July 1851.

[41] *'Uncle Tom's Cabin'*: Harriet Beecher Stowe's *Uncle Tom's Cabin* ran serially in the *National Era* from June 1851 to April 1852 and was published in two volumes in the spring of 1852. For a selection from the novel, see pp. 329–40.

publication, it is well to have another proof of the capability of the Negro intellect. Altogether Mr. Brown has written a pleasing and amusing volume. Contrasted with the caricature and bombast of his white countrymen, Mr. Willis's description of 'People he has met,'[42] a comparison suggested by the similarity of the title, it is both in intellect and in style a superior performance, and we are glad to bear this testimony to the literary merit of a work by a Negro author." — *The Literary Gazette.*

"That a man who was a slave for the first twenty years of his life, and who has never had a day's schooling, should produce such a book as this, cannot but astonish those who speak disparagingly of the African race." — *The Weekly News and Chronicle.*

"This remarkable book of a remarkable man cannot fail to add to the practical protests already entered in Britain against the absolute bondage of 3,000,000 of our fellow creatures. The impression of a self-educated son of slavery here set forth, must hasten the period when the senseless and impious denial of common claims to a common humanity, on the score of color, shall be scouted with scorn in every civilised and Christian country. And when this shall be attained, among the means of destruction of the hideous abomination, his compatriots will remember with respect and gratitude the doings and sayings of William Wells Brown. The volume consists of a sufficient variety of scenes, persons, arguments, inferences, speculations, and opinions, to satisfy and amuse the most *exigeant*[43] of those who read *pour se desennuyer;*[44] while those who look deeper into things, and view with anxious hope the progress of nations and of mankind, will feel that the good cause of humanity and freedom, of Christianity, enlightenment, and brotherhood, cannot fail to be served by such a book as this." — *Morning Advertiser.*

"He writes with ease and ability, and his intelligent observations upon the great question to which he has devoted, and is devoting his life, will be read with interest, and will command influence and respect." — *Daily News.*

Mr. Brown is most assiduous in his studies even at the present time. The following extract from his writings will show how he spends most of his leisure hours: —

[42] *Mr. Willis's . . . 'People he has met'*: Nathaniel Parker Willis (1806–1867) was a popular New York writer, editor, and reviewer who was regarded by some as a dilettante and dandy. His *People I Have Met* was published in 1850.
[43] *exigeant*: Exacting, hard to please.
[44] *pour se desennuyer*: For amusement; to kill time.

"It was eight o'clock before I reached my lodgings. Although fatigued by the day's exertions, I again resumed the reading of Roscoe's 'Leo X.,'[45] and had nearly finished seventy-three pages, when the clock on St. Martin's Church apprised me that it was two. He who escapes from slavery at the age of twenty years without any education, as did the writer of this letter, must read when others are asleep, if he would catch up with the rest of the world. 'To be wise,' says Pope, 'is but to know how little can be known.'[46] The true searcher after truth and knowledge is always like a child; although gaining strength from year to year, he still 'learns to labour and to wait.'[47] The field of labour is ever expanding before him, reminding him that he has yet more to learn; teaching him that he is nothing more than a child in knowledge, and inviting him onward with a thousand varied charms. The son may take possession of the father's goods at his death, but he cannot inherit with the property the father's cultivated mind. He may put on the father's old coat, but that is all; the immortal mind of the first wearer has gone to the tomb. Property may be bequeathed but knowledge cannot. Then let him who would be useful in his generation be up and doing. Like the Chinese student who learned perseverance from the woman whom he saw trying to rub a crowbar into a needle, so should we take the experience of the past to lighten our feet though the paths of the future."

The following testimonial to Mr. Brown's abilities, from an American journal of which Frederick Douglass is editor,[48] shows that his talents are highly appreciated in that country:—

"We have the pleasure to lay before our readers another interesting letter from W. Wells Brown. We rejoice to find our friend still persevering in the pursuit of knowledge, and still more do we rejoice to find such marked evidence of his rapid progress as his several letters afford. But a few years ago he was a despised, degraded, whip-scarred slave, knowing nothing of letters; and now we find him writing accounts of his travels in a distant land, of which a man reared under the most favourable educational advantages might be proud."

[45] *Roscoe's 'Leo X.'*: The British historian William Roscoe (1753–1831) published his four-volume *The Life and Pontificate of Leo the Tenth* in 1805; Leo X (1475–1521) was pope from 1513 to 1521.

[46] *'To be . . . known'*: From Alexander Pope (1688–1744), *An Essay on Man* (1734).

[47] *'learns . . . to wait'*: From Henry Wadsworth Longfellow, "Resignation" (1848).

[48] *"The following . . . editor"*: A testimonial by Frederick Douglass (1818–1895) in the *North Star*, 17 April 1851.

We should have said that it was Mr. Brown's intention to have returned to the United States to his family ere this. But the passage of the infamous "Fugitive Slave Law" prevented his returning.

Mr. Brown's wife[49] died in Buffalo N. Y. in Jan. 1851. He has two daughters[50] who are now in this country, being trained for teachers. Of course we need not add that for their education they are entirely dependent on their father's exertions. During last year, the Rev. Edward Hore, of Ramsgate, through a willingness to assist Mr. Brown in returning to the United States, wrote to his former owner, and offered him £50, if he would relinquish all claim to him, and furnish the fugitive with papers of emancipation, but the following note from the slave-owner speaks for itself:—

"*St. Louis, Feb. 16th*, 1852.

"Rev. sir,—I received your note, dated Jan. 6th, concerning a run-away slave of mine now known by the name of William Wells Brown. You state that I offered to take three hundred and twenty five dollars for him, and give him free papers, in 1848. I did so then, but since that time the laws of the United States are materially changed. The Fugitive Slave Bill has passed since then. I can now take him anywhere in the United States, and I have everything arranged for his arrest if he lands at any port in the United States. But I will give him papers of emancipation, properly authenticated by our statutes, for the sum of five hundred dollars (or £100) that will make him as free as any white person. If this suits your views, you can let me know, and I will have the papers made out and forwarded to Boston, to Joseph Gruley, of the firm of Charles Wilkins and Co., 33, Long Wharf. The money must be paid before the papers are handed over to your agent.[51]

"Respectfully your obedient servant,

"To the Rev. Edward Hore."   "ENOCH PRICE."

---

[49] *Mr. Brown's wife*: Brown married the free black Elizabeth Schooner in 1834; they separated in 1847.

[50] *two daughters*: Brown took custody of Clarissa Brown (1836–?) and Josephine Brown (1839–?) after separating from his wife. For a selection from Josephine Brown, see pp. 360–64.

[51] *money . . . to our agent*: In 1854, Ellen Richardson, who had helped to purchase Frederick Douglass's freedom in 1846, bought Brown's manumission from Enoch Price for $300.

Clotel;
or,
The President's Daughter

CHAPTER I.
THE NEGRO SALE.

"Why stands she near the auction stand,
That girl so young and fair?
What brings her to this dismal place,
Why stands she weeping there?"[1]

With the growing population of slaves in the Southern States of America, there is a fearful increase of half whites, most of whose fathers are slaveowners, and their mothers slaves. Society does not frown upon the man who sits with his mulatto child upon his knee, whilst its mother stands a slave behind his chair. The late Henry Clay, some years since, predicted that the abolition of negro slavery would be brought about by the amalgamation of the races.[2] John Randolph, a distinguished slaveholder of Virginia, and a prominent statesman, said in a speech in the legislature of his native state, that "the blood of the first American statesman coursed through the veins of the slave of the South."[3] In all the cities and towns of the slave states, the real negro, or clear black, does not amount to more than one in every four of the slave population. This fact is, of itself, the best evidence of the

[1] "Why stands she . . . there?": The opening stanza of anon., "The Slave-Auction — A Fact," in The Anti-Slavery Harp, ed. Brown (1848).

[2] The late Henry Clay . . . races: Brown distorts Clay's views by presenting them out of context. Clay saw "amalgamation" as the nightmarish but inevitable outcome of what the abolitionists wanted to impose on the United States. Clay advocated colonizing blacks to Africa precisely because he believed blacks were inferior to whites and that black-white unions were "unnatural." See, for example, his speech to the Senate of 7 February 1839, in which he opposed abolishing slavery in the District of Columbia on the grounds that abolitionists "are in favor of amalgamation" and wish "to contaminate the industrious and laboring classes of society of the North by a revolting admixture of blackness" (The Papers of Henry Clay, vol. 9, ed. Robert Seger II and Melba Porter Hay [Lexington: U of Kentucky, 1988], 282).

[3] John Randolph . . . of the South": The Virginian political leader John Randolph (1773–1833) was a fiery advocate of the doctrine of states' rights and the owner of one of Virginia's largest slave plantations. Nevertheless, he went on record opposing slavery, and in his will he freed his slaves. Consistent with the assertions of this obscure and possibly apocryphal quotation, Randolph regularly boasted of having descended from the Indian princess Pocahontas.

degraded and immoral condition of the relation of master and slave in the United States of America.

In all the slave states, the law says: — "Slaves shall be deemed, sold, taken, reputed, and adjudged in law to be chattels[4] personal in the hands of their owners and possessors, and their executors, administrators and assigns, to all intents, constructions, and purposes whatsoever. A slave is one who is in the power of a master to whom he belongs. The master may sell him, dispose of his person, his industry, and his labour. He can do nothing, possess nothing, nor acquire anything, but what must belong to his master. The slave is entirely subject to the will of his master, who may correct and chastise him, though not with unusual rigour, or so as to maim and mutilate him, or expose him to the danger of loss of life, or to cause his death. The slave, to remain a slave, must be sensible that there is no appeal from his master."[5] Where the slave is placed by law entirely under the control of the man who claims him, body and soul, as property, what else could be expected than the most depraved social condition? The marriage relation, the oldest and most sacred institution given to man by his Creator, is unknown and unrecognised in the slave laws of the United States. Would that we could say, that the moral and religious teaching in the slave states were better than the laws; but, alas! we cannot. A few years since, some slaveholders became a little uneasy in their minds about the rightfulness of permitting slaves to take to themselves husbands and wives, while they still had others living, and applied to their religious teachers for advice; and the following will show how this grave and important subject was treated: —

> "Is a servant, whose husband or wife has been sold by his or her master into a distant country, to be permitted to marry again?"

The query was referred to a committee, who made the following report; which, after discussion, was adopted: —

> "That, in view of the circumstances in which servants in this country are placed, the committee are unanimous in the opinion, that it is better to permit servants thus circumstanced to take another husband or wife."

---

[4] *chattels*: Moveable property; possessions.
[5] *"Slaves shall be deemed . . . from his master"*: An amalgam of slave law, which particularly echoes the famous ruling by Judge Thomas Ruffin (1787–1870), in the 1829 North Carolina Case of *State v. Mann*, that "The power of the master must be absolute to render the submission of the slave perfect."

Such was the answer from a committee of the "Shiloh Baptist Association;" and instead of receiving light, those who asked the question were plunged into deeper darkness!

A similar question was put to the "Savannah River Association,"[6] and the answer, as the following will show, did not materially differ from the one we have already given:—

> "Whether, in a case of involuntary separation, of such a character as to preclude all prospect of future intercourse, the parties ought to be allowed to marry again."

Answer—

> "That such separation among persons situated as our slaves are, is civilly a separation by death; and they believe that, in the sight of God, it would be so viewed. To forbid second marriages in such cases would be to expose the parties, not only to stronger hardships and strong temptation, but to church-censure for acting in obedience to their masters, who cannot be expected to acquiesce in a regulation at variance with justice to the slaves, and to the spirit of that command which regulates marriage among Christians. The slaves are not free agents; and a dissolution by death is not more entirely without their consent, and beyond their control, than by such separation."

Although marriage, as the above indicates, is a matter which the slaveholders do not think is of any importance, or of any binding force with their slaves; yet it would be doing that degraded class an injustice, not to acknowledge that many of them do regard it as a sacred obligation, and show a willingness to obey the commands of God on this subject. Marriage is, indeed, the first and most important institution of human existence—the foundation of all civilisation and culture—the root of church and state. It is the most intimate covenant of heart formed among mankind; and for many persons the only relation in which they feel the true sentiments of humanity. It gives scope for every human virtue, since each of these is developed from the love and confidence which here predominate. It unites all which ennobles and beautifies life,—sympathy, kindness of will and deed, gratitude, devotion, and every delicate, intimate feeling. As the only asylum for true education, it is the first and last sanctuary of human culture. As husband and wife through each other become conscious of complete humanity,

---

[6] *"Savannah River Association"*: Like the aforementioned "Shiloh Baptist Association," a Christian organization based in the South.

and every human feeling, and every human virtue; so children, at their first awakening in the fond covenant of love between parents, both of whom are tenderly concerned for the same object, find an image of complete humanity leagued in free love. The spirit of love which prevails between them acts with creative power upon the young mind, and awakens every germ of goodness within it. This invisible and incalculable influence of parental life acts more upon the child than all the efforts of education, whether by means of instruction, precept, or exhortation. If this be a true picture of the vast influence for good of the institution of marriage, what must be the moral degradation of that people to whom marriage is denied? Not content with depriving them of all the higher and holier enjoyments of this relation, by degrading and darkening their souls, the slaveholder denies to his victim even that slight alleviation of his misery, which would result from the marriage relation being protected by law and public opinion. Such is the influence of slavery in the United States, that the ministers of religion, even in the so-called free states, are the mere echoes, instead of the correctors, of public sentiment.

We have thought it advisable to show that the present system of chattel slavery in America undermines the entire social condition of man, so as to prepare the reader for the following narrative of slave life, in that otherwise happy and prosperous country.

In all the large towns in the Southern States, there is a class of slaves who are permitted to hire their time of their owners, and for which they pay a high price. These are mulatto women, or quadroons,[7] as they are familiarly known, and are distinguished for their fascinating beauty. The handsomest usually pays the highest price for her time. Many of these women are the favourites of persons who furnish them with the means of paying their owners, and not a few are dressed in the most extravagant manner. Reader, when you take into consideration the fact, that amongst the slave population no safeguard is thrown around virtue, and no inducement held out to slave women to be chaste, you will not be surprised when we tell you that immorality and vice pervade the cities of the Southern States in a manner unknown in the cities and towns of the Northern States. Indeed most of the slave women have no higher aspiration than that of becoming the finely-

---

[7] *mulatto . . . or quadroons*: "Quadroon" was a term used in the nineteenth century (and less often in the twentieth century) to refer to people who were thought to be one-fourth "black"; more generally, "quadroon," like "mulatto," was used to refer to light-skinned peoples of mixed racial ancestry.

dressed mistress of some white man. And at negro balls and parties, this class of women usually cut the greatest figure.

At the close of the year——the following advertisement appeared in a newspaper published in Richmond, the capital of the state of Virginia:—"Notice: Thirty-eight negroes will be offered for sale on Monday, November 10th, at twelve o'clock, being the entire stock of the late John Graves, Esq. The negroes are in good condition, some of them very prime; among them are several mechanics, able-bodied field hands, plough-boys, and women with children at the breast, and some of them very prolific in their generating qualities, affording a rare opportunity to any one who wishes to raise a strong and healthy lot of servants for their own use. Also several mulatto girls of rare personal qualities: two of them very superior. Any gentleman or lady wishing to purchase, can take any of the above slaves on trial for a week, for which no charge will be made."[8] Amongst the above slaves to be sold were Currer and her two daughters, Clotel and Althesa; the latter were the girls spoken of in the advertisement as "very superior." Currer was a bright mulatto, and of prepossessing appearance, though then nearly forty years of age. She had hired her time for more than twenty years, during which time she had lived in Richmond. In her younger days Currer had been the housekeeper of a young slaveholder; but of later years had been a laundress or washerwoman, and was considered to be a woman of great taste in getting up linen. The gentleman for whom she had kept house was Thomas Jefferson, by whom she had two daughters. Jefferson being called to Washington to fill a government appointment,[9] Currer was left behind, and thus she took herself to the business of washing, by which means she paid her master, Mr. Graves, and supported herself and two children. At the time of the decease of her master, Currer's daughters, Clotel and Althesa, were aged respectively sixteen and fourteen years, and both, like most of their own sex in America, were well grown. Currer early resolved to bring her daughters up as ladies, as she termed it, and therefore imposed little or no work upon them. As her daughters grew older, Currer had to pay a

---

[8] *"Notice . . . made"*: The advertisement draws on an 1838 advertisement quoted in Theodore Dwight Weld's *American Slavery As It Is* (1839); see pp. 312–16.

[9] *government appointment*: Because Jefferson resided in Washington, D.C., for part of his vice presidency and for all of his presidency, overall from the late 1790s to 1809, the information provided here would suggest that the events in *Clotel* begin around 1815. But this dating is inconsistent with the novel's later account of Nat Turner's rebellion of 1831, the election of 1840, and other historical events. As discussed in the Introduction, Brown deliberately skews historical chronology.

stipulated price for them; yet her notoriety as a laundress of the first
class enabled her to put an extra price upon her charges, and thus she
and her daughters lived in comparative luxury. To bring up Clotel and
Althesa to attract attention, and especially at balls and parties, was the
great aim of Currer.[10] Although the term "negro ball" is applied to
most of these gatherings, yet a majority of the attendants are often
whites. Nearly all the negro parties in the cities and towns of the
Southern States are made up of quadroon and mulatto girls, and white
men. These are democratic gatherings, where gentlemen, shopkeepers,
and their clerks, all appear upon terms of perfect equality. And there is
a degree of gentility and decorum in these companies that is not surpassed by similar gatherings of white people in the Slave States. It was
at one of these parties that Horatio Green, the son of a wealthy
gentleman of Richmond, was first introduced to Clotel. The young
man had just returned from college, and was in his twenty-second year.
Clotel was sixteen and was admitted by all to be the most beautiful
girl, coloured or white, in the city. So attentive was the young man to
the quadroon during the evening that it was noticed by all, and became
a matter of general conversation; while Currer appeared delighted
beyond measure at her daughter's conquest. From that evening, young
Green became the favourite visitor at Currer's house. He soon promised to purchase Clotel, as speedily as it could be effected, and make
her mistress of her own dwelling; and Currer looked forward with
pride to the time when she should see her daughter emancipated and
free. It was a beautiful moonlight night in August, when all who reside
in tropical climes are eagerly gasping for a breath of fresh air, that
Horatio Green was seated in the small garden behind Currer's cottage,
with the object of his affections by his side. And it was here that Horatio drew from his pocket the newspaper, wet from the press, and read
the advertisement for the sale of the slaves to which we have alluded;
Currer and her two daughters being of the number. At the close of the
evening's visit, and as the young man was leaving, he said to the girl,
"You shall soon be free and your own mistress."

As might have been expected, the day of sale brought an unusual
large number together to compete for the property to be sold. Farmers
who make a business of raising slaves for the market were there; slave-
traders and speculators were also numerously represented; and in the
midst of this throng was one who felt a deeper interest in the result of

---

[10] For a similar discussion of quadroon culture, see the selection from Harriet Martineau's *Society in America* (pp. 317–19).

the sale than any other of the bystanders; this was young Green. True to his promise, he was there with a blank bank check in his pocket, awaiting with impatience to enter the list as a bidder for the beautiful slave. The less valuable slaves were first placed upon the auction block, one after another, and sold to the highest bidder. Husbands and wives were separated with a degree of indifference that is unknown in any other relation of life, except that of slavery. Brothers and sisters were torn from each other; and mothers saw their children leave them for the last time on this earth.

It was late in the day, when the greatest number of persons were thought to be present, that Currer and her daughters were brought forward to the place of sale. Currer was first ordered to ascend the auction stand, which she did with a trembling step. The slave mother was sold to a trader. Althesa, the youngest, and who was scarcely less beautiful than her sister, was sold to the same trader for one thousand dollars. Clotel was the last, and, as was expected, commanded a higher price than any that had been offered for sale that day. The appearance of Clotel on the auction block created a deep sensation amongst the crowd. There she stood, with a complexion as white as most of those who were waiting with a wish to become her purchasers; her features as finely defined as any of her sex of pure Anglo-Saxon; her long black wavy hair done up in the neatest manner; her form tall and graceful, and her whole appearance indicating one superior to her position. The auctioneer commenced by saying, that "Miss Clotel had been reserved for the last, because she was the most valuable. How much gentlemen? Real Albino, fit for a fancy girl for any one. She enjoys good health, and has a sweet temper. How much do you say?" "Five hundred dollars." "Only five hundred for such a girl as this? Gentlemen, she is worth a deal more than that sum; you certainly don't know the value of the article you are bidding upon. Here, gentlemen, I hold in my hand a paper certifying that she has a good moral character." "Seven hundred." "Ah, gentlemen, that is something like. This paper also states that she is very intelligent." "Eight hundred." "She is a devoted Christian, and perfectly trustworthy." "Nine hundred." "Nine fifty." "Ten." "Eleven." "Twelve hundred." Here the sale came to a dead stand. The auctioneer stopped, looked around, and began in a rough manner to relate some anecdotes relative to the sale of slaves, which, he said, had come under his own observation. At this juncture the scene was indeed strange. Laughing, joking, swearing, smoking, spitting, and talking kept up a continual hum and noise amongst the crowd; while the slave-girl stood with tears in her eyes, at one time looking towards her mother and sister, and at another towards the young man whom she hoped would become her purchaser. "The chastity of this girl is pure; she has never been from under her mother's care; she is a virtuous creature." "Thirteen." "Fourteen." "Fifteen." "Fifteen hundred dollars," cried the auctioneer, and the maiden was struck for that sum. This was a Southern auction, at which the bones, muscles, sinews, blood, and nerves of a young lady of sixteen were sold for five hundred dollars; her moral character for two hundred; her improved intellect for one hundred; her Christianity for three hundred; and her chastity and virtue for four hundred dollars more. And this, too, in a city thronged with churches, whose tall spires look like so many signals pointing to heaven, and whose ministers preach that slavery is a God-ordained institution![11]

What words can tell the inhumanity, the atrocity, and the immorality of that doctrine which, from exalted office, commends such a crime to the favour of enlightened and Christian people? What indignation from all the world is not due to the government and people who put forth all their strength and power to keep in existence such an institution? Nature abhors it; the age repels it; and Christianity needs all her meekness to forgive it.

Clotel was sold for fifteen hundred dollars, but her purchaser was Horatio Green. Thus closed a negro sale, at which two daughters of Thomas Jefferson, the writer of the Declaration of American Independence, and one of the presidents of the great republic, were disposed of to the highest bidder!

> "O God! my every heart-string cries,
>   Dost thou these scenes behold
> In this our boasted Christian land,
>   And must the truth be told?
>
> "Blush, Christian, blush! for e'en the dark,
>   Untutored heathen see
> Thy inconsistency; and, lo!
>   They scorn thy God, and thee!"[12]

---

[11] *God-ordained institution!*: For an early version of a similar auction scene, see William Wells Brown's "A True Story of Slave Life," *Anti-Slavery Advocate*, December 1852 (pp. 373–77 in this volume).

[12] *"Oh God! . . . and thee!"*: From anon., "The Slave-Auction—A Fact," in *The Anti-Slavery Harp*, ed. Brown.

CHAPTER II.
GOING TO THE SOUTH.

"My country, shall thy honoured name,
    Be as a bye-word through the world?
Rouse! for, as if to blast thy fame,
    This keen reproach is at thee hurled;
The banner that above thee waves,
    Is floating o'er three million slaves."[1]

Dick Walker, the slave speculator, who had purchased Currer and Althesa, put them in prison until his gang was made up, and then, with his forty slaves, started for the New Orleans market. As many of the slaves had been brought up in Richmond, and had relations residing there, the slave trader determined to leave the city early in the morning, so as not to witness any of those scenes so common where slaves are separated from their relatives and friends, when about departing for the Southern market. This plan was successful; for not even Clotel, who had been every day at the prison to see her mother and sister, knew of their departure. A march of eight days through the interior of the state, and they arrived on the banks of the Ohio river, where they were all put on board a steamer, and then speedily sailed for the place of their destination.

Walker had already advertised in the New Orleans papers, that he would be there at a stated time with "a prime lot of able-bodied slaves ready for field service; together with a few extra ones, between the ages of fifteen and twenty-five." But, like most who make a business of buying and selling slaves for gain, he often bought some who were far advanced in years, and would always try to sell them for five or ten years younger than they actually were. Few persons can arrive at anything like the age of a negro, by mere observation, unless they are well acquainted with the race. Therefore the slave-trader very frequently carried out this deception with perfect impunity. After the steamer had left the wharf, and was fairly on the bosom of the Father of Waters,[2] Walker called his servant Pompey to him, and instructed him as to "getting the negroes ready for market." Amongst the forty negroes

---

[1] *"My country . . . slaves"*: From R. C. Wateston, "Freedom's Banner," in *The Anti-Slavery Harp*, ed. Brown.

[2] *Father of Waters*: The Mississippi River—a principal U.S. river with numerous tributaries.

were several whose appearance indicated that they had seen some years, and had gone through some services. Their grey hair and whiskers at once pronounced them to be above the ages set down in the trader's advertisement. Pompey had long been with the trader, and knew his business; and if he did not take delight in discharging his duty, he did it with a degree of alacrity, so that he might receive the approbation of his master. "Pomp," as Walker usually called him, was of real negro blood, and would often say, when alluding to himself, "Dis nigger is no countefit; he is de genewine artekil." Pompey was of low stature, round face, and, like most of his race, had a set of teeth, which for whiteness and beauty could not be surpassed; his eyes large, lips thick, and hair short and woolly. Pompey had been with Walker so long, and had seen so much of the buying and selling of slaves, that he appeared perfectly indifferent to the heartrending scenes which daily occurred in his presence. It was on the second day of the steamer's voyage that Pompey selected five of the old slaves, took them into a room by themselves, and commenced preparing them for the market. "Well," said Pompey, addressing himself to the company, "I is de gentman dat is to get you ready, so dat you will bring marser a good price in de Orleans market. How old is you?" addressing himself to a man who, from appearance, was not less than forty. "If I live to see next corn-planting time I will either be forty-five or fifty-five, I don't know which." "Dat may be," replied Pompey; "but now you is only thirty years old; dat is what marser says you is to be." "I know I is more den dat," responded the man. "I knows nothing about dat," said Pompey; "but when you get in de market, an anybody axe you how old you is, an you tell 'em forty-five, marser will tie you up an gib you de whip like smoke. But if you tell 'em dat you is only thirty, den he wont." "Well den, I guess I will only be thirty when dey axe me," replied the chattel.

"What your name?" inquired Pompey. "Geemes," answered the man. "Oh, Uncle Jim, is it?" "Yes." "Den you must have off dem dare whiskers of yours, an when you get to Orleans you must grease dat face an make it look shiney." This was all said by Pompey in a manner which clearly showed that he knew what he was about. "How old is you?" asked Pompey of a tall, strong-looking man. "I was twenty-nine last potato-digging time," said the man. "What's your name?" "My name is Tobias, but dey call me 'Toby.'" "Well, Toby, or Mr. Tobias, if dat will suit you better, you is now twenty-three years old, an no more. Dus you hear dat?" "Yes," responded Toby. Pompey gave each to understand how old he was to be when asked by persons who wished to purchase, and then reported to his master that the "old boys" were all right. At eight o'clock on the evening of the third day, the lights of another steamer were seen in the distance, and apparently coming up very fast. This was a signal for a general commotion on the Patriot, and everything indicated that a steamboat race was at hand.[3] Nothing can exceed the excitement attendant upon a steamboat on the Mississippi river. By the time the boats had reached Memphis, they were side by side, and each exerting itself to keep the ascendancy in point of speed. The night was clear, the moon shining brightly, and the boats so near to each other that the passengers were calling out from one boat to the other. On board the Patriot, the firemen were using oil, lard, butter, and even bacon, with the wood, for the purpose of raising the steam to its highest pitch. The blaze, mingled with the black smoke, showed plainly that the other boat was burning more than wood. The two boats soon locked, so that the hands of the boats were passing from vessel to vessel, and the wildest excitement prevailed throughout amongst both passengers and crew. At this moment the engineer of the Patriot was seen to fasten down the safety-valve, so that no steam should escape. This was, indeed, a dangerous resort. A few of the boat hands who saw what had taken place, left that end of the boat for more secure quarters.

The Patriot stopped to take in passengers, and still no steam was permitted to escape. At the starting of the boat cold water was forced into the boilers by the machinery, and, as might have been expected, one of the boilers immediately exploded. One dense fog of steam filled every part of the vessel, while shrieks, groans, and cries were heard on every hand. The saloons and cabins soon had the appearance of a hospital. By this time the boat had landed, and the Columbia, the other boat, had come alongside to render assistance to the disabled steamer. The killed and scalded (nineteen in number) were put on shore, and the Patriot, taken in tow by the Columbia, was soon again on its way.

It was now twelve o'clock at night, and instead of the passengers being asleep the majority were gambling in the saloons. Thousands of dollars change hands during a passage from Louisville or St. Louis to New Orleans on a Mississippi steamer, and many men, and even ladies, are completely ruined. "Go call my boy, steward," said Mr. Smith, as

---

[3] *steamboat race was at hand*: The likely source for the subsequent account of this disastrous steamboat race was the widely reported race of 28 July 1852 between the steamboats *Henry Clay* and *Armenia* on the Hudson, which resulted in an explosion killing over sixty people; for an account of the explosion, see the New York *Daily Tribune*, 31 July 1852.

"BETTING" A NEGRO IN THE SOUTHERN STATES.

he took his cards one by one from the table. In a few moments a fine looking, bright-eyed mulatto boy, apparently about fifteen years of age, was standing by his master's side at the table. "I will see you, and five hundred dollars better," said Smith, as his servant Jerry approached the table. "What price do you set on that boy?" asked Johnson, as he took a roll of bills from his pocket. "He will bring a thousand dollars, any day, in the New Orleans market," replied Smith. "Then you bet the whole of the boy, do you?" "Yes." "I call you, then," said Johnson, at the same time spreading his cards out upon the table. "You have beat me," said Smith, as soon as he saw the cards. Jerry, who was standing on top of the table, with the bank notes and silver dollars round his feet, was now ordered to descend from the table. "You will not forget that you belong to me," said Johnson, as the young slave was stepping from the table to a chair. "No, sir," replied the chattel. "Now go back to your bed, and be up in time to-morrow morning to brush my clothes and clean my boots, do you hear?" "Yes, sir," responded Jerry, as he wiped the tears from his eyes.

Smith took from his pocket the bill of sale and handed it to Johnson; at the same time saying, "I claim the right of redeeming that boy, Mr. Johnson. My father gave him to me when I came of age, and I promised not to part with him." "Most certainly, sir, the boy shall be yours, whenever you hand me over a cool thousand," replied Johnson. The next morning, as the passengers were assembling in the breakfast saloon and upon the guards of the vessel, and the servants were seen running about waiting upon or looking for their masters, poor Jerry was entering his new master's state-room with his boots. "Who do you belong to?" said a gentleman to an old black man, who came along leading a fine dog that he had been feeding. "When I went to sleep last night, I belonged to Governor Lucas; but I understand dat he is bin gambling all night, so I don't know who owns me dis morning." Such is the uncertainty of a slave's position. He goes to bed at night the property of the man with whom he has lived for years, and gets up in the morning the slave of some one whom he has never seen before! To behold five or six tables in a steamboat's cabin, with half-a-dozen men playing at cards, and money, pistols, bowie-knives, &c. all in confusion on the tables, is what may be seen at almost any time on the Mississippi river.

On the fourth day, while at Natchez,[4] taking in freight and passengers, Walker, who had been on shore to see some of his old customers,

---

[4] *Natchez*: A port town in southwest Mississippi on the Mississippi River.

returned, accompanied by a tall, thin-faced man, dressed in black, with a white neckcloth, which immediately proclaimed him to be a clergyman. "I want a good, trusty woman for house service," said the stranger, as they entered the cabin where Walker's slaves were kept. "Here she is, and no mistake," replied the trader. "Stand up, Currer, my gal; here's a gentleman who wishes to see if you will suit him." Althesa clung to her mother's side, as the latter rose from her seat. "She is a rare cook, a good washer, and will suit you to a T, I am sure." "If you buy me, I hope you will buy my daughter too," said the woman, in rather an excited manner. "I only want one for my own use, and would not need another," said the man in black, as he and the trader left the room. Walker and the parson went into the saloon, talked over the matter, the bill of sale was made out, the money paid over, and the clergyman left, with the understanding that the woman should be delivered to him at his house. It seemed as if poor Althesa would have wept herself to death, for the first two days after her mother had been torn from her side by the hand of the ruthless trafficker in human flesh. On the arrival of the boat at Baton Rouge, an additional number of passengers were taken on board; and, amongst them, several persons who had been attending the races. Gambling and drinking were now the order of the day. Just as the ladies and gentlemen were assembling at the supper-table, the report of a pistol was heard in the direction of the Social Hall, which caused great uneasiness to the ladies, and took the gentlemen to that part of the cabin. However, nothing serious had occurred. A man at one of the tables where they were gambling had been seen attempting to conceal a card in his sleeve, and one of the party seized his pistol and fired; but fortunately the barrel of the pistol was knocked up, just as it was about to be discharged, and the ball passed through the upper deck, instead of the man's head, as intended. Order was soon restored; all went on well the remainder of the night, and the next day, at ten o'clock, the boat arrived at New Orleans, and the passengers went to the hotels and the slaves to the market!

> "Our eyes are yet on Afric's shores,
>   Her thousand wrongs we still deplore;
>   We see the grim slave trader there;
>   We hear his fettered victim's prayer;
>   And hasten to the sufferer's aid,
>   Forgetful of *our own 'slave trade.'*

> "The Ocean 'Pirate's' fiend-like form
>   Shall sink beneath the vengeance-storm;
>   His heart of steel shall quake before

The battle-din and havoc roar;
The knave shall die, the Law hath said,
While it protects *our own 'slave trade.'*

"What earthly eye presumes to scan
The wily Proteus-heart[5] of man? —
What potent hand will e'er unroll
The mantled treachery of his soul! —
O where is he who hath surveyed
The horrors of *our own 'slave trade?'*

"There is an eye that wakes in light,
There is a hand of peerless might;
Which, soon or late, shall yet assail
And rend dissimulation's veil:
Which *will* unfold the masquerade
Which justifies *our own 'slave trade.'*"

---

[5] *Proteus-heart*: In Greek mythology, Proteus was a prophetic old man of the sea who could change himself into any shape he pleased.

CHAPTER III.
THE NEGRO CHASE.

We shall now return to Natchez, where we left Currer in the hands of the Methodist parson. For many years, Natchez has enjoyed a notoriety for the inhumanity and barbarity of its inhabitants, and the cruel deeds perpetrated there, which have not been equalled in any other city in the Southern States. The following advertisements, which we take from a newspaper published in the vicinity, will show how they catch their negroes who believe in the doctrine that "all men are created free."

> "NEGRO DOGS.—The undersigned, having bought the entire pack of negro dogs (of the Hay and Allen stock), *he now proposes to catch runaway negroes*. His charges will be three dollars a day for hunting, and fifteen dollars for catching a runaway. He resides three and one half miles north of Livingston, near the lower Jones' Bluff Road.
>
> "WILLIAM GAMBREL."
>
> "Nov. 6, 1845."

> "NOTICE.—The subscriber, living on Carroway Lake, on Hoe's Bayou, in Carroll parish, sixteen miles on the road leading from Bayou Mason to Lake Providence, is ready with a pack of dogs to hunt runaway negroes at any time. These dogs are well trained, and are known throughout the parish. Letters addressed to me at Providence will secure immediate attention. My terms are five dollars per day for hunting the trails, whether the negro is caught or not. Where a twelve hours' trail is shown, and the negro not taken, no charge is made. For taking a negro, twenty-five dollars, and no charge made for hunting.
>
> "JAMES W. HALL"
>
> "Nov. 26, 1847."

These dogs will attack a negro at their master's bidding and cling to him as the bull-dog will cling to a beast. Many are the speculations, as to whether the negro will be secured alive or dead, when these dogs once get on his track. A slave hunt took place near Natchez, a few days after Currer's arrival, which was calculated to give her no favourable opinion of the people. Two slaves had run off owing to severe punishment. The dogs were put upon their trail. The slaves went into the swamps, with the hope that the dogs when put on their scent would be unable to follow them through the water. The dogs soon took to the swamp, which lies between the highlands, which was now covered with water, waist deep: here these faithful animals, *swimming* nearly all the time, followed the zigzag course, the tortuous twistings and windings of these two fugitives, who, it was afterwards discovered, were lost; sometimes scenting the tree wherein they had found a temporary refuge from the mud and water; at other places where the deep mud had pulled off a shoe, and they had not taken time to put it on again. For two hours and a half, for four or five miles, did men and dogs wade through this bushy, dismal swamp, surrounded with grim-visaged alligators, who seemed to look on with jealous eyes at this encroachment of their hereditary domain; now losing the trail—then slowly and dubiously taking it off again, until they triumphantly threaded it out, bringing them back to the river, where it was found that the negroes had crossed their own trail, near the place of starting. In the meantime a heavy shower had taken place, putting out the trail. The negroes were now at least four miles ahead.

It is well known to hunters that it requires the keenest scent and best blood to overcome such obstacles, and yet these persevering and sagacious animals conquered every difficulty. The slaves now made a straight course for the Baton Rouge and Bayou Sara road, about four miles distant.

Feeling hungry now, after their morning walk and perhaps thirsty, too, they went about half a mile off the road, and ate a good, hearty, substantial breakfast. Negroes must eat, as well as other people, but the dogs will tell on them. Here, for a moment, the dogs are at fault, but soon unravel the mystery, and bring them back to the road again; and now what before was wonderful, becomes almost a miracle. Here, in this common highway—the thoroughfare for the whole country around—through mud and through mire, meeting waggons and teams, and different solitary wayfarers, and, what above all is most astonishing, actually running through a gang of negroes, their favourite game, who were working on the road, they pursue the track of the two negroes; they even ran for eight miles to the very edge of the plain— the slaves near them for the last mile. At first they would fain believe it some hunter chasing deer. Nearer and nearer the whimpering pack presses on; the delusion begins to dispel; all at once the truth flashes upon them like a glare of light; their hair stands on end; 'tis Tabor with his dogs. The scent becomes warmer and warmer. What was an irregular cry, now deepens into one ceaseless roar, as the relentless pack rolls on after its human prey. It puts one in mind of Actæon[1] and his dogs.

---

[1] *Actæon*: In Greek mythology, Actæon was transformed by Artemis into a stag in punishment for having viewed her bathing naked, and was subsequently killed by his own dogs.

They grow desperate and leave the road, in the vain hope of shaking them off. Vain hope, indeed! The momentary cessation only adds new zest to the chase. The cry grows louder and louder; the yelp grows short and quick, sure indication that the game is at hand. It is a perfect rush upon the part of the hunters, while the negroes call upon their weary and jaded limbs to do their best, but they falter and stagger beneath them. The breath of the hounds is almost upon their very heels, and yet they have a vain hope of escaping these sagacious animals. They can run no longer; the dogs are upon them; they hastily attempt to climb a tree, and as the last one is nearly out of reach, the catch-dog seizes him by the leg, and brings him to the ground; he sings out lustily and the dogs are called off. After this man was secured, the one in the tree was ordered to come down; this, however, he refused to do, but a gun being pointed at him, soon caused him to change his mind. On reaching the ground, the fugitive made one more bound, and the chase again commenced. But it was of no use to run and he soon yielded. While being tied, he committed an unpardonable offence: he resisted, and for that he must be made an example on their arrival home. A mob was collected together, and a Lynch court[2] was held, to determine what was best to be done with the negro who had had the impudence to raise his hand against a white man. The Lynch court decided that the negro should be burnt at the stake. A Natchez newspaper, the *Free Trader*, giving an account of it says,

"The body was taken and chained to a tree immediately on the banks of the Mississippi, on what is called Union Point. Faggots[3] were then collected and piled around him, to which he appeared quite indifferent. When the work was completed, he was asked what he had to say. He then warned all to take example of him, and asked the prayers of all around; he then called for a drink of water, which was handed to him; he drank it, and said, 'Now set fire—I am ready to go in peace!' The torches were lighted, and placed in the pile, which soon ignited. He watched unmoved the curling flame that grew, until it began to entwine itself around and feed upon his body; then he sent forth cries of agony painful to the ear, begging some one to blow his brains out; at the same time surging with almost superhuman strength, until the staple with which the chain was fastened to the tree (not being well

---

[2] *Lynch court*: Named after Captain William Lynch (1742–1820), the term generally refers to a mob's decision to render summary punishment, usually execution by hanging.
[3] *Faggots*: Bundles of sticks or branches.

secured) drew out, and he leaped from the burning pile. At that moment the sharp ringing of several rifles was heard: the body of the
negro fell a corpse on the ground. He was picked up by some two or
three, and again thrown into the fire, and consumed, not a vestige remaining to show that such a being ever existed."[4]

Nearly 4,000 slaves were collected from the plantations in the
neighbourhood to witness this scene. Numerous speeches were made
by the magistrates and ministers of religion to the large concourse of
slaves, warning them, and telling them that the same fate awaited
them, if they should prove rebellious to their owners. There are hundreds of negroes who run away and live in the woods. Some take refuge in the swamps, because they are less frequented by human beings.
A Natchez newspaper gave the following account of the hiding-place
of a slave who had been captured:—

> "A runaway's den was discovered on Sunday, near the Washington
> Spring, in a little patch of woods where it had been for several months
> so artfully concealed under ground, that it was detected only by acci-
> dent, though in sight of two or three houses, and near the road and
> fields where there has been constant daily passing. The entrance was
> concealed by a pile of pine straw, representing a hog-bed, which being
> removed, discovered a trap-door, and steps that led to a room about six
> feet square, comfortably ceiled with plank, containing a small fire-place,
> the flue of which was ingeniously conducted above ground and con-
> cealed by straw. The inmates took the alarm, and made their escape; *but
> Mr. Adams and his excellent dogs being put upon the trail, soon run
> down and secured one of them*, which proved to be a negro-fellow who
> had been out about a year. He stated that the other occupant was a
> woman, who had been a runaway a still longer time. In the den was
> found a quantity of meal, bacon, corn, potatoes, &c. and various cook-
> ing utensils and wearing apparel."—*Vicksburgh Sentinel*, Dec. 6th,
> 1838.

Currer was one of those who witnessed the execution of the slave at
the stake, and it gave her no very exalted opinion of the people of the
cotton growing district.

---

[4] *"The body . . . ever existed"*: From the Natchez, Mississippi, *Free Trader*, 16 June
1842, which Brown also quoted in the 1848 edition of his *Narrative*.

CHAPTER IV.
THE QUADROON'S HOME.

"How sweetly on the hill-side sleeps
    The sunlight with its quickening rays!
The verdant trees that crown the steeps,
    Grow greener in its quivering blaze."

About three miles from Richmond is a pleasant plain, with here and there a beautiful cottage surrounded by trees so as scarcely to be seen.[1] Among them was one far retired from the public roads, and almost hidden among the trees. It was a perfect model of rural beauty. The piazzas that surrounded it were covered with clematis and passion flower. The pride of China mixed its oriental looking foliage with the majestic magnolia, and the air was redolent with the fragrance of flowers, peeping out of every nook and nodding upon you with a most unexpected welcome. The tasteful hand of art had not learned to imitate the lavish beauty and harmonious disorder of nature, but they lived together in loving amity, and spoke in accordant tones. The gateway rose in a gothic arch, with graceful tracery in iron work, surmounted by a cross, round which fluttered and played the mountain fringe, that lightest and most fragile of vines. This cottage was hired by Horatio Green for Clotel, and the quadroon girl soon found herself in her new home.

The tenderness of Clotel's conscience, together with the care her mother had with her and the high value she placed upon virtue, required an outward marriage; though she well knew that a union with her proscribed race was unrecognised by law, and therefore the ceremony would give her no legal hold on Horatio's constancy. But her high poetic nature regarded reality rather than the semblance of things; and when he playfully asked how she could keep him if he wished to run away, she replied, "If the mutual love we have for each other, and the dictates of your own conscience do not cause you to remain my husband, and your affections fall from me, I would not, if I could, hold you by a single fetter." It was indeed a marriage sanctioned by heaven, although unrecognised on earth. There the young couple lived secluded from the world, and passed their time as happily as cir-

---

[1]*About three miles ... to be seen*: This chapter uses most of the language of the first third of Lydia Maria Child's short story "The Quadroons" (1842). Brown draws on the story for Chapters VIII and XXIII as well. For the text of the complete story, see pp. 319–29.

cumstances would permit. It was Clotel's wish that Horatio should purchase her mother and sister, but the young man pleaded that he was unable, owing to the fact that he had not come into possession of his share of property, yet he promised that when he did, he would seek them out and purchase them. Their first-born was named Mary, and her complexion was still lighter than her mother. Indeed she was not darker than other white children. As the child grew older, it more and more resembled its mother. The iris of her large dark eye had the melting mezzotinto,[2] which remains the last vestige of African ancestry, and gives that plaintive expression, so often observed, and so appropriate to that docile and injured race. Clotel was still happier after the birth of her dear child; for Horatio, as might have been expected, was often absent day and night with his friends in the city, and the edicts of society had built up a wall of separation between the quadroon and them. Happy as Clotel was in Horatio's love, and surrounded by an outward environment of beauty, so well adapted to her poetic spirit, she felt these incidents with inexpressible pain. For herself she cared but little; for she had found a sheltered home in Horatio's heart, which the world might ridicule, but had no power to profane. But when she looked at her beloved Mary, and reflected upon the unavoidable and dangerous position which the tyranny of society had awarded her, her soul filled with anguish. The rare loveliness of the child increased daily, and was evidently ripening into most marvellous beauty. The father seemed to rejoice in it with unmingled pride; but in the deep tenderness of the mother's eye, there was an indwelling sadness that spoke of anxious thoughts and fearful foreboding. Clotel now urged Horatio to remove to France or England, where both her and her child would be free, and where colour was not a crime. This request excited but little opposition, and was so attractive to his imagination, that he might have overcome all intervening obstacles, had not "a change come over the spirit of his dreams."[3] He still loved Clotel; but he was now becoming engaged in political and other affairs which kept him oftener and longer from the young mother; and ambition to become a statesman was slowly gaining the ascendancy over him.

Among those on whom Horatio's political success most depended was a very popular and wealthy man, who had an only daughter. His visits to the house were at first purely of a political nature; but the

---

[2] *mezzotinto*: Literally, a half tint between whiteness and blackness, though the emphasis of the description is on blackness.
[3] *"a change . . . dreams"*: From Lord Byron (1788–1824), "The Dream" (1816). Brown changes the phrasing from the first to third person.

young lady was pleasing, and he fancied he discovered in her a sort of timid preference for himself. This excited his vanity, and awakened thoughts of the great worldly advantages connected with a union. Reminiscences of his first love kept these vague ideas in check for several months; for with it was associated the idea of restraint. Moreover, Gertrude, though inferior in beauty, was yet a pretty contrast to her rival. Her light hair fell in silken ringlets down her shoulders, her blue eyes were gentle though inexpressive, and her healthy cheeks were like opening rosebuds. He had already become accustomed to the dangerous experiment of resisting his own inward convictions; and this new impulse to ambition, combined with the strong temptation of variety in love, met the ardent young man weakened in moral principle, and unfettered by laws of the land. The change wrought upon him was soon noticed by Clotel.

CHAPTER V.
THE SLAVE MARKET.

"What! mothers from their children riven!
What! God's own image bought and sold!
Americans to market driven,
And barter'd as the brute for gold."[1] — *Whittier.*

Not far from Canal-street, in the city of New Orleans, stands a large two story flat building surrounded by a stone wall twelve feet high, the top of which is covered with bits of glass, and so constructed as to prevent even the possibility of any one's passing over it without sustaining great injury. Many of the rooms resemble cells in a prison. In a small room near the "office" are to be seen any number of iron collars, hobbles, handcuffs, thumbscrews, cowhides, whip, chains, gags, and yokes. A back yard inclosed by a high wall looks something like the playground attached to one of our large New England schools, and in which are rows of benches and swings. Attached to the back premises is a good-sized kitchen, where two old negresses are at work, stewing, boiling, and baking, and occasionally wiping the sweat from their furrowed and swarthy brows.

The slave-trader Walker, on his arrival in New Orleans, took up his quarters at this slave pen with his gang of human cattle; and the morning after, at ten o'clock, they were exhibited for sale. There, first of all, was the beautiful Althesa, whose pale countenance and dejected look told how many sad hours she had passed since parting with her mother at Natchez. There was a poor woman who had been separated from her husband and five children. Another woman, whose looks and manner were expressive of deep anguish, sat by her side. There, too, was "Uncle Geemes," with his whiskers off, his face shaved clean, and the grey hair plucked out, and ready to be sold for ten years younger than he was. Toby was also there, with his face shaved and greased, ready for inspection. The examination commenced, and was carried on in a manner calculated to shock the feelings of any one not devoid of the milk of human kindness. "What are you wiping your eyes for?" inquired a fat, red-faced man, with a white hat set on one side of his head, and a cigar in his mouth, of a woman who sat on one of the stools. "I s'pose I have been crying." "Why do you cry?" "Because I have left my man behind." "Oh, if I buy you I will furnish you with a

---

[1] "*What!... for gold*": From John Greenleaf Whittier, "Expostulation" (1834).

better man than you left. I have lots of young bucks on my farm." "I don't want, and will never have, any other man," replied the woman. "What's your name?" asked a man in a straw hat of a tall negro man, who stood with his arms folded across his breast, and leaning against the wall. "My name is Aaron, sir." "How old are you?" "Twenty-five." "Where were you raised?" "In old Virginny, sir." "How many men have owned you?" "Four." "Do you enjoy good health?" "Yes, sir." "How long did you live with your first owner?" "Twenty years." "Did you ever run away?" "No, sir." "Did you ever strike your master?" "No, sir." "Were you ever whipped much?" "No, sir, I s'pose I did not deserve it." "How long did you live with your second master?" "Ten years, sir." "Have you a good appetite?" "Yes, sir." "Can you eat your allowance?" "Yes, sir, when I can get it." "What were you employed at in Virginia?" "I worked in de terbacar feel." "In a tobacco field?" "Yes, sir." "How old did you say you were?" "I will be twenty-five if I live to see next sweet potater-digging time." "I am a cotton planter, and if I buy you, you will have to work in the cotton field. My men pick one hundred and fifty pounds a day, and the women one hundred and forty, and those who fail to pick their task receive five stripes from the cat[2] for each pound that is wanting. Now, do you think you could keep up with the rest of the hands?" "I don't know, sir, I 'spec I'd have to." "How long did you live with your third master?" "Three years, sir." "Why, this makes you thirty-three, I thought you told me you was only twenty-five?" Aaron now looked first at the planter, then at the trader, and seemed perfectly bewildered. He had forgotten the lesson given him by Pompey as to his age, and the planter's circuitous talk (doubtless to find out the slave's real age) had the negro off his guard. "I must see your back, so as to know how much you have been whipped, before I think of buying," said the planter. Pompey, who had been standing by during the examination, thought that his services were now required, and stepping forward with a degree of officiousness, said to Aaron, "Don't you hear de gentman tell you he want to zamon your limbs. Come, unharness yeself, old boy, an' don't be standing dar." Aaron was soon examined and pronounced "sound;" yet the conflicting statement about the age was not satisfactory.

Fortunate for Althesa she was spared the pain of undergoing such an examination. Mr. Crawford, a teller in one of the banks, had just

---

[2] *cat*: Short for cat-o'-nine-tails, a whip which had nine cords fastened to a handle and was said to cut and scratch like a cat.

been married, and wanted a maid-servant for his wife; and passing through the market in the early part of the day, was pleased with the young slave's appearance and purchased her, and in his dwelling the quadroon found a much better home than often falls to the lot of a slave sold in the New Orleans market. The heart-rending and cruel traffic in slaves which has been so often described, is not confined to any particular class of persons. No one forfeits his or her character or standing in society, by buying or selling slaves; or even raising slaves for the market. The precise number of slaves carried from the slave-raising to the slave-consuming states, we have no means of knowing. But it must be very great, as more than forty thousand were sold and taken out of the state of Virginia in one year. Known to God only is the amount of human agony and suffering which sends its cry from the slave markets and negro pens, unheard and unheeded by man, up to his ear; mothers weeping for their children, breaking the night-silence with the shrieks of their breaking hearts. From some you will hear the burst of bitter lamentation, while from others the loud hysteric laugh, denoting still deeper agony. Most of them leave the market for cotton or rice plantations,

> "Where the slave-whip ceaseless swings,
> Where the noisome insect stings,
> Where the fever demon strews
> Poison with the falling dews,
> Where the sickly sunbeams glare
> Through the hot and misty air."[3]

---

[3] "*Where . . . misty air*": From John Greenleaf Whittier, "The Farewell of a Virginia Slave Mother to Her Daughter Sold into Southern Bondage" (1838).

CHAPTER VI.
THE RELIGIOUS TEACHER.

"What! preach and enslave men?
Give thanks—and rob thy own afflicted poor?
Talk of thy glorious liberty, and then
Bolt hard the captive's door?"[1]— *Whittier.*

The Rev. John Peck[2] was a native of the state of Connecticut, where he was educated for the ministry, in the Methodist persuasion. His father was a strict follower of John Wesley,[3] and spared no pains in his son's education, with the hope that he would one day be as renowned as the great leader of his sect. John had scarcely finished his education at New Haven, when he was invited by an uncle, then on a visit to his father, to spend a few months at Natchez in the state of Mississippi. Young Peck accepted his uncle's invitation, and accompanied him to the South. Few young men, and especially clergymen, going fresh from a college to the South, but are looked upon as geniuses in a small way, and who are not invited to all the parties in the neighbourhood. Mr. Peck was not an exception to this rule. The society into which he was thrown on his arrival at Natchez was too brilliant for him not to be captivated by it; and, as might have been expected, he succeeded in captivating a plantation with seventy slaves, if not the heart of the lady to whom it belonged. Added to this, he became a popular preacher, had a large congregation with a snug salary. Like other planters, Mr. Peck confided the care of his farm to Ned Huckelby, an overseer of high reputation in his way. The Poplar Farm, as it was called, was situated in a beautiful valley nine miles from Natchez, and near the river Mississippi. The once unshorn face of nature had given way, and now the farm blossomed with a splendid harvest, the neat cottage stood in a grove where Lombardy poplars lift their tufted tops almost to prop the skies; the willow, locust, and horse-chestnut spread their branches, and flowers never cease to blossom. This was the parson's country house, where the family spent only two months during the year.

The town residence was a fine villa, seated upon the brow of a hill at the edge of the city. It was in the kitchen of this house that Currer

[1] *"What! . . . captive's door?"*: From Whittier, "Clerical Oppressors" (1838).

[2] *Rev. John Peck*: The character was inspired by the hypocritical Reverend Peck of Rochester, whom Brown described in "The New Liberty Party"; see pp. 364–65.

[3] *John Wesley*: The founder of Methodism, the English Protestant evangelical John Wesley (1703–1791) emphasized a methodical devotion to religious duties and practices; he saw good works rather than divine election as the key to salvation.

found her new home. Mr. Peck was, every inch of him, a democrat, and early resolved that his "people," as he called his slaves, should be well fed and not overworked, and therefore laid down the law and gospel to the overseer as well as the slaves.

"It is my wish," said he to Mr. Carlton, an old school-fellow, who was spending a few days with him, "it is my wish that a new system be adopted on the plantations in this estate. I believe that the sons of Ham[4] should have the gospel, and I intend that my negroes shall. The gospel is calculated to make mankind better, and none should be without it." "What say you," replied Carlton, "about the right of man to his liberty?" "Now, Carlton, you have begun again to harp about man's rights; I really wish you could see this matter as I do. I have searched in vain for any authority for man's natural rights; if he had any, they existed before the fall. That is, Adam and Eve may have had some rights which God gave them, and which modern philosophy, in its pretended reverence for the name of God, prefers to call natural rights. I can imagine they had the right to eat of the fruit of the trees of the garden; they were restricted even in this by the prohibition of one. As far as I know without positive assertion, their liberty of action was confined to the garden. These were not 'inalienable rights,' however, for they forfeited both them and life with the first act of disobedience. Had they, after this, any rights? We cannot imagine them; they were condemned beings; they could have no rights, but by Christ's gift as king. These are the only rights man can have as an independent isolated being, if we choose to consider him in this impossible position, in which so many theorists have placed him. If he had no rights, he could suffer no wrongs. Rights and wrongs are therefore necessarily the creatures of society, such as man would establish himself in his gregarious state. They are, in this state, both artificial and voluntary. Though man has no rights, as thus considered, undoubtedly he has the power, by such arbitrary rules of right and wrong as his necessity enforces." "I regret I cannot see eye to eye with you," said Carlton. "I am a disciple of Rousseau,[5]

---

[4] *sons of Ham*: In Genesis, Noah cursed his son Ham for viewing him when he lay naked in a drunken stupor; see Genesis 9.20–27. Oral traditions collected in the Talmud claimed that the curse resulted in Ham having black descendants; this interpretation was echoed by racists in the eighteenth and nineteenth centuries.

[5] *Rousseau*: The influential French philosopher, writer, and social reformer Jean Jacques Rousseau (1712–1778) was best known in America for his political writings, especially *Origin of Inequality Among Men* (1753) and *Social Contract* (1761). In these works he castigated established governmental and religious institutions as sources of evil and called for social amelioration through a surrendering of individual wills to a General Will.

and have for years made the rights of man my study; and I must confess to you that I can see no difference between white men and black
men as it regards liberty." "Now, my dear Carlton, would you really
have the negroes enjoy the same rights with ourselves?" "I would,
most certainly. Look at our great Declaration of Independence; look
even at the constitution of our own Connecticut, and see what is said
in these about liberty." "I regard all this talk about rights as mere humbug. The Bible is older than the Declaration of Independence, and
there I take my stand. The Bible furnishes to us the armour of proof,
weapons of heavenly temper and mould, whereby we can maintain
our ground against all attacks. But this is true only when we obey its
directions, as well as employ its sanctions. Our rights are there established, but it is always in connection with our duties. If we neglect the
one we cannot make good the other. Our domestic institutions can be
maintained against the world, if we but allow Christianity to throw its
broad shield over them. But if we so act as to array the Bible against
our social economy, they must fall. Nothing ever yet stood long against
Christianity. Those who say that religious instruction is inconsistent
with our peculiar civil polity, are the worst enemies of that polity. They
would drive religious men from its defence. Sooner or later, if these
views prevail, they will separate the religious portion of our community from the rest, and thus divided we shall become an easy prey.
Why, is it not better that Christian men should hold slaves than unbe-
lievers? We know how to value the bread of life, and will not keep it
from our slaves."

"Well, every one to his own way of thinking," said Carlton, as he
changed his position. "I confess," added he, "that I am no great admirer
of either the Bible or slavery. My heart is my guide: my conscience is
my Bible. I wish for nothing further to satisfy me of my duty to man. If
I act rightly to mankind, I shall fear nothing." Carlton had drunk too
deeply of the bitter waters of infidelity, and had spent too many hours
over the writings of Rousseau, Voltaire, and Thomas Paine,[6] to place
that appreciation upon the Bible and its teachings that it demands.
During this conversation there was another person in the room, seated
by the window, who, although at work upon a fine piece of lace, paid

---

[6] *Voltaire, and Thomas Paine*: Grouped with Rousseau, the French philosopher
Françoise Marie Arouet Voltaire (1694–1778), best known as the author of *Candide*
(1759), and the Anglo-American political writer Thomas Paine (1737–1809), best
known as the author of *Common Sense* (1776), are presented here as troubling exem-
plars of Enlightenment rationalism. Although they wrote powerfully in support of political freedom, they ultimately rejected Christianity as authoritarian and unreasonable.

every attention to what was said. This was Georgiana, the only daughter of the parson. She had just returned from Connecticut, where she had finished her education. She had had the opportunity of contrasting the spirit of Christianity and liberty in New England with that of slavery in her native state, and had learned to feel deeply for the injured Negro. Georgiana was in her nineteenth year, and had been much benefited by a residence of five years at the North. Her form was tall and graceful; her features regular and well defined; and her complexion was illuminated by the freshness of youth, beauty, and health. The daughter differed from both the father and his visitor upon the subject which they had been discussing, and as soon as an opportunity offered, she gave it as her opinion, that the Bible was both the bulwark of Christianity and of liberty. With a smile she said, "Of course, papa will overlook my differing from him, for although I am a native of the South, I am by education and sympathy a Northerner." Mr. Peck laughed and appeared pleased, rather than otherwise, at the manner in which his daughter had expressed herself.

From this Georgiana took courage and said, "We must try the character of slavery, and our duty in regard to it, as we should try any other question of character and duty. To judge justly of the character of anything, we must know what it does. That which is good does good, and that which is evil does evil. And as to duty, God's designs indicate his claims. That which accomplishes the manifest design of God is right; that which counteracts it, wrong. Whatever, in its proper tendency and general effect, produces, secures, or extends human welfare, is according to the will of God, and is good; and our duty is to favour and promote, according to our power, that which God favours and promotes by the general law of his providence. On the other hand, whatever in its proper tendency and general effect destroys, abridges, or renders insecure, human welfare, is opposed to God's will, and is evil. And as whatever accords with the will of God, in any manifestation of it should be done and persisted in, so whatever opposes that will should not be done, and if done, should be abandoned. Can that then be right, be well doing—can that obey God's behest, which makes a man a slave? which dooms him and all his posterity, in limitless generations, to bondage, to unrequited toil through life? 'Thou shalt love thy neighbour as thyself.'[7] This single passage of Scripture should cause us to have respect to the rights of the slave. True Christian love is

---

[7] *'Thou shalt love . . . as thyself.'*: Leviticus 19.18.

of an enlarged, disinterested nature. It loves all who love the Lord Jesus Christ in sincerity, without regard to color or condition." "Georgiana, my dear, you are an abolitionist; your talk is fanaticism," said Mr. Peck in rather a sharp tone; but the subdued look of the girl, and the presence of Carlton, caused the father to soften his language. Mr. Peck having lost his wife by consumption, and Georgiana being his only child, he loved her too dearly to say more, even if he felt displeased. A silence followed this exhortation from the young Christian. But her remarks had done a noble work. The father's heart was touched; and the sceptic, for the first time, was viewing Christianity in its true light.

"I think I must go out to your farm," said Carlton, as if to break the silence. "I shall be pleased to have you go," returned Mr. Peck. "I am sorry I can't go myself, but Huckelby will show you every attention; and I feel confident that when you return to Connecticut, you will do me the justice to say, that I am one who looks after my people, in a moral, social, and religious point of view." "Well, what do you say to my spending next Sunday there?" "Why, I think that a good move; you will then meet with Snyder, our missionary." "Oh, you have missionaries in these parts, have you?" "Yes," replied Mr. Peck; "Snyder is from New York, and is our missionary to the poor, and preaches to our 'people' on Sunday; you will no doubt like him; he is a capital fellow." "Then I shall go," said Carlton, "but only wish I had company." This last remark was intended for Miss Peck, for whom he had the highest admiration.

It was on a warm Sunday morning, in the month of May, that Miles Carlton found himself seated beneath a fine old apple tree, whose thick leaves entirely shaded the ground for some distance round. Under similar trees and near by, were gathered together all the "people" belonging to the plantation. Hontz Snyder was a man of about forty years of age, exceedingly low in stature, but of a large frame. He had been brought up in the Mohawk Valley, in the state of New York, and claimed relationship with the oldest Dutch families in that vicinity. He had once been a sailor, and had all the roughness of character that a sea-faring man might expect to possess; together with the half-Yankee, half-German peculiarities of the people of the Mohawk Valley. It was nearly eleven o'clock when a one-horse waggon drove up in haste, and the low squatty preacher got out and took his place at the foot of one of the trees, where a sort of rough board table was placed, and took his books from his pocket and commenced.

"As it is rather late," said he, "we will leave the singing and praying for the last, and take our text, and commence immediately.[8] I shall base my remarks on the following passage of Scripture, and hope to have that attention which is due to the cause of God: — 'All things whatsoever ye would that men should do unto you, do ye even so unto them;'[9] that is, do by all mankind just as you would desire they should do by you, if you were in their place and they in yours.

"Now, to suit this rule to your particular circumstances, suppose you were masters and mistresses, and had servants under you, would you not desire that your servants should do their business faithfully and honestly, as well when your back was turned as while you were looking over them? Would you not expect that they should take notice of what you said to them? that they should behave themselves with respect towards you and yours, and be as careful of every thing belonging to you as you would be yourselves? You are servants: do, therefore, as you would wish to be done by, and you will be both good servants to your masters and good servants to God, who requires this of you, and will reward you well for it, if you do it for the sake of conscience, in obedience to his commands.

"You are not to be eye-servants. Now, eye-servants are such as will work hard, and seem mighty diligent, while they think anybody is taking notice of them; but, when their masters' and mistresses' backs are turned they are idle, and neglect their business. I am afraid there are a great many such eye-servants among you, and that you do not consider how great a sin it is to be so, and how severely God will punish you for it. You may easily deceive your owners, and make them have an opinion of you that you do not deserve, and get the praise of men by it; but remember that you cannot deceive Almighty God, who sees your wickedness and deceit, and will punish you accordingly. For the rule is, that you must obey your masters in all things, and do the work they set you about with fear and trembling, in singleness of heart as unto Christ; not with eye-service, as men-pleasers, but as the servants of Christ, doing the will of God from the heart; with good-will doing service as to the Lord, and not as to men.

"*Take care that you do not fret or murmur, grumble or repine at your condition; for this will not only make your life uneasy, but will*

---

[8] "*. . . and commence immediately.*": For Snyder's sermon, Brown drew on Thomas Bacon's *Sermons Addressed to Masters and Servants* (1813); see pp. 297–300.

[9] '*All . . . unto them*': Matthew 7.12.

greatly offend Almighty God. Consider that this is not yourselves, it is not the people that you belong to, it is not the men who have brought you to it, but *it is the will of God who hath by providence made you servants, because, no doubt, he knew that condition would be best for you in this world, and help you the better towards heaven, if you would but do your duty in it.* So that any discontent at your not being free, or rich, or great, as you see some others, is quarrelling with your heavenly Master, and finding fault with God himself, who hath made you what you are, and hath promised you as large a share in the kingdom of heaven as the greatest man alive, if you will but behave yourself aright, and do the business he hath set you about in this world honestly and cheerfully. Riches and power have proved the ruin of many an unhappy soul, by drawing away the heart and affections from God, and fixing them on mean and sinful enjoyments; so that, when God, who knows our hearts better than we know them ourselves, sees that they would be hurtful to us, and therefore keeps them from us, it is the greatest mercy and kindness he could show us.

"You may perhaps fancy that, if you had riches and freedom, you could do your duty to God and man with greater pleasure than you can now. But pray consider that, if you can but save your souls through the mercy of God, you will have spent your time to the best of purposes in this world; and he that at last can get to heaven has performed a noble journey, let the road be ever so rugged and difficult. Besides, you really have a great advantage over most white people, who have not only the care of their daily labour upon their hands, but the care of looking forward and providing necessaries for to-morrow and next day, and of clothing and bringing up their children, and of getting food and raiment[10] for as many of you as belong to their families, which often puts them to great difficulties, and distracts their minds so as to break their rest, and take off their thoughts from the affairs of another world. Whereas you are quite eased from all these cares, and have nothing but your daily labour to look after, and, when that is done, take your needful rest. Neither is it necessary for you to think of laying up anything against old age, as white people are obliged to do; for the laws of the country have provided that you shall not be turned off when you are past labour, but shall be maintained, while you live, by those you belong to, whether you are able to work or not.

---

[10] *raiment*: Clothing.

"There is only one circumstance which may appear grievous, that I shall now take notice of, and that is correction.

"Now, when correction is given you, you either deserve it, or you do not deserve it. But whether you really deserve it or not, it is your duty, and Almighty God requires that you bear it patiently. You may perhaps think that this is hard doctrine; but, if you consider it right, you must needs thinks otherwise of it. Suppose, then, that you deserve correction, you cannot but say that it is just and right you should meet with it. Suppose you do not, or at least you do not deserve so much, or so severe a correction, for the fault you have committed, you perhaps have escaped a great many more and are at last paid for all. Or suppose you are quite innocent of what is laid to your charge, and suffer wrongfully in that particular thing, is it not possible you may have done some other bad thing which was never discovered, and that Almighty God who saw you doing it would not let you escape without punishment one time or another? And ought you not, in such a case, to give glory to him, and be thankful that he would rather punish you in this life for your wickedness than destroy your souls for it in the next life? But suppose even this was not the case (a case hardly to be imagined), and that you have by no means, known or unknown, deserved the correction you suffered, there is this great comfort in it, that, if you bear it patiently, and leave your cause in the hands of God, he will reward you for it in heaven, and the punishment you suffer unjustly here shall turn to your exceeding great glory hereafter.

"Lastly, you should serve your masters faithfully, because of their goodness to you. See to what trouble they have been on your account. Your fathers were poor ignorant and barbarous creatures in Africa, and the whites fitted out ships at great trouble and expense and brought you from that benighted land to Christian America, where you can sit under your own vine and fig tree and no one molest or make you afraid. Oh, my dear black brothers and sisters, you are indeed a fortunate and a blessed people. Your masters have many troubles that you know nothing about. If the banks break, your masters are sure to lose something. If the crops turn out poor, they lose by it. If one of you die, your master loses what he paid for you, while you lose nothing. Now let me exhort you once more to be faithful."

Often during the delivery of the sermon did Snyder cast an anxious look in the direction where Carlton was seated; no doubt to see if he had found favour with the stranger. Huckelby, the overseer, was also there, seated near Carlton. With all Snyder's gesticulations, sonorous voice, and occasionally bringing his fist down upon the table with the force of a sledge hammer, he could not succeed in keeping the negroes all interested: four or five were fast asleep, leaning against the trees; as many more were nodding, while not a few were stealthily cracking and eating hazelnuts. "Uncle Simon, you may strike up a hymn," said the preacher as he closed his Bible. A moment more, and the whole company (Carlton excepted) had joined in the well known hymn, commencing with

> "When I can read my title clear
> To mansions in the sky."[11]

After the singing, Sandy closed with prayer, and the following questions and answers read, and the meeting was brought to a close.

"*Q.* What command has God given to servants concerning obedience to their masters?—*A.* 'Servants, obey in all things your masters according to the flesh, not with eye-service as men-pleasers, but in singleness of heart, fearing God.'

"*Q.* What does God mean by masters according to the flesh?—*A.* 'Masters in this world.'

"*Q.* What are servants to count their masters worthy of?—*A.* 'All honour.'

"*Q.* How are they to do the service of their masters?—*A.* '*With good will*, doing service as unto the Lord, and not unto men.'

"*Q.* How are they to try to please their masters?—*A.* 'Please him well in all things, not answering again.'

"*Q.* Is a servant who is an eye-servant to his earthly master an eye-servant to his heavenly master?—*A.* 'Yes.'

"*Q.* Is it right in a servant, when commanded to do any thing, to be sullen and slow, and answer his master again?—*A.* 'No.'

"*Q.* If the servant professes to be a Christian, ought he not to be *as a Christian servant*, an example to all other servants of love and obedience to his master?—*A.* 'Yes.'

"*Q.* And, should his master be a Christian also, ought he not on that account specially to love and obey him?—*A.* 'Yes.'

"*Q.* But suppose the master is hard to please, and threatens and punishes more than he ought, what is the servant to do?—*A.* 'Do his best to please him.'

"*Q.* When the servant suffers *wrongfully* at the hands of his master, and, to please God, takes it patiently, will God reward him for it?—*A.* 'Yes.'

---

[11] "*When . . . the sky*": From Isaac Watts (1674–1748), *Hymns and Spiritual Songs* (1707).

"*Q*. Is it right for the servant to *run away*, or is it right to *harbour* a runaway?—*A*. 'No.'

"*Q*. If a servant runs away, what should be done with him?—*A*. 'He should be caught and brought back.'

"*Q*. When he is brought back, what should be done with him?—*A*. 'Whip him well.'

"*Q*. Why may not the whites be slaves as well as the blacks?—*A*. 'Because the Lord intended the negroes for slaves.'

"*Q*. Are they better calculated for servants than the whites?—*A*. 'Yes, their hands are large, the skin thick and tough, and they can stand the sun better than the whites.'

"*Q*. Why should servants not complain when they are whipped?—*A*. 'Because the Lord has commanded that they should be whipped.'

"*Q*. Where has He commanded it?—*A*. 'He says, He that knoweth his master's will, and doeth it not, shall be beaten with many stripes.'

"*Q*. Then is the master to blame for whipping his servant?—*A*. 'Oh, no! he is only doing his duty as a Christian.'"

Snyder left the ground in company with Carlton and Huckelby, and the three dined together in the overseer's dwelling.

"Well," said Joe, after the three white men were out of hearing, "Marser Snyder bin try hesef to-day." "Yes," replied Ned; "he want to show de strange gentman how good he can preach." "Dat's a new sermon he gib us to-day," said Sandy. "Dees white fokes is de very dibble," said Dick; "and all dey whole study is to try to fool de black people." "Didn't you like de sermon?" asked Uncle Simon. "No," answered four or five voices. "He rared and pitched enough," continued Uncle Simon.

Now Uncle Simon was himself a preacher, or at least he thought so, and was rather pleased than otherwise, when he heard others spoken of in a disparaging manner. "Uncle Simon can beat dat sermon all to pieces," said Ned, as he was filling his mouth with hazelnuts. "I got no notion of dees white fokes, no how," returned Aunt Dafney. "Dey all de time tellin' dat de Lord made us for to work for dem, and I don't believe a word of it." "Marser Peck give dat sermon to Snyder, I know," said Uncle Simon. "He jest de one for dat," replied Sandy. "I think de people dat made de Bible was great fools," said Ned. "Why?" Uncle Simon. "'Cause dey made such a great big book and put nuttin' in it, but servants obey yer masters." "Oh," replied Uncle Simon, "thars more in de Bible den dat, only Snyder never reads any other part to us; I use to hear it read in Maryland, and thar was more den what Snyder lets us hear." In the overseer's house there was another scene going on, and far indifferent from what we have here described.

CHAPTER VII.
THE POOR WHITES, SOUTH.

"No seeming of logic can ever convince the American people, that thousands of our slave-holding brethren are not excellent, humane, and even Christian men, fearing God, and keeping His commandments."
— *Rev. Dr. Joel Parker.*[1]

"You like these parts better than New York," said Carlton to Snyder, as they were sitting down to dinner in the overseer's dwelling. "I can't say that I do," was the reply; "I came here ten years ago as missionary, and Mr. Peck wanted me to stay, and I have remained. I travel among the poor whites during the week, and preach for the niggers on Sunday." "Are there many poor whites in this district?" "Not here, but about thirty miles from here, in the Sand Hill district; they are as ignorant as horses. Why it was no longer than last week I was up there, and really you would not believe it, that people were so poor off. In New England, and, I may say, in all the free states, they have free schools, and everybody gets educated.[2] Not so here. In Connecticut there is only one out of every five hundred above twenty-one years that can neither read nor write. Here there is one out of every eight that can neither read nor write. There is not a single newspaper taken in five of the counties in this state. Last week I was at Sand Hill for the first time, and I called at a farmhouse. The man was out. It was a low log-hut, and yet it was the best house in that locality. The woman and nine children were there, and the geese, ducks, chickens, pigs, and children were all running about the floor. The woman seemed scared at me when I entered the house. I inquired if I could get a little dinner, and my horse fed. She said, yes, if I would only be good enough to feed him myself, as her 'gal,' as she called her daughter, would be afraid of the horse. When I returned into the house again from the stable, she kept her eyes upon me all the time. At last she said, 'I s'pose you aint never bin in these parts afore?' 'No,' said I. 'Is you gwine to stay here long?' 'Not very long,' I replied. 'On business, I s'pose.' 'Yes,' said I,

---

[1] *Rev. Dr. Joel Parker*: A Presbyterian clergyman in Philadelphia, Joel Parker (1799–1873) was criticized in Stowe's *Uncle Tom's Cabin* for his equivocating sermons on slavery. His sermons were regularly printed in the New York *Observer*.

[2] *everybody gets educated*: Though public schooling was more readily available in the Northeast than in the South, Snyder exaggerates the extent of that availability: Many poor white children worked by the age of twelve, and most free black children were excluded from public schools or put in separate, poorly funded schools.

'I am hunting up the lost sheep of the house of Israel.' 'Oh,' exclaimed she, 'hunting for lost sheep is you? Well, you have a hard time to find 'em here. My husband lost an old ram last week, and he aint found him yet, and he's hunted every day.' 'I am not looking for four-legged sheep,' said I, 'I am hunting for sinners.' 'Ah;' she said, 'then you are a preacher.' 'Yes,' said I. 'You are the first of that sort that's bin in these diggins for many a day.' Turning to her eldest daughter, she said in an excited tone, 'Clar out the pigs and ducks, and sweep up the floor; this is a preacher.' And it was some time before any of the children would come near me; one remained under the bed (which, by the by, was in the same room), all the while I was there. 'Well,' continued the woman, 'I was a tellin' my man only yesterday that I would like once more to go to meetin' before I died, and he said as he should like to do the same. But as you have come, it will save us the trouble of going out of the district.' " "Then you found some of the lost sheep," said Carlton. "Yes," replied Snyder, "I did not find anything else up there. The state makes no provision for educating the poor: they are unable to do it themselves, and they grow up in a state of ignorance and degradation. The men hunt and the women have to go in the fields and labour." "What is the cause of it?" inquired Carlton. "Slavery," answered Snyder, "slavery,—and nothing else. Look at the city of Boston; it pays more taxes for the support of the government than this entire state. The people of Boston do more business than the whole population of Mississippi put together. I was told some very amusing things while at Sand Hill. A farmer there told me a story about an old woman, who was very pious herself. She had a husband and three sons, who were sad characters, and she had often prayed for their conversion but to no effect. At last, one day while working in the corn-field, one of her sons was bitten by a rattlesnake. He had scarce reached home before he felt the poison, and in his agony called loudly on his Maker.

"The pious old woman, when she heard this, forgetful of her son's misery, and everything else but the glorious hope of his repentance, fell on her knees, and prayed as follows,—'Oh! Lord, I thank thee, that thou hast at last opened Jimmy's eyes to the error of his ways; and I pray that, in thy Divine mercy, thou wilt send a rattlesnake to bite the old man, and another to bite Tom, and another to bite Harry, for I am certain that nothing but a rattle-snake, or something of the kind, will ever turn them from their sinful ways, they are so hard-headed.' When returning home, and before I got out of the Sand Hill district, I saw a funeral, and thought I would fasten my horse to a post and attend. The coffin was carried in a common horse cart, and followed by fifteen or twenty persons very shabbily dressed, and attended by a man whom I took to be the religious man of the place. After the coffin had been placed near the grave, he spoke as follows, —

> 'Friends and neighbours! you have congregated to see this lump of mortality put into a hole in the ground. You all know the deceased—a worthless, drunken, good-for-nothing vagabond. He lived in disgrace and infamy, and died in wretchedness. You all despised him—you all know his brother Joe, who lives on the hill? He's not a bit better though he has scrap'd together a little property by cheating his neighbours. His end will be like that of this loathsome creature, whom you will please put into the hole as soon as possible. I wont ask you to drop a tear, but brother Bohow will please raise a hymn while we fill up the grave.'"

"I am rather surprised to hear that any portion of the whites in this state are in so low a condition." "Yet it is true," returned Snyder.

"These are very onpleasant facts to be related to ye, Mr. Carlton," said Huckelby; "but I can bear witness to what Mr. Snyder has told ye." Huckelby was from Maryland, where many of the poor whites are in as sad a condition as the Sand Hillers of Mississippi. He was a tall man, of iron constitution, and could neither read nor write, but was considered one of the best overseers in the country. When about to break a slave in, to do a heavy task, he would make him work by his side all day; and if the new hand kept up with him, he was set down as an able bodied man. Huckelby had neither moral, religious, or political principles, and often boasted that conscience was a matter that never "cost" him a thought. "Mr. Snyder aint told ye half about the folks in these parts;" continued he; "we who comes from more enlightened parts don't know how to put up with 'em down here. I find the people here knows mighty little indeed; in fact, I may say they are univarsaly onedicated. I goes out among none on 'em, 'cause they aint such as I have been used to 'sociate with. When I gits a little richer, so that I can stop work, I tend to go back to Maryland, and spend the rest of my days." "I wonder the negroes don't attempt to get their freedom by physical force." "It aint no use for 'em to try that, for if they do, we puts 'em through by daylight," replied Huckelby. "There are some desperate fellows among the slaves," said Snyder. "Indeed," remarked Carlton. "Oh, yes," replied the preacher. "A case has just taken place near here, where a neighbour of ours, Mr. J. Higgerson, attempted to correct a negro man in his employ, who resisted, drew a knife, and stabbed him (Mr. H.) in several places. Mr. J. C. Hobbs (a Tennessean) ran to his assistance. Mr. Hobbs stooped to pick up a stick to strike the negro, and, while in that position, the negro rushed upon him, and caused his immediate death. The negro then fled to the woods, but was pursued with dogs, and soon overtaken. He had stopped in a swamp to fight the dogs, when the party who were pursuing him came upon him, and commanded him to give up, which he refused to do. He then made several efforts to stab them. Mr. Roberson, one of the party, gave him several blows on the head with a rifle gun; but this, instead of subduing, only increased his desperate revenge. Mr. R. then discharged his gun at the negro, and missing him, the ball struck Mr. Boon in the face, and felled him to the ground. The negro, seeing Mr. Boon prostrated, attempted to rush up and stab him, but was prevented by the timely interference of some one of the party. He was then shot three times with a revolving pistol, and once with a rifle, and after having his throat cut, he still kept the knife firmly grasped in his hand, and tried to cut their legs when they approached to put an end to his life. This chastisement was given because the negro grumbled, and found fault with his master for flogging his wife." "Well, this is a bad state of affairs indeed, and especially the condition of the poor whites," said Carlton. "You see," replied Snyder, "no white man is respectable in these slave states who works for a living. No community can be prosperous, where honest labour is not honoured. No society can be rightly constituted, where the intellect is not fed. Whatever institution reflects discredit on industry, whatever institution forbids the general culture of the understanding, is palpably hostile to individual rights, and to social well-being. Slavery is the incubus[3] that hangs over the Southern States." "Yes," interrupted Huckelby; "them's just my sentiments now, and no mistake. I think that, for the honour of our country, this slavery business should stop. I don't own any, no how, and I would not be an overseer if I wern't paid for it."

---

[3] *incubus*: Evil spirit.

CHAPTER VIII.
THE SEPARATION.

"In many ways does the full heart reveal
  The presence of the love it would conceal;
  But in far more the estranged heart lets know
  The absence of the love, which yet it fain would show."[1]

At length the news of the approaching marriage of Horatio met the ear of Clotel. Her head grew dizzy, and her heart fainted within her; but, with a strong effort at composure, she inquired all the particulars, and her pure mind at once took its resolution. Horatio came that evening, and though she would fain have met him as usual, her heart was too full not to throw a deep sadness over her looks and tones. She had never complained of his decreasing tenderness, or of her own lonely hours; but he felt that the mute appeal of her heart-broken looks was more terrible than words. He kissed the hand she offered, and with a countenance almost as sad as her own, led her to a window in the recess shadowed by a luxuriant passion flower. It was the same seat where they had spent the first evening in this beautiful cottage, consecrated to their first loves. The same calm, clear moonlight looked in through the trellis. The vine then planted had now a luxuriant growth; and many a time had Horatio fondly twined its sacred blossoms with the glossy ringlets of her raven hair. The rush of memory almost overpowered poor Clotel; and Horatio felt too much oppressed and ashamed to break the long deep silence. At length, in words scarcely audible, Clotel said: "Tell me, dear Horatio, are you to be married next week?" He dropped her hand as if a rifle ball had struck him; and it was not until after long hesitation, that he began to make some reply about the necessity of circumstances. Mildly but earnestly the poor girl begged him to spare apologies. It was enough that he no longer loved her, and that they must bid farewell. Trusting to the yielding tenderness of her character, he ventured, in the most soothing accents, to suggest that as he still loved her better than all the world, she would ever be his real wife, and they might see each other frequently. He was not prepared for the storm of indignant emotion his words excited. True, she was his slave; her bones, and sinews had been purchased by his gold, yet she had the heart of a true woman, and hers was a passion too deep

---

[1] "*In many ways . . . would show*": From Samuel T. Coleridge's "Prose in Rhyme" (1828).

120

and absorbing to admit of partnership, and her spirit was too pure to form a selfish league with crime.

At length this painful interview came to an end. They stood together by the Gothic gate, where they had so often met and parted in the moonlight. Old remembrances melted their souls. "Farewell, dearest Horatio," said Clotel. "Give me a parting kiss." Her voice was choked for utterance, and the tears flowed freely, as she bent her lips toward him. He folded her convulsively in his arms, and imprinted a long impassioned kiss on that mouth, which had never spoken to him but in love and blessing. With efforts like a death-pang she at length raised her head from his heaving bosom, and turning from him with bitter sobs, "It is our last. To meet thus is henceforth crime. God bless you. I would not have you so miserable as I am. Farewell. A last farewell." "The last?" exclaimed he, with a wild shriek. "Oh God, Clotel, do not say that;" and covering his face with his hands, he wept like a child. Recovering from his emotion, he found himself alone. The moon looked down upon him mild, but very sorrowfully; as the Madonna seems to gaze upon her worshipping children, bowed down with consciousness of sin. At that moment he would have given worlds to have disengaged himself from Gertrude, but he had gone so far, that blame, disgrace, and duels with angry relatives would now attend any effort to obtain his freedom. Oh, how the moonlight oppressed him with its friendly sadness! It was like the plaintive eye of his forsaken one, like the music of sorrow echoed from an unseen world. Long and earnestly he gazed at that cottage, where he had so long known earth's purest foretaste of heavenly bliss. Slowly he walked away; then turned again to look on that charmed spot, the nestling-place of his early affections. He caught a glimpse of Clotel, weeping beside a magnolia, which commanded a long view of the path leading to the public road. He would have sprung toward her but she darted from him, and entered the cottage. That graceful figure, weeping in the moonlight, haunted him for years. It stood before his closing eyes, and greeted him with the morning dawn. Poor Gertrude, had she known all, what a dreary lot would hers have been; but fortunately she could not miss the impassioned tenderness she never experienced; and Horatio was the more careful in his kindness, because he was deficient in love. After Clotel had been separated from her mother and sister, she turned her attention to the subject of Christianity, and received that consolation from her Bible that is never denied to the children of God. Although it was against the laws of Virginia, for a slave to be taught to read, Currer had employed an old free negro, who lived near her, to teach her two daughters to read and write. She felt that the step she had taken in resolving never to meet Horatio again would no doubt expose her to his wrath, and probably cause her to be sold, yet her heart was too guileless for her to commit a crime, and therefore she had ten times rather have been sold as a slave than do wrong. Some months after the marriage of Horatio and Gertrude their barouche[2] rolled along a winding road that skirted the forest near Clotel's cottage, when the attention of Gertrude was suddenly attracted by two figures among the trees by the wayside; and touching Horatio's arm, she exclaimed, "Do look at that beautiful child." He turned and saw Clotel and Mary. His lips quivered, and his face became deadly pale. His young wife looked at him intently, but said nothing. In returning home, he took another road; but his wife seeing this, expressed a wish to go back the way they had come. He objected, and suspicion was awakened in her heart, and she soon after learned that the mother of that lovely child bore the name of Clotel, a name which she had often heard Horatio murmur in uneasy slumbers. From gossiping tongues she soon learned more than she wished to know. She wept, but not as poor Clotel had done; for she never had loved, and been beloved like her, and her nature was more proud: henceforth a change came over her feelings and her manners, and Horatio had no further occasion to assume a tenderness in return for hers. Changed as he was by ambition, he felt the wintry chill of her polite propriety, and sometimes, in agony of heart, compared it with the gushing love of her who was indeed his wife. But these and all his emotions were a sealed book to Clotel, of which she could only guess the contents. With remittances for her and her child's support, there sometimes came earnest pleadings that she would consent to see him again; but these she never answered, though her heart yearned to do so. She pitied his young bride, and would not be tempted to bring sorrow into her household by any fault of hers. Her earnest prayer was, that she might not know of her existence. She had not looked on Horatio since she watched him under the shadow of the magnolia, until his barouche passed her in her rambles some months after. She saw the deadly paleness of his countenance, and had he dared to look back, he would have seen her tottering with faintness. Mary brought water from a rivulet, and sprinkled her face. When she revived, she clasped the beloved child to her heart with a vehemence that made her scream.

---

[2] *barouche*: A four-wheeled carriage, with a seat for a driver and facing seats for two couples.

Soothingly she kissed away her fears, and gazed into her beautiful eyes with a deep, deep sadness of expression, which poor Mary never forgot. Wild were the thoughts that passed round her aching heart, and almost maddened her poor brain; thoughts which had almost driven her to suicide the night of that last farewell. For her child's sake she had conquered the fierce temptation then; and for her sake, she struggled with it now. But the gloomy atmosphere of their once happy home overclouded the morning of Mary's life. Clotel perceived this, and it gave her unutterable pain.

> "Tis ever thus with woman's love,
>   True till life's storms have passed;
> And, like the vine around the tree,
>   It braves them to the last."

CHAPTER IX.
THE MAN OF HONOUR.

"My tongue could never learn sweet soothing words,
But now thy beauty is propos'd, my fee,
My proud heart sues, and prompts my tongue to speak."[1]
—*Shakspeare.*

James Crawford, the purchaser of Althesa, was from the green mountains of Vermont, and his feelings were opposed to the holding of slaves. But his young wife persuaded him into the idea that it was no worse to own a slave than to hire one and pay the money to another. Hence it was that he had been induced to purchase Althesa. Henry Morton, a young physician from the same state, and who had just commenced the practice of his profession in New Orleans, was boarding with Crawford when Althesa was brought home.[2] The young physician had been in New Orleans but a few weeks, and had seen very little of slavery. In his own mountain home he had been taught that the slaves of the Southern states were negroes, if not from the coast of Africa, the descendants of those who had been imported. He was unprepared to behold with composure a beautiful young white girl of fifteen in the degraded position of a chattel slave. The blood chilled in his young heart as he heard Crawford tell how, by bantering with the trader, he had bought her for two hundred dollars less than he first asked. His very looks showed that the slave girl had the deepest sympathy of his heart. Althesa had been brought up by her mother to look after the domestic concerns of her cottage in Virginia, and knew well the duties imposed upon her. Mrs. Crawford was much pleased with her new servant, and often made mention of her in presence of Morton. The young man's sympathy ripened into love, which was reciprocated by the friendless and injured child of sorrow. There was but one course left; that was, to purchase the young girl and make her his wife, which he did six months after her arrival in Crawford's family. The young physician and his wife immediately took lodgings in another part of the city; a private teacher was called in, and the young wife taught some of those accomplishments which are necessary for one's taking a position in society. Dr. Morton soon obtained a large practice

---

[1] "*My Tongue . . . to speak*": Shakespeare, *Richard the Third* I.ii.183–85.
[2] *Henry Morton . . . home*: The story of Althesa and Henry Morton draws on "View Eighth" of Brown's *A Description of William Wells Brown's Original Panoramic Views* (1850); see pp. 371–73.

in his profession, and with it increased in wealth—but with all his wealth he never would own a slave. Mrs. Morton was now in a position to seek out and redeem her mother, whom she had not heard of since they parted at Natchez. An agent was immediately despatched to hunt out the mother and to see if she could be purchased. The agent had no trouble in finding out Mr. Peck: but all overtures were unavailable; he would not sell Currer. His excuse was, that she was such a good housekeeper that he could not spare her. Poor Althesa felt sad when she found that her mother could not be bought. However, she felt a consciousness of having done her duty in the matter, yet waited with the hope that the day might come when she should have her mother by her side.

CHAPTER X.
THE YOUNG CHRISTIAN.

"Here we see *God dealing in slaves*; giving them to his own favourite
child [Abraham], a man of superlative worth, and as a reward for his
eminent goodness."

—Rev. Theodore Clapp, of New Orleans.[1]

On Carlton's return the next day from the farm, he was overwhelmed with questions from Mr. Peck, as to what he thought of the
plantation, the condition of the negroes, Huckelby and Snyder; and
especially how he liked the sermon of the latter. Mr. Peck was a kind of
a patriarch in his own way. To begin with, he was a man of some talent. He not only had a good education, but was a man of great eloquence, and had a wonderful command of language. He too either
had, or thought he had, poetical genius; and was often sending contributions to the *Natchez Free Trader*, and other periodicals. In the way
of raising contributions for foreign missions, he took the lead of all
others in his neighbourhood. Everything he did, he did for the "glory
of God," as he said: he quoted Scripture for almost everything he did.
Being in good circumstances, he was able to give to almost all benevolent causes to which he took a fancy. He was a most loving father, and
his daughter exercised considerable influence over him, and, owing
to her piety and judgment, that influence had a beneficial effect. Carlton, though a schoolfellow of the parson's, was nevertheless nearly ten
years his junior; and though not an avowed infidel, was, however, a
free-thinker, and one who took no note of to-morrow. And for this
reason Georgiana took peculiar interest in the young man, for Carlton
was but little above thirty and unmarried. The young Christian felt
that she would not be living up to that faith that she professed and
believed in, if she did not exert herself to the utmost to save the
thoughtless man from his downward career; and in this she succeeded
to her most sanguine expectations. She not only converted him, but in
placing the Scriptures before him in their true light, she redeemed those
sacred writings from the charge of supporting the system of slavery,
which her father had cast upon them in the discussion some days
before.

---

[1] *Rev. Theodore Clapp, of New Orleans*: A well-known Unitarian clergyman, Theodore Clapp (1792–1866) was born in Easthampton, Massachusetts, and moved to New
Orleans in 1822. In 1834 he founded New Orleans's Unitarian Church of the Messiah.

Georgiana's first object, however, was to awaken in Carlton's breast a love for the Lord Jesus Christ. The young man had often sat under the sound of the gospel with perfect indifference. He had heard men talk who had grown grey bending over the Scriptures, and their conversation had passed by him unheeded; but when a young girl, much younger than himself, reasoned with him in that innocent and persuasive manner that woman is wont to use when she has entered with her whole soul upon an object, it was too much for his stout heart, and he yielded. Her next aim was to vindicate the Bible from sustaining the monstrous institution of slavery. She said, " 'God has created of one blood all the nations of men, to dwell on all the face of the earth.'[2] To claim, hold, and treat a human being as property is felony against God and man. The Christian religion is opposed to slaveholding in its spirit and its principles; it classes men-stealers among murderers; and it is the duty of all who wish to meet God in peace, to discharge that duty in spreading these principles. Let us not deceive ourselves into the idea that slavery is right, because it is profitable to us. Slaveholding is the highest possible violation of the eighth commandment. To take from a man his earnings, is theft; but to take the earner is a compound, life-long theft; and we who profess to follow in the footsteps of our Redeemer, should do our utmost to extirpate slavery from the land. For my own part, I shall do all I can. When the Redeemer was about to ascend to the bosom of the Father, and resume the glory which he had with him before the world was, he promised his disciples that the power of the Holy Ghost should come upon them, and that they should be witnesses for him to the uttermost parts of the earth. What was the effect upon their minds? 'They all continued with one accord in prayer and supplication with the women.'[3] Stimulated by the confident expectation that Jesus would fulfil his gracious promise, they poured out their hearts in fervent supplications, probably for strength to do the work which he had appointed them unto, for they felt that without him they could do nothing, and they consecrated themselves on the altar of God, to the great and glorious enterprise of preaching the unsearchable riches of Christ to a lost and perishing world. Have we less precious promises in the Scriptures of truth? May we not claim of our God the blessing promised unto those who consider the poor: the Lord will preserve them and keep them alive, and they shall be

---

[2] *'God has created . . . earth'*: Act 17.26. Abolitionists regularly cited St. Paul's anti-racist preachings.

[3] *'They . . . the women'*: Acts 1.14.

blessed upon the earth? Does not the language, 'Inasmuch as ye did it unto one of the least of these my brethren, ye did it unto me,'[4] belong to all who are rightly engaged in endeavouring to unloose the bondman's fetters? Shall we not then do as the apostles did? Shall we not, in view of the two millions of heathen in our very midst, in view of the souls that are going down in an almost unbroken phalanx to utter perdition, continue in prayer and supplication, that God will grant us the supplies of his Spirit to prepare us for that work which he has given us to do? Shall not the wail of the mother as she surrenders her only child to the grasp of the ruthless kidnapper, or the trader in human blood, animate our devotions? Shall not the manifold crimes and horrors of slavery excite more ardent outpourings at the throne of grace to grant repentance to our guilty country, and permit us to aid in preparing the way for the glorious second advent of the Messiah, by preaching deliverance to the captives, and the opening of the prison doors to those who are bound."[5]

Georgiana had succeeded in rivetting the attention of Carlton during her conversation, and as she was finishing her last sentence, she observed the silent tear stealing down the cheek of the newly born child of God. At this juncture her father entered, and Carlton left the room. "Dear papa," said Georgiana, "will you grant me one favour; or, rather, make me a promise?" "I can't tell, my dear, till I know what it is," replied Mr. Peck. "If it is a reasonable request, I will comply with your wish," continued he. "I hope, my dear," answered she, "that papa would not think me capable of making an unreasonable request." "Well, well," returned he; "tell me what it is." "I hope," said she, "that in your future conversation with Mr. Carlton, on the subject of slavery, you will not speak of the Bible as sustaining it." "Why, Georgiana, my dear, you are mad, aint you?" exclaimed he, in an excited tone. The poor girl remained silent; the father saw in a moment that he had spoken too sharply; and taking her hand in his he said, "Now, my child, why do you make that request?" "Because," returned she, "I think he is on the stool of repentance, if he has not already been received among the elect. He, you know, was bordering upon infidelity, and if the Bible sanctions slavery, then he will naturally enough say that it is not from

---

[4] '*Inasmuch . . . unto me*': Matthew 25.40.

[5] "*. . . who are bound*": For Georgiana's speech, Brown draws on *An Address to Free Colored Americans. Issued by an Anti-Slavery Convention of American Women, Held in the City of New-York, by adjournments from 9th to 12th May, 1837* (New York: William S. Dorr, 1837). The address has generally been attributed to the South Carolinian antislavery activist Sarah Grimké (1792–1873).

God; for the argument from internal evidence is not only refuted, but actually turned against the Bible. If the Bible sanctions slavery, then it misrepresents the character of God. Nothing would be more dangerous to the soul of a young convert than to satisfy him that the Scriptures favoured such a system of sin." "Don't you suppose that I understand the Scriptures better than you? I have been in the world longer." "Yes," said she, "you have been in the world longer, and amongst slaveholders so long that you do not regard it in the same light that those do who have not become so familiar with its every-day scenes as you. I once heard you say, that you were opposed to the institution, when you first came to the South." "Yes," answered he, "I did not know so much about it then." "With great deference to you, papa," replied Georgiana, "I don't think that the Bible sanctions slavery. The Old Testament contains this explicit condemnation of it, 'He that stealeth a man, and selleth him, or if he be found in his hand, he shall surely be put to death;' and 'Woe unto him that buildeth his house by unrighteousness, and his chambers by wrong; that useth his neighbour's service without wages, and giveth him not for his work;' when also the New Testament exhibits such words to rebuke as these, 'Behold the hire of the labourers who have reaped down your fields, which is of you kept back by fraud, crieth; and the cries of them who have reaped are entered into the ears of the Lord of Sabaoth.' 'The law is not made for a righteous man, but for the lawless and disobedient, for the ungodly and for sinners, for unholy and profane, for murderers of fathers and murderers of mothers, for manslayers, for whoremongers, for them that defile themselves with mankind, for *menstealers*, for liars, for perjured persons.'[6] A more scathing denunciation of the sin in question is surely to be found on record in no other book. I am afraid," continued the daughter, "that the acts of the professed friends of Christianity in the South do more to spread infidelity than the writings of all the atheists which have ever been published. The infidel watches the religious world. He surveys the church, and, lo! thousands and tens of thousands of her accredited members actually hold slaves. Members 'in good and regular standing,' fellowshipped throughout Christendom except by a few anti-slavery churches generally despised as ultra and radical, reduce their fellow men to the condition of chattels, and by force keep them in that state of degradation. Bishops, ministers,

[6] '*He that stealeth . . . persons*': A compendium of passages intended to demonstrate that the Bible is an antislavery document; the sources are Exodus 21.16, Jeremiah 22.13, James 5.4, and 1 Timothy 1.9.

elders, and deacons are engaged in this awful business, and do not consider their conduct as at all inconsistent with the precepts of either the Old or New Testaments. Moreover, those ministers and churches who do not themselves hold slaves, very generally defend the conduct of those who do, and accord to them a fair Christian character, and in the way of business frequently take mortgages and levy executions on the bodies of their fellow men, and in some cases of their fellow Christians.

"Now is it a wonder that infidels, beholding the practice and listening to the theory of professing Christians, should conclude that the Bible inculcates a morality not inconsistent with chattelising human beings? And must not this conclusion be strengthened, when they hear ministers of talent and learning declare that the Bible does sanction slaveholding, and that it ought not to be made a disciplinable offence in churches? And must not all doubt be dissipated, when one of the most learned professors[7] in our theological seminaries asserts that the Bible 'recognises that the relation may still exist, *salva fide et salva ecclesia*' (without injury to the Christian faith or church) and that only 'the *abuse* of it is the essential and fundamental wrong?' Are not infidels bound to believe that these professors, ministers, and churches understand their own Bible, and that, consequently, notwithstanding solitary passages which appear to condemn slaveholding, the Bible sanctions it? When nothing can be further from the truth. And as for Christ, his whole life was a living testimony against slavery and all that it inculcates. When he designed to do us good, he took upon himself the form of a servant. He took his station at the bottom of society. He voluntarily identified himself with the poor and the despised. The warning voices of Jeremiah and Ezekiel were raised in olden time, against sin. Let us not forget what followed. 'Therefore, thus saith the Lord—ye have not hearkened unto me in proclaiming liberty every one to his brother, and every one to his neighbour—behold I proclaim a liberty for you saith the Lord, to the sword, to the pestilence, and to the famine.'[8] Are we not virtually as a nation adopting the same impious language, and are we not exposed to the same tremendous judgments? Shall we not, in view of those things, use every laudable means to awaken our beloved country from the slumbers of death and baptize all our efforts with tears and with prayers, that God may bless them. Then, should our labour fail to accomplish the end for which we

---

[7] *one of the most learned professors*: In all likelihood a reference to the Reverend Joel Parker; see p. 116, note 1.

[8] *'Therefore . . . the famine'*: Jeremiah 34.15.

pray, we shall stand acquitted at the bar of Jehovah, and although we may share in the national calamities which await unrepented sins, yet that blessed approval will be ours.—'Well done good and faithful servants, enter ye into the joy of your Lord.'"[9]

"My dear Georgiana," said Mr. Peck, "I must be permitted to entertain my own views on this subject, and to exercise my own judgment."

"Believe me, dear papa," she replied, "I would not be understood as wishing to teach you, or to dictate to you in the least; but only grant my request, not to allude to the Bible as sanctioning slavery, when speaking with Mr. Carlton."

"Well," returned he, "I will comply with your wish."

The young Christian had indeed accomplished a noble work; and whether it was admitted by the father, or not, she was his superior and his teacher. Georgiana had viewed the right to enjoy perfect liberty as one of those inherent and inalienable rights which pertain to the whole human race, and of which they can never be divested, except by an act of gross injustice. And no one was more able than herself to impress those views upon the hearts of all with whom she came in contact. Modest and self-possessed, with a voice of great sweetness, and a most winning manner, she could, with the greatest ease to herself, engage their attention.

---

[9] *Well done . . . Lord*: Matthew 25.23.

CHAPTER XI.
THE PARSON POET.

"Unbind, unbind my galling chain,
  And set, oh! set me free:
No longer say that I'll disdain
  The gift of liberty."

Through the persuasion of Mr. Peck, and fascinated with the charms of Georgiana, Carlton had prolonged his stay two months with his old school-fellow. During the latter part of the time he had been almost as one of the family. If Miss Peck was invited out, Mr. Carlton was, as a matter of course. She seldom rode out, unless with him. If Mr. Peck was absent, he took the head of the table; and, to the delight of the young lady, he had on several occasions taken part in the family worship. "I am glad," said Mr. Peck, one evening while at the tea table, "I am glad, Mr. Carlton, that my neighbour Jones has invited you to visit him at his farm. He is a good neighbour, but a very ungodly man; I want that you should see his people, and then, when you return to the North, you can tell how much better a Christian's slaves are situated than one who does nothing for the cause of Christ." "I hope, Mr. Carlton," said Georgiana, "that you will spend the Sabbath with him, and have a religious interview with the negroes." "Yes," replied the parson, "that's well thought of, Georgy." "Well, I think I will go up on Thursday next, and stay till Monday," said Carlton; "and I shall act upon your suggestion, Miss Peck," continued he; "and try to get a religious interview with the blacks. By-the-by," remarked Carlton, "I saw an advertisement in the *Free Trader* to-day that rather puzzled me. Ah, here it is now; and," drawing the paper from his pocket, "I will read it, and then you can tell me what it means:

'To Planters and Others.— *Wanted fifty negroes.* Any person having *sick negroes*, considered *incurable* by their respective physicians, (their owners of course,) and wishing to dispose of them, Dr. Stillman will pay cash for negroes affected with scrofula or king's evil,[1] confirmed hypochondriacism, apoplexy, or diseases of the brain, kidneys, spleen, stomach and intestines, bladder and its appendages, diarrhœa, dysentery, &c. *The highest cash price will be paid as above.*'

---

[1] *scrofula or king's evil*: A tuberculous disorder, characterized by lymphatic swelling; legend had it that the disorder could be cured by the touch of the reigning sovereign.

When I read this to-day I thought that the advertiser must be a man of eminent skill as a physician, and that he intended to cure the sick negroes; but on second thought I find that some of the diseases enumerated are certainly incurable. What can he do with these sick negroes?" "You see," replied Mr. Peck, laughing, "that he is a doctor, and has use for them in his lectures. The doctor is connected with a small college. Look at his prospectus, where he invites students to attend, and that will explain the matter to you." Carlton turned to another column, and read the following:

> "Some advantages of a peculiar character are connected with this institution, which it may be proper to point out. No place in the United States offers as great opportunities for the acquisition of anatomical knowledge. Subjects being obtained from among the coloured population in sufficient numbers *for every purpose*, and proper dissections carried on *without offending any individuals in the community!*"[2]

"These are for dissection, then?" inquired Carlton with a trembling voice. "Yes," answered the parson. "Of course they wait till they die before they can use them." "They keep them on hand, and when they need one they bleed him to death," returned Mr. Peck. "Yes, but that's murder." "Oh, the doctors are licensed to commit murder, you know; and what's the difference, whether one dies owing to the loss of blood, or taking too many pills? For my own part, if I had to choose, I would rather submit to the former." "I have often heard what I consider hard stories in abolition meetings in New York about slavery; but now I shall begin to think that many of them are true." "The longer you remain here the more you will be convinced of the iniquity of the institution," remarked Georgiana. "Now, Georgy, my dear, don't give us another abolition lecture, if you please," said Mr. Peck. "Here, Carlton," continued the parson, "I have written a short poem for your sister's album, as you requested me; it is a domestic piece, as you will see." "She will prize it the more for that," remarked Carlton; and taking the sheet of paper, he laughed as his eyes glanced over it. "Read it out, Mr. Carlton," said Georgiana, "and let me hear what it is; I know papa gets off some very droll things at times." Carlton complied with the young lady's request, and read aloud the following rare specimen of poetical genius:

---

[2] *"Some advantages . . . in the community!"*: This passage, and the passage above requesting *"sick negroes,"* were drawn from Theodore Dwight Weld's *American Slavery As It Is* (1839); for selections from Weld's book, see pp. 312–16.

"MY LITTLE NIG.

"I have a little nigger, the blackest thing alive,
  He'll be just four years old if he lives till forty-five;
  His smooth cheek hath a glossy hue, like a new polished boot,
  And his hair curls o'er his little head as black as any soot.
  His lips bulge from his countenance—his little ivories shine—
  His nose is what we call a little pug, but fashioned very fine:
  Although not quite a fairy, he is comely to behold,
  And I wouldn't sell him, 'pon my word, for a hundred all in gold.

"He gets up early in the morn, like all the other nigs,
  And runs off to the hog-lot, where he squabbles with the pigs—
  And when the sun gets out of bed, and mounts up in the sky,
  The warmest corner of the yard is where my nig doth lie.
  And there extended lazily, he contemplates and dreams,
  (I cannot qualify to this, but plain enough it seems;)
  Until 'tis time to take in grub, when you can't find him there,
  For, like a politician, he has gone to hunt his share.

"I haven't said a single word concerning my plantation,
  Though a prettier, I guess, cannot be found within the nation;
  When he gets a little bigger, I'll take and to him show it,
  And then I'll say, 'My little nig, now just prepare to go it!'
  I'll put a hoe into his hand—he'll soon know what it means,
  And every day for dinner, he shall have bacon and greens."

CHAPTER XII.
A NIGHT IN THE PARSON'S KITCHEN.

"And see the servants met,
Their daily labour's o'er;
And with the jest and song they set
The kitchen in a roar."

Mr. Peck kept around him four servants besides Currer, of whom we have made mention: of these, Sam was considered the first. If a dinner-party was in contemplation, or any company to be invited to the parson's, after all the arrangements had been talked over by the minister and his daughter, Sam was sure to be consulted upon the subject by "Miss Georgy," as Miss Peck was called by the servants. If furniture, crockery, or anything else was to be purchased, Sam felt that he had been slighted if his opinion had not been asked. As to the marketing, he did it all. At the servants' table in the kitchen, he sat at the head, and was master of ceremonies. A single look from him was enough to silence any conversation or noise in the kitchen, or any other part of the premises. There is, in the Southern States, a great amount of prejudice against color amongst the negroes themselves. The nearer the negro or mulatto approaches to the white, the more he seems to feel his superiority over those of a darker hue. This is, no doubt, the result of the prejudice that exists on the part of the whites towards both mulattoes and blacks. Sam was originally from Kentucky, and through the instrumentality of one of his young masters whom he had to take to school, he had learned to read so as to be well understood; and, owing to that fact, was considered a prodigy among the slaves, not only of his own master's, but those of the town who knew him. Sam had a great wish to follow in the footsteps of his master, and be a poet; and was, therefore, often heard singing doggrels of his own composition. But there was one great drawback to Sam, and that was his colour. He was one of the blackest of his race. This he evidently regarded as a great misfortune. However, he made up for this in his dress. Mr. Peck kept his house servants well dressed; and as for Sam, he was seldom seen except in a ruffled shirt. Indeed, the washerwoman feared him more than all others about the house.

Currer, as we have already stated, was chief of the kitchen department, and had a general supervision of the household affairs. Alfred the coachman, Peter, and Hetty made up the remainder of the house servants. Besides these, Mr. Peck owned eight slaves who were masons.

These worked in the city. Being mechanics, they were let out to greater advantage than to keep them on the farm. However, every Sunday night, Peck's servants, including the bricklayers, usually assembled in the kitchen, when the events of the week were freely discussed and commented on. It was on a Sunday evening, in the month of June, that there was a party at Mr. Peck's, and, according to custom in the Southern States, the ladies had their maid-servants with them. Tea had been served in "the house," and the servants, including the strangers, had taken their seats at the tea table in the kitchen. Sam, being a "single gentleman," was unusually attentive to the "ladies" on this occasion. He seldom or ever let the day pass without spending at least an hour in combing and brushing up his "hair." Sam had an idea that fresh butter was better for his hair than any other kind of grease; and therefore, on churning days, half a pound of butter had always to be taken out before it was salted. When he wished to appear to great advantage, he would grease his face, to make it "shiny." On the evening of the party therefore, when all the servants were at the table, Sam cut a big figure. There he sat with his wool well combed and buttered, face nicely greased, and his ruffles extending five or six inches from his breast. The parson in his own drawing-room did not make a more imposing appearance than did his servant on this occasion. "I jist bin had my fortune told last Sunday night," said Sam, as he helped one of the girls to some sweet hash. "Indeed," cried half-a-dozen voices. "Yes," continued he; "Aunt Winny told me I is to hab de prettiest yaller gall in town, and dat I is to be free." All eyes were immediately turned toward Sally Johnson, who was seated near Sam. "I speck I see somebody blush at dat remark," said Alfred. "Pass dem pancakes and molasses up dis way, Mr. Alf, and none of your insinawaysion here," rejoined Sam. "Dat reminds me," said Currer, "dat Dorcas Simpson is gwine to git married." "Who to, I want to know?" inquired Peter. "To one of Mr. Darby's field-hands," answered Currer. "I should tink dat dat gal would not trow herself away in dat manner," said Sally. "She good enough looking to get a house servant, and not to put up wid a fiel' nigger," continued she. "Yes," said Sam, "dat's a wery insensible remark of yours, Miss Sally. I admire your judgment wery much, I assure you. Dah's plenty of suspectible and well-dressed house servants dat a gal of her looks can get, wid out taken up wid dem common darkies." "Is de man black or a mulatto?" inquired one of the company. "He's nearly white," replied Currer. "Well den, dat's some exchuse for her," remarked Sam; "for I don't like to see dis malgemation of blacks and mulattoes, no how," continued Sam. "If I had my rights I would be a mulatto too, for my mother was almost as light-coloured as Miss

Sally," said he. Although Sam was one of the blackest men living, he nevertheless contended that his mother was a mulatto, and no one was more prejudiced against the blacks than he. A good deal of work, and the free use of fresh butter, had no doubt done wonders for his "hare" in causing it to grow long, and to this he would always appeal when he wished to convince others that he was part of an Anglo-Saxon. "I always thought you was not clear black, Mr. Sam," said Agnes. "You are right dahr, Miss Agnes. My hare tells what company I belong to," answered Sam. Here the whole company joined in the conversation about colour, which lasted for some time, giving unmistakeable evidence that caste is owing to ignorance. The evening's entertainment concluded by Sam's relating a little of his own experience while with his first master in old Kentucky.

Sam's former master was a doctor, and had a large practice among his neighbours, doctoring both masters and slaves. When Sam was about fifteen years of age, his old master set him to grinding up the ointment, then to making pills. As the young student grew older and became more practised in his profession, his services were of more importance to the doctor. The physician having a good business, and a large number of his patients being slaves, the most of whom had to call on the doctor when ill, he put Sam to bleeding, pulling teeth, and administering medicine to the slaves. Sam soon acquired the name amongst the slaves of the "Black Doctor." With this appellation he was delighted, and no regular physician could possibly have put on more airs than did the black doctor when his services were required. In bleeding, he must have more bandages, and rub and smack the arm more than the doctor would have thought of. We once saw Sam taking out a tooth for one of his patients, and nothing appeared more amusing. He got the poor fellow down on his back, and he got a straddle of the man's chest, and getting the turnkeys on the wrong tooth, he shut both eyes and pulled for his life. The poor man screamed as loud as he could, but to no purpose. Sam had him fast. After a great effort, out came the sound grinder, and the young doctor saw his mistake; but consoled himself with the idea that as the wrong tooth was out of the way, there was more room to get at the right one. Bleeding and a dose of calomel[1] was always considered indispensable by the "Old Boss;" and, as a matter of course, Sam followed in his footsteps.

---

[1] *Bleeding and a dose of calomel*: At the time, the practice of bleeding patients, usually through the use of bloodsucking leeches, was believed by many to restore a healthy balance to the body's blood. Calomel pills consisted of organic mercury compounds and were used as purgatives.

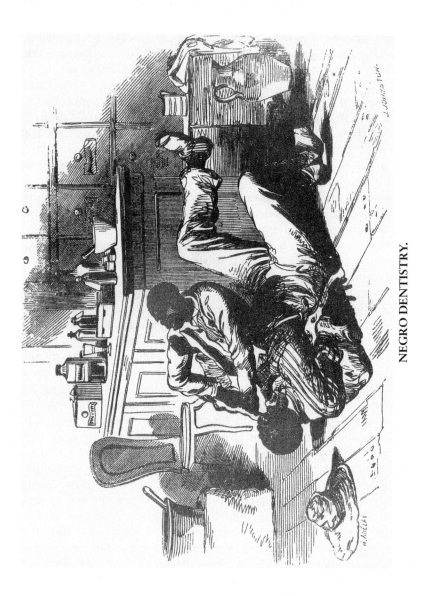

NEGRO DENTISTRY.

On one occasion the old doctor was ill himself, so as to be unable to attend to his patients. A slave, with pass in hand, called to receive medical advice, and the master told Sam to examine him and see what he wanted. This delighted him beyond measure, for although he had been acting his part in the way of giving out medicine as the master ordered it, he had never been called upon by the latter to examine a patient, and this seemed to convince him that, after all, he was no sham doctor. As might have been expected, he cut a rare figure in his first examination, placing himself directly opposite his patient, and folding his arms across his breast, and looking very knowingly, he began, "What's de matter wid you?" "I is sick." "Where is you sick?" "Here," replied the man, putting his hand upon his stomach. "Put out your tongue," continued the doctor. The man run out his tongue at full length. "Let me feel your pulse," at the same time taking his patient's hand in his, placing his fingers on his pulse, he said, "Ah, your case is a bad one; if I don't do something for you, and dat pretty quick, you i'll be a gone coon, and dat's sartin." At this the man appeared frightened and inquired what was the matter with him: in answer, Sam said, "I done told you dat your case is a bad one, and dat's enough." On Sam's returning to his master's bedside, the latter said, "Well, Sam, what do you think is the matter with him?" "His stomach is out of order, sir," he replied. "What do you think had best be done for him?" "I think I better bleed him and give him a dose of calomel," returned Sam. So to the latter's gratification the master let him have his own way. We need not further say, that the recital of Sam's experience as a physician gave him a high position amongst the servants that evening, and made him a decided favourite with the ladies, one of whom feigned illness, when the black doctor, to the delight of all, and certainly to himself, gave medical advice. Thus ended the evening amongst the servants in the parson's kitchen.

CHAPTER XIII.
A SLAVE HUNTING PARSON.

" 'Tis too much prov'd—that with devotion's visage,
And pious action, we do sugar o'er the devil himself."[1]
—*Shakspeare*

"You will, no doubt, be well pleased with neighbour Jones," said Mr. Peck, as Carlton stepped into the chaise[2] to pay his promised visit to the "ungodly man." "Don't forget to have a religious interview with the negroes," remarked Georgiana, as she gave the last nod to her young convert. "I will do my best," returned Carlton, as the vehicle left the door. As might have been expected, Carlton met with a cordial reception at the hands of the proprietor of the Grove Farm. The servants in the "Great House" were well dressed, and appeared as if they did not want for food. Jones knew that Carlton was from the North, and a non-slaveholder, and therefore did everything in his power to make a favourable impression on his mind. "My negroes are well clothed, well fed, and not over worked," said the slaveholder to his visitor, after the latter had been with him nearly a week. "As far as I can see, your slaves appear to good advantage," replied Carlton. "But," continued he, "if it is a fair question, do you have preaching among your slaves on Sunday, Mr. Jones?" "No, no," returned he, "I think that's all nonsense; my negroes do their own preaching." "So you do permit them to have meetings."[3] "Yes, when they wish. There's some very intelligent and clever chaps among them." "As to-morrow is the Sabbath," said Carlton, "if you have no objection, I will attend meeting with them." "Most certainly you shall, if you will do the preaching," returned the planter. Here the young man was about to decline, but he remembered the parting words of Georgiana, and he took courage and said, "Oh, I have no objection to give the negroes a short talk." It was then understood that Carlton was to have a religious interview with the blacks the next day, and the young man waited with a degree of impatience for the time.

In no part of the South are slaves in a more ignorant and degraded state than in the cotton, sugar, and rice districts.

If they are permitted to cease labour on the Sabbath, the time is spent in hunting, fishing, or lying beneath the shade of a tree, resting

[1] " *'Tis . . . the devil himself*": Shakespeare, *Hamlet* III.i.51–53.
[2] *chaise*: A horse-drawn carriage.
[3] *meetings*: Religious gatherings.

for the morrow. Religious instruction is unknown in the far South, except among such men as the Rev. C. C. Jones, John Peck, and some others who regard religious instruction, such as they impart to their slaves, as calculated to make them more trustworthy and valuable as property. Jones, aware that his slaves would make rather a bad show of intelligence if questioned by Carlton, resolved to have them ready for him, and therefore gave his driver orders with regard to their preparation. Consequently, after the day's labour was over, Dogget, the driver, assembled the negroes together and said, "Now, boys and gals, your master is coming down to the quarters to-morrow with his visitor, who is going to give you a preach, and I want you should understand what he says to you. Now many of you who came of Old Virginia and Kentuck, know what preaching is, and others who have been raised in these parts do not. Preaching is to tell you that you are mighty wicked and bad at heart. This, I suppose, you all know. But if the gentleman should ask you who made you, tell him the Lord; if he ask if you wish to go to heaven, tell him yes. Remember that you are all Christians, all love the Lord, all want to go to heaven, all love your masters, and all love me. Now, boys and gals, I want you to show yourselves smart to-morrow: be on your p's and q's, and, Monday morning, I will give you all a glass of whiskey bright and early." Agreeable to arrangement the slaves were assembled together on Sunday morning under the large tree near the great house, and after going through another drilling from the driver, Jones and Carlton made their appearance. "You see," said Jones to the negroes, as he approached them, "you see here's a gentleman that's come to talk to you about your souls, and I hope you 'ill all pay that attention that you ought." Jones then seated himself in one of the two chairs placed there for him and the stranger.

Carlton had already selected a chapter in the Bible to read to them, which he did, after first prefacing it with some remarks of his own. Not being accustomed to speak in public, he determined, after reading the Bible, to make it more of a conversational meeting than otherwise. He therefore began asking them questions. "Do you feel that you are a Christian?" asked he of a full-blooded negro that sat near him. "Yes, sir," was the response. "You feel, then, that you shall go to heaven." "Yes, sir." "Of course you know who made you?" The man put his hand on his head and began to scratch his wool; and, after a little hesitation, answered, "De overseer told us last night who made us, but indeed I forgot the gentmun's name." This reply was almost too much for Carlton, and his gravity was not a little moved. However, he bit his tongue, and turned to another man, who appeared, from his looks, to be more intelligent. "Do you serve the Lord?" asked he. "No, sir, I don't serve anybody but Mr. Jones; I neber belong to anybody else." To hide his feelings at this juncture, Carlton turned and walked to another part of the grounds, to where the women were seated, and said to a mulatto woman who had rather an anxious countenance, "Did you ever hear of John the Baptist?"[4] "Oh yes, marser, John de Baptist; I know dat nigger bery well indeed; he libs in Old Kentuck, where I come from." Carlton's gravity here gave way, and he looked at the planter and laughed right out. The old woman knew a slave near her old master's farm in Kentucky, and was ignorant enough to suppose that he was the John the Baptist inquired about. Carlton occupied the remainder of the time in reading Scripture and talking to them. "My niggers aint shown off very well to-day," said Jones, as he and his visitor left the grounds. "No" replied Carlton. "You did not get hold of the bright ones," continued the planter. "So it seems," remarked Carlton. The planter evidently felt that his neighbour, Parson Peck, would have a nut to crack over the account that Carlton would give of the ignorance of the slaves, and said and did all in his power to remove the bad impression already made; but to no purpose. The report made by Carlton, on his return, amused the parson very much. It appeared to him the best reason why professed Christians like himself should be slave-holders. Not so with Georgiana. She did not even smile when Carlton was telling his story, but seemed sore at heart that such ignorance should prevail in their midst. The question turned upon the heathen of other lands, and the parson began to expatiate upon his own efforts in foreign missions, when his daughter, with a child-like simplicity, said,

> "Send Bibles to the heathen;
>   On every distant shore,
>   From light that's beaming o'er us,
>   Let streams increasing pour
>   But keep it from the millions
>   Down-trodden at our door.
>
> "Send Bibles to the heathen,
>   Their famished spirits feed;
>   Oh! haste, and join your efforts,

---

[4] *John the Baptist*: Jewish prophet and forerunner of Jesus, John baptized Jesus, whom he recognized as the Son of God. He was beheaded at the request of Salome, daughter of the aristocrats Herod and Herodias.

The priceless gift to speed;
Then flog the trembling negro
If he should learn to read."

"I saw a curiosity while at Mr. Jones's that I shall not forget soon," said Carlton. "What was it?" inquired the parson. "A kennel of bloodhounds; and such dogs I never saw before. They were of a species between the bloodhound and the foxhound, and were ferocious, gaunt, and savage-looking animals. They were part of a stock imported from Cuba, he informed me. They were kept in an iron cage, and fed on Indian corn bread. This kind of food, he said, made them eager for their business. Sometimes they would give the dogs meat, but it was always after they had been chasing a negro." "Were those the dogs you had, papa, to hunt Harry?" asked Georgiana. "No, my dear," was the short reply: and the parson seemed anxious to change the conversation to something else. When Mr. Peck had left the room, Carlton spoke more freely of what he had seen, and spoke more pointedly against slavery; for he well knew that Miss Peck sympathised with him in all he felt and said.

"You mentioned about your father hunting a slave," said Carlton, in an under tone. "Yes," replied she; "papa went with some slave-catchers and a parcel of those nasty negro-dogs, to hunt poor Harry. He belonged to papa and lived on the farm. His wife lies in town, and Harry had been to see her, and did not return quite as early as he should; and Huckelby was flogging him, and he got away and came here. I wanted papa to keep him in town, so that he could see his wife more frequently; but he said they could not spare him from the farm, and flogged him again, and sent him back. The poor fellow knew that the overseer would punish him over again, and instead of going back he went into the woods." "Did they catch him?" asked Carlton. "Yes," replied she. "In chasing him through the woods, he attempted to escape by swimming across a river, and the dogs were sent in after him, and soon caught him. But Harry had great courage and fought the dogs with a big club; and papa seeing the negro would escape from the dogs, shot at him, as he says, only to wound him, that he might be caught; but the poor fellow was killed." Overcome by relating this incident, Georgiana burst into tears.

Although Mr. Peck fed and clothed his house servants well, and treated them with a degree of kindness, he was, nevertheless, a most cruel master. He encouraged his driver to work the field-hands from early dawn till late at night; and the good appearance of the house-servants, and the preaching of Snyder to the field negroes, was to cause

A NEGRO HUNT IN THE SOUTHERN STATES.

144

himself to be regarded as a Christian master. Being on a visit one day at the farm, and having with him several persons from the Free States, and wishing to make them believe that his slaves were happy, satisfied, and contented, the parson got out the whiskey and gave each one a dram, who in return had to drink the master's health, or give a toast of some kind. The company were not a little amused at some of the sentiments given, and Peck was delighted at every indication of contentment on the part of the blacks. At last it came to Jack's turn to drink, and the master expected something good from him, because he was considered the cleverest and most witty slave on the farm.

"Now," said the master, as he handed Jack the cup of whiskey; "now, Jack, give us something rich. You know," continued he, "we have raised the finest crop of cotton that's been seen in these parts for many a day. Now give us a toast on cotton; come, Jack give us something to laugh at." The negro felt not a little elated at being made the hero of the occasion, and taking the whiskey in his right hand, put his left to his head and began to scratch his wool, and said,

> "The big bee flies high,
> The little bee make the honey;
> The black folks makes the cotton,
> And the white folks gets the money."

CHAPTER XIV.
A FREE WOMAN REDUCED TO SLAVERY.

Althesa found in Henry Morton a kind and affectionate husband; and his efforts to purchase her mother, although unsuccessful, had doubly endeared him to her. Having from the commencement resolved not to hold slaves, or rather not to own any, they were compelled to hire servants[1] for their own use. Five years had passed away, and their happiness was increased by two lovely daughters. Mrs. Morton was seated, one bright afternoon, busily engaged with her needle, and near her sat Salome, a servant that she had just taken into her employ. The woman was perfectly white; so much so, that Mrs. Morton had expressed her apprehensions to her husband, when the woman first came, that she was not born a slave. The mistress watched the servant, as the latter sat sewing upon some coarse work, and saw the large silent tear in her eye. This caused an uneasiness to the mistress, and she said, "Salome, don't you like your situation here?" "Oh yes, madam," answered the woman in a quick tone, and then tried to force a smile. "Why is it that you often look sad, and with tears in your eyes?" The mistress saw that she had touched a tender chord, and continued, "I am your friend; tell me your sorrow, and, if I can, I will help you." As the last sentence was escaping the lips of the mistress, the slave woman put her check apron to her face and wept. Mrs. Morton saw plainly that there was cause for this expression of grief, and pressed the woman more closely. "Hear me, then," said the woman calming herself: "I will tell you why I sometimes weep. I was born in Germany, on the banks of the Rhine. Ten years ago my father came to this country, bringing with him my mother and myself. He was poor, and I, wishing to assist all I could, obtained a situation as nurse to a lady in this city. My father got employment as a labourer on the wharf, among the steamboats; but he was soon taken ill with the yellow fever, and died. My mother then got a situation for herself, while I remained with my first employer. When the hot season came on, my master, with his wife, left New Orleans until the hot season was over, and took me with them. They stopped at a town on the banks of the Mississippi river, and said they should remain there some weeks. One day they went out for a ride, and they had not been gone more than half an hour, when two men came into the room and told me that they had bought me, and that I was their slave. I was bound and taken to prison,

[1] *hire servants*: The practice of paying slave masters for the use of their slaves.

146

and that night put on a steamboat and taken up the Yazoo river,[2] and set to work on a farm. I was forced to take up with a negro, and by him had three children. A year since my master's daughter was married, and I was given to her. She came with her husband to this city, and I have ever since been hired out."

"Unhappy woman," whispered Althesa, "why did you not tell me this before?" "I was afraid," replied Salome, "for I was once severely flogged for telling a stranger that I was not born a slave." On Mr. Morton's return home, his wife communicated to him the story which the slave woman had told her an hour before, and begged that something might be done to rescue her from the situation she was then in. In Louisiana as well as many others of the slave states, great obstacles are thrown in the way of persons who have been wrongfully reduced to slavery regaining their freedom. A person claiming to be free must prove his right to his liberty. This, it will be seen, throws the burden of proof upon the slave, who, in all probability, finds it out of his power to procure such evidence. And if any free person shall attempt to aid a freeman in regaining his freedom, he is compelled to enter into security in the sum of one thousand dollars, and if the person claiming to be free shall fail to establish such fact, the thousand dollars are forfeited to the state. This cruel and oppressive law has kept many a freeman from espousing the cause of persons unjustly held as slaves. Mr. Morton inquired and found that the woman's story was true, as regarded the time she had lived with her present owner; but the latter not only denied that she was free, but immediately removed her from Morton's. Three months after Salome had been removed from Morton's and let out to another family, she was one morning cleaning the door steps, when a lady passing by, looked at the slave and thought she recognised some one that she had seen before. The lady stopped and asked the woman if she was a slave. "I am," said she. "Were you born a slave?" "No, I was born in Germany." "What's the name of the ship in which you came to this country?" inquired the lady. "I don't know," was the answer. "Was it the *Amazon*?" At the sound of this name, the slave woman was silent for a moment, and then the tears began to flow freely down her care-worn cheeks. "Would you know Mrs. Marshall, who was a passenger in the *Amazon*, if you should see her?" inquired the lady. At this the woman gazed at the lady with a degree of intensity that can be imagined better than described, and

[2] *Yazoo river*: A river flowing from northern Mississippi into the Mississippi River at Vicksburg.

then fell at the lady's feet. The lady was Mrs. Marshall. She had crossed the Atlantic in the same ship with this poor woman. Salome, like many of her countrymen, was a beautiful singer, and had often entertained Mrs. Marshall and the other lady passengers on board the *Amazon*. The poor woman was raised from the ground by Mrs. Marshall, and placed upon the door step that she had a moment before been cleaning. "I will do my utmost to rescue you from the horrid life of a slave," exclaimed the lady, as she took from her pocket her pencil, and wrote down the number of the house, and the street in which the German woman was working as a slave.

After a long and tedious trial of many days, it was decided that Salome Miller was by birth a free woman, and she was set at liberty. The good and generous Althesa had contributed some of the money toward bringing about the trial, and had done much to cheer on Mrs. Marshall in her benevolent object. Salome Miller is free, but where are her three children? They are still slaves, and in all human probability will die as such.

This, reader, is no fiction; if you think so, look over the files of the New Orleans newspaper of the years 1845–6, and you will there see reports of the trial.[3]

[3] *the trial*: Brown draws on the Louisiana trial of Salome Müller, who in 1844 lost her suit to regain her freedom but triumphed in the state's supreme court in 1845. An article about the trial appeared in the *National Anti-Slavery Standard*, 1 January 1846. The case is also discussed in William Craft's *Running a Thousand Miles for Freedom* (1860).

CHAPTER XV.
TO-DAY A MISTRESS, TO-MORROW A SLAVE.

> "I promised thee a sister tale
> Of man's perfidious cruelty;
> Come, then, and hear what cruel wrong
> Befel the dark ladie."[1]
> — *Coleridge.*

Let us return for a moment to the home of Clotel. While she was passing lonely and dreary hours with none but her darling child, Horatio Green was trying to find relief in that insidious enemy of man, the intoxicating cup. Defeated in politics, forsaken in love by his wife, he seemed to have lost all principle of honour, and was ready to nerve himself up to any deed, no matter how unprincipled. Clotel's existence was now well known to Horatio's wife, and both her and her father demanded that the beautiful quadroon and her child should be sold and sent out of the state. To this proposition he at first turned a deaf ear; but when he saw that his wife was about to return to her father's roof, he consented to leave the matter in the hands of his father-in-law. The result was, that Clotel was immediately sold to the slave-trader, Walker, who, a few years previous, had taken her mother and sister to the far South. But, as if to make her husband drink of the cup of humiliation to its very dregs, Mrs. Green resolved to take his child under her own roof for a servant. Mary was, therefore, put to the meanest work that could be found, and although only ten years of age, she was often compelled to perform labour, which, under ordinary circumstances, would have been thought too hard for one much older. One condition of the sale of Clotel to Walker was, that she should be taken out of the state, which was accordingly done. Most quadroon women who are taken to the lower countries to be sold are either purchased by gentlemen for their own use, or sold for waiting-maids; and Clotel, like her sister, was fortunate enough to be bought for the latter purpose. The town of Vicksburgh stands on the left bank of the Mississippi, and is noted for the severity with which slaves are treated. It was here that Clotel was sold to Mr. James French, a merchant.

Mrs. French was severe in the extreme to her servants. Well dressed, but scantily fed, and overworked were all who found a home with her.

---

[1] *"I promised . . . dark ladie"*: From Samuel T. Coleridge, "Introduction to the Tale of the Dark Ladie" (1799).

The quadroon had been in her new home but a short time ere she found that her situation was far different from what it was in Virginia. What social virtues are possible in a society of which injustice is the primary characteristic? in a society which is divided into two classes, masters and slaves? Every married woman in the far South looks upon her husband as unfaithful, and regards every quadroon servant as a rival. Clotel had been with her new mistress but a few days, when she was ordered to cut off her long hair. The negro, constitutionally, is fond of dress and outward appearance. He that has short, woolly hair, combs it and oils it to death. He that has long hair, would sooner have his teeth drawn than lose it. However painful it was to the quadroon, she was soon seen with her hair cut as short as any of the full-blooded negroes in the dwelling.

Even with her short hair, Clotel was handsome. Her life had been a secluded one, and though now nearly thirty years of age, she was still beautiful. At her short hair, the other servants laughed, "Miss Clo needn't strut round so big, she got short nappy har well as I," said Nell, with a broad grin that showed her teeth. "She tinks she white, when she come here wid dat long har of hers," replied Mill. "Yes," continued Nell; "missus make her take down her wool so she no put it up to-day."

The fairness of Clotel's complexion was regarded with envy as well by the other servants as by the mistress herself. This is one of the hard features of slavery. To-day the woman is mistress of her own cottage; to-morrow she is sold to one who aims to make her life as intolerable as possible. And be it remembered, that the house servant has the best situation which a slave can occupy. Some American writers have tried to make the world believe that the condition of the labouring classes of England is as bad as the slaves of the United States.[2]

The English labourer may be oppressed, he may be cheated, defrauded, swindled, and even starved; but it is not slavery under which he groans. He cannot be sold; in point of law he is equal to the prime minister. "It is easy to captivate the unthinking and the prejudiced, by eloquent declamation about the oppression of English operatives being worse than that of American slaves, and by exaggerating the wrongs on one side and hiding them on the other. But all informed and reflecting minds, knowing that bad as are the social evils of England, those

---

[2] *Some American writers . . . United States*: Proslavery writers regularly argued that "wage slavery" in the North and in European industrial centers was far worse than slavery on the plantation. See, for example, George Fitzhugh's *Sociology for the South* (1854) and *Cannibals All!, or Slaves without Masters* (1857).

of Slavery are immeasurably worse."[3] But the degradation and harsh treatment that Clotel experienced in her new home was nothing compared with the grief she underwent at being separated from her dear child. Taken from her without scarcely a moment's warning, she knew not what had become of her. The deep and heartfelt grief of Clotel was soon perceived by her owners, and fearing that her refusal to take food would cause her death, they resolved to sell her. Mr. French found no difficulty in getting a purchaser for the quadroon woman, for such are usually the most marketable kind of property. Clotel was sold at private sale to a young man for a housekeeper; but even he had missed his aim.

---

[3] "*It is . . . worse*": Probably an example of self-quotation, as Brown delivered a number of lectures with similar arguments; see, for example, the transcription of a speech he gave in the Lecture Hall at Croyden, Surrey, on 5 September 1849, in the *Liberator*, 28 September 1849.

CHAPTER XVI.
DEATH OF THE PARSON.

Carlton was about thirty years of age, standing on the last legs of a young man, and entering on the first of a bachelor. He had never dabbled in matters of love, and looked upon all women alike. Although he respected woman for her virtues, and often spoke of the goodness of heart of the sex, he had never dreamed of marriage. At first he looked upon Miss Peck as a pretty young woman, but after she became his religious teacher, he regarded her in that light, that every one will those whom they know to be their superiors. It was soon seen, however, that the young man not only respected and reverenced Georgiana for the incalculable service she had done him, in awakening him to a sense of duty to his soul, but he had learned to bow to the shrine of Cupid. He found, weeks after he had been in her company, that when he met her at table, or alone in the drawingroom, or on the piazza, he felt a shortness of breath, a palpitating of the heart, a kind of dizziness of the head; but he knew not its cause.

This was love in its first stage. Mr. Peck saw, or thought he saw, what would be the result of Carlton's visit, and held out every inducement in his power to prolong his stay. The hot season was just commencing, and the young Northerner was talking of his return home, when the parson was very suddenly taken ill. The disease was the cholera, and the physicians pronounced the case incurable. In less than five hours John Peck was a corpse. His love for Georgiana, and respect for her father, had induced Carlton to remain by the bedside of the dying man, although against the express orders of the physician. The act of kindness caused the young orphan henceforth to regard Carlton as her best friend. He now felt it his duty to remain with the young woman until some of her relations should be summoned from Connecticut. After the funeral, the family physician advised that Miss Peck should go to the farm, and spend the time at the country seat; and also advised Carlton to remain with her, which he did.

At the parson's death his negroes showed little or no signs of grief. This was noticed by both Carlton and Miss Peck, and caused no little pain to the latter. "They are ungrateful," said Carlton, as he and Georgiana were seated on the piazza. "What," asked she, "have they to be grateful for?" "Your father was kind, was he not?" "Yes, as kind as most men who own slaves; but the kindness meted out to blacks would be unkindness if given to whites. We would think so, should we not?" "Yes," replied he. "If we would not consider the best treatment which a slave receives good enough for us, we should not think he ought to be grateful for it. Everybody knows that slavery in its best and mildest form is wrong. Whoever denies this, his lips libel his heart. Try him! Clank the chains in his ears, and tell him they are for him; give him an hour to prepare his wife and children for a life of slavery; bid him make haste, and get ready their necks for the yoke, and their wrists for the coffle chains,[1] then look at his pale lips and trembling knees, and you have nature's testimony against slavery."

"Let's take a walk," said Carlton, as if to turn the conversation. The moon was just appearing through the tops of the trees, and the animals and insects in an adjoining weed kept up a continued din of music. The croaking of bull-frogs, buzzing of insects, cooing of turtle-doves, and the sound from a thousand musical instruments, pitched on as many different keys, made the welkin[2] ring. But even all this noise did not drown the singing of a party of the slaves, who were seated near a spring that was sending up its cooling waters. "How prettily the negroes sing," remarked Carlton, as they were wending their way towards the place from whence the sound of the voices came. "Yes," replied Georgiana; "master Sam is there, I'll warrant you: he's always on hand when there's any singing or dancing. We must not let them see us, or they will stop singing." "Who makes their songs for them?" inquired the young man. "Oh, they make them up as they sing them; they are all impromptu songs." By this time they were near enough to hear distinctly every word; and, true enough, Sam's voice was heard above all others. At the conclusion of each song they all joined in a hearty laugh, with an expression of "Dats de song for me;" "Dems dems."

"Stop," said Carlton, as Georgiana was rising from the log upon which she was seated; "stop, and let's hear this one." The piece was sung by Sam, the others joining in the chorus, and was as follows:

Sam.
"Come, all my brethren, let us take a rest,
  While the moon shines so brightly and clear;
Old master is dead, and left us at last,
  And had gone at the Bar to appear.
Old master has died, and lying in his grave,
  And our blood will awhile cease to flow;
He will no more trample on the neck of the slave;
  For he's gone where the slaveholders go.

---

[1] *coffle chains*: Used to chain slaves together to form a train.
[2] *welkin*: Sky or heavens.

Chorus.

"Hang up the shovel and the hoe—
Take down the fiddle and the bow—
Old master has gone to the slaveholder's rest;
He has gone where they all ought to go.

Sam.

"I heard the old doctor say the other night,
    As he passed by the dining-room door—
'Perhaps the old man may live through the night,
    But I think he will die about four.'
Young mistress sent me, at the peril of my life,
    For the parson to come down and pray,
For she says, 'Your old master is now about to die,'
    And says I, 'God speed him on his way.'

    "Hang up the shovel, &c.

"At four o'clock at morn the family was called
    Around the old man's dying bed;
And oh! but I laughed to myself when I heard
    That the old man's spirit had fled.
Mr. Carlton cried, and so did I pretend;
    Young mistress very nearly went mad;
And the old parson's groans did the heavens fairly rend;
    But I tell you I felt mighty glad.

    "Hang up the shovel, &c.

"We'll no more be roused by the blowing of his horn,
    Our backs no longer he will score;
He no more will feed us on cotton-seeds and corn;
    For his reign of oppression now is o'er.
He no more will hang our children on the tree,
    To be ate by the carrion crow;
He no more will send our wives to Tennessee;
    For he's gone where the slaveholders go.

"Hang up the shovel and the hoe,
    Take down the fiddle and the bow,
We'll dance and sing,
And make the forest ring,
With the fiddle and the old banjo."

The song was not half finished before Carlton regretted that he had caused the young lady to remain and hear what to her must be anything but pleasant reflections upon her deceased parent. "I think we will walk," said he, at the same time extending his arm to Georgiana.

"No," said she; "let's hear them out. It is from these unguarded expressions of the feelings of the negroes, that we should learn a lesson." At its conclusion they walked towards the house in silence: as they were ascending the steps, the young man said, "They are happy, after all. The negro, situated as yours are, is not aware that he is deprived of any just rights." "Yes, yes," answered Georgiana: "you may place the slave where you please; you may dry up to your utmost the fountains of his feelings, the springs of his thought; you may yoke him to your labour, as an ox which liveth only to work, and worketh only to live; you may put him under any process which, without destroying his value as a slave, will debase and crush him as a rational being; you may do this, and *the idea that he was born to be free will survive it all.* It is allied to his hope of immortality; it is the ethereal part of his nature, which oppression cannot reach; it is a torch lit up in his soul by the hand of Deity, and never meant to be extinguished by the hand of man."

On reaching the drawing-room, they found Sam snuffing the candles, and looking as solemn and as dignified as if he had never sung a song or laughed in his life. "Will Miss Georgy have de supper got up now?" asked the negro. "Yes," she replied. "Well," remarked Carlton, "that beats anything I ever met with. Do you think that was Sam we heard singing?" "I am sure of it," was the answer. "I could not have believed that that fellow was capable of so much deception," continued he. "Our system of slavery is one of deception; and Sam, you see, has only been a good scholar. However, he is as honest a fellow as you will find among the slave population here. If we would have them more honest, we should give them their liberty, and then the inducement to be dishonest would be gone. I have resolved that these creatures shall all be free." "Indeed!" exclaimed Carlton. "Yes, I shall let them all go free, and set an example to those about me." "I honour your judgment," said he. "But will the state permit them to remain?"[3] "If not, they can go where they can live in freedom. I will not be unjust because the state is."

---

[3] "*. . . will the state permit them to remain?*": In order to discourage mass emancipations, most slave states had legal or de facto requirements that slaves liberated under such circumstances must emigrate to nonslave states.

CHAPTER XVII.
RETALIATION.

"I had a dream, a happy dream;
I thought that I was free:
That in my own bright land again
A home there was for me."

With the deepest humiliation Horatio Green saw the daughter of
Clotel, his own child, brought into his dwelling as a servant. His wife
felt that she had been deceived, and determined to punish her deceiver.
At first Mary was put to work in the kitchen, where she met with little
or no sympathy from the other slaves, owing to the fairness of her
complexion. The child was white, what should be done to make her
look like other negroes, was the question Mrs. Green asked herself. At
last she hit upon a plan: there was a garden at the back of the house
over which Mrs. Green could look from her parlour window. Here the
white slave-girl was put to work, without either bonnet or handkerchief upon her head. A hot sun poured its broiling rays on the naked
face and neck of the girl, until she sank down in the corner of the garden, and was actually broiled to sleep. "Dat little nigger ain't working
a bit, missus," said Dinah to Mrs. Green, as she entered the kitchen.
"She's lying in the sun, seasoning; she will work better by and by,"
replied the mistress. "Dees white niggers always tink dey sef good as
white folks," continued the cook. "Yes, but we will teach them better;
won't we, Dinah?" "Yes, missus, I don't like dees mularter niggers, no
how; dey always want to set dey sef up for something big." The cook
was black, and was not without that prejudice which is to be found
among the negroes, as well as among the whites of the Southern States.
The sun had the desired effect, for in less than a fortnight Mary's fair
complexion had disappeared, and she was but little whiter than any
other mulatto children running about the yard. But the close resemblance between the father and child annoyed the mistress more than
the mere whiteness of the child's complexion. Horatio made proposition after proposition to have the girl sent away, for every time he
beheld her countenance it reminded him of the happy days he had
spent with Clotel. But his wife had commenced, and determined to
carry out her unfeeling and fiendish designs. This child was not only
white, but she was the granddaughter of Thomas Jefferson, the man
who, when speaking against slavery in the legislature of Virginia, said,

"The whole commerce between master and slave is a perpetual exercise of the most boisterous passions; *the most unremitting despotism on the one part, and degrading submission on the other.* With what execration should the statesman be loaded who, permitting one half the citizens thus to trample on the rights of the other, transforms those into despots and these into enemies, destroys the morals of the one part, and the *amor patriæ*[1] of the other! For if the slave can have a country in this world, it must be any other in preference to that in which he is born to live and labour for another; in which he must lock up the faculties of his nature, contribute as far as depends on his individual endeavours to the evanishment of the human race, or entail his own miserable condition on the endless generations proceeding from him. And can the liberties of a nation be thought secure when we have removed their only firm basis, a conviction in the minds of the people that these liberties are a gift of God? that they are not to be violated but with his wrath? Indeed, I tremble for my country when I reflect that God is just; that his justice cannot sleep for ever; that, considering numbers, nature, and natural means only, a revolution of the wheel of fortune, an exchange of situation, is among possible events; that it may become probable by supernatural interference! The Almighty has no attribute which can take side with us in such a contest.

. . . .

"What an incomprehensible machine is man! Who can endure toil, famine, stripes, imprisonment, and death itself, in vindication of his own liberty, and the next moment be deaf to all those motives, whose power supported him through his trial, and inflict on his fellow-men a bondage, *one hour of which is fraught with more misery than ages of that which he rose in rebellion to oppose!* But we must wait with patience the workings of an overruling Providence, and hope that that is preparing the deliverance of these our suffering brethren. When the measure of their tears shall be full—when their tears shall have involved heaven itself in darkness—doubtless a God of justice will awaken to their distress, and by diffusing light and liberality among their oppressors, or at length by his exterminating thunder, manifest his attention to things of this world, and that they are not left to the guidance of blind fatality."[2]

The same man, speaking of the probability that the slaves might some day attempt to gain their liberties by a revolution, said,

[1] *amor patriæ*: Love of native land.
[2] "*The whole commerce . . . blind fatality*": The first passage is from Thomas Jefferson's *Notes on the State of Virginia* (1785); the second is from his "Observations" (1786). For selections from *Notes*, see pp. 242–51.

"I tremble for my country, when I recollect that God is just, and that His justice cannot sleep for ever. The Almighty has no attribute that can take sides with us in such a struggle."[3]

But, sad to say, Jefferson is not the only American statesman who has spoken high-sounding words in favour of freedom, and then left his own children to die slaves.

[3] *"I tremble . . . struggle"*: From Jefferson's *Notes on the State of Virginia.*

CHAPTER XVIII.
THE LIBERATOR.

"We hold these truths to be self-evident, that all men are created free and equal; that they are endowed by their Creator with certain inalienable rights; among these are life, *liberty*, and the pursuit of happiness."
— *Declaration of American Independence.*

The death of the parson was the commencement of a new era in the history of his slaves. Only a little more than eighteen years of age, Georgiana could not expect to carry out her own wishes in regard to the slaves, although she was sole heir to her father's estate. There were distant relations whose opinions she had at least to respect. And both laws and public opinion in the state were against any measure of emancipation that she might think of adopting; unless, perhaps, she might be permitted to send them to Liberia.[1] Her uncle in Connecticut had already been written to, to come down and aid in settling up the estate. He was a Northern man, but she knew him to be a tight-fisted yankee, whose whole counsel would go against liberating the negroes. Yet there was one way in which the thing could be done. She loved Carlton, and she well knew that he loved her; she read it in his countenance every time they met, yet the young man did not mention his wishes to her. There were many reasons why he should not. In the first place, her father was just deceased, and it seemed only right that he should wait a reasonable time. Again, Carlton was poor, and Georgiana was possessed of a large fortune; and his high spirit would not, for a moment, allow him to place himself in a position to be regarded as a fortune-hunter. The young girl hinted, as best she could, at the probable future; but all to no purpose. He took nothing to himself. True, she had read much of "woman's rights;" and had even attended a meeting, while at the North, which had been called to discuss the wrongs of woman;[2] but she could not nerve herself up to the point of putting the question to Carlton, although she felt sure that she should not be rejected. She waited, but in vain. At last, one evening, she came out of her room rather late, and was walking on the piazza for fresh air. She passed near Carlton's room, and heard the voice of Sam. The negro had just come in to get the young man's boots, and had stopped, as he usually

---

[1] *Liberia*: The American Colonization Society founded this West African colony in the early 1820s as the appropriate "home" for the colonized free blacks.

[2] *the wrongs of woman*: The first women's rights convention was held at Seneca Falls, New York, in 1848.

159

did, to have some talk. "I wish," said Sam, "dat Marser Carlton an Miss Georgy would get married; den, I 'spec, we'd have good times." "I don't think your mistress would have me," replied the young man. "What make tink dat, Marser Carlton?" "Your mistress would marry no one, Sam, unless she loved him." "Den I wish she would lub you, cause I tink we have good times den. All our folks is de same 'pinion like me," returned the negro, and then left the room with the boots in his hands. During the conversation between the Anglo-Saxon and the African, one word had been dropped by the former that haunted the young lady the remainder of the night—"Your mistress would marry no one unless she loved them." That word awoke her in the morning, and caused her to decide upon this important subject. Love and duty triumphed over the woman's timid nature, and that day Georgiana informed Carlton that she was ready to become his wife. The young man, with grateful tears, accepted and kissed the hand that was offered to him. The marriage of Carlton and Miss Peck was hailed with delight by both the servants in the house and the negroes on the farm. New rules were immediately announced for the working and general treatment of the slaves on the plantation. With this, Huckelby, the overseer, saw his reign coming to an end; and Snyder, the Dutch preacher, felt that his services would soon be dispensed with, for nothing was more repugnant to the feelings of Mrs. Carlton than the sermons preached by Snyder to the slaves. She regarded them as something intended to make them better satisfied with their condition, and more valuable as pieces of property, without preparing them for the world to come. Mrs. Carlton found in her husband a congenial spirit, who entered into all her wishes and plans for bettering the condition of their slaves. Mrs. Carlton's views and sympathies were all in favour of immediate emancipation; but then she saw, or thought she saw, a difficulty in that. If the slaves were liberated, they must be sent out of the state. This, of course, would incur additional expense; and if they left the state, where had they better go? "Let's send them to Liberia," said Carlton. "Why should they go to Africa, any more than the Free States or to Canada?" asked the wife. "They would be in their native land," he answered. "Is not this their native land? What right have we, more than the negro, to the soil here, or to style ourselves native Americans? Indeed it is as much their homes as ours, and I have sometimes thought it was more theirs. The negro has cleared up the lands, built towns, and enriched the soil with his blood and tears; and in return, he is to be sent to a country of which he knows nothing. Who fought more bravely for American independence than the blacks? A negro, by the name of Attucks,[3] was the first that fell in Boston at the commencement of the revolutionary war; and, throughout the whole of the struggles for liberty in this country, the negroes have contributed their share. In the last war with Great Britain,[4] the country was mainly indebted to the blacks in New Orleans for the achievement of the victory at that place; and even General Jackson, the commander in chief, called the negroes together at the close of the war, and addressed them in the following terms:—

> "Soldiers!—When on the banks of the Mobile I called you to take up arms, inviting you to partake the perils and glory of your *white fellow citizens, I expected much from you*; for I was not ignorant that you possessed qualities most formidable to an invading enemy. I knew with what fortitude you could endure hunger and thirst, and all the fatigues of a campaign. *I knew well how you loved your native country*, and that you, as well as ourselves, had to defend what *man* holds most dear—his parents, wife, children, and property. *You have done more than I expected.* In addition to the previous qualities I before knew you to possess, I found among you a noble enthusiasm, which leads to the performance of great things.
>
> " 'Soldiers! The President of the United States shall hear how praiseworthy was your conduct in the hour of danger, and the representatives of the American people will give you the praise your exploits entitle you to. Your general anticipates them in applauding your noble ardour.' " [5]

"And what did these noble men receive in return for their courage, their heroism? Chains and slavery. Their good deeds have been consecrated only in their own memories. Who rallied with more alacrity in response to the summons of danger? If in that hazardous hour, when our homes were menaced with the horrors of war, we did not disdain to call upon the negro to assist in repelling invasion, why should we, now that the danger is past, deny him a home in his native land?" "I see," said Carlton, "you are right, but I fear you will have difficulty in persuading others to adopt your views." "We will set the example," replied she, "and then hope for the best; for I feel that the people of the Southern States will one day see their error. Liberty has always been

[3] *Attucks*: On 5 March 1770, Crispus Attucks (1723–1770), a mulatto who had escaped from slavery in Framingham, Massachusetts, led a group protesting the British army's presence in Boston. British soldiers fired into the crowd, killing Attucks and four others. Attucks's bravery and patriotism were regularly celebrated by nineteenth-century African Americans.

[4] *the last war with Great Britain*: The War of 1812.

[5] *"Soldiers! . . . noble ardour' "*: For Andrew Jackson's complete speech to the black troops on this famous battle of 1815, see "Two Proclamations" on pp. 301–3.

our watchword, as far as profession is concerned. Nothing has been held so cheap as our common humanity, on a national average. If every man had his aliquot proportion[6] of the injustice done in this land, by law and violence, the present freemen of the northern section would many of them commit suicide in self-defence, and would court the liberties awarded by Ali Pasha of Egypt[7] to his subjects. Long ere this we should have tested, in behalf of our bleeding and crushed American brothers of every hue and complexion, every new constitution, custom, or practice, by which inhumanity was supposed to be upheld, the injustice and cruelty they contained, emblazoned before the great tribunal of mankind for condemnation; and the good and available power they possessed, for the relief, deliverance and elevation of oppressed men, permitted to shine forth from under the cloud, for the refreshment of the human race."

Although Mr. and Mrs. Carlton felt that immediate emancipation was the right of the slave and the duty of the master, they resolved on a system of gradual emancipation, so as to give them time to accomplish their wish, and to prepare the negro for freedom. Huckelby was one morning told that his services would no longer be required. The negroes, ninety-eight in number, were called together and told that the whip would no longer be used, and that they would be allowed a certain sum for every bale of cotton produced. Sam, whose long experience in the cotton-field before he had been taken into the house, and whose general intelligence justly gave him the first place amongst the negroes on the Poplar Farm, was placed at their head. They were also given to understand that the money earned by them would be placed to their credit; and when it amounted to be a certain sum, they should all be free.

The joy with which the news was received by the slaves, showed their grateful appreciation of the boon their benefactors were bestowing upon them. The house servants were called and told that wages would be allowed them, and what they earned set to their credit, and they too should be free. The next were the bricklayers. There were eight of these, who had paid their master two dollars per day, and boarded and clothed themselves. An arrangement was entered into with them, by which the money they earned should be placed to their

---

[6] *aliquot proportion*: Comprising a definite, fixed part of a whole.

[7] *Ali Pasha of Egypt*: Known as a despotic military governor of a province of the Ottoman Empire, Ali Pasha (1744?–1822) battled the French, made an alliance with England in 1814, and was eventually assassinated by a Turkish agent.

credit; and they too should be free, when a certain amount should be accumulated; and great was the change amongst all these people. The bricklayers had been to work but a short time, before their industry was noticed by many. They were no longer apparently the same people. A sedateness, a care, an economy, an industry, took possession of them, to which there seemed to be no bounds but in their physical strength. They were never tired of labouring, and seemed as though they could never effect enough. They became temperate, moral, religious, setting an example of innocent, unoffending lives to the world around them, which was seen and admired by all. Mr. Parker, a man who worked nearly forty slaves at the same business, was attracted by the manner in which these negroes laboured. He called on Mr. Carlton, some weeks after they had been acting on the new system, and offered 2,000 dollars for the head workman, Jim. The offer was, of course, refused. A few days after the same gentleman called again, and made an offer of double the sum that he had on the former occasion. Mr. Parker, finding that no money would purchase either of the negroes, said, "Now, Mr. Carlton, pray tell me what it is that makes your negroes work so? What kind of people are they?" "I suppose," observed Carlton, "that they are like other people, flesh and blood." "Why, sir," continued Parker, "I have never seen such people; building as they are next door to my residence, I see and have my eye on them from morning till night. You are never there, for I have never met you, or seen you once at the building. Why, sir, I am an early riser, getting up before day; and do you think that I am not awoke every morning in my life by the noise of their trowels at work, and their singing and noise before day; and do you suppose, sir, that they stop or leave off work at sundown? No, sir, but they work as long as they can see to lay a brick, and then they carry up brick and mortar for an hour or two afterward, to be ahead of their work the next morning. And again, sir, do you think that they walk at their work? No, sir, they run all day. You see, sir, those immensely long ladders, five stories in height; do you suppose they walk up them? No, sir, they run up and down them like so many monkeys all day long. I never saw such people as these in my life. I don't know what to make of them. Were a white man with them and over them with a whip, then I should see and understand the cause of the running and incessant labour; but I cannot comprehend it; there is something in it, sir. Great man, sir, that Jim; great man; I should like to own him." Carlton here informed Parker that their liberties depended upon their work; when the latter replied, "If niggers can work so for the promise of freedom, they ought to be made to work without it." This last remark was in the true spirit of the slaveholder, and reminds us of the fact that, some years since, the overseer of General Wade Hampton[8] offered the niggers under him a suit of clothes to the one that picked the most cotton in one day; and after that time that day's work was given as a task to the slaves on that plantation; and, after a while, was adopted by other planters.

The negroes on the farm, under "Marser Sam," were also working in a manner that attracted the attention of the planters round about. They no longer feared Huckelby's whip, and no longer slept under the preaching of Snyder. On the Sabbath, Mr. and Mrs. Carlton read and explained the Scriptures to them; and the very great attention paid by the slaves showed plainly that they appreciated the gospel when given to them in its purity. The death of Currer, from yellow fever, was a great trial to Mrs. Carlton; for she had not only become much attached to her, but had heard with painful interest the story of her wrongs, and would, in all probability, have restored her to her daughter in New Orleans.

---

[8] *Wade Hampton:* A prominent South Carolina slave owner, Wade Hampton (1818–1902) owned over nine hundred slaves on six plantations.

CHAPTER XIX.
ESCAPE OF CLOTEL.

"The fetters galled my weary soul —
A soul that seemed but thrown away:
I spurned the tyrant's base control,
Resolved at last the man to play."[1]

No country has produced so much heroism in so short a time, connected with escapes from peril and oppression, as has occurred in the United States among fugitive slaves, many of whom show great shrewdness in their endeavours to escape from this land of bondage. A slave was one day seen passing on the high road from a border town in the interior of the state of Virginia to the Ohio river. The man had neither hat upon his head or coat upon his back. He was driving before him a very nice fat pig, and appeared to all who saw him to be a labourer employed on an adjoining farm. "No negro is permitted to go at large in the Slave States without a written pass from his or her master, except on business in the neighbourhood." "Where do you live, my boy?" asked a white man of the slave, as he passed a white house with green blinds. "Jist up de road, sir," was the answer. "That's a fine pig." "Yes, sir, marser like dis choat[2] berry much." And the negro drove on as if he was in great haste. In this way he and the pig travelled more than fifty miles before they reached the Ohio river. Once at the river they crossed over; the pig was sold; and nine days after the runaway slave passed over the Niagara river,[3] and, for the first time in his life, breathed the air of freedom. A few weeks later, and, on the same road, two slaves were seen passing; one was on horseback, the other was walking before him with his arms tightly bound, and a long rope leading from the man on foot to the one on horseback. "Oh, ho, that's a runaway rascal, I suppose," said a farmer, who met them on the road. "Yes, sir, he bin runaway, and I got him fast. Marser will tan his jacket for him nicely when he gets him." "You are a trustworthy fellow, I imagine," continued the farmer. "Oh yes, sir; marser puts a heap of confidence in dis nigger." And the slaves travelled on. When the one on foot was fatigued they would change positions, the

---

[1] "The fetters . . . play": From Elizur Wright Jr. (1814–1885), "The Fugitive Slave to the Christian," in The Anti-Slavery Harp, ed. Brown.

[2] choat: Shoat, a weaned pig.

[3] the Niagara river: A river along the New York-Canada border flowing from Lake Erie to Lake Ontario.

other being tied and driven on foot. This they called "ride and tie."
After a journey of more than two hundred miles they reached the Ohio
river,[4] turned the horse loose, told him to go home, and proceeded on
their way to Canada. However they were not to have it all their own
way. There are men in the Free States, and especially in the states adja-
cent to the Slave States, who make their living by catching the runaway
slave, and returning him for the reward that may be offered. As the
two slaves above mentioned were travelling on towards the land of
freedom, led by the North Star, they were set upon by four of these
slave-catchers, and one of them unfortunately captured. The other
escaped. The captured fugitive was put under the torture, and compelled to reveal the name of his owner and his place of residence. Filled
with delight, the kidnappers started back with their victim. Overjoyed
with the prospect of receiving a large reward, they gave themselves up
on the third night to pleasure. They put up at an inn. The negro was
chained to the bed-post, in the same room with his captors. At dead
of night, when all was still, the slave arose from the floor upon which
he had been lying, looked around, and saw that the white men were
fast asleep. The brandy punch had done its work. With palpitating
heart and trembling limbs he viewed his position. The door was fast,
but the warm weather had compelled them to leave the window open.
If he could but get his chains off, he might escape through the window
to the piazza, and reach the ground by one of the posts that supported
the piazza. The sleeper's clothes hung upon chairs by the bedside; the
slave thought of the padlock key, examined the pockets and found it.
The chains were soon off, and the negro stealthily making his way to
the window: he stopped and said to himself, "These men are villains,
they are enemies to all who like me are trying to be free. Then why not
I teach them a lesson?" He then undressed himself, took the clothes of
one of the men, dressed himself in them, and escaped through the window, and, a moment more, he was on the high road to Canada. Fifteen
days later, and the writer of this gave him a passage across Lake Erie,
and saw him safe in her Britannic Majesty's dominions.[5]

We have seen Clotel sold to Mr. French in Vicksburgh, her hair cut
short, and everything done to make her realise her position as a servant. Then we have seen her re-sold, because her owners feared she
would die through grief. As yet her new purchaser treated her with

[4] *the Ohio river:* The Ohio river marked an important boundary between free (Ohio
and Pennsylvania) and slave (Kentucky and Virginia) states.
[5] *Britannic Majesty's dominions:* Canada.

respectful gentleness, and sought to win her favour by flattery and presents, knowing that whatever he gave her he could take back again. But she dreaded every moment lest the scene should change, and trembled at the sound of every footfall. At every interview with her new master Clotel stoutly maintained that she had left a husband in Virginia, and would never think of taking another. The gold watch and chain, and other glittering presents which he purchased for her, were all laid aside by the quadroon, as if they were of no value to her. In the same house with her was another servant, a man, who had from time to time hired himself from his master. William was his name. He could feel for Clotel, for he, like her, had been separated from near and dear relatives, and often tried to console the poor woman. One day the quadroon observed to him that her hair was growing out again. "Yes," replied William, "you look a good deal like a man with your short hair." "Oh," rejoined she, "I have often been told that I would make a better looking man than a woman. If I had the money," continued she, "I would bid farewell to this place." In a moment more she feared that she had said too much, and smilingly remarked, "I am always talking nonsense." William was a tall, full-bodied negro, whose very counte-nance beamed with intelligence. Being a mechanic, he had, by his own industry, made more than what he paid his owner; this he laid aside, with the hope that some day he might get enough to purchase his free-dom. He had in his chest one hundred and fifty dollars. His was a heart that felt for others, and he had again and again wiped the tears from his eyes as he heard the story of Clotel as related by herself. "If she can get free with a little money, why not give her what I have?" thought he, and then he resolved to do it. An hour after, he came into the quadroon's room, and laid the money in her lap, and said, "There, Miss Clotel, you said if you had the means you would leave this place; there is money enough to take you to England, where you will be free. You are much fairer than many of the white women of the South, and can easily pass for a free white lady." At first Clotel feared that it was a plan by which the negro wished to try her fidelity to her owner; but she was soon convinced by his earnest manner, and the deep feeling with which he spoke, that he was honest. "I will take the money only on one condition," said she; "and that is, that I effect your escape as well as my own." "How can that be done?" he inquired. "I will assume the disguise of a gentleman and you that of a servant, and we will take passage on a steamboat and go to Cincinnati, and thence to Canada." Here William put in several objections to the plan. He feared detection, and he well knew that, when a slave is once caught when attempting to escape, if returned is sure to be worse treated than before. However, Clotel satisfied him that the plan could be carried out if he would only play his part.[6]

The resolution was taken, the clothes for her disguise procured, and before night everything was in readiness for their departure. That night Mr. Cooper, their master, was to attend a party, and this was their opportunity. William went to the wharf to look out for a boat, and had scarcely reached the landing ere he heard the puffing of a steamer. He returned and reported the fact. Clotel had already packed her trunk, and had only to dress and all was ready. In less than an hour they were on board the boat. Under the assumed name of "Mr. Johnson," Clotel went to the clerk's office and took a private state room for herself, and paid her own and servant's fare. Besides being attired in a neat suit of black, she had a white silk handkerchief tied round her chin, as if she was an invalid. A pair of green glasses covered her eyes; and fearing that she would be talked to too much and thus render her liable to be detected, she assumed to be very ill. On the other hand, William was playing his part well in the servants' hall; he was talking loudly of his master's wealth. Nothing appeared as good on the boat as in his master's fine mansion. "I don't like dees steamboats no how," said William; "I hope when marser goes on a journey agin he will take de carriage and de hosses." Mr. Johnson (for such was the name by which Clotel now went) remained in his room, to avoid, as far as possible, conversation with others. After a passage of seven days they arrived at Louisville, and put up at Gough's Hotel.[7] Here they had to await the departure of another boat for the North. They were now in their most critical position. They were still in a slave state, and John C. Calhoun,[8] a distinguished slave-owner, was a guest at this hotel. They feared, also, that trouble would attend their attempt to leave this place for the North, as all persons taking negroes with them have to give bail that such negroes are not runaway slaves. The law upon this point is very stringent: all steamboat and other public conveyances are liable to a fine for every slave that escapes by them, besides paying the full

---

[6] *the plan . . . part*: Clotel and William's plan is modeled on the 1848 escape of Ellen and William Craft. In a letter printed in the *Liberator*, Brown was the first to report on their amazing escape; see "Singular Escape," pp. 368–70.

[7] *Gough's Hotel*: One of many hotels named in honor of the popular British temperance reformer John Bartholomew Gough (1817–1886).

[8] *John C. Calhoun*: The South Carolina politician and political theorist John C. Calhoun (1782–1850) was the South's most prominent advocate of the doctrine of states' rights.

value for the slave. After a delay of four hours, Mr. Johnson and servant took passage on the steamer Rodolph, for Pittsburgh. It is usual,
before the departure of the boats, for an officer to examine every part
of the vessel to see that no slave secretes himself on board. "Where are
you going?" asked the officer of William, as he was doing his duty on
this occasion. "I am going with marser," was the quick reply. "Who is
your master?" "Mr. Johnson, sir, a gentleman in the cabin." "You
must take him to the office and satisfy that captain that all is right, or
you can't go on this boat." William informed his master what the officer had said. The boat was on the eve of going, and no time could be
lost, yet they knew not what to do. At last they went to the office, and
Mr. Johnson, addressing the captain, said, "I am informed that my
boy can't go with me unless I give security that he belongs to me."
"Yes," replied the captain, "that is the law." "A very strange law
indeed," rejoined Mr. Johnson, "that one can't take his property with
him." After a conversation of some minutes, and a plea on the part of
Johnson that he did not wish to be delayed owing to his illness, they
were permitted to take their passage without farther trouble, and the
boat was soon on its way up the river. The fugitives had now passed
the Rubicon,[9] and the next place at which they would land would be
in a Free State. Clotel called William to her room, and said to him,
"We are now free, you can go on your way to Canada, and I shall go
to Virginia in search of my daughter." The announcement that she was
going to risk her liberty in a Slave State was unwelcome news to William. With all the eloquence he could command, he tried to persuade
Clotel that she could not escape detection, and was only throwing her
freedom away. But she had counted the cost, and made up her mind
for the worst. In return for the money he had furnished, she had
secured for him his liberty, and their engagement was at an end.

After a quick passage the fugitives arrived at Cincinnati, and there
separated. William proceeded on his way to Canada, and Clotel again
resumed her own apparel, and prepared to start in search of her child.
As might have been expected, the escape of these two valuable slaves
created no little sensation in Vicksburgh. Advertisements and messages
were sent in every direction in which the fugitives were thought to
have gone. It was soon, however, known that they had left the town
as master and servant; and many were the communications which

---

[9] *Rubicon:* In 49 B.C.E., in defiance of the Roman senate, Julius Caesar crossed the
Rubicon, a stream flowing into the Adriatic Sea, to invade Pompey. Crossing or passing
the Rubicon has come to signify taking a bold and irrevocable action.

appeared in the newspapers, in which the writers thought, or pretended, that they had seen the slaves in their disguise. One was to the effect that they had gone off on a chaise; one as master, and the other as servant. But the most probable was an account given by a correspondent of one of the Southern newspapers, who happened to be a passenger in the same steamer in which the slaves escaped, and which we here give:—

"One bright starlight night, in the month of December last, I found myself in the cabin of the steamer Rodolph, then lying in the port of Vicksburgh, and bound to Louisville. I had gone early on board, in order to select a good berth, and having got tired of reading the papers, amused myself by watching the appearance of the passengers as they dropped in, one after another, and I being a believer in physiognomy, formed my own opinion of their characters.

"The second bell rang, and as I yawningly returned my watch to my pocket, my attention was attracted by the appearance of a young man who entered the cabin supported by his servant, a strapping negro.

"The man was bundled up in a capacious overcoat; his face was bandaged with a white handkerchief, and its expression entirely hid by a pair of enormous spectacles.

"There was something so mysterious and unusual about the young man as he sat restless in the corner, that curiosity led me to observe him more closely.

"He appeared anxious to avoid notice, and before the steamer had fairly left the wharf, requested, in a low, womanly voice, to be shown his berth, as he was an invalid, and must retire early: his name he gave as Mr. Johnson. His servant was called, and he was put quietly to bed. I paced the deck until Tybee light[10] grew dim in the distance, and then went to my berth.

"I awoke in the morning with the sun shining in my face; we were then just passing St. Helena.[11] It was a mild beautiful morning, and most of the passengers were on deck, enjoying the freshness of the air, and stimulating their appetites for breakfast. Mr. Johnson soon made his appearance, arrayed as on the night before, and took his seat quietly upon the guard of the boat.

"From the better opportunity afforded by daylight, I found that he was a slight built, apparently handsome young man, with black hair and eyes, and of a darkness of complexion that betokened Spanish extraction. Any notice from others seemed painful to him; so to satisfy

[10] *Tybee light*: Light from the Tybee Lighthouse, one of the tallest lighthouses in the nineteenth-century United States. The lighthouse was located on the Georgia coast.

[11] *St. Helena*: One of the sea islands off the coast of South Carolina.

my curiosity, I questioned his servant, who was standing near, and gained the following information.

"His master was an invalid—he had suffered for a long time under a complication of diseases, that had baffled the skill of the best physicians in Mississippi; he was now suffering principally with the 'rheumatism,' and he was scarcely able to walk or help himself in any way. He came from Vicksburgh and was now on his way to Philadelphia, at which place resided his uncle, a celebrated physician, and through whose means he hoped to be restored to perfect health.

"This information, communicated in a bold, off-hand manner, enlisted my sympathies for the sufferer, although it occurred to me that he walked rather too gingerly for a person afflicted with so many ailments."

After thanking Clotel for the great service she had done him in bringing him out of slavery, William bade her farewell. The prejudice that exists in the Free States against coloured persons, on account of their color, is attributable solely to the influence of slavery, and is but another form of slavery itself. And even the slave who escapes from the Southern plantations, is surprised when he reaches the North, at the amount and withering influence of this prejudice. William applied at a railway station for a ticket for the train going to Sandusky,[12] and was told that if he went by that train he would have to ride in the luggage-van. "Why?" asked the astonished negro. "We don't send a Jim Crow[13] carriage but once a day, and that went this morning." The "Jim Crow" carriage is the one in which the blacks have to ride. Slavery is a school in which its victims learn much shrewdness, and William had been an apt scholar. Without asking any more questions, the negro took his seat in one of the first-class carriages. He was soon seen and ordered out. Afraid to remain in the town longer, he resolved to go by that train; and consequently seated himself on a goods' box in the luggage-van. The train started at its proper time, and all went on well. Just before arriving at the end of the journey, the conductor called on William for his ticket. "I have none," was the reply. "Well, then, you can pay your fare with me," said the officer. "How much is it?" asked the black man. "Two dollars." "What do you charge those in the passenger-carriage?" "Two dollars." "And do you charge me the same as you do those who ride in the best carriage?" asked the negro.

---

[12] *Sandusky*: A port town in northern Ohio, on Lake Erie.

[13] *Jim Crow*: A term first used in the 1830s to describe a song and dance routine by blackface minstrel performers, "Jim Crow" came to be understood as an adjective indicating discrimination based on race.

"Yes," was the answer. "I shan't pay it," returned the man. "You black scamp, do you think you can ride on this road without paying your fare?" "No, I don't want to ride for nothing; I only want to pay what's right." "Well, launch out two dollars, and that's right." "No, I shan't; I will pay what I ought, and won't pay any more." "Come, come, nigger, your fare and be done with it," said the conductor, in a manner that is never used except by Americans to blacks. "I won't pay you two dollars, and that enough," said William. "Well, as you have come all the way in the luggage-van, pay me a dollar and a half and you may go." "I shan't do any such thing." "Don't you mean to pay for riding?" "Yes, but I won't pay a dollar and a half for riding up here in the freight-van. If you had let me come in the carriage where others ride, I would have paid you two dollars." "Where were you raised? You seem to think yourself as good as white folks." "I want nothing more than my rights." "Well, give me a dollar, and I will let you off." "No, sir, I shan't do it." "What do you mean to do then—don't you wish to pay anything?" "Yes, sir, I want to pay you the full price." "What do you mean by full price?" "What do you charge per hundred-weight for goods?" inquired the negro with a degree of gravity that would have astonished Diogenes[14] himself. "A quarter of a dollar per hundred," answered the conductor. "I weigh just one hundred and fifty pounds," returned William, "and will pay you three-eighths of a dollar." "Do you expect that you will pay only thirty-seven cents for your ride?" "This, sir, is your own price. I came in a luggage-van, and I'll pay for luggage." After a vain effort to get the negro to pay for more, the conductor took the thirty-seven cents, and noted in his cash-book, "Received for one hundred and fifty pounds of luggage, thirty-seven cents." This, reader, is no fiction;[15] it actually occurred in the railway above described.

Thomas Corwin,[16] a member of the American Congress, is one of the blackest white men in the United States. He was once on his way to Congress, and took passage in one of the Ohio river steamers. As he came just at the dinner hour, he immediately went into the dining saloon, and took his seat at the table. A gentleman with his whole

---

[14] *Diogenes*: A Greek Cynic philosopher, Diogenes (412?–323 B.C.E.) expounded on the virtues of self-control.

[15] *This, reader, is no fiction*: For a description of Brown's own encounter with such discriminatory practices, see the selection from Josephine Brown, pp. 360–64.

[16] *Thomas Corwin*: Thomas Corwin (1794–1865) held a number of political offices in Ohio, including the governorship and a senate seat. He was best known for an 1847 speech in Congress that attacked the Mexican War and predicted increasing sectional conflict.

party of five ladies at once left the table. "Where is the captain," cried the man in an angry tone. The captain soon appeared, and it was sometime before he could satisfy the old gent. that Governor Corwin was not a nigger. The newspapers often have notices of mistakes made by innkeepers and others who undertake to accommodate the public, one of which we give below.

On the 6th inst.,[17] the Hon. Daniel Webster[18] and family entered Edgartown,[19] on a visit for health and recreation. Arriving at the hotel, without alighting from the coach, the landlord was sent for to see if suitable accommodation could be had. That dignitary appearing, and surveying Mr. Webster, while the hon. senator addressed him, seemed woefully to mistake the dark features of the traveller as he sat back in the corner of the carriage, and to suppose him a *coloured man*, particularly as there were two coloured servants of Mr. W. outside. So he promptly declared that there was no room for him and his family, and he could not be accommodated there—at the same time suggesting that he might perhaps find accommodation at some of the huts "up back," to which he pointed. So deeply did the prejudice of looks possess him, that he appeared not to notice that the stranger introduced himself to him as Daniel Webster, or to be so ignorant as not to have heard of such a personage; and turning away, he expressed to the driver his astonishment that he should bring *black* people there for *him* to take in. It was not till he had been repeatedly assured and made to understand that the said Daniel Webster was a real live senator of the United States, that he perceived his awkward mistake and the distinguished honour which he and his house were so near missing.

In most of the Free States, the coloured people are disfranchised on account of their color. The following scene, which we take from a newspaper in the state of Ohio, will give some idea of the extent to which this prejudice is carried.

> "The whole of Thursday last was occupied by the Court of Common Pleas for this county in trying to find out whether one Thomas West was of the VOTING COLOUR, as some had very *constitutional doubts* as to whether his colour was orthodox, and whether his hair was of the official crisp! Was it not a dignified business? Four profound judges, four acute lawyers, twelve grave jurors, and I don't know how many venerable

---

[17] *inst.:* Of the present month; from the Latin "instans."
[18] *Hon. Daniel Webster:* A much admired senator from Massachusetts, Daniel Webster (1782–1852) alienated many abolitionists when he supported the Compromise of 1850. For a selection from Webster, see pp. 345–47.
[19] *Edgartown:* A town in Martha's Vineyard, an island off southeast Massachusetts.

witnesses, making in all about thirty men, perhaps, all engaged in the profound, laborious, and illustrious business, of finding out whether a man who pays tax, works on the road, and is an industrious farmer, has been born according to the republican, Christian constitution of Ohio—so that he can vote! And they wisely, gravely and 'JUDGMATI- CALLY' decided that he should not vote! What wisdom—what research it must have required to evolve this truth! It was left for the Court of Common Pleas for Columbian county, Ohio, in the United States of North America, to find out what Solomon never dreamed of—the courts of all civilised, heathen, or Jewish countries, never contemplated. Lest the wisdom of our courts should be circumvented by some such men as might be named, who are so near being born constitutionally that they might be taken for white by sight, I would suggest that our court be invested with SMELLING powers, and that if a man don't exhale the constitutional smell, he shall not vote! This would be an additional security to our liberties."

William found, after all, that liberty in the so-called Free States was more a name than a reality; that prejudice followed the coloured man into every place that he might enter. The temples erected for the wor- ship of the living God are no exception. The finest Baptist church in the city of Boston has the following paragraph in the deed that con- veys its seats to pewholders:[20]

"And it is a further condition of these presents, that if the owner or owners of said pew shall determine hereafter to sell the same, it shall first be offered, in writing, to the standing committee of said society for the time being, at such price as might otherwise be obtained for it; and the said committee shall have the right, for ten days after such offer, to purchase said pew for said society, at that price, first deducting there- from all taxes and assessments on said pew then remaining unpaid. And if the said committee shall not so complete such purchase within said ten days, then the pew may be sold by the owner or owners thereof (after payment of all such arrears) to any one respectable *white person*, but upon the same conditions as are contained in this instrument; and immediate notice of such sale shall be given in writing, by the vendor, to the treasurer of said society."

Such are the conditions upon which the Rowe Street Baptist Church, Boston, disposes of its seats. The writer of this is able to put that whole congregation, minister and all, to flight, by merely putting his coloured

---

[20]*pewholders*: Those who rent or own a pew, an enclosed area of seats or benches in a church. The system of pewholding was widespread in nineteenth-century churches.

face in that church. We once visited a church in New York that had a place set apart for the sons of Ham. It was a dark, dismal looking place in one corner of the gallery, grated in front like a hen-coop, with a black border around it. It had two doors; over one was B. M. — black men; over the other B. W. — black women.

CHAPTER XX.
A TRUE DEMOCRAT.

"Who can, with patience, for a moment see
The medley mass of pride and misery,
Of whips and charters, manacles and rights,
Of slaving blacks and democratic whites,
And all the piebald policy that reigns
In free confusion o'er Columbia's plains?
To think that man, thou just and gentle God!
Should stand before thee with a tyrant's rod,
O'er creatures like himself, with souls from thee,
Yet dare to boast of perfect liberty!"[1]
— *Thomas Moore.*

Educated in a free state, and marrying a wife who had been a victim to the institution of slavery, Henry Morton became strongly opposed to the system. His two daughters, at the age of twelve years, were sent to the North to finish their education, and to receive that refinement that young ladies cannot obtain in the Slave States. Although he did not publicly advocate the abolition of slavery, he often made himself obnoxious to private circles, owing to the denunciatory manner in which he condemned the "peculiar institution." Being one evening at a party, and hearing one of the company talking loudly of the glory and freedom of American institutions, he gave it as his opinion that, unless slavery was speedily abolished, it would be the ruin of the Union. "It is not our boast of freedom," said he, "that will cause us to be respected abroad. It is not our loud talk in favour of liberty that will cause us to be regarded as friends of human freedom; but our acts will be scrutinised by the people of other countries. We say much against European despotism; let us look to ourselves. That government is despotic where the rulers govern subjects by their own mere will—by decrees and laws emanating from their uncontrolled will, in the enactment and execution of which the ruled have no voice, and under which they have no right except at the will of the rulers. Despotism does not depend upon the numbers of the rulers, or the number of the subjects. It may have one ruler or many. Rome was a despotism under Nero; so she was under the triumvirate. Athens was a despotism under Thirty Tyrants; under her Four Hundred Tyrants; under her Three Thousand

---

[1] "*Who can . . . perfect liberty!*": From Thomas Moore (1779–1852), "To the Lord Viscount Forbes. From the City of Washington," in *The Poetical Works* (1840–41).

Tyrants.[2] It has been generally observed that despotism increases in severity with the number of despots; the responsibility is more divided, and the claims more numerous. The triumvirs each demanded his victims. The smaller the number of subjects in proportion to the tyrants, the more cruel the oppression, because the less danger from rebellion. In this government, the free white citizens are the rulers—the sovereigns, as we delight to be called. All others are subjects. There are, perhaps, some sixteen or seventeen millions of sovereigns, and four millions of subjects.

"The rulers and the ruled are of all colours, from the clear white of the Caucasian[3] tribes to the swarthy Ethiopian. The former, by courtesy, are all called white, the latter black. In this government the subject has no rights, social, political, or personal. He has no voice in the laws which govern him. He can hold no property. His very wife and children are not his. His labour is another's. He, and all that appertain to him, are the absolute property of his rulers. He is governed, bought, sold, punished, executed, by laws to which he never gave his assent, and by rulers whom he never chose. He is not a serf merely, with half the rights of men like the subjects of despotic Russia; but a native slave, stripped of every right which God and nature gave him, and which the high spirit of our revolution declared inalienable—which he himself could not surrender, and which man could not take from him. Is he not then the subject of despotic sway?

"The slaves of Athens and Rome were free in comparison.[4] They had some rights—could acquire some property; could choose their own masters, and purchase their own freedom; and, when free, could rise in social and political life. The slaves of America, then, lie under the most absolute and grinding despotism that the world ever saw. But who are the despots? The rulers of the country—the sovereign people!

---

[2] *Rome . . . Tyrants*: Nero was emperor of Rome, 54–68 C.E.; a triumvirate, a ruling body of three men, governed in ancient Rome circa 60–31 B.C.E. Athens's oligarchical Thirty Tyrants were overthrown in 403 B.C.E. Morton's references to the Four Hundred and Three Thousand Tyrants are more likely jabs at what Brown regards as Southerners' false forms of democracy.

[3] *Caucasian*: A term coined by the German naturalist and anthropologist Johann Friedrich Blumenbach (1752–1840) to designate what he classified as the white race. Based on a comparative study of human skulls, his widely disseminated *On the Natural Varieties of Mankind* (1775) divided mankind into five racial classifications and helped give rise to racial "science."

[4] *The slaves . . . comparison*: In his *Appeal* (1829), the black nationalist David Walker similarly argued that the Roman slaves were better off than U.S. slaves; for selections from the *Appeal*, see pp. 256–64.

Not merely the slaveholder who cracks the lash. He is but the instrument in the hands of despotism. That despotism is the government of the Slave States, and the United States, consisting of all its rulers—all the free citizens. Do not look upon this as a paradox, because you and I and the sixteen millions of rulers are free. The rulers of every despotism are free. Nicholas of Russia is free. The grand Sultan of Turkey is free. The butcher of Austria is free. Augustus, Anthony, and Lepidus were free, while they drenched Rome in blood.[5] The Thirty Tyrants—the Four Hundred—the Three Thousand, were free while they bound their countrymen in chains. You, and I, and the sixteen millions are free, while we fasten iron chains, and rivet manacles on four millions of our fellow-men—tear their wives and children from them—separate them—sell them, and doom them to perpetual, eternal bondage. Are we not then despots—despots such as history will brand and God abhor?

"We, as individuals, are fast losing our reputation for honest dealing. Our nation is losing its character. The loss of a firm national character, or the degradation of a nation's honour, is the inevitable prelude to her destruction. Behold the once proud fabric of a Roman empire—an empire carrying its arts and arms into every part of the Eastern continent; the monarchs of mighty kingdoms dragged at the wheels of her triumphal chariots; her eagle waving over the ruins of desolated countries;—where is her splendour, her wealth, her power, her glory? Extinguished for ever. Her mouldering temples, the mournful vestiges of her former grandeur, afford a shelter to her muttering monks. Where are her statesmen, her sages, her philosophers, her orators, generals? Go to their solitary tombs and inquire? She lost her national character, and her destruction followed. The ramparts of her national pride were broken down, and Vandalism[6] desolated her classic fields. Then let the people of our country take warning ere it is too late. But most of us say to ourselves,

---

[5] *Nicholas ... blood*: A listing of representative despots: Nicholas I (1796–1855) was czar of Russia from 1825 to 1855; Abd al-Majid (1823–1861) reigned as the Ottoman sultan from 1839 to 1861; Franz Joseph (1830–1916) was emperor of Austria from 1848 to 1916; Augustus (63 B.C.E.–14 C.E.) was the first Roman emperor; Marc Anthony (c.83–30 B.C.E.) and Marcus Aemilius Lepidus (?–13 B.C.E.) formed Rome's Second Triumvirate circa 43 B.C.E.

[6] *Vandalism*: Derives from the Vandals, the Germanic people who sacked Rome in 455 B.C.E.

> " 'Who questions the right of mankind to be free?
> Yet, what are the rights of the *negro* to me?
> I'm well fed and clothed, I have plenty of pelf[7] —
> I'll care for the blacks when I turn black myself.'

"New Orleans is doubtless the most immoral place in the United States. The theatres are open on the Sabbath. Bull-fights, horse-racing, and other cruel amusements are carried on in this city to an extent unknown in any other part of the Union. The most stringent laws have been passed in that city against negroes, yet a few years since the State Legislature passed a special act to enable a white man to marry a coloured woman, on account of her being possessed of a large fortune. And, very recently, the following paragraph appeared in the city papers: —

> " 'There has been quite a stir recently in this city, in consequence of a marriage of a white man, named Buddington, a teller in the Canal Bank, to the negro daughter of one of the wealthiest merchants. Buddington, before he could be married, was obliged to swear that he had negro blood in his veins, and to do this he made an incision in his arm, and put some of her blood in the cut. The ceremony was performed by a Catholic clergyman, and the bridegroom has received with his wife a fortune of fifty or sixty thousand dollars.'

"It seems that the fifty or sixty thousand dollars entirely covered the negro woman's black skin, and the law prohibiting marriage between blacks and whites was laid aside for the occasion."

Althesa felt proud, as well she might, at her husband's taking such high ground in a slaveholding city like New Orleans.

---

[7] *pelf*: Money (generally a disparaging term).

CHAPTER XXI.
THE CHRISTIAN'S DEATH.

"O weep, ye friends of freedom weep!
Your harps to mournful measure sweep."[1]

On the last day of November, 1620, on the confines of the Grand Bank of Newfoundland, lo! we behold one little solitary tempest-tost and weather-beaten ship; it is all that can be seen on the length and breadth of the vast intervening solitudes, from the melancholy wilds of Labrador[2] and New England's iron-bound shores, to the western coasts of Ireland and the rock-defended Hebrides,[3] but one lonely ship greets the eyes of angels or of men, on this great thoroughfare of nations in our age. Next in moral grandeur, was this ship, to the great discoverer's: Columbus found a continent; the May-flower[4] brought the seed-wheat of states and empire. That is the May-flower, with its servants of the living God, their wives and little ones, hastening to lay the foundations of nations in the occidental lands of the setting-sun. Hear the voice of prayer to God for his protection, and the glorious music of praise, as it breaks into the wild tempest of the mighty deep, upon the ear of God. Here in this ship are great and good men. Justice, mercy, humanity, respect for the rights of all; each man honoured, as he was useful to himself and others; labour respected, law-abiding men, constitution-making and respecting men; men, whom no tyrant could conquer, or hardship overcome, with the high commission sealed by a Spirit divine, to establish religious and political liberty for all. This ship had the embryo elements of all that is useful, great, and grand in Northern institutions; it was the great type of goodness and wisdom, illustrated in two and a quarter centuries gone by; it was the good genius of America.

But look far in the South-east, and you behold on the same day, in 1620, a low rakish ship hastening from the tropics, solitary and alone, to the New World. What is she? She is freighted with the elements of unmixed evil. Hark! hear those rattling chains, hear that cry of despair

---

[1] "*O Weep . . . measures sweep*": From D. H. Jacques, "Your Brother Is a Slave," in *The Anti-Slavery Harp*, ed. Brown.

[2] *Labrador*: Peninsula containing the Canadian provinces of Newfoundland and Quebec.

[3] *Hebrides*: Scottish islands west of Scotland.

[4] *May-flower*: The *Mayflower* brought William Bradford (1590–1657) and other English Puritans to Cape Cod on 9 November 1620.

and wail of anguish, as they die away in the unpitying distance. Listen to those shocking oaths, the crack of that flesh-cutting whip. Ah! it is the first cargo of slaves on their way to Jamestown, Virginia.[5] Behold the May-flower anchored at Plymouth Rock, the slave-ship in James River. Each a parent, one of the prosperous, labour-honouring, law-sustaining institutions of the North; the other the mother of slavery, idleness, lynch-law, ignorance, unpaid labour, poverty, and duelling, despotism, the ceaseless swing of the whip, and the peculiar institutions of the South. These ships are the representation of good and evil in the New World, even to our day. When shall one of those parallel lines come to an end?

The origin of American slavery is not lost in the obscurity of by-gone ages. It is a plain historical fact, that it owes its birth to the African slave trade, now pronounced by every civilised community the greatest crime ever perpetrated against humanity. Of all causes intended to benefit mankind, the abolition of chattel slavery must necessarily be placed amongst the first, and the negro hails with joy every new advocate that appears in his cause. Commiseration for human suffering and human sacrifices awakened the capacious mind, and brought into action the enlarged benevolence, of Georgiana Carlton. With respect to her philosophy—it was of a noble cast. It was, that all men are by nature equal; that they are wisely and justly endowed by the Creator with certain rights, which are irrefragable; and that, however human pride and human avarice may depress and debase, still God is the author of good to man—and of evil, man is the artificer to himself and to his species. Unlike Plato and Socrates,[6] her mind was free from the gloom that surrounded theirs; her philosophy was founded in the school of Christianity; though a devoted member of her father's church, she was not a sectarian.

We learn from Scripture, and it is a little remarkable that it is the only exact definition of religion found in the sacred volume, that "pure religion and undefiled before God, even the Father, is this, to visit the fatherless and widows in their affliction, and to keep oneself unspotted from the world." "Look not every man on his own things, but every

---

[5] *the first cargo of slaves on their way to Jamestown, Virginia*: In fact, twenty slaves purchased from a Dutch man-of-war were brought to the early English settlement of Jamestown in August 1619.

[6] *Plato and Socrates*: Committed to a philosophical idealism that conceived of the Good as the divine, ordering principle of the cosmos, the ancient Greek philosophers Plato (427?–347 B.C.E.) and Socrates (469–399 B.C.E.) are presented as gloomy for lacking a sense of the Christian God.

man also on the things of others." "Remember them that are in bonds as bound with them." "Whatsoever ye would that others should do to you, do ye even so to them."[7]

This was her view of Christianity, and to this end she laboured with all her energies to convince her slaveholding neighbours that the negro could not only take care of himself, but that he also appreciated liberty, and was willing to work and redeem himself. Her most sanguine wishes were being realized when she suddenly fell into a decline. Her mother had died of consumption, and her physician pronounced this to be her disease. She was prepared for this sad intelligence, and received it with the utmost composure. Although she had confidence in her husband that he would carry out her wishes in freeing the negroes after her death, Mrs. Carlton resolved upon their immediate liberation. Consequently the slaves were all summoned before the noble woman, and informed that they were no longer bondsmen. "From this hour," said she, "you are free, and all eyes will be fixed upon you. I dare not predict how far your example may affect the welfare of your brethren yet in bondage. If you are temperate, industrious, peaceable, and pious, you will show to the world that slaves can be emancipated without danger. Remember what a singular relation you sustain to society. The necessities of the case require not only that you should behave as well as the whites, but better than the whites; and for this reason: if you behave no better than they, your example will lose a great portion of its influence. Make the Lord Jesus Christ your refuge and exemplar. His is the only standard around which you can successfully rally. If ever there was a people who needed the consolations of religion to sustain them in their grievous afflictions, you are that people. You had better trust in the Lord than to put confidence in man. Happy is that people whose God is the Lord. Get as much education as possible for yourselves and your children. An ignorant people can never occupy any other than a degraded station in society; they

---

[7] *"pure religion. . . . to them"*: James 1.27, Philippians 2.4, Hebrews 13.3, Matthew 7.12. Much of the opening of this chapter draws on a speech that the New York lawyer and abolitionist Alvan Stewart (1790–1849) delivered before the New Jersey State Supreme Court in 1845 as counsel for two African Americans still held as slaves, despite the fact that the Bill of Rights attached to the state's new Constitution, ratified in 1844, prohibited slavery. See Alvan Stewart, *A Legal Argument before the Supreme Court of the State of New Jersey, at the May Term, 1845, at Trenton, for the Deliverance of Four Thousand Persons from Bondage* (New York: Finch and Weed, 1845); reprinted in *Abolitionists in Northern Courts: The Pamphlet Literature*, ed. Paul Finkelman (New York: Garland, 1988).

can never be truly free until they are intelligent. In a few days you will start for the state of Ohio, where land will be purchased for some of you who have families, and where I hope you will all prosper. We have been urged to send you to Liberia, but we think it wrong to send you from your native land. We did not wish to encourage the Colonization Society,[8] for it originated in hatred of the free coloured people. Its pretences are false, its doctrines odious, its means contemptible. Now, whatever may be your situation in life, 'Remember those in bonds as bound with them.'[9] You must get ready as soon as you can for your journey to the North."

Seldom was there ever witnessed a more touching scene than this. There sat the liberator,—pale, feeble, emaciated, with death stamped upon her countenance, surrounded by the sons and daughters of Africa; some of whom had in former years been separated from all that they had held near and dear, and the most of whose backs had been torn and gashed by the negro whip. Some were upon their knees at the feet of their benefactress; others were standing round her weeping. Many begged that they might be permitted to remain on the farm and work for wages, for some had wives and some husbands on other plantations in the neighbourhood, and would rather remain with them.

But the laws of the state forbade any emancipated negroes remaining, under penalty of again being sold into slavery. Hence the necessity of sending them out of the state. Mrs. Carlton was urged by her friends to send the emancipated negroes to Africa. Extracts from the speeches of Henry Clay, and other distinguished Colonization Society men, were read to her to induce her to adopt this course. Some thought they should be sent away because the blacks are vicious; others because they would be missionaries to their brethren in Africa. "But," said she, "if we send away the negroes because they are profligate and vicious, what sort of missionaries will they make? Why not send away the vicious among the whites for the same reason, and the same purpose?"

Death is a leveller, and neither age, sex, wealth, nor usefulness can avert when he is permitted to strike. The most beautiful flowers soon fade, and droop, and die; this is also the case with man; his days are uncertain as the passing breeze. This hour he glows in the blush of health and vigour, but the next he may be counted with the number no more known on earth.

---

[8] *Colonization Society*: Founded in 1816 in Washington, D.C., the American Colonization Society sought to ship the free blacks to Africa.
[9] *'Remember . . . with them'*: Hebrews 13.3.

Although in a low state of health, Mrs. Carlton had the pleasure of seeing all her slaves, except Sam and three others, start for a land of freedom. The morning they were to go on board the steamer, bound for Louisville, they all assembled on the large grass plot, in front of the drawing-room window, and wept while they bid their mistress farewell. When they were on the boat, about leaving the wharf, they were heard giving the charge to those on shore— "Sam, take care of Misus, take care of Marser, as you love us, and hope to meet us in de Hio (Ohio), and in heben; be sure and take good care of Misus and Marser."

In less than a week after her emancipated people had started for Ohio, Mrs. Carlton was cold in death. Mr. Carlton felt deeply, as all husbands must who love their wives, the loss of her who had been a lamp to his feet, and a light to his path. She had converted him from infidelity to Christianity; from the mere theory of liberty to practical freedom. He had looked upon the negro as an ill-treated distant link of the human family; he now regarded them as a part of God's children. Oh, what a silence pervaded the house when the Christian had been removed. His indeed was a lonesome position.

> " 'Twas midnight, and he sat alone—
> The husband of the dead,
> That day the dark dust had been thrown
> Upon the buried head."

In the midst of the buoyancy of youth, this cherished one had drooped and died. Deep were the sounds of grief and mourning heard in that stately dwelling, when the stricken friends, whose office it had been to nurse and soothe the weary sufferer, beheld her pale and motionless in the sleep of death.

Oh what a chill creeps through the breaking heart when we look upon the insensible form, and feel that it no longer contains the spirit we so dearly loved! How difficult to realise that the eye which always glowed with affection and intelligence—that the ear which had so often listened to the sounds of sorrow and gladness—that the voice whose accents had been to us like sweet music, and the heart, the habitation of benevolence and truth, are now powerless and insensate as the bier[10] upon which the form rests. Though faith is strong enough to penetrate the cloud of gloom which hovers near, and to behold the freed spirit safe, *for ever*, safe in its home in heaven, yet the thoughts *will* linger sadly and cheerlessly upon the grave.

[10] *bier*: A stand holding a corpse or coffin.

Peace to her ashes! she fought the fight, obtained the Christian's victory, and wears the crown. But if it were that departed spirits are permitted to note the occurrences of this world, with what a frown of disapprobation would hers view the effort being made in the United States to retard the work of emancipation for which she laboured and so wished to see brought about.

In what light would she consider that hypocritical priesthood who gave their aid and sanction to the infamous "Fugitive Slave Law." If true greatness consists in doing good to mankind, then was Georgiana Carlton an ornament to human nature. Who can think of the broken hearts made whole, of sad and dejected countenances now beaming with contentment and joy, of the mother offering her free-born babe to heaven, and of the father whose cup of joy seems overflowing in the presence of his family, where none can molest or make him afraid. Oh, that God may give more such persons to take the whip-scarred negro by the hand, and raise him to a level with our common humanity! May the professed lovers of freedom in the new world see that true liberty is freedom for all! and may every American continually hear it sounding in his ear: —

> "Shall every flap of England's flag
>   Proclaim that all around are free,
> From 'farthest Ind' to each blue crag
>   That beetles o'er the Western Sea?
> And shall we scoff at Europe's kings,
>   When Freedom's fire is dim with us,
> And round our country's altar clings
>   The damning shade of Slavery's curse?"[11]

---

[11] *"Shall . . . Slavery's curse?"*: From John Greenleaf Whittier, "Expostulation" (1834).

CHAPTER XXII.
A RIDE IN A STAGE-COACH.

We shall now return to Cincinnati, where we left Clotel preparing to go to Richmond in search of her daughter. Tired of the disguise in which she had escaped, she threw it off on her arrival at Cincinnati. But being assured that not a shadow of safety would attend her visit to a city in which she was well known, unless in some disguise, she again resumed men's apparel on leaving Cincinnati. This time she had more the appearance of an Italian or Spanish gentleman. In addition to the fine suit of black cloth, a splendid pair of dark false whiskers covered the sides of her face, while the curling moustache found its place upon the upper lip. From practice she had become accustomed to high-heeled boots, and could walk without creating any suspicion as regarded her sex. It was on a cold evening that Clotel arrived at Wheeling,[1] and took a seat in the coach going to Richmond. She was already in the state of Virginia, yet a long distance from the place of her destination.

A ride in a stage-coach, over an American road, is unpleasant under the most favourable circumstances. But now that it was winter, and the roads unusually bad, the journey was still more dreary. However, there were eight passengers in the coach, and I need scarcely say that such a number of genuine Americans could not be together without whiling away the time somewhat pleasantly. Besides Clotel, there was an elderly gentleman with his two daughters—one apparently under twenty years, the other a shade above. The pale, spectacled face of another slim, tall man, with a white neckerchief, pointed him out as a minister. The rough featured, dark countenance of a stout looking man, with a white hat on one side of his head, told that he was from the sunny South. There was nothing remarkable about the other two, who might pass for ordinary American gentlemen. It was on the eve of a presidential election, when every man is thought to be a politician. Clay, Van Buren, and Harrison were the men who expected the endorsement of the Baltimore Convention.[2] "Who does this town go

---

[1] *Wheeling*: A city in the northwest section of Virginia (now West Virginia) on the Ohio River.

[2] *Clay... Convention*: In 1839, Henry Clay and William Henry Harrison (1773–1841) competed as presidential candidates at the Whig nominating convention in Harrisburg, Pennsylvania; the incumbent president Martin Van Buren (1782–1862) was renominated at the Democratic convention in Baltimore in 1840. The Whigs' nominee, Harrison, defeated Van Buren to become the nation's ninth president, and died shortly after his inauguration.

for?" asked the old gent. with the ladies, as the coach drove up to an inn, where groups of persons were waiting for the latest papers. "We are divided," cried the rough voice of one of the outsiders. "Well, who do you think will get the majority here?" continued the old gent. "Can't tell very well; I go for 'Old Tip,' "[3] was the answer from without. This brought up the subject fairly before the passengers, and when the coach again started a general discussion commenced, in which all took a part except Clotel and the young ladies. Some were for Clay, some for Van Buren, and others for "Old Tip." The coach stopped to take in a real farmer-looking man, who no sooner entered than he was saluted with "Do you go for Clay?" "No," was the answer. "Do you go for Van Buren?" "No." "Well, then, of course you will go for Harrison." "No." "Why, don't you mean to work for any of them at the election?" "No." "Well, who will you work for?" asked one of the company. "I work for Betsy and the children, and I have a hard job of it at that," replied the farmer, without a smile. This answer, as a matter of course, set the new comer down as one upon whom the rest of the passengers could crack their jokes with the utmost impunity. "Are you an Odd Fellow?"[4] asked one. "No, sir, I've been married more than a month." "I mean, do you belong to the order of Odd Fellows?" "No, no; I belong to the order of married men." "Are you a mason?"[5] "No, I am a carpenter by trade." "Are you a Son of Temperance?"[6] "Bother you, no; I am a son of Mr. John Gosling." After a hearty laugh in which all joined, the subject of Temperance became the theme for discussion. In this the spectacled gent. was at home. He soon showed that he was a New Englander, and went the whole length of the "Maine Law."[7] The minister was about having it all his own way, when the Southerner, in the white hat, took the opposite side of the question. "I don't bet a red cent on these teetotlars,"[8] said he, and at the same time

[3] "*Old Tip*": Nickname of William Henry Harrison, which he acquired for having led U.S. forces against the Shawnee Indians in the 1811 Battle of Tippecanoe at what was later named Battle Ground, Indiana.

[4] *Odd Fellow*: A secretive, benevolent organization founded in England in the eighteenth century.

[5] *mason*: Like the Odd Fellows, the Free and Accepted Masons are a secretive, fraternal organization. Modern Masonry had its origins in early-eighteenth-century England.

[6] *Son of Temperance*: Founded in 1843, the Sons of Temperance was a secretive, fraternal organization committed to the cause of total abstinence from alcoholic beverages. By 1850, the organization boasted of having 250,000 dues-paying members.

[7] "*Maine Law*": Passed by Maine's state legislature in 1851, the law banned the sale and manufacture of alcoholic beverages within the state.

[8] *teetotlers*: People who abstain from intoxicating beverages.

looking round to see if he had the approbation of the rest of the company. "Why?" asked the minister. "Because they are a set who are afraid to spend a cent. They are a bad lot, the whole on 'em." It was evident that the white hat gent. was an uneducated man. The minister commenced in full earnest, and gave an interesting account of the progress of temperance in Connecticut, the state from which he came, proving, that a great portion of the prosperity of the state was attributable to the disuse of intoxicating drinks. Every one thought the white hat had got the worst of the argument, and that he was settled for the remainder of the night. But not he; he took fresh courage and began again. "Now," said he, "I have just been on a visit to my uncle's in Vermont, and I guess I knows a little about these here teetotlars. You see, I went up there to make a little stay of a fortnight. I got there at night, and they seemed glad to see me, but they didn't give me a bit of anything to drink. Well, thinks I to myself, the jig's up: I sha'n't get any more liquor till I get out of the state. We all sat up till twelve o'clock that night, and I heard nothing but talk about the 'Juvinal Temperance Army,' the 'Band of Hope,' the 'Rising Generation,' the 'Female Dorcas Temperance Society,' 'The None Such,'[9] and I don't know how many other names they didn't have. As I had taken several pretty large 'Cock Tails' before I entered the state, I thought upon the whole that I would not spile for the want of liquor. The next morning, I commenced writing back to my friends, and telling them what's what. Aunt Polly said, 'Well, Johnny, I s'pose you are given 'em a pretty account of us all here.' 'Yes,' said I; 'I am tellin' 'em if they want anything to drink when they come up here, they had better bring it with 'em.' 'Oh,' said aunty, 'they would search their boxes; can't bring any spirits in the state.' Well, as I was saying, jist as I got my letters finished, and was going to the post office (for uncle's house was two miles from the town), aunty says, 'Johnny, I s'pose you'll try to get a little somethin' to drink in town won't you?' Says I, 'I s'pse it's no use.' 'No,' said she, 'you can't; it aint to be had no how, for love nor money.' So jist as I was puttin' on my hat, 'Johnny,' cries out aunty, 'What,' says I. 'Now I'll tell you, I don't want you to say nothin' about it, but I keeps a little rum to rub my head with, for I am troubled with a headache; now I don't want you to mention it for the world, but I'll give you a little taste, the old man is such a teetotaller, that I should never hear the last of it, and I would not like for the boys to know it, they are members of the "Cold Water Army." '[10]

---

[9] *'Juvinal . . . None Such'*: Various temperance organizations.
[10] *"Cold Water Army"*: Founded in 1834, an organization of Sunday-school youth that campaigned against alcohol as a destroyer of families.

"Aunty now brought out a black bottle and gave me a cup, and told me to help myself, which I assure you I did. I now felt ready to face the cold. As I was passing the barn I heard uncle thrashing oats, so I went to the door and spoke to him. 'Come in, John,' says he. 'No,' said I; 'I am goin' to post some letters,' for I was afraid that he would smell my breath if I went too near to him. 'Yes, yes, come in.' So I went in, and says he, 'It's now eleven o'clock; that's about the time you take your grog,[11] I s'pose, when you are at home.' 'Yes,' said I. 'I am sorry for you, my lad; you can't get anything up here; you can't even get it at the chemist's, except as medicine, and then you must let them mix it and you take it in their presence.' 'This is indeed hard,' replied I; 'Well, it can't be helped,' continued he: 'and it ought not to be if it could. It's best for society; people's better off without drink. I recollect when your father and I, thirty years ago, used to go out on a spree and spend more than half a dollar in a night. Then here's the rising generation; there's nothing like settin' a good example. Look how healthy your cousins are—there's Benjamin, he never tasted spirits in his life. Oh, John, I would you were a teetotaller.' 'I suppose,' said I, 'I'll have to be one till I leave the state.' 'Now,' said he, 'John, I don't want you to mention it, for your aunt would go into hysterics if she thought there was a drop of intoxicating liquor about the place, and I would not have the boys to know it for anything, but I keep a little brandy to rub my joints for the rheumatics, and being it's you, I'll give you a little dust.' So the old man went to one corner of the barn, took out a brown jug and handed it to me, and I must say it was a little the best cogniac that I had tasted for many a day. Says I, 'Uncle, you are a good judge of brandy.' 'Yes,' said he, 'I learned when I was young.' So off I started for the post office. In returnin' I thought I'd jist go through the woods where the boys were chopping wood, and wait and go to the house with them when they went to dinner. I found them hard at work, but as merry as crickets. 'Well, cousin John, are you done writing?' 'Yes,' answered I. 'Have you posted them?' 'Yes.' 'Hope you didn't go to any place inquiring about grog.' 'No, I knowed it was no good to do that.' 'I suppose a cock-tail would taste good now.' 'Well, I guess it would,' said I. The three boys then joined in a hearty laugh. 'I suppose you have told 'em that we are a dry set up here?' 'Well, I aint told 'em anything else.' 'Now, cousin John,' said Edward, 'if you wont say anything, we will give you a small taste. For mercy's sake don't let father or mother know it; they are such rabid teetotallers, that they would not sleep a wink to-night if they thought there was any spirits about

---

[11] *grog*: Generally refers to a mixture of water and hard liquor.

the place.' 'I am mum,' says I. And the boys took a jug out of a hollow stump, and gave me some first-rate peach brandy. And during the fortnight that I was in Vermont, with my teetotal relations, I was kept about as well corned[12] as if I had been among my hot water friends in Tennessee."

This narrative, given by the white hat man, was received with unbounded applause by all except the pale gent. in spectacles, who showed, by the way in which he was running his fingers between his cravat and throat, that he did not intend to "give it up so." The white hat gent. was now the lion of the company.

"Oh, you did not get hold of the right kind of teetotallers." said the minister. "I can give you a tale worth a dozen of yours," continued he. "Look at society in the states where temperance views prevail, and you will there see real happiness. The people are taxed less, the poor houses are shut up for want of occupants, and extreme destitution is unknown. Every one who drinks at all is liable to become an habitual drunkard. Yes, I say boldly, that no man living who uses intoxicating drinks, is free from the danger of at least occasional, and if of occasional, ultimately of habitual excess. There seems to be no character, position, or circumstances that free men from the danger. *I have known* many young men of the finest promise, led by the drinking habit into vice, ruin, and early death. *I have known* many tradesmen whom it has made bankrupt. *I have known* Sunday scholars whom it has led to prison—teachers, and even superintendents, whom it has dragged down to profligacy. *I have known* ministers of high academic honours, of splendid eloquence, nay, of vast usefulness, whom it has fascinated, and hurried over the precipice of public infamy with their eyes open, and gazing with horror on their fate. *I have known* men of the strongest and clearest intellect and of vigorous resolution, whom it has made weaker than children and fools—gentlemen of refinement and taste whom it has debased into brutes—poets of high genius whom it has bound in a bondage worse than the galleys, and ultimately cut short their days. *I have known* statesmen, lawyers, and judges whom it has killed—kind husbands and fathers whom it has turned into monsters. *I have known* honest men whom it has made villains—elegant and Christian *ladies* whom it has *converted into bloated sots*."[13]

---

[12] *well corned*: Well supplied with hard drink; the expression derived from the popularity of corn whiskey.

[13] *"Look at society . . . bloated sots"*: The likely source of the minister's remarks on temperance is "Important Testimony to the Maine Law from a Minister at Large," in *Frederick Douglass' Paper*, 1 April 1852.

"But you talk too fast," replied the white hat man. "You don't give a feller a chance to say nothin'." "I heard you," continued the minister, "and now you hear me out. It is indeed wonderful how people become lovers of strong drink. Some years since, before I became a teetotaller I kept spirits about the house, and I had a servant who was much addicted to strong drink. He used to say that he could not make my boots shine, without mixing the blacking with whiskey. So to satisfy myself that the whisky was put in the blacking, one morning I made him bring the dish in which he kept the blacking, and poured in the whiskey myself. And now, sir, what do you think?" "Why, I s'pose your boots shined better than before," replied the white hat. "No," continued the minister. "He took the blacking out, and I watched him, and he drank down the whiskey, blacking, and all."

This turned the joke upon the advocate of strong drink, and he began to put his wits to work for arguments. "You are from Connecticut, are you?" asked the Southerner. "Yes, and we are an orderly, pious, peaceable people. Our holy religion is respected, and we do more for the cause of Christ than the whole Southern States put together." "I don't doubt it," said the white hat gent. "You sell wooden nutmegs and other spurious articles enough to do some good. You talk of your 'holy religion;' but your robes' righteousness are woven at Lowell and Manchester;[14] your paradise is high per centum on factory stocks; your palms of victory and crowns of rejoicing are triumphs over a rival party in politics, on the questions of banks and tariffs. If you could, you would turn heaven into Birmingham,[15] make every angel a weaver, and with the eternal din of looms and spindles drown all the anthems of the morning star. Ah! I know you Connecticut people like a book. No, no, all hoss;[16] you can't come it on me." This last speech of the rough featured man again put him in the ascendant, and the spectacled gent. once more ran his fingers between his cravat and throat. "You live in Tennessee, I think," said the minister. "Yes," replied the Southerner, "I used to live in Orleans, but now I claim to be a Tennessean." "Your people of New Orleans are the most ungodly set in the United States," said the minister. Taking a New Orleans newspaper from his pocket he continued, "Just look here, there are not less than three advertisements of bull fights to take place on the Sabbath.

---

[14] *Lowell and Manchester*: In the mid-nineteenth century, Lowell, Massachusetts, and Manchester, England, were major manufacturing centers.

[15] *Birmingham*: A factory town in central England.

[16] *hoss*: Horse (slang), suggestive of feistiness (or horse manure).

You people of the Slave States have no regard for the Sabbath, religion, morality or anything else intended to make mankind better." Here Clotel could have borne ample testimony, had she dared to have taken sides with the Connecticut man. Her residence in Vicksburgh had given her an opportunity of knowing something of the character of the inhabitants of the far South. "Here is an account of a grand bull fight that took place in New Orleans a week ago last Sunday. I will read it to you." And the minister read aloud the following:

"Yesterday, pursuant to public notice, came off at Gretna,[17] opposite the Fourth District, the long heralded fight between the famous grizzly bear, General Jackson[18] (victor in fifty battles), and the Attakapas[19] bull, Santa Anna.[20]

"The fame of the coming conflict had gone forth to the four winds, and women and children, old men and boys, from all parts of the city, and from the breezy banks of Lake Pontchartrain and Borgne,[21] brushed up their Sunday suit, and prepared to see the fun. Long before the published hour, the quiet streets of the rural Gretna were filled with crowds of anxious denizens, flocking to the arena, and before the fight commenced, such a crowd had collected as Gretna had not seen, nor will be likely to see again.

"The arena for the sports was a cage, twenty feet square, built upon the ground, and constructed of heavy timbers and iron bars. Around it were seats, circularly placed, and intended to accommodate many thousands. About four or five thousand persons assembled, covering the seats as with a cloud, and crowding down around the cage, were within reach of the bars.

"The bull selected to sustain the honour and verify the pluck of Attakapas on this trying occasion was a black animal from the Opelousas,[22] lithe and sinewy as a four year old courser,[23] and with eyes like burning coals. His horns bore the appearance of having been filed at the

---

[17] *Gretna*: City in southeastern Louisiana, along the west bank of the Mississippi River.

[18] *General Jackson*: The bear is named for Andrew Jackson (1767–1845), who, during his career as general and president, achieved a reputation as a pugnacious fighter for having battled the British, the Spanish, and the Indians; Jackson also fought several duels.

[19] *Attakapas*: City in southern Louisiana.

[20] *Santa Anna*: Mexican politician and general, Antonio López de Santa Anna (1794–1876) was regarded by many in the United States as particularly brutal for having led the 1836 attack on the Alamo, which resulted in the deaths of approximately 150 Texan revolutionaries.

[21] *Lake Pontchartrain and Borgne*: Connected lakes north of New Orleans.

[22] *Opelousas*: A town in southeast Louisiana.

[23] *courser*: A swift horse.

tips, and wanted that keen and slashing appearance so common with others of his kith and kin; otherwise it would have been 'all day' with Bruin at the first pass, and no mistake.

"The bear was an animal of note, and called General Jackson, from the fact of his licking up everything that came in his way, and taking 'the responsibility' on all occasions. He was a wicked looking beast, very lean and unamiable in aspect, with hair all standing the wrong way. He had fought some fifty bulls (so they said), always coming out victorious, but that either one of the fifty had been an Attakapas bull, the bills of the performances did not say. Had he tackled Attakapas first it is likely his fifty battles would have remained unfought.

"About half past four o'clock the performances commenced.

"The bull was first seen, standing in the cage alone, with head erect, and looking a very monarch in his capacity. At an appointed signal, a cage containing the bear was placed alongside the arena, and an opening being made, bruin stalked into the battle ground—not, however, without sundry stirrings up with a ten foot pole, he being experienced in such matters, and backwards in raising a row.

"Once on the battle-field, both animals stood, like wary champions, eyeing each other, the bear cowering low, with head upturned and fangs exposed, while Attakapas stood wondering, with his eyes dilated, lashing his sides with his long and bushy tail, and pawing up the earth in very wrath.

"The bear seemed little inclined to begin the attack, and the bull, standing a moment, made steps first backward and then forward, as if measuring his antagonist, and meditating where to plant a blow. Bruin wouldn't come to the scratch no way, till one of the keepers, with an iron rod, tickled his ribs and made him move. Seeing this, Attakapas took it as a hostile demonstration, and, gathering his strength, dashed savagely at the enemy, catching him on the points of his horns, and doubling him up like a sack of bran against the bars. Bruin 'sung out' at this, and made a dash for his opponent's nose.

"Missing this, the bull turned to the 'about face,' and the bear caught him by the ham, inflicting a ghastly wound. But Attakapas with a kick shook him off, and renewing the attack, went at him again, head on and with a rush. This time he was not so fortunate, for the bear caught him above the eye, burying his fangs in the tough hide, and holding him as in a vice. It was now the bull's turn to 'sing out,' and he did it, bellowing forth with a voice more hideous than that of all the bulls of Bashan.[24] Some minutes stood matters thus, and the cries of the bull, mingled with the hoarse growls of the bear, made hideous music, fit only for a dance of devils. Then came a pause (the bear having relinquished his hold),

---

[24] *Bashan*: Region in ancient Palestine.

and for a few minutes it was doubtful whether the fun was not up. But the magic wand of the keeper (the ten foot pole) again stirred up bruin, and at it they went, and with a rush.

"Bruin now tried to fasten on the bull's back, and drove his tusks in him in several places, making the red blood flow like wine from the vats of Luna.[25] But Attakapas was pluck to the back bone, and, catching bruin on the tips of his horns, shuffled him up right merrily, making the fur fly like feather in a gale of wind. Bruin cried 'Nuff' (in bear language), but the bull followed up his advantage, and, making one furious plunge full at the figure head of the enemy, struck a horn into his eye, burying it there, and dashing the tender organ into darkness and atoms. Blood followed the blow, and poor bruin, blinded, bleeding, and in mortal agony, turned with a howl to leave, but Attakapas caught him in the retreat, and rolled him over like a ball. Over and over again this rolling over was enacted, and finally, after more than an hour, bruin curled himself up on his back, bruised, bloody, and dead beat. The thing was up with California,[26] and Attakapas was declared the victor amidst the applause of the multitude that made the heavens ring."

"There," said he, "can you find anything against Connecticut equal to that?" The Southerner had to admit that he was beat by the Yankee. During all this time, it must not be supposed that the old gent. with the two daughters, and even the young ladies themselves, had been silent. Clotel and they had not only given their opinions as regarded the merits of the discussion, but that sly glance of the eye, which is ever given where the young of both sexes meet, had been freely at work. The American ladies are rather partial to foreigners, and Clotel had the appearance of a fine Italian. The old gentleman was now near his home, and a whisper from the eldest daughter, who was unmarried but marriageable, induced him to extend to "Mr. Johnson" an invitation to stop and spend a week with the young ladies at their family residence. Clotel excused herself upon various grounds, and at last, to cut short the matter, promised that she would pay them a visit on her return. The arrival of the coach at Lynchburgh[27] separated the young ladies from the Italian gent., and the coach again resumed its journey.

[25] *Luna*: Roman goddess of the moon.

[26] *The thing was up with California*: An allusion to the end of the California gold rush of 1849, or perhaps an allusion to the bruins of California. Because the United States acquired California following the war with Mexico, Brown may have used this newspaper story to comment ironically on U.S. expansionism as incarnated by Andrew Jackson.

[27] *Lynchburgh*: A city in central Virginia.

CHAPTER XXIII.
TRUTH STRANGER THAN FICTION.

"Is the poor privilege to turn the key
Upon the captive, freedom? He's as far
From the enjoyment of the earth and air
Who watches o'er the chains, as they who wear."[1]
— *Byron.*

During certain seasons of the year, all tropical climates are subject
to epidemics of a most destructive nature. The inhabitants of New
Orleans look with as much certainty for the appearance of the yellow-
fever, small-pox, or cholera, in the hot-season, as the Londoner does
for fog in the month of November. In the summer of 1831, the people
of New Orleans were visited with one of these epidemics.[2] It appeared
in a form unusually repulsive and deadly. It seized persons who were
in health, without any premonition. Sometimes death was the immediate consequence. The disorder began in the brain, by an oppressive
pain accompanied or followed by fever. The patient was devoured
with burning thirst. The stomach, distracted by pains, in vain sought
relief in efforts to disburden itself. Fiery veins streaked the eye; the face
was inflamed, and dyed of a dark dull red color; the ears from time to
time rang painfully. Now mucous secretions surcharged the tongue,
and took away the power of speech; now the sick one spoke, but in
speaking had a foresight of death. When the violence of the disease
approached the heart, the gums were blackened. The sleep, broken,
troubled by convulsions, or by frightful visions, was worse than the
waking hours; and when the reason sank under a delirium which had
its seat in the brain, repose utterly forsook the patient's couch. The
progress of the heat within was marked by yellowish spots, which
spread over the surface of the body. If, then, a happy crisis came not,
all hope was gone. Soon the breath infected the air with a fetid odour,
the lips were glazed, despair painted itself in the eyes, and sobs, with
long intervals of silence, formed the only language. From each side of
the mouth spread foam, tinged with black and burnt blood. Blue
streaks mingled with the yellow all over the frame. All remedies were
useless. This was the Yellow Fever. The disorder spread alarm and

---

[1] "*Is the poor . . . who wear*": From Lord Byron, *Don Juan* (1819–24), Canto X.
[2] *epidemics*: In fact a cholera outbreak hit New Orleans in the summer of 1832. For
his descriptions of yellow fever, Brown borrowed from John R. Beard, *The Life of Toussaint L'Ouverture, the Negro Patriot of Hayti* (London, 1853).

confusion throughout the city. On an average, more than 400 died daily. In the midst of disorder and confusion, death heaped victims on victims. Friend followed friend in quick succession. The sick were avoided from the fear of contagion, and for the same reason the dead were left unburied. Nearly 2000 dead bodies lay uncovered in the burial-ground, with only here and there a little lime[3] thrown over them, to prevent the air becoming infected.

The negro, whose home is in a hot climate, was not proof against the disease. Many plantations had to suspend their work for want of slaves to take the places of those carried off by the fever. Henry Morton and wife were among the thirteen thousand swept away by the raging disorder that year.[4] Like too many, Morton had been dealing extensively in lands and stocks; and though apparently in good circumstances was, in reality, deeply involved in debt. Althesa, although as white as most white women in a southern clime, was, as we already know, born a slave. By the laws of all the Southern States the children follow the condition of the mother. If the mother is free the children are free; if a slave, they are slaves. Morton was unacquainted with the laws of the land; and although he had married Althesa, it was a marriage which the law did not recognise; and therefore she whom he thought to be his wife was, in fact, nothing more than his slave. What would have been his feelings had he known this, and also known that his two daughters, Ellen and Jane, were his slaves? Yet such was the fact. After the disappearance of the disease with which Henry Morton had so suddenly been removed, his brother went to New Orleans to give what aid he could in settling up the affairs. James Morton, on his arrival in New Orleans, felt proud of his nieces, and promised them a home with his own family in Vermont; little dreaming that his brother had married a slave woman, and that his nieces were slaves. The girls themselves had never heard that their mother had been a slave, and therefore knew nothing of the danger hanging over their heads. An inventory of the property was made out by James Morton and placed in the hands of the creditors; and the young ladies, with their uncle, were about leaving the city to reside for a few days on the banks of Lake Pontchartrain, where they could enjoy a fresh air that the city could not afford. But just as they were about taking the train, an officer arrested the whole party; the young ladies as slaves, and the uncle

---

[3] *lime*: An odorless calcium compound.

[4] *Henry Morton . . . that year*: Brown skews chronology and historical facts, for if the Mortons died in 1831 they would have been unable to help Salome Miller in the mid-1840s.

upon the charge of attempting to conceal the property of his deceased brother. Morton was overwhelmed with horror at the idea of his nieces being claimed as slaves, and asked for time, that he might save them from such a fate. He even offered to mortgage his little farm in Vermont for the amount which young slave women of their ages would fetch. But the creditors pleaded that they were "an extra article," and would sell for more than common slaves; and must, therefore, be sold at auction. They were given up, but neither ate nor slept, nor separated from each other, till they were taken into the New Orleans slave market, where they were offered to the highest bidder. There they stood, trembling, blushing, and weeping; compelled to listen to the grossest language, and shrinking from the rude hands that examined the graceful proportions of their beautiful frames.

After a fierce contest between the bidders, the young ladies were sold, one for 2,300 dollars, and the other for 3,000 dollars. We need not add that had those young girls been sold for mere house servants or field hands, they would not have brought one half the sums they did. The fact that they were the grand-daughters of Thomas Jefferson, no doubt, increased their value in the market. Here were two of the softer sex, accustomed to the fondest indulgence, surrounded by all the refinements of life, and with all the timidity that such a life could produce, bartered away like cattle in Smithfield market.[5] Ellen, the eldest, was sold to an old gentleman, who purchased her, as he said, for a housekeeper. The girl was taken to his residence, nine miles from the city. She soon, however, knew for what purpose she had been bought; and an educated and cultivated mind and taste, which made her see and understand how great was her degradation, now armed her hand with the ready means of death. The morning after her arrival, she was found in her chamber, a corpse. She had taken poison. Jane was purchased by a dashing young man, who had just come into the possession of a large fortune. The very appearance of the young Southerner pointed him out as an unprincipled profligate; and the young girl needed no one to tell her of her impending doom. The young maid of fifteen was immediately removed to his country seat, near the junction of the Mississippi river with the sea. This was a most singular spot, remote, in a dense forest spreading over the summit of a cliff that rose abruptly to a great height above the sea; but so grand in its situation, in the desolate sublimity which reigned around, in the reverential murmur of the waves that washed its base, that, though picturesque, it was

---

[5] *Smithfield market*: London's main meat market is in the Smithfield district.

a forest prison. Here the young lady saw no one, except an old negress who acted as her servant. The smiles with which the young man met her were indignantly spurned. But she was the property of another, and could hope for justice and mercy only through him.

Jane, though only in her fifteenth year, had become strongly attached to Volney Lapuc, a young Frenchman, a student in her father's office. The poverty of the young man, and the youthful age of the girl, had caused their feelings to be kept from the young lady's parents. At the death of his master, Volney had returned to his widowed mother at Mobile, and knew nothing of the misfortune that had befallen his mistress, until he received a letter from her. But how could he ever obtain a sight of her, even if he wished, locked up as she was in her master's mansion? After several days of what her master termed "obstinacy" on her part, the young girl was placed in an upper chamber, and told that that would be her home, until she should yield to her master's wishes. There she remained more than a fortnight, and with the exception of a daily visit from her master, she saw no one but the old negress who waited upon her. One bright moonlight evening as she was seated at the window, she perceived the figure of a man beneath her window. At first, she thought it was her master; but the tall figure of the stranger soon convinced her that it was another. Yes, it was Volney! He had no sooner received her letter, than he set out for New Orleans; and finding on his arrival there, that his mistress had been taken away, resolved to follow her. There he was; but how could she communicate with him? She dared not trust the old negress with her secret, for fear that it might reach her master. Jane wrote a hasty note and threw it out the window, which was eagerly picked up by the young man, and he soon disappeared in the woods. Night passed away in dreariness to her, and the next morning she viewed the spot beneath her window with the hope of seeing the footsteps of him who had stood there the previous night. Evening returned, and with it the hope of again seeing the man she loved. In this she was not disappointed; for daylight had scarcely disappeared, and the moon once more rising through the tops of the tall trees, when the young man was seen in the same place as on the previous night. He had in his hand a rope ladder. As soon as Jane saw this, she took the sheets from her bed, tore them into strings, tied them together, and let one end down the side of the house. A moment more, and one end of the rope ladder was in her hand, and she fastened it inside the room. Soon the young maiden was seen descending, and the enthusiastic lover, with his arms extended, waiting to receive his mistress. The planter had been out on an hunting excursion, and returning home, saw his victim as her lover was receiving her in his arms. At this moment the sharp sound of a rifle was heard and the young man fell weltering in his blood, at the feet of his mistress. Jane fell senseless by his side. For many days she had a confused consciousness of some great agony, but knew not where she was, or by whom surrounded. The slow recovery of her reason settled into the most intense melancholy, which gained at length the compassion even of her cruel master. The beautiful bright eyes, always pleading in expression, were now so heart-piercing in their sadness, that he could not endure their gaze. In a few days the poor girl died of a broken heart, and was buried at night at the back of the garden by the negroes; and no one wept at the grave of her who had been so carefully cherished, and so tenderly beloved.

This, reader, is an unvarnished narrative of one doomed by the laws of the Southern States to be a slave. It tells not only its own story of grief, but speaks of a thousand wrongs and woes beside, which never see the light; all the more bitter and dreadful, because no help can relieve, no sympathy can mitigate, and no hope can cheer.

CHAPTER XXIV.
THE ARREST.

"The fearful storm—it threatens lowering,
  Which God in mercy long delays;
Slaves yet may see their masters cowering,
  While whole plantations smoke and blaze!"[1]
                                    —*Carter.*

It was late in the evening when the coach arrived at Richmond, and Clotel once more alighted in her native city. She had intended to seek lodgings somewhere in the outskirts of the town, but the lateness of the hour compelled her to stop at one of the principal hotels for the night. She had scercely entered the inn, when she recognised among the numerous black servants one to whom she was well known; and her only hope was, that her disguise would keep her from being discovered. The imperturbable calm and entire forgetfulness of self which induced Clotel to visit a place from which she could scarcely hope to escape, to attempt the rescue of a beloved child, demonstrate that over-willingness of woman to carry out the promptings of the finer feelings of her heart. True to woman's nature, she had risked her own liberty for another.

She remained in the hotel during the night, and the next morning, under the plea of illness, she took her breakfast alone. That day the fugitive slave paid a visit to the suburbs of the town, and once more beheld the cottage in which she had spent so many happy hours. It was winter, and the clematis and passion flowers were not there; but there were the same walks she had so often pressed with her feet, and the same trees which had so often shaded her as she passed through the garden at the back of the house. Old remembrances rushed upon her memory, and caused her to shed tears freely. Clotel was now in her native town, and near her daughter; but how could she communicate with her? How could she see her? To have made herself known, would have been a suicidal act; betrayal would have followed, and she arrested. Three days had passed away, and Clotel still remained in the hotel at which she had first put up; and yet she had got no tidings of her child. Unfortunately for Clotel, a disturbance had just broken out amongst the slave population in the state of Virginia, and all strangers were eyed with suspicion.

---

[1] *"The fearful . . . blaze!"*: From Mrs. J. G. Carter, "Ye Sons of Freedom," in *The Anti-Slavery Harp*, ed. Brown.

The evils consequent on slavery are not lessened by the incoming of one or two rays of light. If the slave only becomes aware of his condition, and conscious of the injustice under which he suffers, if he obtains but a faint idea of these things, he will seize the first opportunity to possess himself of what he conceives to belong him. The infusion of Anglo-Saxon with African blood has created an insurrectionary feeling among the slaves of America hitherto unknown. Aware of their blood connection with their owners, these mulattoes labour under the sense of their personal and social injuries; and tolerate, if they do not encourage in themselves, low and vindictive passions. On the other hand, the slave owners are aware of their critical position, and are ever watchful, always fearing an outbreak among the slaves.[2]

True, the Free States are equally bound with the Slave States to suppress any insurrectionary movement that may take place among the slaves. The Northern freemen are bound by their constitutional obligations to aid the slaveholder in keeping his slaves in their chains. Yet there are, at the time we write, four millions of bond slaves in the United States. The insurrection to which we now refer was headed by a full-blooded negro, who had been born and brought up a slave. He had heard the twang of the driver's whip, and saw the warm blood streaming from the negro's body; he had witnessed the separation of parents and children, and was made aware, by too many proofs, that the slave could expect no justice at the hand of the slave owner. He went by the name of "Nat Turner."[3] He was a preacher among the negroes, and distinguished for his eloquence, respected by the whites, and loved and venerated by the negroes. On the discovery of the plan for the outbreak, Turner fled to the swamps, followed by those who had joined in the insurrection. Here the revolted negroes numbered some hundreds, and for a time bade defiance to their oppressors. The Dismal Swamps cover many thousands of acres of wild land, and a dense forest, with wild animals and insects, such as are unknown in any other part of Virginia. Here runaway negroes usually seek a hiding-place, and some have been known to reside here for years. The revolters were joined by one of these. He was a large, tall, full-blooded negro, with a stern and savage countenance; the marks on his face showed that he was from one of the barbarous tribes in Africa, and claimed

[2] *The evils . . . slaves*: For this paragraph, Brown borrowed from John R. Beard's *The Life of Toussaint L'Ouverture* (1853).

[3] *"Nat Turner"*: Nat Turner's bloody slave rebellion occurred in Southampton County, Virginia, in 1831. For a selection from *The Confessions of Nat Turner*, see pp. 304–12.

that country as his native land; his only covering was a girdle around his loins, made of skins of wild beasts which he had killed; his only token of authority among those that he led, was a pair of epaulettes made from the tail of a fox, and tied to his shoulder by a cord. Brought from the coast of Africa when only fifteen years of age to the island of Cuba, he was smuggled from thence into Virginia. He had been two years in the swamps, and considered it his future home. He had met a negro woman who was also a runaway; and, after the fashion of his native land, had gone through the process of oiling her as the marriage ceremony. They had built a cave on a rising mound in the swamp; this was their home. His name was Picquilo. His only weapon was a sword, made from the blade of a scythe, which he had stolen from a neighbouring plantation. His dress, his character, his manners, his mode of fighting, were all in keeping with the early training he had received in the land of his birth. He moved about with the activity of a cat, and neither the thickness of the trees, nor the depth of the water could stop him. He was a bold, turbulent spirit; and from revenge imbrued his hands in the blood of all the whites he could meet. Hunger, thirst, fatigue, and loss of sleep he seemed made to endure as if by peculiarity of constitution. His air was fierce, his step oblique, his look sanguinary. Such was the character of one of the leaders in the Southampton insurrection.[4] All negroes were arrested who were found beyond their master's threshold, and all strange whites watched with a great degree of alacrity.

Such was the position in which Clotel found affairs when she returned to Virginia in search of her Mary. Had not the slave-owners been watchful of strangers, owing to the outbreak, the fugitive could not have escaped the vigilance of the police; for advertisements, announcing her escape and offering a large reward for her arrest, had been received in the city previous to her arrival, and the officers were therefore on the look-out for the runaway slave. It was on the third day, as the quadroon was seated in her room at the inn, still in the disguise of a gentleman, that two of the city officers entered the room, and informed her that they were authorised to examine all strangers, to assure the authorities that they were not in league with the revolted negroes. With trembling heart the fugitive handed the key of her trunk

---

[4] *He was a large . . . insurrection*: For his description of the fictional Picquilo, Brown borrowed from Beard's description of the Haitian revolutionary Lamour de Rance in *The Life of Toussaint L'Ouverture*. Again, Brown skews chronology, for Clotel returns to Virginia in the wake of the 1831 Nat Turner rebellion after taking a stagecoach ride set during the 1839 election campaign.

to the officers. To their surprise, they found nothing but a woman's apparel in the box, which raised their curiosity, and caused a further investigation that resulted in the arrest of Clotel as a fugitive slave. She was immediately conveyed to prison, there to await the orders of her master. For many days, uncheered by the voice of kindness, alone, hopeless, desolate, she waited for the time to arrive when the chains were to be placed on her limbs, and she returned to her inhuman and unfeeling owner.

The arrest of the fugitive was announced in all the newspapers, but created little or no sensation. The inhabitants were too much engaged in putting down the revolt among the slaves; and although all the odds were against the insurgents, the whites found it no easy matter, with all their caution. Every day brought news of fresh outbreaks. Without scruple and without pity, the whites massacred all blacks found beyond their owners' plantations: the negroes, in return, set fire to houses, and put those to death who attempted to escape from the flames. Thus carnage was added to carnage, and the blood of the whites flowed to avenge the blood of the blacks. These were the ravages of slavery. No graves were dug for the negroes; their dead bodies became food for dogs and vultures, and their bones, partly calcined by the sun, remained scattered about, as if to mark the mournful fury of servitude and lust of power. When the slaves were subdued, except a few in the swamps, bloodhounds were put in this dismal place to hunt out the remaining revolters. Among the captured negroes was one of whom we shall hereafter make mention.

CHAPTER XXV.
DEATH IS FREEDOM.

"I asked but freedom, and ye gave
Chains, and the freedom of the grave."[1]
—*Snelling.*

There are, in the District of Columbia, several slave prisons, or "negro pens," as they are termed. These prisons are mostly occupied by persons to keep their slaves in, when collecting their gangs together for the New Orleans market. Some of them belong to the government, and one, in particular, is noted for having been the place where a number of free coloured persons have been incarcerated from time to time. In this district is situated the capital of the United States. Any free coloured persons visiting Washington, if not provided with papers asserting and proving their rights to be free, may be arrested and placed in one of these dens. If they succeed in showing that they are free, they are set at liberty, provided they are able to pay the expenses of their arrest and imprisonment; if they cannot pay these expenses, they are sold out. Through this unjust and oppressive law, many persons born in the Free States have been consigned to a life of slavery on the cotton, sugar, or rice plantations of the Southern States. By order of her master, Clotel was removed from Richmond and placed in one of these prisons, to await the sailing of a vessel for New Orleans. The prison in which she was put stands midway between the capitol at Washington and the president's house. Here the fugitive saw nothing but slaves brought in and taken out, to be placed in ships and sent away to the same part of the country to which she herself would soon be compelled to go. She had seen or heard nothing of her daughter while in Richmond, and all hope of seeing her now had fled. If she was carried back to New Orleans, she could expect no mercy from her master.

At the dusk of the evening previous to the day when she was to be sent off, as the old prison was being closed for the night, she suddenly darted past her keeper, and ran for her life. It is not a great distance from the prison to the Long Bridge,[2] which passes from the lower part

---

[1] "*I asked . . . grave*": From a poem by William J. Snelling (1804–1848), whose anti-slavery poems regularly appeared in the *Liberator.*

[2] *Long Bridge*: Crossing the Potomac River and linking Washington, D.C., to Virginia, the Long Bridge was built in 1835 and remained in use until 1903. For a photograph of the Long Bridge circa 1863, see p. 343.

of the city across the Potomac, to the extensive forests and woodlands of the celebrated Arlington Place, occupied by that distinguished relative and descendant of the immortal Washington, Mr. George W. Custis.[3] Thither the poor fugitive directed her flight. So unexpected was her escape, that she had quite a number of rods[4] the start before the keeper had secured the other prisoners, and rallied his assistants in pursuit. It was at an hour when, and in a part of the city where, horses could not be readily obtained for the chase; no bloodhounds were at hand to run down the flying woman; and for once it seemed as though there was to be a fair trial of speed and endurance between the slave and slave-catchers. The keeper and the forces raised the hue and cry on her pathway close behind; but so rapid was the flight along the wild avenue, that the astonished citizens, as they poured forth from their dwellings to learn the cause of alarm, were only able to comprehend the nature of the case in time to fall in with the motley mass in pursuit, (as many a one did that night,) to raise an anxious prayer to heaven, as they refused to join in the pursuit, that the panting fugitive might escape, and the merciless soul dealer for once be disappointed of his prey. And now with the speed of an arrow—having passed the avenue—with the distance between her and her pursuers constantly increasing, this poor hunted female gained the *"Long Bridge,"* as it is called, where interruption seemed improbable, and already did her heart begin to beat high with the hope of success. She had only to pass three-fourths of a mile across the bridge, and she could bury herself in a vast forest, just in time when the curtain of night would close around her, and protect her from the pursuit of her enemies.

But God by his Providence had otherwise determined. He had determined that an appalling tragedy should be enacted that night, within plain sight of the President's house and the capital of the Union, which should be an evidence wherever it should be known, of the unconquerable love of liberty the heart may inherit; as well as a fresh admonition to the slave dealer, of the cruelty and enormity of his crimes. Just as the pursuers crossed the high draw for the passage of sloops,[5] soon after entering upon the bridge, they beheld three men slowly approaching from the Virginia side. They immediately called to them to arrest the fugitive, whom they proclaimed a runaway slave. True to their

[3] *George W. Custis*: Grandson of Martha Washington and heir to part of Washington's Mt. Vernon estate, George W. Custis (1781–1857) gained repute as a playwright and in 1860 published *Recollections and Private Memoirs of Washington.*

[4] *rods*: A unit of linear measurement, a rod equals five-and-a-half yards.

[5] *sloops*: Sailing vessels.

THE DEATH OF CLOTEL.

Virginian instincts as she came near, they formed in line across the narrow bridge, and prepared to seize her. Seeing escape impossible in that
quarter, she stopped suddenly, and turned upon her pursuers. On came
the profane and ribald crew, faster than ever, already exulting in her
capture, and threatening punishment for her flight. For a moment she
looked wildly and anxiously around to see if there was no hope of
escape. On either hand, far down below, rolled the deep foamy water
of the Potomac, and before and behind the rapidly approaching step
and noisy voices of pursuers, showing how vain would be any further
effort for freedom. Her resolution was taken. She clasped her *hands*
convulsively, and raised *them*, as she at the same time raised her *eyes*
towards heaven, and begged for that mercy and compassion *there*,
which had been denied her on earth; and then, with a single bound,
she vaulted over the railings of the bridge, and sunk for ever beneath
the waves of the river!

Thus died Clotel, the daughter of Thomas Jefferson, a president of
the United States; a man distinguished as the author of the Declaration of American Independence, and one of the first statesmen of that
country.

Had Clotel escaped from oppression in any other land, in the disguise in which she fled from Mississippi to Richmond, and reached the
United States, no honour within the gift of the American people would
have been too good to have been heaped upon the heroic woman. But
she was a slave, and therefore out of the pale of their sympathy. They
have tears to shed over Greece and Poland; they have an abundance of
sympathy for "poor Ireland;" they can furnish a ship of war to convey
the Hungarian refugees from a Turkish prison to the "land of the free
and home of the brave." They boast that America is the "cradle of
liberty;" if it is, I fear they have rocked the child to death.[6] The body of
Clotel was picked up from the bank of the river, where it had been
washed by the strong current, a hole dug in the sand, and there depos-
ited, without either inquest being held over it, or religious service being
performed. Such was the life and such the death of a woman whose
virtues and goodness of heart would have done honour to one in a
higher station of life, and who, if she had been born in any other land

---

[6] *They have tears . . . to death*: In this passage, Brown joins with many abolitionists
in decrying nineteenth-century Americans' tendencies to rally behind various European
revolutionary movements while ignoring the plight of U.S. slaves. Brown and William
Lloyd Garrison were particularly disturbed by the hero's welcome accorded the Hungarian revolutionary Louis Kossuth (1802–1894) during his 1851–52 tour of the United
States, for Kossuth insisted on remaining neutral on abolitionism.

but that of slavery, would have been honoured and loved.[7] A few days after the death of Clotel, the following poem appeared in one of the newspapers:

"Now, rest for the wretched! the long day is past,
And night on yon prison descendeth at last.
Now lock up and bolt! Ha, jailor, look there!
Who flies like a wild bird escaped from the snare?
    A woman, a slave—up, out in pursuit,
      While linger some gleams of day!
    Let thy call ring out!—now a rabble rout
      Is at thy heels—speed away!

"A bold race for freedom!—On, fugitive, on!
Heaven help but the right, and thy freedom is won.
How eager she drinks the free air of the plains;
Every limb, every nerve, every fibre she strains;
    From Columbia's glorious capitol,
      Columbia's daughter flees
    To the sanctuary God has given—
      The sheltering forest trees.

"Now she treads the Long Bridge—joy lighteth her eye—
Beyond her the dense wood and darkening sky—
Wild hopes thrill her heart as she neareth the shore:
O, despair! there are *men* fast advancing before!
    Shame, shame on their manhood! they hear, they heed
      The cry, her flight to stay,
    And like demon forms with their outstretched arms,
      They wait to seize their prey!

"She pauses, she turns! Ah, will she flee back?
Like wolves, her pursuers howl loud on their track;
She lifteth to Heaven one look of despair—
Her anguish breaks forth in one hurried prayer—
    Hark! her jailor's yell! like a bloodhound's bay
      On the low night wind it sweeps!
    Now, death or the chain! to the stream she turns,
      And she leaps! O God, she leaps!

"The dark and the cold, yet merciful wave,
Received to its bosom the form of the slave:
She rises—earth's scenes on her dim vision gleam,
Yet she struggleth not with the strong rushing stream:

---

[7] "*. . . honoured and loved*": For a possible source, see the selection from Frederick Douglass's *Reception Speech*, pp. 341–42.

And low are the death-cries her woman's heart gives,
  As she floats adown the river,
  Faint and more faint grows the drowning voice,
    And her cries have ceased for ever!

"Now back, jailor, back to thy dungeons, again,
 To swing the red lash and rivet the chain!
 The form thou would'st fetter — returned to its God;
    The universe holdeth no realm of night
     More drear than her slavery —
    More merciless fiends than here stayed her flight —
     Joy! the hunted slave is free!

"That bond woman's corse[8] — let Potomac's proud wave
 Go bear it along *by our Washington's grave,*
 And heave it high up on that hallowed strand,
 To tell of the freedom he won for our land.
    A weak woman's corse, by freemen chased down;
     Hurrah for our country! hurrah!
    To freedom she leaped, through drowning and death —
     Hurrah for our country! hurrah!"[9]

---

[8] *corse*: Corpse.

[9] *"Now, rest . . . hurrah!"*: The poem, titled "The Leap from the Long Bridge," is by Grace Greenwood (1823–1904), and is included in her *Poems* (1851). Brown changed some of the wording and added the final stanza; for the text of the original, see pp. 342–45.

CHAPTER XXVI.
THE ESCAPE.

"No refuge is found on our unhallowed ground,
　For the wretched in Slavery's manacles bound;
While our star spangled banner in vain boasts to wave
O'er the land of the free and the home of the brave!"[1]

We left Mary,[2] the daughter of Clotel, in the capacity of a servant in her own father's house, where she had been taken by her mistress for the ostensible purpose of plunging her husband into the depths of humiliation. At first the young girl was treated with great severity; but after finding that Horatio Green had lost all feeling for his child, Mrs. Green's own heart became touched for the offspring of her husband, and she became its friend. Mary had grown still more beautiful, and, like most of her sex in that country, was fast coming to maturity.

The arrest of Clotel, while trying to rescue her daughter, did not reach the ears of the latter till her mother had been removed from Richmond to Washington. The mother had passed from time to eternity before the daughter knew that she had been in the neighbourhood. Horatio Green was not in Richmond at the time of Clotel's arrest; had he been there, it is not probable but he would have made an effort to save her. She was not his slave, and therefore was beyond his power, even had he been there and inclined to aid her. The revolt amongst the slaves had been brought to an end, and most of the insurgents either were put to death or sent out of the state. One, however, remained in prison. He was the slave of Horatio Green, and had been a servant in his master's dwelling. He, too, could boast that his father was an American statesman. His name was George. His mother had been employed as a servant in one of the principal hotels in Washington, where members of Congress usually put up. After George's birth his mother was sold to a slave trader, and he to an agent of Mr. Green, the father of Horatio. George was as white as most white persons. No one would suppose that any African blood coursed through his veins. His hair was straight, soft, fine, and light; his eyes blue, nose prominent, lips thin, his head well formed, forehead high and prominent; and he was often taken for a free white person by those who did know

---

[1] "No refuge . . . brave!": From A. E. Atlee, "The Star Spangled Banner," in the *Liberator*, 13 September 1844.

[2] *Mary*: For the story of Mary in this and the next two chapters, Brown reworked the story he initially told in Letter XXII of his *Three Years in Europe* (London, 1852).

him. This made his condition still more intolerable; for one so white seldom ever receives fair treatment at the hands of his fellow slaves; and the whites usually regard such slaves as persons who, if not often flogged, and otherwise ill treated, to remind them of their condition, would soon "forget" that they were slaves, and "think themselves as good as white folks." George's opportunities were far greater than most slaves. Being in his master's house, and waiting on educated white people, he had become very familiar with the English language. He had heard his master and visitors speak of the down-trodden and oppressed Poles; he heard them talk of going to Greece to fight for Grecian liberty, and against the oppressors of that ill-fated people. George, fired with the love of freedom, and zeal for the cause of his enslaved countrymen, joined the insurgents, and with them had been defeated and captured. He was the only one remaining of these unfortunate people, and he would have been put to death with them but for a circumstance that occurred some weeks before the breakout. The court house had, by accident, taken fire, and was fast consuming. The engines could not be made to work, and all hope of saving the building seemed at an end. In one of the upper chambers there was a small box containing some valuable deeds belonging to the city; a ladder was placed against the house, leading from the street to the window of the room in which the box stood. The wind blew strong, and swept the flames in that direction. Broad sheets of fire were blown again and again over that part of the building, and then the wind would lift the pall of smoke, which showed that the work of destruction was not yet accomplished. While the doomed building was thus exposed, and before the destroying element had made its final visit, as it did soon after, George was standing by, and hearing that much depended on the contents of the box, and seeing no one disposed to venture through the fiery element to save the treasure, mounted the ladder and made his way to the window, entered the room, and was soon seen descending with the much valued box. Three cheers rent the air as the young slave fell from the ladder near the ground; the white men took him up in their arms, to see if he had sustained any injury. His hair was burnt, eyebrows closely singed, and his clothes smelt strongly of smoke; but the heroic young slave was unhurt. The city authorities, at their next meeting, passed a vote of thanks to George's master for the lasting benefit that the slave had rendered the public, and commended the poor boy to the special favour of his owner. When George was on trial for participating in the revolt, this "meritorious act," as they were pleased to term it, was brought up in his favour. His trial was put off from session to session, till he had been in prison more than a year. At last, however, he was convicted of high treason, and sentenced to be hanged within ten days of that time. The judge asked the slave if he had anything to say why sentence of death should not be passed on him. George stood for a moment in silence, and then said, "As I cannot speak as I should wish, I will say nothing." "You may say what you please," said the judge. "You had a good master," continued he, "and still you were dissatisfied; you left your master and joined the negroes who were burning our houses and killing our wives." "As you have given me permission to speak," remarked George, "I will tell you why I joined the revolted negroes.[3] I have heard my master read in the Declaration of Independence 'that all men are created free and equal,' and this caused me to inquire of myself why I was a slave. I also heard him talking with some of his visitors about the war with England, and he said, all wars and fightings for freedom were just and right. If so, in what am I wrong? The grievances of which your fathers complained, and which caused the Revolutionary War, were trifling in comparison with the wrongs and sufferings of those who were engaged in the late revolt. Your fathers were never slaves, ours are; your fathers were never bought and sold like cattle, never shut out from the light of knowledge and religion, never subjected to the lash of brutal taskmasters. For the crime of having a dark skin, my people suffer the pangs of hunger, the infliction of stripes, and the ignominy of brutal servitude. We are kept in heathenish darkness by laws expressly enacted to make our instruction a criminal offence. What right has one man to the bones, sinews, blood, and nerves of another? Did not one God make us all? You say your fathers fought for freedom—so did we. You tell me that I am to be put to death for violating the laws of the land. Did not the American revolutionists violate the laws when they struck for liberty? They were revolters, but their success made them patriots—we were revolters, and our failure makes us rebels. Had we succeeded, we would have been patriots too. Success makes all the difference. You make merry on the 4th of July; the thunder of cannon and ringing of bells announce it as the birthday of American independence. Yet while these cannons are roaring and bells ringing, one-sixth of the people of this land are in chains and slavery. You boast that this is the 'Land of the Free;' but a traditionary freedom will not save you. It will not do to praise your fathers and build their sepulchres.[4]

---

[3] *"I will tell you . . . negroes:* George's speech echoes Frederick Douglass's "What to the Slave Is the Fourth of July?" (1852); see pp. 267–72.

[4] *sepulchres:* Tombs or burial places.

Worse for you that you have such an inheritance, if you spend it fool-
ishly and are unable to appreciate its worth. Sad if the genius of a true
humanity, beholding you with tearful eyes from the mount of vision,
shall fold his wings in sorrowing pity, and repeat the strain, 'O land of
Washington, how often would I have gathered thy children together,
as a hen doth gather her brood under her wings, and ye would not;
behold your house is left unto you desolate.'[5] This is all I have to say;
I have done." Nearly every one present was melted to tears; even the
judge seemed taken by surprise at the intelligence of the young slave.
But George was still a slave, and an example must be made of him,
and therefore he was sentenced. Being employed in the same house
with Mary, the daughter of Clotel, George had become attached to
her, and the young lovers fondly looked forward to the time when they
should be husband and wife.

After George had been sentenced to death, Mary was still more
attentive to him, and begged and obtained leave of her mistress to visit
him in his cell. The poor girl paid a daily visit to him to whom she had
pledged her heart and hand. At one of these meetings, and only four
days from the time fixed for the execution, while Mary was seated in
George's cell, it occurred to her that she might yet save him from a fel-
on's doom. She revealed to him the secret that was then occupying her
thoughts, viz. that George should exchange clothes with her, and thus
attempt his escape in disguise. But he would not for a single moment
listen to the proposition. Not that he feared detection; but he would
not consent to place an innocent and affectionate girl in a position
where she might have to suffer for him. Mary pleaded, but in vain—
George was inflexible. The poor girl left her lover with a heavy heart,
regretting that her scheme had proved unsuccessful.

Towards the close of the next day, Mary again appeared at the
prison door for admission, and was soon by the side of him whom she
so ardently loved. While there the clouds which had overhung the city
for some hours broke, and the rain fell in torrents amid the most ter-
rific thunder and lightning. In the most persuasive manner possible,
Mary again importuned George to avail himself of her assistance to
escape from an ignominious death. After assuring him that she, not
being the person condemned, would not receive any injury, he at last
consented, and they began to exchange apparel. As George was of
small stature, and both were white, there was no difficulty in his passing out without detection; and as she usually left the cell weeping, with

[5] *'O land . . . desolate'*: A paraphrase of Jesus's admonition in Matthew 23.37–38.
In his speech, George substitutes "Washington" for "Jerusalem."

handkerchief in hand, and sometimes at her face, he had only to adopt this mode and his escape was safe. They had kissed each other, and Mary had told George where he would find a small parcel of provisions which she had placed in a secluded spot, when the prison-keeper opened the door and said, "Come, girl, it is time for you to go." George again embraced Mary, and passed out of the jail. It was already dark, and the street lamps were lighted, so that our hero in his new dress had no dread of detection. The provisions were sought out and found, and poor George was soon on the road to Canada. But neither of them had once thought of a change of dress for George when he should have escaped, and he had walked but a short distance before he felt that a change of his apparel would facilitate his progress. But he dared not go amongst even his coloured associates for fear of being betrayed. However, he made the best of his way on towards Canada, hiding in the woods during the day, and travelling by the guidance of the North Star at night.

With the poet he could truly say,

> "Star of the North! while blazing day
> Pours round me its full tide of light,
> And hides thy pale but faithful ray,
> I, too, lie hid, and long for night."[6]

One morning, George arrived on the banks of the Ohio river, and found his journey had terminated, unless he could get some one to take him across the river in a secret manner, for he would not be permitted to cross in any of the ferry boats, it being a penalty for crossing a slave, besides the value of the slave. He concealed himself in the tall grass and weeds near the river, to see if he could embrace an opportunity to cross. He had been in his hiding place but a short time, when he observed a man in a small boat, floating near the shore, evidently fishing. His first impulse was to call out to the man and ask him to take him over to the Ohio side, but the fear that the man was a slaveholder, or one who might possibly arrest him, deterred him from it. The man after rowing and floating about for some time fastened the boat to the root of a tree, and started to a neighbouring farmhouse.

This was George's moment, and he seized it. Running down the bank, he unfastened the boat, jumped in, and with all the expertness of one accustomed to a boat, rowed across the river and landed on the Ohio side.

---

[6] *"Star . . . for night"*: From John Pierpont (1785–1866), "The Fugitive Slave's Apostrophe to the North Star," in *Airs of Palestine and Other Poems* (1840).

Being now in a Free State, he thought he might with perfect safety travel toward Canada. He had, however, gone but a very few miles when he discovered two men on horseback coming behind him. He felt sure that they could not be in pursuit of him, yet he did not wish to be seen by them, so he turned into another road leading to a house near by. The men followed, and were but a short distance from George, when he ran up to a farmhouse, before which was standing a farmer-looking man, in a broad-brimmed hat and straight-collared coat, whom he implored to save him from the "slave-catchers." The farmer told him to go into the barn near by; he entered by the front door, the farmer following, and closing the door behind George, but remaining outside, and gave directions to his hired man as to what should be done with George. The slaveholders by this time had dismounted, and were in front of the barn demanding admittance, and charging the farmer with secreting their slave woman, for George was still in the dress of a woman. The Friend, for the farmer proved to be a member of the Society of Friends,[7] told the slave-owners that if they wished to search his barn, they must first get an officer and a search warrant. While the parties were disputing, the farmer began nailing up the front door, and the hired man served the back door the same way. The slaveholders, finding that they could not prevail on the Friend to allow them to get the slave, determined to go in search of an officer. One was left to see that the slave did not escape from the barn, while the other went off at full speed to Mount Pleasant, the nearest town. George was not the slave of either of these men, nor were they in pursuit of him, but they had lost a woman who had been seen in that vicinity, and when they saw poor George in the disguise of a female, and attempting to elude pursuit, they felt sure they were close upon their victim. However, if they had caught him, although he was not their slave, they would have taken him back and placed him in jail, and there he would have remained until his owner arrived.

After an absence of nearly two hours, the slave-owner returned with an officer and found the Friend still driving large nails into the door. In a triumphant tone and with a corresponding gesture, he handed the search-warrant to the Friend, and said, "There, sir, now I will see if I can't get my nigger." "Well," said the Friend, "thou hast gone to work according to law, and thou canst now go into my barn." "Lend me your hammer that I may get the door open," said the slaveholder. "Let me see the warrant again." And after reading it over once more, he

[7] *Society of Friends*: Quakers.

said, "I see nothing in this paper which says I must supply thee with tools to open my door; if thou wishest to go in, thou must get a hammer elsewhere." The sheriff said, "I will go to a neighbouring farm and borrow something which will introduce us to Miss Dinah;" and he immediately went in search of tools. In a short time the officer returned, and they commenced an assault and battery upon the barn door, which soon yielded; and in went the slaveholder and officer, and began turning up the hay and using all other means to find the lost property; but, to their astonishment, the slave was not there. After all hope of getting Dinah was gone, the slave-owner in a rage said to the Friend, "My nigger is not here." "I did not tell thee there was any one here." "Yes, but I saw her go in, and you shut the door behind her, and if she was not in the barn, what did you nail the door for?" "Can't I do what I please with my own barn door? Now I will tell thee; thou need trouble thyself no more, for the person thou art after entered the front door and went out at the back door, and is a long way from here by this time. Thou and thy friend must be somewhat fatigued by this time; wont thou go in and take a little dinner with me?" We need not say that this cool invitation of the good Quaker was not accepted by the slaveholders. George in the meantime had been taken to a friend's dwelling some miles away, where, after laying aside his female attire, and being snugly dressed up in a straight collared coat, and pantaloons to match, was again put on the right road towards Canada.

The fugitive now travelled by day, and laid by during night. After a fatiguing and dreary journey of two weeks, the fugitive arrived in Canada, and took up his abode in the little town of St. Catherine's,[8] and obtained work on the farm of Colonel Street. Here he attended a night-school, and laboured for his employer during the day. The climate was cold, and wages small, yet he was in a land where he was free, and this the young slave prized more than all the gold that could be given him. Besides doing his best to obtain education for himself, he imparted what he could to those of his fellow-fugitives about him, of whom there were many.

---

[8] *St. Catherine's*: A town in southern Ontario.

CHAPTER XXVII.
THE MYSTERY.

George, however, did not forget his promise to use all the means in his power to get Mary out of slavery. He, therefore, laboured with all his might to obtain money with which to employ some one to go back to Virginia for Mary. After nearly six months' labour at St. Catherine's, he employed an English missionary to go and see if the girl could be purchased, and at what price. The missionary went accordingly, but returned with the sad intelligence that, on account of Mary's aiding George to escape the court had compelled Mr. Green to sell her out of the state, and she had been sold to a negro trader, and taken to the New Orleans market. As all hope of getting the girl was now gone, George resolved to quit the American continent for ever. He immediately took passage in a vessel laden with timber, bound for Liverpool, and in five weeks from that time he was standing on the quay of the great English seaport. With little or no education, he found many difficulties in the way of getting a respectable living. However he obtained a situation as porter in a large house in Manchester, where he worked during the day, and took private lessons at night. In this way he laboured for three years, and was then raised to the situation of clerk. George was so white as easily to pass for a white man, and being somewhat ashamed of his African descent, he never once mentioned the fact of having been a slave. He soon became a partner in the firm that employed him, and was now on the road to wealth.

In the year 1842, just ten years after George Green (for he adopted his master's name) arrived in England, he visited France, and spent some time at Dunkirk.[1] It was towards sunset, on a warm day in the month of October, that Mr. Green, after strolling some distance from the Hotel de Leon, entered a burial ground, and wandered long alone among the silent dead, gazing upon the many green graves and marble tombstones of those who once moved on the theatre of busy life, and whose sounds of gaiety once fell upon the ear of man. All nature around was hushed in silence, and seemed to partake of the general melancholy which hung over the quiet resting-place of departed mortals. After tracing the varied inscriptions which told the characters or conditions of the departed, and viewing the mounds beneath which the dust of mortality slumbered, he had now reached a secluded spot, near to where an aged weeping willow bowed its thick foliage to the ground,

---

[1] *Dunkirk*: A seaport in northern France.

as though anxious to hide from the scrutinising gaze of curiosity the grave beneath it. Mr. Green seated himself upon a marble tomb, and began to read Roscoe's *Leo X.*,[2] a copy of which he had under his arm. It was then about twilight, and he had scarcely gone through half a page, when he observed a lady in black, leading a boy, some five years old, up one of the paths; and as the lady's black veil was over her face, he felt somewhat at liberty to eye her more closely. While looking at her, the lady gave a scream, and appeared to be in a fainting position, when Mr. Green sprang from his seat in time to save her from falling to the ground. At this moment, an elderly gentleman was seen approaching with a rapid step, who, from his appearance, was evidently the lady's father, or one intimately connected with her. He came up, and, in a confused manner, asked what was the matter. Mr. Green explained as well as he could. After taking up the smelling bottle which had fallen from her hand, and holding it a short time to her face, she soon began to revive. During all this time the lady's veil had so covered her face, that Mr. Green had not seen it. When she had so far recovered as to be able to raise her head, she again screamed, and fell back into the arms of the old man. It now appeared quite certain, that either the countenance of George Green, or some other object, was the cause of these fits of fainting; and the old gentleman, thinking it was the former, in rather a petulant tone said, "I will thank you, sir, if you will leave us alone." The child whom the lady was leading, had now set up a squall; and amid the death-like appearance of the lady, the harsh look of the old man, and the cries of the boy, Mr. Green left the grounds, and returned to his hotel.

Whilst seated by the window, and looking out upon the crowded street, with every now and then the strange scene in the grave-yard vividly before him, Mr. Green thought of the book he had been reading, and, remembering that he had left it on the tomb, where he had suddenly dropped it when called to the assistance of the lady, he immediately determined to return in search of it. After a walk of some twenty minutes, he was again over the spot where he had been an hour before, and from which he had been so unceremoniously expelled by the old man. He looked in vain for the book; it was nowhere to be found: nothing save the bouquet which the lady had dropped, and which lay half-buried in the grass from having been trodden upon, indicated that any one had been there that evening. Mr. Green took up the bunch of flowers, and again returned to the hotel.

[2] *Roscoe's Leo X.*: See p. 79, note 45.

After passing a sleepless night, and hearing the clock strike six, he dropped into a sweet sleep, from which he did not awake until roused by the rap of a servant, who, entering his room, handed him a note which ran as follows: — "Sir, — I owe you an apology for the inconvenience to which you were subjected last evening, and if you will honour us with your presence to dinner to-day at four o'clock, I shall be most happy to give you due satisfaction. My servant will be in waiting for you at half-past three. I am, sir, your obedient servant, J. Devenant. October 23. To George Green, Esq."

The servant who handed this note to Mr. Green, informed him that the bearer was waiting for a reply. He immediately resolved to accept the invitation, and replied accordingly. Who this person was, and how his name and the hotel where he was stopping had been found out, was indeed a mystery. However, he waited impatiently for the hour when he was to see this new acquaintance, and get the mysterious meeting in the grave-yard solved.

CHAPTER XXVIII.
THE HAPPY MEETING.

"Man's love is of man's life, a thing apart;
'Tis woman's whole existence."[1]
—*Byron.*

The clock on a neighbouring church had scarcely ceased striking three, when the servant announced that a carriage had called for Mr. Green. In less than half an hour he was seated in a most sumptuous barouche, drawn by two beautiful iron greys, and rolling along over a splendid gravel road completely shaded by large trees, which appeared to have been the accumulating growth of many centuries. The carriage soon stopped in front of a low villa, and this too was embedded in magnificent trees covered with moss. Mr. Green alighted and was shown into a superb drawing room, the walls of which were hung with fine specimens from the hands of the great Italian painters, and one by a German artist representing a beautiful monkish legend connected with "The Holy Catherine," an illustrious lady of Alexandria.[2] The furniture had an antique and dignified appearance. High backed chairs stood around the room; a venerable mirror stood on the mantle shelf; rich curtains of crimson damask hung in folds at either side of the large windows; and a rich Turkey carpet covered the floor. In the centre stood a table covered with books, in the midst of which was an old-fashioned vase filled with fresh flowers, whose fragrance was exceedingly pleasant. A faint light, together with the quietness of the hour, gave beauty beyond description to the whole scene.

Mr. Green had scarcely seated himself upon the sofa, when the elderly gentleman whom he had met the previous evening made his appearance, followed by the little boy, and introduced himself as Mr. Devenant. A moment more, and a lady—a beautiful brunette—dressed in black, with long curls of a chestnut color hanging down on her cheeks, entered the room. Her eyes were of a dark hazel, and her whole appearance indicated that she was a native of a southern clime. The door at which she entered was opposite to where the two gentlemen were seated. They immediately rose; and Mr. Devenant was in the act of introducing her to Mr. Green, when he observed that the latter had sunk back upon the sofa, and the last word that he remem-

---

[1] *"Man's love . . . existence"*: From Lord Byron, *Don Juan* (1819–24), Canto I.
[2] *illustrious lady of Alexandria*: Virgin martyr of the fourth century, St. Catherine was popularly represented in Renaissance art as married to Christ.

bered to have heard was, "It is her." After this, all was dark and dreamy: how long he remained in this condition it was for another to tell. When he awoke, he found himself stretched upon the sofa, with his boots off, his neckerchief removed, shirt collar unbuttoned, and his head resting upon a pillow. By his side sat the old man, with the smelling bottle in the one hand, and a glass of water in the other, and the little boy standing at the foot of the sofa. As soon as Mr. Green had so far recovered as to be able to speak, he said, "Where am I, and what does this mean?" "Wait a while," replied the old man, "and I will tell you all." After a lapse of some ten minutes he rose from the sofa, adjusted his apparel, and said, "I am now ready to hear anything you have to say." "You were born in America?" said the old man. "Yes," he replied. "And you were acquainted with a girl named Mary?" continued the old man. "Yes, and I loved her as I can love none other." "The lady whom you met so mysteriously last evening is Mary," replied Mr. Devenant. George Green was silent, but the fountains of mingled grief and joy stole out from beneath his eye-lashes, and glistened like pearls upon his pale and marble-like cheeks. At this juncture that lady again entered the room. Mr. Green sprang from the sofa, and they fell into each other's arms, to the surprise of the old man and little George, and to the amusement of the servants who had crept up one by one, and were hid behind the doors, or loitering in the hall. When they had given vent to their feelings, they resumed their seats, and each in turn related the adventures through which they had passed. "How did you find out my name and address?" asked Mr. Green. "After you had left us in the grave-yard, our little George said, 'O, mamma, if there aint a book!' and picked it up and brought it to us. Papa opened it, and said, 'The gentleman's name is written in it, and here is a card of the Hotel de Leon, where I suppose he is stopping.' Papa wished to leave the book, and said it was all a fancy of mine that I had ever seen you before, but I was perfectly convinced that you were my own George Green. Are you married?" "No, I am not." "Then, thank God!" exclaimed Mrs. Devenant. "And are you single now?" inquired Mr. Green. "Yes," she replied. "This is indeed the Lord's doings," said Mr. Green, at the same time bursting into a flood of tears. Mr. Devenant was past the age when men should think upon matrimonial subjects, yet the scene brought vividly before his eyes the days when he was a young man, and had a wife living. After a short interview, the old man called their attention to the dinner, which was then waiting. We need scarcely add, that Mr. Green and Mrs. Devenant did very little towards diminishing the dinner that day.

After dinner the lovers (for such we have to call them) gave their experience from the time that George left the jail dressed in Mary's clothes. Up to that time Mr. Green's was substantially as we have related it. Mrs. Devenant's was as follows: — "The night after you left the prison," said she, "I did not shut my eyes in sleep. The next morning, about eight o'clock, Peter the gardener came to the jail to see if I had been there the night before, and was informed that I had, and that I had left a little after dark. About an hour after, Mr. Green came himself, and I need not say that he was much surprised on finding me there, dressed in your clothes. This was the first tidings they had of your escape." "What did Mr. Green say when he found that I had fled?" "Oh!" continued Mrs. Devenant, "he said to me when no one was near, I hope George will get off, but I fear you will have to suffer in his stead. I told him that if it must be so I was willing to die if you could live." At this moment George Green burst into tears, threw his arms around her neck, and exclaimed, "I am glad I have waited so long, with the hope of meeting you again."

Mrs. Devenant again resumed her story: — "I was kept in jail three days, during which time I was visited by the magistrates, and two of the judges. On the third day I was taken out, and master told me that I was liberated, upon condition that I should be immediately sent out of the state. There happened to be just at the time in the neighbourhood a negro-trader, and he purchased me, and I was taken to New Orleans. On the steam-boat we were kept in a close room, where slaves are usually confined, so that I saw nothing of the passengers on board, or the towns we passed. We arrived in New Orleans, and were all put into the slave-market for sale. I was examined by many person, but none seemed willing to purchase me, as all thought me too white, and said I would run away and pass as a free white woman. On the second day, while in the slave-market, and while planters and others were examining slaves and making their purchases, I observed a tall young man, with long black hair, eyeing me very closely, and then talking to the trader. I felt sure that my time had now come, but the day closed without my being sold. I did not regret this, for I had heard that foreigners made the worst of masters, and I felt confident that the man who eyed me so closely was not an American.

"The next day was the Sabbath. The bells called the people to the different places of worship. Methodists sang, and Baptists immersed, and Presbyterians sprinkled, and Episcopalians read their prayers, while the ministers of the various sects preached that Christ died for all; yet there were some twenty-five or thirty of us poor creatures confined in the 'Negro Pen,' awaiting the close of the holy Sabbath, and the dawn of another day, to be again taken into the market, there to be examined like so many beasts of burden. I need not tell you with what anxiety we waited for the advent of another day. On Monday we were again brought out and placed in rows to be inspected; and, fortunately for me, I was sold before we had been on the stand an hour. I was purchased by a gentleman residing in the city, for a waiting-maid for his wife, who was just on the eve of starting for Mobile, to pay a visit to a near relation. I was then dressed to suit the situation of a maid-servant; and upon the whole, I thought that, in my new dress, I looked as much the lady as my mistress.

"On the passage to Mobile, who should I see among the passengers but the tall, long-haired man that had eyed me so closely in the slave-market a few days before. His eyes were again on me, and he appeared anxious to speak to me, and I was reluctant to be spoken to. The first evening after leaving New Orleans, soon after twilight had let her curtain down, and pinned it with a star, and while I was seated on the deck of the boat near the ladies' cabin, looking upon the rippled waves, and the reflection of the moon upon the sea, all at once I saw the tall young man standing by my side. I immediately rose from my seat, and was in the act of returning to my cabin, when he in a broken accent said, 'Stop a moment; I wish to have a word with you. I am your friend.' I stopped and looked him full in the face, and he said, 'I saw you some days since in the slave-market, and I intended to have purchased you to save you from the condition of a slave. I called on Monday, but you had been sold and had left the market. I inquired and learned who the purchaser was, and that you had to go to Mobile, so I resolved to follow you. If you are willing I will try and buy you from your present owner, and you shall be free.' Although this was said in an honest and off-hand manner, I could not believe the man to be sincere in what he said. 'Why should you wish to set *me* free?' I asked. 'I had an only sister,' he replied. 'who died three years ago in France, and you are so much like her that had I not known of her death, I would most certainly have taken you for her.' 'However much I may resemble your sister, you are aware that I am not her, and why take so much interest in one whom you never saw before?' 'The love,' said he, 'which I had for my sister is transferred to you.' I had all along suspected that the man was a knave, and this profession of love confirmed me in my former belief, and I turned away and left him.

"The next day, while standing in the cabin and looking through the window, the French gentleman (for such he was) came to the window while walking on the guards, and again commenced as on the previous evening. He took from his pocket a bit of paper and put it into my hand, at the same time saying, 'Take this, it may some day be of service to you; remember it is from a friend,' and left me instantly. I unfolded the paper, and found it to be a 100 dollars bank note, on the United States Branch Bank, at Philadelphia. My first impulse was to give it to my mistress, but, upon a second thought, I resolved to seek an opportunity, and to return the hundred dollars to the stranger.

"Therefore I looked for him, but in vain; and had almost given up the idea of seeing him again, when he passed me on the guards of the boat and walked towards the stem of the vessel. It being now dark, I approached him and offered the money to him. He declined, saying at the same time, 'I gave it to you—keep it.' 'I do not want it,' I said. 'Now,' said he, 'you had better give your consent for me to purchase you, and you shall go with me to France.' 'But you cannot buy me now,' I replied, 'for my master is in New Orleans, and he purchased me not to sell, but to retain in his own family.' 'Would you rather remain with your present mistress than be free?' 'No,' said I. 'Then fly with me to-night; we shall be in Mobile in two hours from this, and when the passengers are going on shore, you can take my arm, and you can escape unobserved. The trader who brought you to New Orleans exhibited to me a certificate of your good character, and one from the minister of the church to which you were attached in Virginia; and upon the faith of these assurances, and the love I bear you, I promise before high heaven that I will marry you as soon as it can be done.' This solemn promise, coupled with what had already transpired, gave me confidence in the man; and rash as the act may seem, I determined in an instant to go with him. My mistress had been put under the charge of the captain; and as it would be past ten o'clock when the steamer would land, she accepted an invitation of the captain to remain on board with several other ladies till morning. I dressed myself in my best clothes, and put a veil over my face, and was ready on the landing of the boat. Surrounded by a number of passengers, we descended the stage leading to the wharf, and were soon lost in the crowd that thronged the quay. As we went on shore we encountered several persons announcing the names of hotels, the starting of boats for the interior, and vessels bound for Europe. Among these was the ship Utica, Captain Pell, bound for Havre.[3] 'Now,' said Mr. Devenant, 'this is our chance.' The ship was to sail at twelve o'clock that night, at high tide; and following the men who were seeking passengers, we

[3] *Havre*: Le Havre is a seaport in northern France.

went immediately on board. Devenant told the captain of the ship that I was his sister, and for such we passed during the voyage. At the hour of twelve the Utica set sail, and we were soon out at sea.

"The morning after we left Mobile, Devenant met me as I came from my state-room, and embraced me for the first time. I loved him, but it was only that affection which we have for one who has done us a lasting favour: it was the love of gratitude rather than that of the heart. We were five weeks on the sea, and yet the passage did not seem long, for Devenant was so kind. On our arrival at Havre we were married and came to Dunkirk, and I have resided here ever since."

At the close of this narrative, the clock struck ten, when the old man, who was accustomed to retire at an early hour, rose to take leave, saying at the same time, "I hope you will remain with us to-night." Mr. Green would fain have excused himself, on the ground that they would expect him and wait at the hotel, but a look from the lady told him to accept the invitation. The old man was the father of Mrs. Devenant's deceased husband, as you will no doubt long since have supposed. A fortnight from the day on which they met in the graveyard, Mr. Green and Mrs. Devenant were joined in holy wedlock; so that George and Mary, who had loved each other so ardently in their younger days, were now husband and wife.[4]

A celebrated writer has justly said of woman, "A woman's whole life is a history of the affections. The heart is her world; it is there her ambition strives for empire; it is there her avarice seeks for hidden treasures. She sends forth her sympathies on adventure; she embarks her whole soul in the traffic of affection; and, if shipwrecked, her case is hopeless, for it is a bankruptcy of the heart."[5]

Mary had every reason to believe that she would never see George again; and although she confesses that the love she bore him was never transferred to her first husband, we can scarcely find fault with her for marrying Mr. Devenant. But the adherence of George Green to the resolution never to marry, unless to Mary, is, indeed, a rare instance of the fidelity of man in the matter of love. We can but blush for our country's shame when we recall to mind the fact, that while George and Mary Green, and numbers of other fugitives from American slavery, can receive protection from any of the governments of Europe, they cannot return to their native land without becoming slaves.

---

[4] "... were now husband and wife": Brown first told the story of George Green in *Three Years in Europe* (1852), letter XXII.

[5] "A woman's ... heart": From Washington Irving (1783–1859), "The Broken Heart," in *The Sketch Book* (1819–20).

CHAPTER XXIX.
CONCLUSION.

My narrative has now come to a close. I may be asked, and no doubt shall, Are the various incidents and scenes related founded in truth? I answer, Yes. I have personally participated in many of those scenes. Some of the narratives I have derived from other sources; many from the lips of those who, like myself, have run away from the land of bondage. Having been for nearly nine years employed on Lake Erie, I had many opportunities for helping the escape of fugitives, who, in return for the assistance they received, made me the depositary of their sufferings and wrongs. Of their relations I have made free use. To Mrs. Child, of New York, I am indebted for part of a short story.[1] American Abolitionist journals are another source from whence some of the characters appearing in my narrative are taken. All these combined have made up my story. Having thus acknowledged my resources, I invite the attention of my readers to the following statement, from which I leave them to draw their own conclusions: — "It is estimated that in the United States, members of the Methodist church own 219,363 slaves; members of the Baptist church own 226,000 slaves; members of the Episcopalian church own 88,000 slaves; members of the Presbyterian church own 77,000 slaves; members of all other churches own 50,000 slaves; in all, 660,563 slaves owned by members of the Christian church in this pious democratic republic!"[2]

May these facts be pondered over by British Christians, and at the next anniversaries of the various religious denominations in London may their influence be seen and felt! The religious bodies of American Christians will send their delegates to these meetings. Let British feeling be publicly manifested. Let British sympathy express itself in tender sorrow for the condition of my unhappy race. Let it be understood, unequivocally understood, that no fellowship can be held with slaveholders professing the same common Christianity as yourselves. And until this stain from America's otherwise fair escutcheon[3] be wiped away, let no Christian association be maintained with those who traffic

---

[1] *To Mrs. Child . . . story*: Brown's acknowledgment of his use of Lydia Maria Child's "The Quadroons" (1842).

[2] *"It is estimated . . . republic"*: From Reverend Edward S. Mathews (1812–?), "Statistical Account of the Connection of the Religious Bodies in America with Slavery" (1851). A Welsh-born clergyman, Mathews worked as a lecturing agent for the American Baptist Free Mission Society.

[3] *escutcheon*: Shield bearing a coat of arms; reputation.

in the blood and bones of those whom God has made of one flesh as yourselves. Finally, let the voice of the whole British nation be heard across the Atlantic, and throughout the length and breadth of the land of the Pilgrim Fathers, beseeching their descendants, as they value *the* common salvation, which knows no distinction between the bond and the free, to proclaim the Year of Jubilee.[4] Then shall the "earth indeed yield her increase, and God, even our own God, shall bless us; and all the ends of the earth shall fear Him."[5]

[4] *Year of Jubilee*: A yearlong period during which all the slaves would be freed; see Leviticus 25.

[5] *"earth indeed . . . fear him"*: Psalms 67.6–7.

Part Two

Clotel;
or,
The President's Daughter
Cultural Contexts

1

Thomas Jefferson and the Declaration of Independence

William Wells Brown chose as his epigraph to *Clotel* the most famous lines in Jefferson's Declaration of Independence: "We hold these truths to be self-evident: that all men are created equal; that they are endowed by their Creator with certain inalienable rights, and that among these are LIFE, LIBERTY, and the PURSUIT OF HAPPINESS." By placing this inspirational passage on the title page of his novel about slavery in the United States, Brown underscored the unfinished and contradictory nature of the American Revolution. Ironically, the very person who penned the Declaration's ringing assertion of human equality and, during the Revolutionary period, proposed a plan to abolish slavery, owned what would become one of the largest slave plantations in Virginia. In the Declaration, Jefferson set forth the principles that would be enlisted by many abolitionists to challenge the slave system that he himself would come to defend. For antislavery writers ranging from Benjamin Banneker to Frederick Douglass, Jefferson emerged as both the enemy and a source of inspiration. Even a militant antislavery writer like David Walker, who disdained Jefferson for his racism, regarded the Declaration as a document of liberation.

In the spirit of Walker's *Appeal*, *Clotel* simultaneously invokes and talks back to Jefferson's Declaration of Independence. There is both anger at Jefferson the slaveholder and awe at the visionary reach of his egalitarian ideals. Like William Lloyd Garrison and Douglass, Brown seems to be saying that the sources for antislavery reform lie in the nation's key founding document; and in a Jeffersonian mode, he underscores that U.S. culture isn't set and fixed for all time, that it can be challenged, questioned, and reformed. Several of the documents in this section similarly suggest that antislavery reform can proceed by engaging the legacy of Jefferson. In this respect, Brown can be seen as participating in a "conversation" with Jefferson that extends from the post-Revolutionary moment to the publication of *Clotel* in 1853. But aspects of the conversation are deeply troubling, for the fact is that, despite his affirmations, Jefferson the empirical scientist wasn't entirely convinced of human equality. His 1776 draft of the Declaration expresses his anger about slavery, but in his 1787 *Notes on the State of Virginia*, he not only conveys his concerns about the damage slavery can do to blacks and whites alike, but he also elaborates his "suspicion" that blacks are morally and intellectually inferior to whites.

Considered as a group, the selections in this chapter can be viewed as a unit of proposition and rebuttal on the interrelated matters of slavery and race. On the proposition side are Jefferson's inspirational Declaration and his highly influential remarks on slavery and race in *Notes on the State of Virginia*; on the rebuttal side are a letter exchange between Jefferson and the black scientist Banneker, an excerpt from Walker's 1829 *Appeal* (which mainly responds to Jefferson's *Notes*), and selections from Garrison and Douglass on the paradoxical status of the Declaration in a slave culture. Race is central to this cultural conversation. According to the historian Winthrop D. Jordan, Jefferson's reflections on slavery and race in *Notes* "were more widely read, in all probability, than any others until the mid-nineteenth century" and "became a fixed and central point of reference and influence" (429). Influenced by the racist theories of David Hume and other Enlightenment philosophers who regarded blacks as less "civilized" than whites, Jefferson became convinced of blacks' inferiority, and wondered if they might not belong to a different species. At the same time, he was attracted to the views of late-eighteenth-century naturalists, such as the German physical anthropologist Friedrich Blumenbach and the influential French geographer George Leclerc Buffon, who argued that despite apparent racial differences, all humans belonged to a common species. This led Jefferson to a moral and intellectual conundrum. On the one hand he believed that blacks had the same moral sense and natural rights as whites; on the other, he was a slave owner who found it useful to regard blacks as less human than whites. In *Notes*, he attempts to make the "scientific" case for black inferiority and difference, commenting on blacks' supposed failings as artists and purveyors of culture, and almost obsessively sharing his impressions of blacks' physical unattractiveness and sensuality. Ultimately, despite efforts to rationalize the practice of slavery by invoking notions of racial hierarchy, he presents a bleak picture of the institution, portraying anything but the kind masters and loyal slaves who would populate the fabled plantation of antebellum proslavery writers. Contemplating the future, Jefferson worries over the possibility of a bloody war of extermination between the races. Given this fear, and his inability to imagine blacks and whites living together in free society, it is not surprising that several decades later he would support the American Colonization Society's program of shipping free blacks to Africa.

A number of Northern antislavery writers responded to Jefferson's remarks on slavery and race, most prominently the Princeton theologian Samuel Stanhope Smith (1751–1819), who insisted on the intellectual and moral equality of blacks and whites, and the Philadelphia physician Benjamin Rush (1745–1813), who theorized that blacks' dark skin was a biologically transmitted response to leprosy but that otherwise blacks were intellectually, physically, and morally equal to whites. Some of the most compelling responses to Jefferson, however, came from African Americans. In his letter to Jefferson, Banneker posed a challenge to Jefferson's racialism; and one can detect some bending in Jefferson's position on black inferiority when he concedes to Banneker that his "empirical" observations on the plantation may not have done justice to African Americans' capabilities. In addition to responding warmly to Banneker, Jefferson wrote a follow-up letter to the French scientist the Marquis de Condorcet, in which he proclaimed: "I am happy to be able to inform you that we have now in the United States a negro, the son of a black man born in Africa, and of a black woman born in the United States, who is a very respectable mathematician. . . . I have seen very elegant solutions of Geometrical problems by him. Add to this that he is a very worthy & respectable member of society. He is a free man. I shall be delighted to see these instances of moral eminence so multiplied as to prove that the want of talent observed in them is merely the effect of their degraded condition, and not proceeding from any difference in the structure of the parts on which intellect depends" (*Works* VI: 311). Similarly, nearly twenty years later, Jefferson remarked in a letter of 25 February 1809 to the Abbé Henri Gregoire, who had sent him a volume on blacks' accomplishments in literature: "Be assured that no person living wishes more sincerely than I do, to see a complete refutation of the doubts I have myself entertained and expressed on the grade of understanding allotted to them [blacks] by nature, and to find that in this respect they are on a par with ourselves. My doubts were the result of personal observation on the limited sphere of my own State, where the opportunities for the development of their genius were not favorable, and those of exercising it still less so" (*Writings* 1202). Of course the possibility exists that Jefferson was being disingenuous in his letters to Condorcet and Gregoire, and that like many Southerners he was incapable of regarding blacks as fully human. Such is the unattractive image of Jefferson that emerges in David Walker's *Appeal* (1829), published just three years after Jefferson's death on 4 July 1826. According to Walker, Jefferson was a hypocrite who bequeathed to the nation a loathsome racist ideology of white supremacy. In Walker's view, Jefferson also bequeathed to the nation a host of unresolved political and cultural conflicts that made the apocalyptic racial war he envisioned in *Notes* little more than a self-fulfilling prophecy.

The year 1831 is generally regarded as a turning point in the antislavery movement. That year Garrison's highly influential newspaper, the *Liberator*, was founded in Massachusetts; the first annual black convention took place in Philadelphia; and a small group of slaves staged the bloodiest slave revolt in U.S. history, Nat Turner's rebellion in Virginia, which Jefferson's *Notes* to some extent anticipated. (For more on Turner, see Chapter 3.) According to Garrison's editorial on Turner, which appeared in the 3 September 1831 issue of the *Liberator*, the rebellion was "the vengeance of heaven" on the "crime of oppression." Horrified by the bloody violence, Garrison called for "IMMEDIATE EMANCIPATION" (143), arguing that evangelical appeals to conscience were the most effective means for combating slavery. As is clear from his editorial in the inaugural January 1831 issue of the *Liberator*, Garrison also sought to mobilize black and white abolitionists by invoking the egalitarian ideals of the Declaration. Approximately twenty years later, Douglass in his famous Fifth of July address mockingly noted the continued failure of U.S. culture to live up to those ideals, angrily asking white Americans how they could celebrate the Fourth of July in good conscience. Delivered a year before the publication of *Clotel*, Douglass's speech highlights the hypocrisies of a nation that tells a progressive democratic story about its commitment to the principles of the Declaration even as it enslaves millions of African descent.

In the four selections included with the Jefferson texts, then, we see a range of responses. Banneker attempts literally to converse with

Jefferson, sending him a letter and a copy of one of his books with the hope of instructing him on the relevance of the Declaration for black Americans. But for the more militant free black Walker, Jefferson's moral failings as slave owner and racist are just too great, and he responds to the recently deceased Jefferson by refuting the racism of *Notes*, even as he marshals the fighting spirit of the Declaration. The reformist energies and anger of Garrison and Douglass are directed more at American culture than at Jefferson, with Jefferson's own writings providing some of the terms of their critiques. Brown may well have been familiar with all of these cultural texts, which can be taken, in a way, as source texts. But compared to the writers included in this chapter, his response to Jefferson seems more oblique, pointing to the larger irony that Jefferson, who spoke passionately about human equality but remained suspicious of blacks, would ultimately become the father of slaves.

THOMAS JEFFERSON

A Declaration by the Representatives of the United States of America, in General Congress Assembled

Thomas Jefferson (1743–1826), the great Virginian polymath and politician, was the nation's first secretary of state, second vice president, and third president (1801–09). As the principal author of the Declaration of Independence, he continues to occupy a sacred place in American culture for having expressed the nation's ideals of democracy and equality in their most powerful written form. Yet because he was a slave owner, his reputation has fluctuated and the genuineness of his commitment to freedom has come under repeated scrutiny. In his defense, Jefferson seemed uncomfortable with slavery and was reluctant to present the institution as a "positive good." But the fact remains that he owned slaves throughout his career and at his death manumitted only the slaves of the Hemings family. Some therefore view Jefferson as a hypocrite who extolled human liberty while simultaneously defending his — and his fellow Southerners' — rights to enslave black people; others regard him as a visionary Founding Father who, despite being influenced by the sectional and racist ideologies of his day, championed humankind's inalienable rights to freedom and equality. The tensions and contradictions informing Jefferson's (and the new nation's) founding ideals are displayed with no greater clarity than in the draft of the Declaration of Independence printed in his "Autobiography." The draft, "Declaration by the Representatives of the United States of America," includes his original attack on the slave trade, along with the revisions made by the General Congress that cut those antislavery sentiments from the final document. Jefferson wrote the "Autobiography" in 1821 but it was left unpublished until after his death. The text is from *The Works of Thomas Jefferson*, vol. 1, ed. Paul Leicester Ford (New York: G. P. Putnam's Sons, 1904), 32–43.

Congress proceeded the same day to consider the declaration of Independance which had been reported & lain on the table the Friday preceding, and on Monday referred to a commee[1] of the whole. The pusillanimous idea that we had friends in England worth keeping terms with, still haunted the minds of many. For this reason those passages which conveyed censures on the people of England were struck out, lest they should give them offence. The clause too, reprobating the enslaving the inhabitants of Africa, was struck out in complaisance to South Carolina and Georgia, who had never attempted to restrain the importation of slaves, and who on the contrary still wished to continue it. Our northern brethren also I believe felt a little tender under those censures; for tho' their people have very few slaves themselves yet they had been pretty considerable carriers of them to others. The debates having taken up the greater parts of the 2d 3d & 4th days of July were, in the evening of the last, closed the declaration was reported by the commee, agreed to by the house and signed by every member present except Mr. Dickinson.[2] As the sentiments of men are known not only by what they receive, but what they reject also, I will state the form of the declaration as originally reported. The parts struck out by Congress shall be distinguished by a black line drawn under them; & those inserted by them shall be placed in the margin or in a concurrent column.[3]

[1] *commee*: Committee.
[2] *Mr. Dickinson*: The Pennsylvanian John Dickinson (1732–1808) was a leader of the conservative patriots who hoped for reconciliation with England.
[3] *The parts . . . column*: Jefferson fails to note that he uses brackets to indicate where Congress added words to the body of the text.

A Declaration

When in the course of human events it becomes necessary for one people to dissolve the political bands which have connected them with another, and to assume among the powers of the earth the separate & equal station to which the laws of nature and of nature's God entitle them, a decent respect to the opinions of mankind requires that they should declare the causes which impel them to the separation.

We hold these truths to be self-evident: that all men are created equal; that they are endowed by their creator with inherent and* inalienable rights; that among these are life, liberty, & the pursuit of happiness:[4] that to secure these rights, governments are instituted among men, deriving their just powers from the consent of the governed; that whenever any form of government becomes destructive of these ends, it is the right of the people to alter or abolish it, & to institute new government, laying it's foundation on such principles, & organizing it's powers in such form, as to them shall seem most likely to effect their safety & happiness. Prudence indeed will dictate that governments long established should not be changed for light & transient causes; and accordingly all experience hath shown that mankind are more disposed to suffer while evils are sufferable, than to right themselves by abolishing the forms to which they are accustomed. But when a long train of abuses & usurpations begun at a distinguished period and pursuing invariably the same object, evinces a design to reduce them under absolute despotism, it is their right, it is their duty to throw off such government, & to provide new guards for their future security. Such has been the patient sufferance of these colonies; & such is now the necessity which constrains them to expunge† their former systems of government. The history of the present king of Great Britain[5] is a history of unremitting‡ injuries & usurpations, among which appears no solitary fact to contradict the uniform tenor of the

---

Note: In this edition, Jefferson's marginal notations, which contain Congress's inserted text, have been replaced by footnotes with symbols (*, †, ‡, §, ||, #).

 * certain
 † alter
 ‡ repeated

---

[4] *life, liberty, & the pursuit of happiness*: Principles derived from John Locke (1632–1704), *Treatises of Civil Government* (1690); Locke also emphasized the right to own property.
[5] *the present king of Great Britain*: George III (1738–1820), who reigned from 1760 to 1820.

rest but all have* in direct object the establishment of an absolute tyranny over these states. To prove this let facts be submitted to a candid world for the truth of which we pledge a faith yet unsullied by falsehood.

He has refused his assent to laws the most wholesome & necessary for the public good.

He has forbidden his governors to pass laws of immediate & pressing importance, unless suspended in their operation till his assent should be obtained; & when so suspended, he has utterly neglected to attend to them.

He has refused to pass other laws for the accommodation of large districts of people, unless those people would relinquish the right of representation in the legislature, a right inestimable to them, & formidable to tyrants only.

He has called together legislative bodies at places unusual, uncomfortable, and distant from the depository of their public records, for the sole purpose of fatiguing them into compliance with his measures.

He has dissolved representative houses repeatedly & continually for opposing with manly firmness his invasions on the rights of the people.

He has refused for a long time after such dissolutions to cause others to be elected, whereby the legislative powers, incapable of annihilation, have returned to the people at large for their exercise, the state remaining in the meantime exposed to all the dangers of invasion from without & convulsions within.

He has endeavored to prevent the population of these states; for that purpose obstructing the laws for naturalization of foreigners, refusing to pass others to encourage their migrations hither, & raising the conditions of new appropriations of lands.

He has suffered† the administration of justice totally to cease in some of these states‡ refusing his assent to laws for establishing judiciary powers.

He has made our judges dependant on his will alone, for the tenure of their offices, & the amount & paiment of their salaries.

He has erected a multitude of new offices by a self assumed power and sent hither swarms of new officers to harass our people and eat out their substance.

* all having
† obstructed
‡ by

He has kept among us in times of peace standing armies <u>and ships</u> <u>of war</u> without the consent of our legislatures.

He has affected to render the military independant of, & superior to the civil power.

He has combined with others[6] to subject us to a jurisdiction foreign to our constitutions & unacknowledged by our laws, giving his assent to their acts of pretended legislation for quartering large bodies of armed troops among us; for protecting them by a mock-trial from punishment for any murders which they should commit on the inhabitants of these states; for cutting off our trade with all parts of the world; for imposing taxes on us without our consent; for depriving us [ ]* of the benefits of trial by jury; for transporting us beyond seas to be tried for pretended offences; for abolishing the free system of English laws in a neighboring province,[7] establishing therein an arbitrary government, and enlarging it's boundaries, so as to render it at once an example and fit instrument for introducing the same absolute rule into these <u>states</u>†; for taking away our charters, abolishing our most valuable laws, and altering fundamentally the forms of our governments; for suspending our own legislatures, & declaring themselves invested with power to legislate for us in all cases whatsoever.

He has abdicated government here <u>withdrawing his governors, and</u> <u>declaring us out of his allegiance & protection.</u>‡

He has plundered our seas, ravaged our coasts, burnt our towns, & destroyed the lives of our people.

He is at this time transporting large armies of foreign mercenaries[8] to compleat the works of death, desolation & tyranny already begun with circumstances of cruelty and perfidy [ ]§ unworthy the head of a civilized nation.

He has constrained our fellow citizens taken captive on the high seas to bear arms against their country, to become the executioners of their friends & brethren, or to fall themselves by their hands.

---

* in many cases
† colonies
‡ by declaring us out of his protection, and waging war against us.
§ scarcely paralleled in the most barbarous ages, & totally

---

[6] *others*: The British Parliament.

[7] *abolishing ... province*: A reference to the Quebec Act of 1774, which recognized Roman Catholicism in Quebec and allowed the province to extend its boundaries to the Ohio River. The colonists' Protestant majority regarded this act as but one of the "Intolerable Acts" of 1774.

[8] *foreign mercenaries*: German soldiers, financed by the British.

He has [ ]* endeavored to bring on the inhabitants of our frontiers the merciless Indian savages, whose known rule of warfare is an undistinguished destruction of all ages, sexes, & conditions of existence.

He has incited treasonable insurrections of our fellow-citizens, with the allurements of forfeiture & confiscation of our property.

He has waged cruel war against human nature itself, violating it's most sacred rights of life and liberty in the persons of a distant people who never offended him, captivating & carrying them into slavery in another hemisphere, or to incur miserable death in their transportation thither. This piratical warfare, the opprobrium of INFIDEL powers, is the warfare of the CHRISTIAN king of Great Britain. Determined to keep open a market where MEN should be bought & sold, he has prostituted his negative for suppressing every legislative attempt to prohibit or to restrain this execrable commerce. And that this assemblage of horrors might want no fact of distinguished die, he is now exciting those very people to rise in arms among us, and to purchase that liberty of which he has deprived them, by murdering the people on whom he also obtruded them: thus paying off former crimes committed against the LIBERTIES of one people, with crimes which he urges them to commit against the LIVES of another.

In every stage of these oppressions we have petitioned for redress in the most humble terms: our repeated petitions have been answered only by repeated injuries.

A prince whose character is thus marked by every act which may define a tyrant is unfit to be the ruler of a [ ]† people who mean to be free. Future ages will scarcely believe that the hardiness of one man adventured, within the short compass of twelve years only, to lay a foundation so broad & so undisguised for tyranny over a people fostered & fixed in principles of freedom.

Nor have we been wanting in attention to our British brethren. We have warned them from time to time of attempts by their legislature to extend a‡ jurisdiction over these our states.§ We have reminded them of the circumstances of our emigration & settlement here, no one of which could warrant so strange a pretension: that these were effected at the expense of our own blood & treasure, unassisted by the wealth or the strength of Great Britain: that in constituting indeed our several

---

* excited domestic insurrection among us, & has
† free
‡ an unwarrantable
§ us

forms of government, we had adopted one common king, thereby laying a foundation for perpetual league & amity with them: but that submission to their parliament was no part of our constitution, nor ever in idea, if history may be credited: and, we [ ]* appealed to their native justice and magnanimity as well as to† the ties of our common kindred to disavow these usurpations which were likely to‡ interrupt our connection and correspondence. They too have been deaf to the voice of justice & of consanguinity, and when occasions have been given them, by the regular course of their laws, of removing from their councils the disturbers of our harmony, they have, by their free election, re-established them in power. At this very time too they are permitting their chief magistrate to send over not only soldiers of our common blood, but Scotch & foreign mercenaries to invade & destroy us. These facts have given the last stab to agonizing affection, and manly spirit bids us to renounce forever these unfeeling brethren. We must endeavor to forget our former love for them, and hold them as we hold the rest of mankind, enemies in war, in peace friends. We might have been a free and a great people together; but a communication of grandeur & of freedom it seems is below their dignity. Be it so, since they will have it. The road to happiness & to glory is open to us too. We will tread it apart from them, and§ acquiesce in the necessity which denounces[9] our eternal separation [ ]!‖

We[10] therefore the representatives of the United States of America in General Congress assembled do in the same & by authority of the good people of these states reject & renounce all allegiance & subjection to the kings of Great Britain & all others who may hereafter claim by, through or under

We therefore the representatives of the United States of America in General Congress assembled, appealing to the supreme judge of the world for the rectitude of our intentions, do in the name, & by the authority of the good people of these colonies, solemnly publish & declare that these united colonies

---

* have
† and we have conjured them by
‡ would inevitably
§ We must therefore
‖ and hold them as we hold the rest of mankind, enemies in war, in peace friends.

[9] *denounces*: Announces.
[10] *We . . .*: In this closing section Jefferson prints his version in the left column and the final adopted version in the right column.

them: we utterly dissolve all political connection which may heretofore have subsisted between us & the people or parliament of Great Britain: & finally we do assert & declare these colonies to be free & independent states, & that as free & independent states, they have full power to levy war, conclude peace, contract alliances, establish commerce, & to do all other acts & things which independent states may of right do.

And for the support of this declaration we mutually pledge to each other our lives, our fortunes, & our sacred honor.

are & of right ought to be free & independent states; that they are absolved from all allegiance to the British crown, and that all political connection between them & the state of Great Britain is, & ought to be, totally dissolved; & that as free & independent states they have full power to levy war, conclude peace, contract alliances, establish commerce & to do all other acts & things which independant states may of right do.

And for the support of this declaration, with a firm reliance on the protection of divine providence we mutually pledge to each other our lives, our fortunes, & our sacred honor.

The Declaration thus signed on the 4th, on paper was engrossed on parchment, & signed again on the 2d of August.

THOMAS JEFFERSON

From *Notes on the State of Virginia*

Jefferson wrote *Notes on the State of Virginia* (1787) in response to a series of queries about the state from the Marquis de Barbé-Marbois, secretary to the French legation in Philadelphia. The main purpose of the text was to refute Europe's leading naturalists, Abbé Reynal and the Count de Buffon, who had argued that the New World showed signs of physical and natural degeneration. Jefferson, then governor of Virginia, devoted a number of his chapters to careful, naturalistic descriptions of landscapes, animals, and even the Native Americans, with an aim toward demonstrating the nation's bounty, vigor, and future potential. His discussion of slavery constituted a small but important part of the book. At the time Jefferson disapproved of slavery, but his antislavery views were grounded in a racialist belief in black inferiority and a conviction that blacks could never become citizens of the United States. As he became more economically dependent on his slaves, Jefferson became more of a defender of the South's right to own slaves for the time being, particularly after slavery was banned from the Northwest territories by the Missouri Compromise of 1820. But he continued to look forward to a national future in which slavery had come to an end and blacks had gone to other countries. The selection is taken from *The Works of Thomas Jefferson*, ed. Paul Leicester Ford, vol. 4 (New York: G. P. Putnam's Sons, 1904), 47, 48–54, 55–59, 82–84.

QUERY XIV
The administration of justice and the description of the laws?

Many of the laws which were in force during the monarchy being relative merely to that form of government, or inculcating principles inconsistent with republicanism, the first assembly which met after the establishment of the commonwealth, appointed a committee to revise the whole code, to reduce it into proper form and volume, and report it to the assembly. This work has been executed by three gentlemen, and reported; but probably will not be taken up till a restoration of peace shall leave to the legislature leisure to go through such a work.[1] . . .

The following are the most remarkable alterations proposed:

To change the rules of descent, so as that the lands of any person dying intestate shall be divisible equally among all his children, or other representatives, in equal degree.

To make slaves distributable among the next of kin, as other movables.

To have all public expences, whether of the general treasury, or of a parish or county, (as for the maintenance of the poor, building bridges, courthouses, &c.,) supplied by assessments on the citizens, in proportion to their property.

To hire undertakers for keeping the public roads in repair, and indemnify individuals through whose lands new roads shall be opened.

To define with precision the rules whereby aliens should become citizens, and citizens make themselves aliens.

---

[1] *such a work*: A reference to the *Report of the Revisors*, a revision of Virginia's state laws, which was prepared by Thomas Jefferson, George Wythe (1726–1806), and Edmund Pendleton (1721–1803), and submitted to the state legislature on 18 June 1779.

To establish religious freedom on the broadest bottom.

To emancipate all slaves born after passing the act. The bill reported by the revisers does not itself contain this proposition; but an amendment containing it was prepared, to be offered to the legislature whenever the bill should be taken up, and further directing, that they should continue with their parents to a certain age, then be brought up, at the public expence, to tillage, arts, or sciences, according to their geniusses, till the females should be eighteen, and the males twenty-one years of age, when they should be colonized to such place as the circumstances of the time should render most proper, sending them out with arms, implements of household and of the handicraft arts, seeds, pairs of the useful domestic animals, &c. to declare them a free and independant people, and extend to them our alliance and protection, till they shall have acquired strength; and to send vessels at the same time to other parts of the world for an equal number of white inhabitants; to induce whom to migrate hither, proper encouragements were to be proposed. It will probably be asked, Why not retain and incorporate the blacks into the state, and thus save the expence of supplying by importation of white settlers, the vacancies they will leave? Deep rooted prejudices entertained by the whites; ten thousand recollections, by the blacks, of the injuries they have sustained; new provocations; the real distinctions which nature has made; and many other circumstances will divide us into parties, and produce convulsions, which will probably never end but in the extermination of the one or the other race.—To these objections, which are political, may be added others, which are physical and moral. The first difference which strikes us is that of colour. Whether the black of the negro resides in the reticular membrane between the skin and scarfskin,[2] or in the scarfskin itself; whether it proceeds from the colour of the blood, the colour of the bile, or from that of some other secretion, the difference is fixed in nature, and is as real as if its seat and cause were better known to us. And is this difference of no importance? Is it not the foundation of a greater or less share of beauty in the two races? Are not the fine mixtures of red and white, the expressions of every passion by greater or less suffusions of colour in the one, preferable to that eternal monotony, which reigns in the countenances, that immovable veil of black which covers all the emotions of the other race? Add to these, flowing hair, a more elegant symmetry of form, their own judgment in favour

---

[2] *scarfskin*: The outermost layer of skin.

of the whites, declared by their preference of them as uniformly as in the preference of the Oran ootan[3] for the black woman over those of his own species. The circumstance of superior beauty, is thought worthy attention in the propagation of our horses, dogs, and other domestic animals; why not in that of man? Besides those of colour, figure and hair, there are other physical distinctions proving a difference of race. They have less hair on the face and body. They secrete less by the kidnies, and more by the glands of the skin, which gives them a very strong and disagreeable odour. This greater degree of transpiration, renders them more tolerant of heat, and less so of cold than the whites. Perhaps too a difference of structure in the pulmonary apparatus, which a late ingenious experimentalist[4] has discovered to be the principal regulator of animal heat, may have disabled them from extricating, in the act of inspiration, so much of that fluid from the outer air, or obliged them in expiration, to part with more of it. They seem to require less sleep. A black after hard labour through the day, will be induced by the slightest amusements to sit up till midnight or later, though knowing he must be out with the first dawn of the morning. They are at least as brave, and more adventuresome. But this may perhaps proceed from a want of forethought, which prevents their seeing a danger till it be present. When present, they do not go through it with more coolness or steadiness than the whites. They are more ardent after their female; but love seems with them to be an eager desire, than a tender delicate mixture of sentiment and sensation. Their griefs are transient. Those numberless afflictions, which render it doubtful whether heaven has given life to us in mercy or in wrath, are less felt, and sooner forgotten with them. In general, their existence appears to participate more of sensation than reflection. To this must be ascribed their disposition to sleep when abstracted from their diversions, and unemployed in labour. An animal whose body is at rest, and who does not reflect, must be disposed to sleep of course. Comparing them by their faculties of memory, reason, and imagination, it appears to me that in memory they are equal to the whites; in reason much inferior, as I think one could scarcely be found capable of tracing and comprehending the investigations of Euclid:[5] and that in imagination they are dull, tasteless,

---

[3] *Oran ootan*: Orangutan.

[4] *a late ingenious experimentalist*: A reference to Adair Crawford (1748–1795), a British physician and chemist best known for his *Experiments and Observations on Animal Heat* (1779).

[5] *Euclid*: Greek mathematician circa 300 B.C.

and anomalous. It would be unfair to follow them to Africa for this investigation. We will consider them here, on the same stage with the whites, and where the facts are not apochryphal on which a judgment is to be formed. It will be right to make great allowances for the difference of condition, of education, of conversation, of the sphere in which they move. Many millions of them have been brought to, and born in America. Most of them, indeed, have been confined to tillage, to their own homes, and their own society: yet many have been so situated, that they might have availed themselves of the conversation of their masters; many have been brought up to the handicraft arts, and from that circumstance have always been associated with the whites. Some have been liberally educated, and all have lived in countries where the arts and sciences are cultivated to a considerable degree, and have had before their eyes samples of the best works from abroad. The Indians, with no advantages of this kind, will often carve figures on their pipes not destitute of design and merit. They will crayon out an animal, a plant, or a country, so as to prove the existence of a germ in their minds which only wants cultivation. They astonish you with strokes of the most sublime oratory; such as prove their reason and sentiment strong, their imagination glowing and elevated. But never yet could I find that a black had uttered a thought above the level of plain narration; never seen even an elementary trait of painting or sculpture. In music they are more generally gifted than the whites, with accurate ears for tune and time, and they have been found capable of imagining a small catch.[6] Whether they will be equal to the composition of a more extensive run of melody, or of complicated harmony, is yet to be proved. Misery is often the parent of the most affecting touches in poetry. — Among the blacks is misery enough, God knows, but no poetry. Love is the peculiar œstrum[7] of the poet. Their love is ardent, but it kindles the senses only, not the imagination. Religion, indeed, has produced a Phyllis Whately[8]; but it could not produce a poet. The compositions published under her name are below the dignity of criticism. The heroes of the Dunciad[9] are to her, as Hercules to the author

[6] "The instrument proper to them is the Banjar, which they brought hither from Africa, and which is the original of the guitar, its chords being precisely the four lower chords of the guitar." [Jefferson's note]

[7] *oestrum*: Passionate impulse.

[8] *Phyllis Whately*: A condescending reference to the African American poet Phillis Wheatley (1753–1784), whose *Poems* (1773) was popular in England, going through at least four printings.

[9] *Dunciad*: Alexander Pope's satirical poem on Dullness, first published in 1728.

of that poem. Ignatius Sancoh[10] has approached nearer to merit in composition; yet his letters do more honour to the heart than the head. They breathe the purest effusions of friendship and general philanthropy, and show how great a degree of the latter may be compounded with strong religious zeal. He is often happy in the turn of his compliments, and his style is easy and familiar, except when he affects a Shandean[11] fabrication of words. But his imagination is wild and extravagant, escapes incessantly from every restraint of reason and taste, and, in the course of its vagaries, leaves a tract of thought as incoherent and eccentric, as is the course of a meteor through the sky. His subjects should often have led him to a process of sober reasoning; yet we find him always substituting sentiment for demonstration. Upon the whole, though we admit him to the first place among those of his own color who have presented themselves to the public judgment, yet when we compare him with the writers of the race among whom he lived and particularly with the epistolary[12] class in which he has taken his own stand, we are compelled to enrol him at the bottom of the column. This criticism supposes the letters published under his name to be genuine, and to have received amendment from no other hand; points which would not be of easy investigation. The improvement of the blacks in body and mind, in the first instance of their mixture with the whites, has been observed by every one, and proves that their inferiority is not the effect merely of their condition of life. We know that among the Romans, about the Augustan age[13] especially, the condition of their slaves was much more deplorable than that of the blacks on the continent of America. The two sexes were confined in separate apartments, because to raise a child cost the master more than to buy one. . . . With the Romans, the regular method of taking the evidence of their slaves was under torture. Here it has been thought better never to resort to their evidence. When a master was murdered, all his slaves, in the same house, or within hearing, were condemned to death. Here punishment falls on the guilty only, and as precise proof is required against him as against a freeman. Yet notwithstanding these

---

[10] *Ignatius Sancoh*: Charles Ignatius Sancho (1729–1780), born a slave on a slave ship, was eventually taken to England, where he emerged as an internationally prominent man of letters. His *Letters of the Late Ignatius Sancho, an African* was published in London in 1782.

[11] *Shandean*: In imitation of the eponymous antihero of Laurence Sterne's *Tristram Shandy* (1760–1767).

[12] *epistolary*: Letter writing.

[13] *Augustan age*: The Roman Emperor Augustus ruled from 27 B.C. to A.D. 14.

and other discouraging circumstances among the Romans, their slaves were often their rarest artists. They excelled too in science, insomuch as to be usually employed as tutors to their master's children. Epictetus, Terence, and Phædrus, were slaves.[14] But they were of the race of whites. It is not their condition then, but nature, which has produced the distinction.—Whether further observation will or will not verify the conjecture, that nature has been less bountiful to them in the endowments of the head, I believe that in those of the heart she will be found to have done them justice. That disposition to theft with which they have been branded, must be ascribed to their situation, and not to any depravity of the moral sense. The man in whose favour no laws of property exist, probably feels himself less bound to respect those made in favour of others. When arguing for ourselves, we lay it down as a fundamental, that laws, to be just, must give a reciprocation of right: that, without this, they are mere arbitrary rules of conduct, founded in force, and not in conscience; and it is a problem which I give to the master to solve, whether the religious precepts against the violation of property were not framed for him as well as his slave? And whether the slave may not as justifiably take a little from one who has taken all from him, as he may slay one who would slay him? That a change in the relations in which a man is placed should change his ideas of moral right and wrong, is neither new, nor peculiar to the colour of the blacks. Homer[15] tells us it was so 2600 years ago.

> Ἥμισυ, γὰρ τ᾽ ἀρετῆς ἀποαίνυται εὐρύοπα Ζεὺ
> Ἀφνερος, ευτ᾽ ἂν μιν κατὰ δουλιον ἦμαρ ἕλησιν.
> —Od. 17, 323.

> Jove fix'd it certain, that whatever day
> Makes man a slave, take half his worth away.

But the slaves of which Homer speaks were whites. Notwithstanding these considerations which must weaken their respect for the laws of property, we find among them numerous instances of the most rigid integrity, and as many as among their better instructed masters, of benevolence, gratitude, and unshaken fidelity. The opinion that they are inferior in the faculties of reason and imagination, must be haz-

---

[14] *Epictetus, Terence, and Phædrus, were slaves*: Epictetus (A.D. c.50–c.138) was a philosopher, Terence (c.190 B.C.–c.159 B.C.) a comic playwright, and Phædrus (first century A.D.) a writer of fables.

[15] *Homer*: The passage that follows is from the epic poem *The Odyssey*, generally attributed to the Greek poet Homer, who lived sometime before 700 B.C.

arded with great diffidence. To justify a general conclusion, requires many observations, even where the subject may be submitted to the Anatomical knife, to Optical glasses, to analysis by fire or by solvents. How much more then where it is a faculty, not a substance, we are examining; where it eludes the research of all the senses; where the conditions of its existence are various and variously combined; where the effects of those which are present or absent bid defiance to calculation; let me add too, as a circumstance of great tenderness, where our conclusion would degrade a whole race of men from the rank in the scale of beings which their Creator may perhaps have given them. To our reproach it must be said, that though for a century and a half we have had under our eyes the races of black and of red men, they have never yet been viewed by us as subjects of natural history. I advance it, therefore, as a suspicion only, that the blacks, whether originally a distinct race, or made distinct by time and circumstances, are inferior to the whites in the endowments both of body and mind. It is not against experience to suppose that different species of the same genus, or varieties of the same species, may possess different qualifications. Will not a lover of natural history then, one who views the gradations in all the races of animals with the eye of philosophy, excuse an effort to keep those in the department of man as distinct as nature has formed them? This unfortunate difference of colour, and perhaps of faculty, is a powerful obstacle to the emancipation of these people. Many of their advocates, while they wish to vindicate the liberty of human nature, are anxious also to preserve its dignity and beauty. Some of these, embarrassed by the question, 'What further is to be done with them?' join themselves in opposition with those who are actuated by sordid avarice only. Among the Romans emancipation required but one effort. The slave, when made free, might mix with, without staining the blood of his master. But with us a second is necessary, unknown to history. When freed, he is to be removed beyond the reach of mixture. . . .

QUERY XVIII
The particular customs and manners that may happen to be received in that State?

It is difficult to determine on the standard by which the manners of a nation may be tried, whether *catholic*[16] or *particular*. It is more

---

[16] *catholic*: Universal; wide-ranging.

difficult for a native to bring to that standard the manners of his own nation, familiarized to him by habit. There must doubtless be an unhappy influence on the manners of our people produced by the existence of slavery among us. The whole commerce between master and slave is a perpetual exercise of the most boisterous passions, the most unremitting despotism on the one part, and degrading submissions on the other. Our children see this, and learn to imitate it; for man is an imitative animal. This quality is the germ of all education in him. From his cradle to his grave he is learning to do what he sees others do. If a parent could find no motive either in his philanthropy or his self-love, for restraining the intemperance of passion towards his slave, it should always be a sufficient one that his child is present. But generally it is not sufficient. The parent storms, the child looks on, catches the lineaments of wrath, puts on the same airs in the circle of smaller slaves, gives a loose to the worst of passions, and thus nursed, educated, and daily exercised in tyranny, cannot but be stamped by it with odious peculiarities. The man must be a prodigy who can retain his manners and morals undepraved by such circumstances. And with what execrations should the statesman be loaded, who permitting one half the citizens thus to trample on the rights of the other, transforms those into despots, and these into enemies, destroys the morals of the one part, and the amor patriæ of the other. For if a slave can have a country in this world, it must be any other in preference to that in which he is born to live and labour for another: in which he must lock up the faculties of his nature, contribute as far as depends on his individual endeavours to the evanishment of the human race, or entail his own miserable condition on the endless generations proceeding from him. With the morals of the people, their industry also is destroyed. For in a warm climate, no man will labour for himself who can make another labour for him. This is so true, that of the proprietors of slaves a very small proportion indeed are ever seen to labour. And can the liberties of a nation be thought secure when we have removed their only firm basis, a conviction in the minds of the people that these liberties are of the gift of God? That they are not to be violated but with his wrath? Indeed I tremble for my country when I reflect that God is just: that his justice cannot sleep forever: that considering numbers, nature and natural means only, a revolution of the wheel of fortune, an exchange of situation, is among possible events: that it may become probable by supernatural interference! The Almighty has no attribute which can take side with us in such a contest. — But it is impossible to be temperate and to pursue this subject through the various considerations of policy, of morals, of history natural and civil. We must be contented to hope they will force their way into every one's mind. I think a change already perceptible, since the origin of the present revolution. The spirit of the master is abating, that of the slave rising from the dust, his condition mollifying, the way I hope preparing, under the auspices of heaven, for a total emancipation, and that this is disposed, in the order of events, to be with the consent of the masters, rather than by their extirpation.

BENJAMIN BANNEKER AND THOMAS JEFFERSON

Letter Exchange (1791)

The free black Benjamin Banneker (1731–1806) was an extraordinarily gifted mathematician, astronomer, inventor, and natural historian. His genealogy anticipates the tangled racial genealogies of *Clotel*. Banneker's grandmother on his mother's side, Molly Welsh, was a white Englishwoman who was convicted of a crime and deported to the colony of Maryland as an indentured servant. After serving out her time, she purchased a farm and two slaves, but eventually freed the slaves and married one of them, "Bannaka," who claimed to be an African prince. Their eldest daughter, Mary, married a slave from Guinea, who took on the name Banneker; their first child was Benjamin. Taught to read and write by Molly, Benjamin also attended Baltimore's Quaker schools. When, as an adult, he gained a reputation as a gifted scientist, some of the local Quakers and other abolitionists began to publicize his achievements in order to challenge racist notions of black inferiority.

Banneker completed his first *Almanac* at age sixty, a compilation of his lifelong astronomical studies. The Quaker publishers of the volume sent a copy to then-Secretary of State Thomas Jefferson, along with Banneker's letter to Jefferson, which challenged the racialist views propounded in *Notes on the State of Virginia* and pointed to the ideological contradictions of the Declaration of Independence. Jefferson seemed genuinely impressed with both the *Almanac* and Banneker's eloquent letter. As he remarked in a subsequent letter of 30 August 1791 to the distinguished French mathematician, the Marquis de Condorcet, Banneker's achievements suggest that "the want of talents observed in them [blacks] is merely the effect of their degraded condition, and not proceeding from any difference in the structure of the parts on which intellect depends." Banneker's letter to Jefferson was regularly reprinted by abolitionists; William Wells Brown printed a version of the exchange in a chapter on Banneker in *The Black Man, His Antecedents, His Genius and His Achievements* (1863). The source of the Banneker letter below is John R. B. Latrobe, *Memoir of Benjamin Banneker* (Baltimore: John D. Toy, 1845), 14–16; Jefferson's letter is taken from *The Works of Thomas Jefferson*, vol. 6, ed. Paul Leicester Ford (New York: G. P. Putnam's Sons, 1904), 309–310.

MARYLAND, BALTIMORE COUNTY
Near Ellicotts' Lower Mills, August 19th, 1791.

THOMAS JEFFERSON, *Secretary of State.*

Sir: — I am fully sensible of the greatness of that freedom, which I take with you on the present occasion, a liberty which seemed to me scarcely allowable, when I reflected on that distinguished and dignified station in which you stand, and the almost general prejudice and pre-possession which is so prevalent in the world against those of my complexion.

I suppose it is a truth too well attested to you, to need a proof here, that we are a race of beings who have long laboured under the abuse and censure of the world, that we have long been considered rather as brutish than human, and scarcely capable of mental endowments.

Sir, I hope I may safely admit, in consequence of that report which hath reached me, that you are a man far less inflexible in sentiments of this nature than many others, that you are measurably friendly and well disposed towards us, and that you are ready and willing to lend your aid and assistance to our relief, from those many distressed and numerous calamities, to which we are reduced.

Now, sir, if this is founded in truth, I apprehend you will readily embrace every opportunity to eradicate that train of absurd and false ideas and opinions, which so generally prevails with respect to us, and that your sentiments are concurrent with mine, which are that one universal father hath given being to us all, and that he hath not only made us all of one flesh, but that he hath also without partiality afforded us all the same sensations, and endued us all with the same faculties, and that however variable we may be in society or religion, however diversified in situation or colour, we are all of the same family, and stand in the same relation to him.

Sir, if these are sentiments of which you are fully persuaded, I hope you cannot but acknowledge, that it is the indispensable duty of those who maintain for themselves the rights of human nature, and who profess the obligations of christianity, to extend their power and influence to the relief of every part of the human race, from whatever burthen or oppression they may unjustly labour under, and this I apprehend a full conviction of the truth and obligation of these principles should lead all to.

Sir, I have long been convinced, that if your love for yourselves and for those inestimable laws, which preserve to you the rights of human nature, was founded on sincerity, you could not but be solicitous that every individual of whatever rank or distinction, might with you equally enjoy the blessings thereof, neither could you rest satisfied, short of the most active diffusion of your exertions, in order, to their promotion from any state of degradation, to which the unjustifiable cruelty and barbarism of men may have reduced them.

Sir, I freely and cheerfully acknowledge that I am of the African race, and in that colour which is natural to them of the deepest dye, and it is under a sense of the most profound gratitude to the supreme ruler of the Universe, that I now confess to you, that I am not under that state of tyrannical thraldom, and inhuman captivity, to which too many of my brethren are doomed, but that I have abundantly tasted of the fruition of those blessings, which proceed from that free and unequalled liberty, with which you are favored, and which, I hope you will willingly allow, you have received from the immediate hand of that being, from whom proceedeth every good and perfect gift.

Sir, suffer me to recall to your mind that time in which the arms and tyranny of the British crown were exerted with every powerful effort in order to reduce you to a state of servitude; look back, I entreat you, on the variety of dangers to which you were exposed; reflect on that time in which every human aid appeared unavailable, and in which even hope and fortitude wore the aspect of inability to the conflict, and you cannot but be led to a serious and grateful sense of your miraculous and providential preservation; you cannot but acknowledge, that the present freedom and tranquillity which you enjoy, you have mercifully received, and that it is the peculiar blessing of heaven.

This, sir, was a time in which you clearly saw into the injustice of a state of slavery, and in which you had just apprehension of the horrors of its condition; it was now, sir, that your abhorrence thereof was so excited, that you publicly held forth this true and invaluable doctrine, which is worthy to be recorded and remembered in all succeeding ages. "We hold these truths to be self-evident, that all men are created equal, and that they are endowed by their creator with certain inalienable rights, that among these are life, liberty and the pursuit of happiness."

Here, sir, was a time in which your tender feelings for yourselves had engaged you thus to declare, you were then impressed with proper ideas of the great valuation of liberty, and the free possession of those blessings to which you were entitled by nature; but, sir, how pitiable is it to reflect that although you were so fully convinced of the benevolence of the Father of mankind, and of his equal and impartial distribution of those rights and privileges which he had conferred upon them, that you should at the same time counteract his mercies, in detaining by fraud and violence so numerous a part of my brethren, under groaning captivity and cruel oppression, that you should at the same time be found guilty of that most criminal act, which you professedly detested in others with respect to yourselves.

Sir, I suppose that your knowledge of the situation of my brethren, is too extensive to need a recital here; neither shall I presume to prescribe methods by which they may be relieved, otherwise than by recommending to you and all others, to wean yourselves from those narrow prejudices which you have imbibed with respect to them, and as Job proposed to his friends, "put your souls in their souls stead";[1] thus shall your hearts be enlarged with kindness and benevolence towards them, and thus shall you need neither the direction of myself nor others, in what manner to proceed herein.

And now, sir, although my sympathy and affection for my brethren hath caused my enlargement thus far, I ardently hope that your candour and generosity, will plead with you in my behalf, when I make known to you, that it was not originally my design; but that having taken up my pen in order to direct to you as a present, a copy of an almanac, which I have calculated for the succeeding year, I was unexpectedly and unavoidably led thereto.

This calculation, sir, is the production of my arduous study in this my advanced stage of life; for having long had unbounded desires to become acquainted with the secrets of nature, I have had to gratify my curiosity herein through my own assiduous application to astronomical study, in which I need not to recount to you the many difficulties and disadvantages which I have had to encounter.

And although I had almost declined to make my calculation for the ensuing year, in consequence of that time which I had allotted therefor, being taken up at the Federal Territory, by the request of Mr. Andrew Ellicott,[2] yet finding myself under several engagements to printers of

---

[1] *"put your souls . . . stead"*: Job 16.4.

[2] *Andrew Ellicott*: A surveyor and mathematician from Maryland, Andrew Ellicott (1754–1820) surveyed the site of the national capital with Banneker's assistance during the early 1790s.

this State, to whom I had communicated my design, on my return to my place of residence, I industriously applied myself thereto, which I hope I have accomplished with correctness and accuracy, a copy of which I have taken the liberty to direct to you, and which I humbly request you will favorably receive, and although you may have the opportunity of perusing it after its publication, yet I choose to send it to you in manuscript previous thereto, that thereby you might not only have an earlier inspection, but that you might also view it in my own hand-writing.

And now, sir, I shall conclude and subscribe myself, with the most profound respect, your most obedient humble servant,

B. BANNEKER.

THOMAS JEFFERSON, *Secretary of State. Philadelphia.*

N. B.   Any communication to me, may be had by direction to Mr. Elias Ellicott, merchant, in Baltimore Town.

B. B.

TO BENJAMIN BANNEKER

PHILADELPHIA Aug. 30. 1791.

Sir,—I thank you sincerely for your letter of the 19th instant and for the Almanac it contained. No body wishes more than I do to see such proofs as you exhibit, that nature has given to our black brethren, talents equal to those of the other colors of men, and that the appearance of a want of them is owing merely to the degraded condition of their existence, both in Africa & America. I can add with truth, that no body wishes more ardently to see a good system commenced for raising the condition both of their body & mind to what it ought to be, as fast as the imbecility of their present existence, and other circumstances which cannot be neglected, will admit. I have taken the liberty of sending your Almanac to Monsieur de Condorcet,[3] Secretary of the Academy of Sciences at Paris, and member of the Philanthropic society, because I consider it as a document to which your whole colour had a right for their justification against the doubts which have been entertained of them. I am with great esteem, Sir Your most obedt humble servt.

---

[3] *Condorcet:* The Marquis de Condorcet (1743–1794), a French mathematician and philosopher, was best known for his philosophy of historical progress, particularly his belief in the eventual perfection of man.

DAVID WALKER

From *Walker's Appeal*

David Walker (c. 1790–1830), one of the most influential and contro-
versial black abolitionists of the early national period, was born free in
Wilmington, North Carolina, the son of a slave father (who died before his
birth) and a free mother. As a free black, he traveled widely in the South
and became a vigorous critic of slavery. In 1827 he moved to Boston,
opened a clothing store, and served as the Boston sales agent of *Freedom's
Journal*, the first African American newspaper. A year later he married
Eliza, a fugitive slave, and during the few remaining years of his life
engaged in a number of antislavery and antiracist activities, continuing his
association with black newspapers, speaking before black organizations,
and writing and attempting to disseminate his *Walker's Appeal, in Four
Articles, Together with a Preamble, to the Colored Citizens of the World,
But in Particular, and Very Expressly to those of the United States of
America* (1829). Though the book became notorious for its militant assertion that blacks, when faced with the possibility of enslavement, should
"kill or be killed," an assertion that led Southerners to blame Walker for
Nat Turner's insurrection of 1831, the overarching intention of the volume was not to push blacks toward a race war (unless whites offered no
other choice) but to argue for blacks' rights to freedom and dignity in the
United States. In developing his argument, Walker challenged whites' racist assumptions about black inferiority, particularly as set forth in Jefferson's *Notes on the State of Virginia*, attacked African colonizationism,
and called for blacks to take responsibility for their moral, educational,
and economic uplift. Walker died under uncertain circumstances in 1830.
According to legend, he was murdered by white racists, but evidence suggests he died from consumption a week after his daughter succumbed to a
similar illness. The *Appeal* remained highly influential among black abolitionists. In 1848 it was republished as part of a volume titled *Walker's
Appeal, With a Brief Sketch of His Life. By Henry Highland Garnet. And
also Garnet's Address to the Slaves of the United States of America* (New
York: J. H. Tobitt), from which the selection below is taken.

My beloved brethren: The Indians of North and of South America—the Greeks—the Irish subjected under the king of Great Britain—the Jews that ancient people of the Lord—the inhabitants of the

islands of the sea—in fine, all the inhabitants of the earth, (except however, the sons of Africa) are called *men*, and of course are, and ought to be free. But *we*, (coloured people) and our children are *brutes*!! and of course are and ought to be SLAVES to the American people and their children forever! to dig their mines and work their farms; and thus go on enriching them, from one generation to another with our blood and our tears!!

I promised in a preceding page to demonstrate to the satisfaction of the most incredulous, that we, (colored people of these United States of America) are the *most wretched, degraded* and abject set of beings that ever *lived* since the world began, and that the white Americans having reduced us to the wretched state of *slavery*, treat us in that condition *more cruel* (they being an enlightened and christian people) than any heathen nation did any people whom it had reduced to our condition. These affirmations are so well confirmed in the minds of all unprejudiced men who have taken the trouble to read histories, that they need no elucidation from me. . . .

I have been for years troubling the pages of historians to find out what our fathers have done to the *white Christians of America*, to merit such condign punishment as they have inflicted on them, and do continue to inflict on us their children. But I must aver, that my researches have hitherto been to no effect. I have therefore come to the immovable conclusion, that they (Americans) have, and do continue to punish us for nothing else, but for enriching them and their country. For I cannot conceive of any thing else. Nor will I ever believe otherwise until the Lord shall convince me.

The world knows, that slavery as it existed among the Romans, (which was the primary cause of their destruction) was, comparatively speaking, no more than a *cypher*, when compared with ours under the Americans. Indeed, I should not have noticed the Roman slaves, had not the very learned and penetrating Mr. Jefferson said, "When a mas-"ter was murdered, all his slaves in the same house or within hearing, "were condemned to death."[1]—Here let me ask Mr. Jefferson, (but he is gone to answer at the bar of God, for the deeds done in his body while living,) I therefore ask the whole American people, had I not rather die, or be put to death than to be a slave to any tyrant, who takes not only my own, but my wife and children's lives by the inches? Yea, would I meet death with avidity far! far!! in preference to such *servile submission* to the murderous hands of tyrants. Mr. Jefferson's

[1] See his notes on Virginia. [Walker's note.]

very severe remarks on us have been so extensively argued upon by men whose attainments in literature, I shall never be able to reach, that I would not have meddled with it, were it not to solicit each of my brethren, who has the spirit of a man, to buy a copy of Mr. Jefferson's "Notes on Virginia," and put it in the hand of his son. For let no one of us suppose that the refutations which have been written by our white friends are enough—they are *whites*—we are *blacks*. We, and the world wish to see the charges of Mr. Jefferson refuted by the blacks *themselves*, according to their chance: for we must remember that what the whites have written respecting this subject, is other men's labors and did not emanate from the blacks. I know well, that there are some talents and learning among the coloured people of this country, which we have not a chance to develope, in consequence of oppression; but our oppression ought not to hinder us from acquiring all we can.—For we will have a chance to develope them by and by. God will not suffer us, always to be oppressed. Our sufferings will come to an *end*, in spite of all the Americans this side of *eternity*. Then we will want all the learning and talents among ourselves, and perhaps more, to govern ourselves.—"Every dog must have its day,"[2] the American's is coming to an end.

But let us review Mr. Jefferson's remarks respecting us some further. Comparing our miserable fathers, with the learned philosophers of Greece, he says: "Yet notwithstanding these and other discouraging "circumstances among the Romans, their slaves were often their rar- "est artists. They excelled too in science, insomuch as to be usually "employed as tutors to their master's children; Epictetus, Terence and "Phædrus, were slaves,—but they were of the race of whites. It is not "their *condition* then, but *nature*, which has produced the distinction."[3] See this, my brethren!! Do you believe that this assertion is swallowed by millions of the whites? Do you know that Mr. Jefferson was one of as great characters as ever lived among the whites? See his writings for the world, and public labors for the United States of America. Do you believe that the assertions of such a man, will pass away into oblivion unobserved by this people and the world? If you do you are much mistaken—See how the American people treat us—have we souls in our bodies? are we men who have any spirits at all? I know that there are many *swell-bellied* fellows among us whose greatest object is to fill

---

[2] *"Every dog must have its day"*: Attributed to John Heywood (1497?–1580?), a British writer known for his proverbs and epigrams.

[3] See his notes on Virginia. [Walker's note.]

their stomachs. Such I do not mean—I am after those who know and feel, that we are MEN as well as other people; to them, I say, that unless we try to refute Mr. Jefferson's arguments respecting us, we will only establish them.

But the slaves among the Romans. Every body who has read history, knows, that as soon as a slave among the Romans obtained his freedom, he could rise to the greatest eminence in the State, and there was no law instituted to hinder a slave from buying his freedom. Have not the Americans instituted laws to hinder us from obtaining our freedom. Do any deny this charge? Read the laws of Virginia, North Carolina, &c. Further: have not the Americans instituted laws to prohibit a man of colour from obtaining and holding any office whatever, under the government of the United States of America? Now, Mr. Jefferson tells us that our condition is not so hard, as the slaves were under the Romans!!!!

It is time for me to bring this article to a close. But before I close it, I must observe to my brethren that at the close of the first Revolution in this country with Great Britain, there were but thirteen States in the Union, now there are twenty-four, most of which are slave-holding States, and the whites are dragging us around in chains and hand-cuffs to their new States and Territories to work their mines and farms, to enrich them and their children, and millions of them believing firmly that we being a little darker than they, were made by our creator to be an inheritance to them and their children forever—the same as a parcel of *brutes*!!

Are we MEN!!—I ask you, O my brethren! are we MEN? Did our creator make us to be slaves to dust and ashes like ourselves? Are they not dying worms as well as we? Have they not to make their appearance before the tribunal of heaven, to answer for the deeds done in the body, as well as we? Have we any other master but Jesus Christ alone? Is he not their master as well as ours?—What right then, have we to obey and call any other master, but Himself? How we could be so *submissive* to a gang of men, whom we cannot tell whether they are as *good* as ourselves or not, I never could conceive. However, this is shut up with the Lord and we cannot precisely tell—but I declare, we judge men by their works.

The whites have always been an unjust, jealous unmerciful, avaricious and blood thirsty set of beings, always seeking after power and authority.—We view them all over the confederacy of Greece, where they were first known to be any thing, (in consequence of education) we see them there, cutting each other's throats—trying to subject each other to wretchedness and misery, to effect which they used all kinds of deceitful, unfair and unmerciful means. We view them next in Rome, where the spirit of tyranny and deceit rated still higher. — We view them in Gaul, Spain and in Britain — in fine, we view them all over Europe, together with what were scattered about in Asia and Africa, as heathens, and we see them acting more like devils than accountable men. But some may ask, did not the blacks of Africa, and the mulattoes of Asia, go on in the same way as did the whites of Europe. I answer no — they never were half so avaricious, deceitful and unmerciful as the whites, according to their knowledge.

But we will leave the whites or Europeans as heathens and take a view of them as christians, in which capacity we see them as cruel, if not more so than ever. In fact, take them as a body, they are ten times more cruel, avaricious and unmerciful than ever they were; for while they were heathens they were bad enough it is true, but it is positively a fact that they were not quite so audacious as to go and take vessel loads of men, women and children, and in cold blood and through devilishness, throw them into the sea, and murder them in all kind of ways. While they were heathens, they were too ignorant for such barbarity. But being christians, enlightened and sensible, they are completely prepared for such hellish cruelties. Now suppose God were to give them more sense, what would they do. If it were possible would they not *dethrone* Jehovah and seat themselves upon his throne? I therefore, in the name and fear of the Lord God of heaven and of earth, divested of prejudice either on the side of my colour or that of the whites, advance my suspicion, whether they are *as good by nature* as we are or not. Their actions, since they were known as a people, have been the reverse, I do indeed suspect them, but this, as I before observed, is shut up with the Lord, we cannot exactly tell, it will be proved in succeeding generations. — The whites have had the essence of the gospel as it was preached by my master and his apostles — the Ethiopians have not, who are to have it in its meridian splendor — the Lord will give it to them to their satisfaction. I hope and pray my God, that they will make good use of it, that it may be well with them. . . .

Oh! coloured people of these United States, I ask you, in the name of that God who made us, have we, in consequence of oppression, nearly lost the spirit of man, and, in no very trifling degree, adopted that of brutes? Do you answer, No? — I ask you, then, what set of men can you point me to, in all the world, who are so abjectly employed by their oppressors as we are by our *natural enemies?* How can, Oh! how can those enemies but say that we and our children are not of the

HUMAN FAMILY, but were made by our creator to be an inheritance to them and theirs forever? How can the slave-holders but say that they can bribe the best coloured person in the country, to sell his brethren for a trifling sum of money, and take that atrocity to confirm them in their avaricious opinion, that we were made to be slaves to them and their children? How could Mr. Jefferson but say,[4] "I advance it there-"fore as a suspicion only, that the blacks, whether originally a distinct "race, or made distinct by time and circumstances, are *inferior* to the "whites in the endowments both of body and mind?" "It," says he, "is "not against experience to suppose, that different species of the same "genus, or varieties of the same species, may possess different qualifi-"cations." [Here, my brethren listen to him.] ☞ "Will not a lover of "natural history then, one who views the gradations in all the races of "*animals* with the eye of philosophy, excuse an effort to keep those "in the department of MAN as *distinct* as nature has formed them?" I hope you will try to find out the meaning of this verse—its widest sense and all its bearings: whether you do or not, remember the whites do. This very verse, brethren, having emanated from Mr. Jefferson, a much greater philosopher the world never afforded, has in truth injured us more, and has been as great a barrier to our emancipation as any thing that has ever been advanced against us. I hope you will not let it pass unnoticed. He goes on further and says: "This *unfortu-"nate* difference of colour, and *perhaps* of *faculty*, is a powerful ob-"stacle to the emancipation of these people. Many of their advocates, "while they wish to vindicate the liberty of human nature are anxious "also to preserve its *dignity* and *beauty*. Some of these, embarrassed "by the question, 'What further is to be done with them?' join them-"selves in opposition with those who are actuated by sordid avarice "only." Now I ask you candidly, my suffering brethren in time, who are candidates for the eternal worlds, how could Mr. Jefferson but have given the world these remarks respecting us, when we are so sub-missive to them, and so much servile deceit prevails among ourselves— when we so *meanly* submit to their murderous lashes, to which neither the Indians or any other people under heaven would submit? No, they could die to a man, before they would suffer such things from men who are no better than themselves, and *perhaps not so good*. Yes, how can our friends but be embarrassed, as Mr. Jefferson says, by the ques-tion, "What further is to be done with these people?" for while they are working for our emancipation, we are, by our treachery, wickedness

---

[4] See his notes on Virginia. [Walker's note.]

and deceit, working against ourselves and our children—helping ours, and the enemies of God, to keep us and our dear little children, in their infernal chains of slavery!! Indeed, our friends cannot but relapse and join themselves 'with those who are actuated by *sordid avarice* only!!!!' For my part, I am glad Mr. Jefferson has advanced his position for your sake; for you will either have to contradict or confirm him by your own actions and not by what our friends have said or done for us; for those things are other men's labors and do not satisfy the Americans who are waiting for us to prove to them ourselves that we are MEN before they will be willing to admit the fact; for I pledge you my sacred word of honor that Mr. Jefferson's remarks respecting us have sunk deep into the hearts of millions of the whites and never will be removed this side of eternity. For how can they, when we are confirming him every day by our *groveling submissions* and *treachery*?

I aver that when I look upon these United States and see the ignorant deceptions and consequent wretchedness of my brethren, I am brought ofttimes solemnly to a stand, and in the midst of my reflections I exclaim to my God, 'Lord didst thou make us to be slaves to our brethren, the whites?' But when I reflect that God is just, and that millions of my wretched brethren would meet death with glory—yea, more, would plunge into the very mouths of cannons and be torn into particles as minute as the atoms which compose the elements of the earth, in preference to a mean submission to the lash of tyrants, I am with streaming eyes, compelled to shrink back into nothingness before my Maker, and exclaim again, thy will be done, O Lord God Almighty. . . .

In conclusion, I ask the candid and unprejudiced of the whole world, to search the pages of historians diligently, and see if the Antediluvians—the Sodomites—the Egyptians—the Babylonians—the Ninevites—the Carthagenians—the Persians—the Macedonians—the Greeks—the Romans—the Mahometans—the Jews[5]—or devils, ever treated a set of human beings, as the white Christians of America do us, the blacks, or Africans.—I also ask the attention of the world of mankind to the declaration of these very American people, of the United States.

A Declaration made July 4, 1776.

It says,[6] "When in the course of human events, it becomes neces-"sary for one people to dissolve the political bands which have con-

---

[5] *Antediluvians . . . Jews:* For the most part, references to ancient peoples who once held great power.

[6] See the Declaration of Independence of the United States. [Walker's note.]

"nected them with another, and to assume among the Powers of the
"earth, the separate and equal station to which the laws of nature and
"of nature's God entitle them, a decent respect for the opinions of
"mankind requires that they should declare the causes which impel
"them to the separation. We hold these truths to be self evident, that
"all men are created equal, that they are endowed by their Creator
"with certain unalienable rights; that among these are life, liberty, and
"the pursuit of happiness; that to secure these rights, governments are
"instituted among men, deriving their just powers from the consent
"of the governed; that whenever any form of government becomes
"destructive of these ends it is the right of the people to alter or to
"abolish it, and to institute a new government laying its foundation on
"such principles, and organizing its powers in such form as to them
"shall seem most likely to effect their safety and happiness. Prudence,
"indeed, will dictate that governments long established should not be
"changed for light and transient causes; and accordingly all experience
"hath shewn, that mankind are more disposed to suffer, while evils are
"sufferable, than to right themselves by abolishing the forms to which
"they are accustomed. But when a long train of abuses and usurpa-
"tions, pursuing invariably the same object, evinces a design to reduce
"them under absolute despotism, it is their right, it is their duty to
"throw off such government, and to provide new guards for their
"future security." See your declaration, Americans!! Do you understand your own language? Hear your language, proclaimed to the
world, July 4, 1776 — ☞ "We hold these truths to be self evident —
"that *ALL* MEN ARE CREATED EQUAL! *that they are endowed by their*
"*Creator with certain unalienable rights; that among these are life, lib-*
"*erty, and the pursuit of happiness*!!" Compare your own language
above, extracted from your Declaration of Independence, with your
cruelties and murders inflicted by your cruel and unmerciful fathers on
ourselves on our fathers and on us, men who have never given your
fathers or you the least provocation!!!

Hear your language further! ☞ "But when a long train of abuses
"and usurpations, pursuing invariably the same object, evinces a design
"to reduce them under absolute despotism, it is their *right*, it is their
"*duty*, to throw off such government, and to provide new guards for
their future security."

Now, Americans! I ask you candidly, was your sufferings under
Great Britain one hundredth part as cruel and tyrannical as you have
rendered ours under you? Some of you, no doubt, believe that we will
never throw off your murderous government, and "provide new

"guards for our future security." If Satan has made you believe it, will he not deceive you?[7] Do the whites say, I being a black man, ought to be humble, which I readily admit? I ask them, ought they not to be as humble as I? or do they think they can measure arms with Jehovah? Will not the Lord yet humble them? or will not these very coloured people, whom they now treat worse than brutes, yet under God, humble them low down enough? Some of the whites are ignorant enough to tell us, that we ought to be submissive to them, that they may keep their feet on our throats. And if we do not submit to be beaten to death by them, we are bad creatures and of course must be damned, &c. If any man wishes to hear this doctrine openly preached to us by the American preachers, let him go into the Southern and Western sections of this country—I do not speak from hearsay—what I have written, is what I have seen and heard myself. No man may think that my book is made up of conjecture—I have travelled and observed nearly the whole of those things myself, and what little I did not get by my own observation, I received from those among the whites and blacks, in whom the greatest confidence may be placed.

The Americans may be as vigilant as they please, but they cannot be vigilant enough for the Lord, neither can they hide themselves, where he will not find and bring them out.

---

[7] The Lord has not taught the Americans that we will not some day or other throw off their chains and hand-cuffs, from our hands and feet, and their devilish lashes (which some of them shall have enough of yet) from off our backs. [Walker's note.]

WILLIAM LLOYD GARRISON

To the Public

Born in Newburyport, Massachusetts, William Lloyd Garrison (1805–1879) came to antislavery reform after working for several years as a printer and temperance reformer. In 1828 he joined forces with the abolitionist Benjamin Lundy (1789–1839), who edited the antislavery newspaper *The Genius of Universal Emancipation*. Disillusioned by Lundy's support for gradual emancipation and African colonization, Garrison soon broke with Lundy and by the early 1830s had asserted the principles that would guide his politics for the next thirty years: an unconditional call for immediate emancipation, a condemnation of the Constitution as proslavery, a rejection of union with slaveholding states, and a commitment to moral suasion over violence. In 1833 he organized the American

Anti-Slavery Society, which remained one of the most effective antislavery organizations of the period. His support for women's rights and moral suasion led to a schism in his abolitionist organization in 1840 and the emergence of the more pragmatic American and Foreign Anti-Slavery Society. During the 1840s and 1850s, Brown, who shared Garrison's views on the immorality of the American Constitution and the importance of having women participate in antislavery reform, worked as a lecturing agent for Garrison's American Anti-Slavery Society. In the editorial "To the Public," which appeared in the 1 January 1831 inaugural issue of the *Liberator,* the source of the following selection, Garrison invokes Jefferson's language in the Declaration to point to the unfinished work of the American Revolution.

In the month of August, I issued proposals for publishing "THE LIBERATOR" in Washington city; but the enterprise, though hailed in different sections of the country, was palsied by public indifference. Since that time, the removal of the Genius of Universal Emancipation[1] to the Seat of Government has rendered less imperious the establishment of a similar periodical in that quarter.

During my recent tour for the purpose of exciting the minds of the people by a series of discourses on the subject of slavery, every place that I visited gave fresh evidence of the fact, that a greater revolution in public sentiment was to be effected in the free states—*and particularly in New-England*—than at the south. I found contempt more bitter, opposition more active, detraction more relentless, prejudice more stubborn, and apathy more frozen, than among slave owners themselves. Of course, there were individual exceptions to the contrary. This state of things afflicted, but did not dishearten me. I determined, at every hazard, to lift up the standard of emancipation in the eyes of the nation, *within sight of Bunker Hill*[2] *and in the birth place of liberty.* That standard is now unfurled; and long may it float unhurt by the spoliations of time or the missiles of a desperate foe—yea, till every chain be broken, and every bondman set free! Let southern oppressors tremble—let their secret abettors tremble—let their northern apologists tremble—let all the enemies of the persecuted blacks tremble.

---

[1] *the Genius of Universal Emancipation*: An antislavery paper edited by Benjamin Lundy (1789–1839). Garrison served as an editor from 1829 to 1830.

[2] *Bunker Hill*: The site of a famous Revolutionary battle fought in Boston on 17 June 1775.

I deem the publication of my original Prospectus unnecessary, as it has obtained a wide circulation. The principles therein inculcated will be steadily pursued in this paper, excepting that I shall not array myself as the political partisan of any man. In defending the great cause of human rights, I wish to derive the assistance of all religions and of all parties.

Assenting to the "self-evident truth" maintained in the American Declaration of Independence, "that all men are created equal, and endowed by their Creator with certain inalienable rights—among which are life, liberty and the pursuit of happiness," I shall strenuously contend for the immediate enfranchisement of our slave population. In Park-street Church, on the Fourth of July, 1829, in an address on slavery, I unreflectingly assented to the popular but pernicious doctrine of *gradual* abolition. I seize this opportunity to make a full and unequivocal recantation, and thus publicly to ask pardon of my God, of my country, and of my brethren the poor slaves, for having uttered a sentiment so full of timidity, injustice and absurdity. A similar recantation, from my pen, was published in the Genius of Universal Emancipation at Baltimore, in September, 1829. My conscience is now satisfied.

I am aware, that many object to the severity of my language; but is there not cause for severity? I *will be* as harsh as truth, and as uncompromising as justice. On this subject, I do not wish to think, or speak, or write, with moderation. No! no! Tell a man whose house is on fire, to give a moderate alarm; tell him to moderately rescue his wife from the hands of the ravisher; tell the mother to gradually extricate her babe from the fire into which it has fallen;—but urge me not to use moderation in a cause like the present. I am in earnest—I will not equivocate—I will not excuse—I will not retreat a single inch—AND I WILL BE HEARD. The apathy of the people is enough to make every statue leap from its pedestal, and to hasten the resurrection of the dead.

It is pretended, that I am retarding the cause of emancipation by the coarseness of my invective, and the precipitancy of my measures. *The charge is not true.* On this question my influence,—humble as it is,— is felt at this moment to a considerable extent, and shall be felt in coming years—not perniciously, but beneficially—not as a curse, but as a blessing; and posterity will bear testimony that I was right. I desire to thank God, that he enables me to disregard "the fear of man which bringeth a snare," and to speak his truth in its simplicity and power. And here I close with this fresh dedication:

Oppression! I have seen thee, face to face,
And met thy cruel eye and cloudy brow;
But thy soul-withering glance I fear not now—
For dread to prouder feelings doth give place
Of deep abhorrence! Scorning the disgrace
Of slavish knees that at thy footstool bow
I also kneel—but with far other vow
Do hail thee and thy hord of hirelings base:—
I swear, while life-blood warms my throbbing veins,
Still to oppose and thwart, with heart and hand,
Thy brutalising sway—till Afric's chains
Are burst, and Freedom rules the rescued land,—
Trampling Oppression and his iron rod:
Such is the vow I take—SO HELP ME GOD!

FREDERICK DOUGLASS

What to the Slave Is the Fourth of July?

In a searing indictment of the nation's contradictory Revolutionary origins in slavery and freedom, Frederick Douglass called attention to the limits (and promise) of Jefferson's Declaration in a Fifth of July speech delivered on 5 July 1852 in Rochester, New York, before a racially mixed audience of approximately six hundred people. The best-known and most influential African American leader of the nineteenth century, Douglass (1818–1895) escaped from slavery in Maryland in 1838, and in 1841 was appointed a lecturing agent for William Lloyd Garrison's Anti-Slavery Society. His widely read *The Narrative of the Life of Frederick Douglass*, an important influence on Brown's own *Narrative*, appeared in 1845. Following a British tour, during which his freedom was purchased, Douglass returned to the United States in 1847 and commenced a career in journalism and abolitionism. For the most part Brown and Douglass greatly respected one another. They met in Buffalo in 1843 at the National Convention of Colored Citizens and, as Garrisonians committed to a nonviolent use of moral persuasion, voted against endorsing Henry Highland Garnet's militant "Address to the Slaves." During the early 1850s, Brown contributed a number of letters to *Frederick Douglass' Paper*. In the mid-1850s, however, Brown and Douglass quarreled in print after Douglass publicly repudiated Garrison, whom Brown continued to admire. At an 1855 meeting of the Anti-Slavery Society, Douglass attacked Brown for urging the free states to break from, rather than reform, the slave states. That same year Douglass published a much revised and expanded narrative of his life, *My Bondage and My Freedom* (New York and Auburn: Miller, Orton, and Mulligan, 1855). In the appendix to that volume Douglass included an abridgment of his Fifth of July speech, which is printed below.

FELLOW-CITIZENS—Pardon me, and allow me to ask, why am I called upon to speak here to-day? What have I, or those I represent, to do with your national independence? Are the great principles of political freedom and of natural justice, embodied in that Declaration of Independence, extended to us? and am I, therefore, called upon to bring our humble offering to the national altar, and to confess the benefits, and express devout gratitude for the blessings, resulting from your independence to us?

Would to God, both for your sakes and ours, that an affirmative answer could be truthfully returned to these questions? Then would my task be light, and my burden easy and delightful. For who is there so cold that a nation's sympathy could not warm him? Who so obdurate and dead to the claims of gratitude, that would not thankfully acknowledge such priceless benefits? Who so stolid and selfish, that would not give his voice to swell the hallelujahs of a nation's jubilee, when the chains of servitude had been torn from his limbs? I am not that man. In a case like that, the dumb might eloquently speak, and the "lame man leap as an hart."[1]

But, such is not the state of the case. I say it with a sad sense of the disparity between us. I am not included within the pale of this glorious anniversary! Your high independence only reveals the immeasurable distance between us. The blessings in which you this day rejoice, are not enjoyed in common. The rich inheritance of justice, liberty, prosperity, and independence, bequeathed by your fathers, is shared by you, not by me. The sunlight that brought life and healing to you, has brought stripes and death to me. This Fourth of July is *yours*, not *mine*. *You* may rejoice, *I* must mourn. To drag a man in fetters into the grand illuminated temple of liberty, and call upon him to join you in joyous anthems, were inhuman mockery and sacrilegious irony. Do you mean, citizens, to mock me, by asking me to speak to-day? If so, there is a

---

[1] *"lame . . . hart"*: Isaiah 35.6; a "hart" is a male red deer.

parallel to your conduct. And let me warn you that it is dangerous to copy the example of a nation whose crimes, towering up to heaven, were thrown down by the breath of the Almighty, burying that nation in irrecoverable ruin![2] I can to-day take up the plaintive lament of a peeled and woe-smitten people.

"By the rivers of Babylon, there we sat down. Yea! we wept when we remembered Zion. We hanged our harps upon the willows in the midst thereof. For there, they that carried us away captive, required of us a song; and they who wasted us required of us mirth, saying, Sing us one of the songs of Zion. How can we sing the Lord's song in a strange land? If I forget thee, O Jerusalem, let my right hand forget her cunning. If I do not remember thee, let my tongue cleave to the roof of my mouth."[3]

Fellow-citizens, above your national, tumultuous joy, I hear the mournful wail of millions, whose chains, heavy and grievous yesterday, are to-day rendered more intolerable by the jubilant shouts that reach them. If I do forget, if I do not faithfully remember those bleeding children of sorrow this day, "may my right hand forget her cunning, and may my tongue cleave to the roof of my mouth!" To forget them, to pass lightly over their wrongs, and to chime in with the popular theme, would be treason most scandalous and shocking, and would make me a reproach before God and the world. My subject then, fellow-citizens, is AMERICAN SLAVERY. I shall see this day and its popular characteristics from the slave's point of view. Standing there, identified with the American bondman, making his wrongs mine, I do not hesitate to declare, with all my soul, that the character and conduct of this nation never looked blacker to me than on this Fourth of July. Whether we turn to the declarations of the past, or to the professions of the present, the conduct of the nation seems equally hideous and revolting. America is false to the past, false to the present, and solemnly binds herself to be false to the future. Standing with God and the crushed and bleeding slave on this occasion, I will, in the name of humanity which is outraged, in the name of liberty which is fettered, in the name of the constitution and the bible, which are disregarded and trampled upon, dare to call in question and to denounce, with all the emphasis I can command, everything that serves to perpetuate

---

[2] *a nation whose crimes . . . ruin*: The Israelites of the Old Testament. Douglass here is addressing (and critiquing) nineteenth-century Americans' tendency to regard the United States as a New Israel.

[3] *"By the rivers . . . mouth"*: Psalms 137.1–6.

slavery—the great sin and shame of America! "I will not equivocate; I will not excuse;"[4] I will use the severest language I can command; and yet not one word shall escape me that any man, whose judgment is not blinded by prejudice, or who is not at heart a slaveholder, shall not confess to be right and just.

But I fancy I hear some one of my audience say, it is just in this circumstance that you and your brother abolitionists fail to make a favorable impression on the public mind. Would you argue more, and denounce less, would you persuade more and rebuke less, your cause would be much more likely to succeed. But, I submit, where all is plain there is nothing to be argued. What point in the anti-slavery creed would you have me argue? On what branch of the subject do the people of this country need light? Must I undertake to prove that the slave is a man? That point is conceded already. Nobody doubts it. The slaveholders themselves acknowledge it in the enactment of laws for their government. They acknowledge it when they punish disobedience on the part of the slave. There are seventy-two crimes in the state of Virginia, which, if committed by a black man, (no matter how ignorant he be,) subject him to the punishment of death; while only two of these same crimes will subject a white man to the like punishment. What is this but the acknowledgment that the slave is a moral, intellectual, and responsible being. The manhood of the slave is conceded. It is admitted in the fact that southern statute books are covered with enactments forbidding, under severe fines and penalties, the teaching of the slave to read or write. When you can point to any such laws, in reference to the beasts of the field, then I may consent to argue the manhood of the slave. When the dogs in your streets, when the fowls of the air, when the cattle on your hills, when the fish of the sea, and the reptiles that crawl, shall be unable to distinguish the slave from a brute, then will I argue with you that the slave is a man!

For the present, it is enough to affirm the equal manhood of the negro race. Is it not astonishing that, while we are plowing, planting, and reaping, using all kinds of mechanical tools, erecting houses, constructing bridges, building ships, working in metals of brass, iron, copper, silver, and gold; that, while we are reading, writing, and cyphering, acting as clerks, merchants, and secretaries, having among us lawyers, doctors, ministers, poets, authors, editors, orators, and teachers; that, while we are engaged in all manner of enterprises common to other

---

[4] *"I will . . . not excuse"*: From "To the Public," an editorial by William Lloyd Garrison in the inaugural issue of the *Liberator*, reprinted on pp. 265–67.

men—digging gold in California, capturing the whale in the Pacific, feeding sheep and cattle on the hillside, living, moving, acting, thinking, planning, living in families as husbands, wives, and children, and, above all, confessing and worshiping the christian's God, and looking hopefully for life and immortality beyond the grave,—we are called upon to prove that we are men!

Would you have me argue that man is entitled to liberty? that he is the rightful owner of his own body? You have already declared it. Must I argue the wrongfulness of slavery? Is that a question for republicans? Is it to be settled by the rules of logic and argumentation, as a matter beset with great difficulty, involving a doubtful application of the principle of justice, hard to be understood? How should I look today in the presence of Americans, dividing and subdividing a discourse, to show that men have a natural right to freedom, speaking of it relatively and positively, negatively and affirmatively? To do so, would be to make myself ridiculous, and to offer an insult to your understanding. There is not a man beneath the canopy of heaven that does not know that slavery is wrong *for him.*

What! am I to argue that it is wrong to make men brutes, to rob them of their liberty, to work them without wages, to keep them ignorant of their relations to their fellow-men, to beat them with sticks, to flay their flesh with the lash, to load their limbs with irons, to hunt them with dogs, to sell them at auction, to sunder their families, to knock out their teeth, to burn their flesh, to starve them into obedience and submission to their masters? Must I argue that a system, thus marked with blood and stained with pollution, is wrong? No; I will not. I have better employment for my time and strength than such arguments would imply.

What, then, remains to be argued? Is it that slavery is not divine; that God did not establish it; that our doctors of divinity are mistaken? There is blasphemy in the thought. That which is inhuman cannot be divine. Who can reason on such a proposition! They that can, may; I cannot. The time for such argument is past.

At a time like this, scorching irony, not convincing argument, is needed. Oh! had I the ability, and could I reach the nation's ear, I would to-day pour out a fiery stream of biting ridicule, blasting reproach, withering sarcasm, and stern rebuke. For it is not light that is needed, but fire; it is not the gentle shower, but thunder. We need the storm, the whirlwind, and the earthquake. The feeling of the nation must be quickened; the conscience of the nation must be roused; the propriety of the nation must be startled; the hypocrisy of the nation must be exposed; and its crimes against God and man must be proclaimed and denounced.

What to the American slave is your Fourth of July? I answer, a day that reveals to him, more than all other days in the year, the gross injustice and cruelty to which he is the constant victim. To him, your celebration is a sham; your boasted liberty, an unholy license; your national greatness, swelling vanity; your sounds of rejoicing are empty and heartless; your denunciations of tyrants, brass-fronted impudence; your shouts of liberty and equality, hollow mockery; your prayers and hymns, your sermons and thanksgivings, with all your religious parade and solemnity, are to him mere bombast, fraud, deception, impiety, and hypocrisy — a thin veil to cover up crimes which would disgrace a nation of savages. There is not a nation on the earth guilty of practices more shocking and bloody, than are the people of these United States, at this very hour.

Go where you may, search where you will, roam through all the monarchies and despotisms of the old world, travel through South America, search out every abuse, and when you have found the last, lay your facts by the side of the every-day practices of this nation, and you will say with me, that, for revolting barbarity and shameless hypocrisy, America reigns without a rival.

2

Thomas Jefferson and
Sally Hemings

The full title of William Wells Brown's first novel is *Clotel; or, The President's Daughter: A Narrative of Slave Life in the United States.* The title has a teasing vagueness, pressing the reader to ask: Who is the president and what is the possible relation of his daughter to slave life? But coupled with the epigraph from Thomas Jefferson's Declaration of Independence, the title isn't so vague after all, for there was a long history of rumors about Jefferson's involvement with the slave Sally Hemings. Once it becomes clear that Clotel is the name of a female slave, it would have been equally clear to a number of Brown's readers that he was drawing on that rumored history. As elaborated in the general Introduction, Jefferson first met Hemings in Paris in 1787, when she was fourteen and he was forty-four. There is considerable evidence that they had seven children together, and that Jefferson gave special privileges to both Hemings and their children. Jefferson's political enemies, particularly James Callender, who published details about Jefferson's supposed black family in 1802, saw Jefferson's relationship with Hemings as evidence that he had sullied his name through his connections with a black woman. In other words, Callender and his allies sought to use their knowledge to smear Jefferson as a man who had betrayed his race. But the fact is that many white Southern men had sexual relations with their female slaves, and in Jefferson's case he had become involved with a slave who was the daughter of his father-in-law and one of his slaves (which is to say, Jefferson had become

involved with his deceased wife's half-sister). Mastery afforded Southern slave owners an exploitative sexual power, and their practice of
treating some of their slave women as concubines became an unspoken
part of Southern white culture. Callender's efforts to publicize Jefferson's association with Hemings ultimately worked against his anti–
Jeffersonian politics, at least in the South, because he was regarded as
having violated the Southern code of silence.

Antislavery writers took a completely different perspective on the
matter. Whereas Callender scornfully presented Jefferson as enamored
of a black woman, writers ranging from Frances Trollope to James
McCune Smith saw him as a hypocrite and sexual predator. In a larger
sense, they saw U.S. culture itself, which Jefferson to some extent had
"fathered" through the Declaration, as hypocritical. What sort of culture celebrated human equality and then countenanced slavery and the
practice of rape? To be sure, most antislavery writers emphasized that
the masters' predatory sexual practices were simply another instance
of the evils of slavery. But there was also the possibility, as Brown
suggests in his account of black-white sexual relations in *Clotel*, that
there could be more human and affectionate aspects to these relations
as well. The sarcasm and anger that can be found in abolitionists'
accounts of Jefferson as a father of slaves spoke to their sense that Jefferson took advantage of his power and to their equally strong sense
that he could have treated his black offspring as a father would treat
his children. Jefferson never refuted the racial condescension of his
1787 *Notes*, and by the 1820s he had become adamant in his insis-
tence on the Southern states' rights to sustain the institution of slavery.
Still, at his death he liberated his slave children, which reveals that he
hardly saw slavery as a positive good.

For many proslavery writers, slavery was fundamentally grounded
in ideas of racial difference and white supremacy. But the Jefferson-
Hemings relationship exposes a crucial hole in the proslavery argument: The more prevalent are black-white sexual relations, the more
difficult it becomes to insist upon racial difference. Throughout *Clotel*,
Brown emphasizes that the South is replete with "white" slaves—
those who are white to the eye because of the history over many generations of white masters forcing themselves sexually on slave women.
With such racial and genealogical entanglement, how could anyone be
certain of his or her racial identity? And what is race anyway when
there are gradations of color that unfix stable notions of white and
black? In chapter XIV of *Clotel*, "A Free Woman Reduced to Slavery,"
Brown shows that it is entirely possible for a white woman to be
remanded as a slave because of the uncertainty about connections

between color and race. In the overall novel, which concludes with light-complected "blacks" who are able to pass, Brown underscores the contradictions and illogic of race itself through the long genealogical history based on Jefferson's relationship with the fictional slave Currer, who is the mother and grandmother of the main black female characters of the novel. By drawing on the actual history of Jefferson and Hemings, and coupling that history with the Declaration, Brown suggests that all Americans are in some ways Jefferson's children, and that slavery ultimately has no basis in blood, race, or the nation's founding Revolutionary document.

This chapter presents six selections on Jefferson and Hemings (or an unnamed slave woman), beginning with the charges leveled by Callender in 1802 and then turning to accounts by Frances Trollope and various writers in the abolitionist press. Brown would have been familiar with some of these texts and certainly with the hidden history that these writings were bringing into view. In the concluding post-*Clotel* selection from 1873, Madison Hemings, the son of Jefferson and Hemings, describes in a newspaper interview what it was like to grow up with Jefferson as both his owner and father. Most twentieth-century historians dismissed the possibility that Jefferson could have been the father of Hemings or any other slave, but in 1997, even before the well-publicized DNA evidence pointing to Jefferson's paternity, the historian Annette Gordon-Reed made a compelling case in *Thomas Jefferson and Sally Hemings* for taking seriously the black oral history of that relationship. In Madison Hemings's narrative, we see how his mother was able to exert some power and control over Jefferson, even as Jefferson the slave master clearly differentiated between his white and black children. Brown's depiction of interracial sexual relations in *Clotel* captures the cruelties and sheer irrationality of a system based on the "science" of race that sanctions white patriarchal mastery and denies all possibilities of love across the color line.

JAMES CALLENDER

From *The President, Again*

Born in Scotland, James Thomas Callender (1758–1803) emigrated to the United States in 1793 after British authorities declared him a political outlaw for publishing a pamphlet calling for Scottish independence. His egalitarian sentiments drew him to the Jeffersonian Republicans, and he became known for his fiery attacks on John Adams and other Federalists. In 1797 he met Thomas Jefferson, who gave him two hundred dollars to support his anti-Federalist journalism. Callender's 1799 attack on President Adams, *The Prospect before Us*, may have contributed to Jefferson's victory in the presidential election of 1800, but it also landed Callender in jail for nine months under the terms of the Alien and Sedition Acts. Callender served his jail time in Richmond, Virginia, and he also paid a two hundred dollar fine. Upon his release in 1801, he looked to Jefferson for a federal patronage job and financial remuneration. The money came slowly and he never got the job he wanted. Enraged at Jefferson, he sought to use his editor's position at the *Richmond Recorder* to gain some revenge on the president, and in September 1802 published the first of several articles asserting that Jefferson had sexual relations (and children) with his slave Sally Hemings. Callender, who hated African Americans, got some of his facts wrong. Hemings sailed to France in 1787 with Jefferson's daughter Mary; Jefferson himself had been in Paris since 1784 as U.S. ambassador to France. The slave Callender calls "TOM" wasn't Jefferson and Hemings's child and perhaps was invented by Callender in order mockingly to underscore that there were white and black Toms at Monticello. Overall, though, Callender got most of his facts right, but he miscalculated his audience. Southerners in particular thought that Jefferson acted with propriety toward his slaves, and believed that interracial sexual relations at plantations did not need to be openly acknowledged. Callender died in July 1803 when, during a night of drinking, he fell into Richmond's James River and drowned; but his charges against Jefferson lived on in abolitionist discourse. The text of this excerpt is from the 1 September 1802 issue of the *Richmond Recorder*.

It is well known that the man, *whom it delighteth the people to honor*, keeps, and for many years past has kept, as his concubine, one of his own slaves. Her name is SALLY. The name of her eldest son is TOM. His features are said to bear a striking although sable resemblance to those of the president himself. The boy is ten or twelve years of age. His mother went to France in the same vessel with Mr. Jefferson and his two daughters. The delicacy of this arrangement must strike every person of common sensibility. What a sublime pattern for an American ambassador to place before the eyes of two young ladies!

If the reader does not feel himself *disposed to pause* we beg leave to proceed. Some years ago, this story had once or twice been hinted at in

Rind's Federalist.[1] At that time, we believed the surmise to be an absolute calumny. One reason for thinking so was this. A vast body of people wished to debar Mr. Jefferson from the presidency. The *establishment of this* SINGLE FACT would have rendered his election impossible. We reasoned thus; that if the allegation had been true, it was sure to have been ascertained and advertised by his enemies, in every corner of the continent. The suppression of so decisive an enquiry serves to shew[2] that the common sense of the federal party was overruled by divine providence. It was the predestination of the supreme being that they should be turned out; that they should be expelled from office by the *popularity* of a character, which, at that instant, was lying fettered and gagged, consumed and extinguished at their feet! . . .

By this wench Sally, our president has had several children. There is not an individual in the neighbourhood of Charlottesville who does not believe the story; and not a few who know it.

If Duane[3] sees this account, he will not prate any more about the treaty between Mr. Adams and Toussaint.[4] Behold the favorite, the first born of republicanism! the pinnacle of all that is good and great! in the open consummation of an act which tends to subvert the policy, the happiness, and even the existence of this country!

'Tis supposed that, at the time when Mr. Jefferson wrote so smartly concerning negroes, when he endeavored much to belittle the African race,[5] he had no expectation that the chief magistrate of the United States was to be the ringleader in shewing that his opinion was erroneous; or that he should chuse an African stock whereupon he was to engraft his own descendants. . . .

---

[1] *Rind's Federalist*: In June 1800, William Rind, the editor of the *Virginia Federalist*, had reported that he had "damning proofs" of Jefferson's "depravity," but he never offered specifics. For an excellent overview, see Joshua D. Rothman, "James Callender and Social Knowledge of Interracial Sex in Antebellum Virginia," in *Sally Hemings & Thomas Jefferson: History, Memory, and Civic Culture*, ed. Jan Ellen Lewis and Peter S. Onuf (Charlottesville: University Press of Virginia, 1999), 87–113.

[2] *shew*: show; demonstrate.

[3] *Duane*: William Duane (1760–1835), editor of the Jeffersonian newspaper *The Aurora*. Jefferson came to Duane's defense when he was brought to trial under the Alien and Sedition Acts, and charges were dismissed.

[4] *Mr. Adams and Toussaint*: John Adams (1735–1826), was the second president of the United States (1796–1801); the former slave Toussaint L'Ouverture (c.1744–1803) was a key leader of the Haitian Revolution (1791–1804). (For more on Toussaint, see the selection from Brown's *St. Domingo: Its Revolutions and Its Patriots* [pp. 387–88 in this volume].) During his presidency, Adams was willing to establish diplomatic relations with the black revolutionaries. In 1801, Jefferson ended those diplomatic ties.

[5] *Mr. Jefferson . . . belittle the African race*: A reference to Jefferson's *Notes on the State of Virginia*; see the selections in this edition.

If the friends of Mr. Jefferson are convinced of *his* innocence, *they* will make an appeal of the same sort.[6] If they rest in silence, or if they content themselves with resting upon a *general denial*, they cannot hope for credit. The allegation is of a nature too *black* to be suffered to remain in suspence. We should be glad to hear of its refutation. We give it to the world under the firmest belief that such a refutation *never can be made*. The AFRICAN VENUS[7] is said to officiate, as housekeeper at Monticello. When Mr. Jefferson has read this article, he will find leisure to estimate how much has been lost or gained by so many attacks upon

J. T. CALLENDER

[6] *appeal of the same sort*: In 1797, Callender had exposed an affair between Federalist secretary of treasury Alexander Hamilton (1755–1804) and a married woman, Maria Reynolds (1768–1832), publicly rebutting Hamilton's charges that he had got his facts wrong.

[7] *Venus*: Roman goddess of love. Hemings worked as a house slave at Monticello.

"A Philosophic Cock," by the Federalist James Akin (1773–1846), whose print satirizing Jefferson's relationship with Sally Hemings appeared in 1804. Courtesy American Antiquarian Society.

FRANCES TROLLOPE

From *Domestic Manners of the Americans*

In 1827 the English writer Frances Trollope (1780–1863) traveled from England to America with the intention of setting up a department store in Cincinnati. She also wanted to participate in the racially integrated socialist community founded at Nashoba, Tennessee, by her Scottish-born friend Frances Wright. Unsuccessful in her commercial ventures, though impressed by Wright's radical antislavery efforts, Trollope returned to England three years later and soon afterward published her acerbic, widely read *Domestic Manners of the Americans* (London: Whittaker, Treacher, & Co., 1832), from which this selection about Jefferson is taken. (Some twenty years later, her son Anthony Trollope would emerge as an internationally celebrated novelist.) In his 1839 *A Diary in America, with Remarks on Its Institutions*, a book William Wells Brown probably read, the English novelist Captain Frederick Marryat echoed Trollope's (and others') charges against Jefferson.

Few names are held in higher estimation in America than that of Jefferson; it is the touchstone of the democratic party, and all seem to agree that he was one of the greatest of men; yet I have heard his name coupled with deeds which would make the sons of Europe shudder. The facts I allude to are spoken openly by all, not whispered privately by a few; and in a country where religion is the tea-table talk, and its strict observance a fashionable distinction, these facts are recorded and listened to without horror, nay, without emotion.

Mr. Jefferson is said to have been the father of children by almost all his numerous gang of female slaves. These wretched offspring were also the lawful slaves of their father, and worked in his house and plantations as such; in particular, it is recorded that it was his especial pleasure to be waited upon by them at table, and the hospitable orgies for which his Monticello[1] was so celebrated, were incomplete, unless the goblet he quaffed were tendered by the trembling hand of his own slavish offspring.

---

[1] *Monticello*: Located near Charlottesville, Virginia, the 640-acre estate of Monticello was Jefferson's home for over fifty years. He designed the mansion, which was built with the assistance of some of his slaves.

I once heard it stated by a democratical adorer of this great man, that when, as it sometimes happened, his children by Quadroon slaves were white enough to escape suspicion of their origin, he did not pursue them if they attempted to escape, saying laughingly, "Let the rogues get off, if they can; I will not hinder them." This was stated in a large party, as a proof of his kind and noble nature, and was received by all with approving smiles.

If I know any thing of right or wrong, if virtue and vice be indeed something more than words, then was this great American an unprincipled tyrant and most heartless libertine.

WILLIAM GOODELL

Sale of a Daughter of Tho's Jefferson

Though this selection consists almost entirely of a letter from the obscure New York abolitionist Dr. Gaylord on his conversation with the equally obscure Missouri slavery apologist Otis Reynolds, the piece is ultimately the work of the well-known New York abolitionist William Goodell (1792–1878). Goodell helped to found the American Anti-Slavery Society in 1833, and went on to edit a number of antislavery newspapers, including the *Emancipator*, the *Friend of Man*, and the *Radical Abolitionist*. During the 1840s he championed "Come-Outerism," a movement encouraging abolitionists to withdraw from churches that supported or even remained neutral on slavery. Among his most important books are *Views on American Constitutional Law in Its Bearing on American Slavery* (1844) and *Slavery and Anti-Slavery* (1852). Goodell saw the rumors about Jefferson's sexual involvement with his slaves as performing useful ideological critique; he published Gaylord's account of his putative conversation about Jefferson in the 22 August 1838 issue of his Utica newspaper, *Friend of Man*. The letter, with Goodell's commentary, was reprinted in the 21 September 1838 *Liberator*, which is the source of the text below.

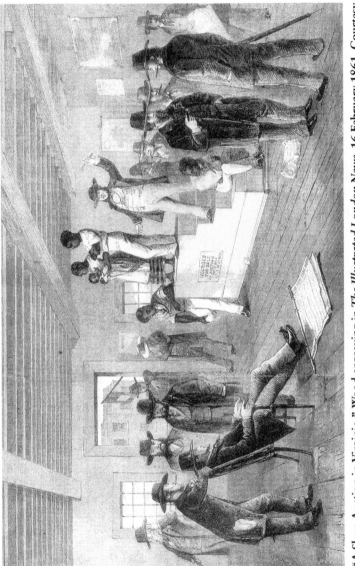

"A Slave Auction in Virginia." Wood engraving in *The Illustrated London News*, 16 February 1861. Courtesy of the Photographs and Prints Division, Schomburg Center for Research in Black Culture, The New York Public Library, Astor, Lennox and Tilden Foundations.

[A SCENE AT NEW ORLEANS]
Sale of a Daughter of Tho's Jefferson.
'Going for a Thousand Dollars! Who Bids?
'Going? going! gone! Who's the buyer?'

The following fact was related in our hearing, by the writer, Dr. GAYLORD, of Sodus,[1] at the Wayne County Anti-Slavery Society's meeting, at Palmyra,[2] last June. At our request, he has now furnished it for publication. Read it, fellow citizens, and ponder. If a daughter of THOMAS JEFFERSON may be sold at auction, what security can you, or any of us, have, that *our* daughters may not, one day, be sold in the same manner? COLOR is NO PROTECTION. *'Bleached or unbleached!'* says Gov. M'Duffie![3] 'CLEAR WHITE *complexion'* — say the slave advertisements!

From the *Friend of Man.*

MR. GOODELL, — My apology for not furnishing you with an earlier communication, in regard to the following fact, must be found in my having been absent to the 'far West,' for several weeks, whence I have just returned.

Gladly, Mr. Editor, would I draw the mantle of oblivion over a transaction disclosing so dark a spot on the moral escutcheon of the man, whose name stands enrolled so high on the archives of our proud republic, did I not believe, that like the faithful delineations on our sacred pages, of the sin of David,[4] and other eminently great men, it should descend on record, as a solemn beacon, not only to excite disgust and warning against the crime, but also to awaken the lovers of our country, of morality, humanity, and religion, to see the *natural results* connected with the *'practical operations'* of slavery — and hoping, also, that it may assist in prostrating the power of lawless passion, and legalized cruelty; and in preventing similar scenes of disgrace from being either enacted or tolerated, by high or low, as they frequently are, to the burning shame of our beloved country.

---

[1] *Sodus:* A city in northern New York.

[2] *Palmyra:* A town in northern New York.

[3] *Gov. M'Duffie:* The South Carolina proslavery politician George McDuffie (1790–1851) served as congressman (1821–34), governor (1834–35), and senator (1842–46).

[4] *the sin of David:* A reference to David's sexual relationship with Bathsheba; see 2 Samuel 11.1–12.

In a recent conversation with Mr. OTIS REYNOLDS, a gentleman from *St. Louis, Missouri,* himself a practical, as well as theoretical supporter of slavery, in our discussion of the subject, Mr. Reynolds endeavored to find an apology for the 'domestic institution' of the South, by assuming, as a fact, the alleged inferiority of the colored race.

I replied, that it was currently reported here, that 'the best blood of Virginia, flowed in the veins of the slaves;' and the argument therefore could have no force, in regard to the amalgamated portion of the slaves. Said he, with much emphasis,

'That's true; I saw myself, the DAUGHTER of THOMAS JEFFERSON SOLD in New Orleans, for ONE THOUSAND DOLLARS.'

What a fact for the contemplation of this free republic!! and what a comment on our *professions* of love of liberty, and practice of slavery!!!

The Daughter of the President of the United States, the boasted land of Freedom, sold into interminable bondage!!! Look at it, citizens of our free republic! Here is no violation of law—you have the natural, legalized, common working of the system.

I do not wonder that Jefferson said, 'I tremble for my country when I remember that God is just, and that his justice cannot sleep forever.'[5] If slavery has so far annihilated parental and kindred ties, that the natural offspring of our highest officers of government, are sold under the hammer of the auctioneer, and driven under the lash of unfeeling tyrants,

> 'With stripes that mercy, with a bleeding heart,
> Weeps when she sees inflicted on a beast,'[6]

or turned over to mercenary lust of involuntary prostitution—let it be sounded longer and louder, through the length and breadth of the land, until a virtuous indignation shall kindle in every American bosom, and the guilty apologists and participators of such deeds of infamy, shall hide their heads in merited shame and contempt.

The authenticity of the above fact, rests on the sober testimony of a southern man, whose credibility is unquestioned, in the presence of some respectable merchants of our village, whose names can be given, if necessary; and as it may be highly important to the full development

---

[5] *I tremble ... forever:* From Jefferson's *Notes on the State of Virginia;* see p. 250.

[6] *With stripes ... inflicted on a beast:* From William Cowper (1731–1800), *The Task* (1784).

of a system, in which amalgamation, and an utter disregard to the claims of consanguinity and domestic ties, are perfectly commonplace, it is my deliberate opinion, that such astounding facts should be spread before the community, to awaken them to the repulsive workings of that system of wrongs and wretchedness, which has so long been the foulest blot on the fair fame of our republic.

Very respectfully, yours,
LEVI GAYLORD.

Sodus, August 13, 1838.

Jefferson's Daughter

"Jefferson's Daughter," along with the epigraph from the *London Morning Chronicle* on Jefferson's alleged trafficking of his alleged slave daughter, first appeared in the July 1839 issue of *Tait's Edinburgh Magazine.* The "American Newspaper" mentioned in the epigraph was in all probability the *Liberator*, which would suggest that Levi Gaylord's 1838 letter to William Goodell, printed above, may well have inspired the poem. A slightly different version of "Jefferson's Daughter" appeared in the 26 May 1848 issue of the *Liberator*, and a virtually identical version of that poem appeared in William Wells Brown's antislavery songbook, *The Anti-Slavery Harp: A Collection of Songs for Anti-Slavery Meetings. Compiled by William W. Brown, A Fugitive Slave* (Boston: Bela Marsh, 1848), which is the source of the selection below. Convinced that the communal singing of songs at antislavery meetings would help to advance the cause, Brown compiled a songbook that included Garrison's "I Am an Abolitionist," John Greenleaf Whittier's "The Yankee Girl," James Russell Lowell's "Stanzas on Freedom," and the anonymous "The Blind Slave Boy." "Jefferson's Daughter" anticipates the concerns about genealogy and ideology that would come to inform Brown's novel of "The President's Daughter."

"It is asserted, on the authority of an American Newspaper, that the daughter of Thomas Jefferson, late President of the United States, was sold at New Orleans for $1,000."

—Morning Chronicle

Can the blood that, at Lexington,[1] poured o'er the plain,
    When the sons warred with tyrants their rights to uphold,
Can the tide of Niagara wipe out the stain?
    No! Jefferson's child has been bartered for gold!

Do you boast of your freedom? Peace, babblers — be still;
    Prate[2] not of the goddess who scarce deigns to hear;
Have ye power to unbind?   Are ye wanting in will?
    Must the groans of your bondman still torture the ear?

The daughter of Jefferson sold for a slave!
    The child of a freeman for dollars and francs!
The roar of applause, when your orators rave,
    Is lost in the sound of her chain, as it clanks.

Peace, then, ye blasphemers of Liberty's name!
    Though red was the blood by your forefathers spilt,
Still redder your cheeks should be mantled with shame,
    Till the spirit of freedom shall cancel the guilt.

But the brand of the slave is the tint of his skin,
    Though his heart may beat loyal and true underneath;
While the soul of the tyrant is rotten within,
    And his white the mere cloak to the blackness of death.

Are ye deaf to the plaints that each moment arise?
    Is it thus ye forget the mild precepts of Penn,[3] —
Unheeding the clamor that "maddens the skies,"
    As ye trample the rights of your dark fellow-men?

When the incense that glows before Liberty's shrine,
    Is unmixed with the blood of the galled and oppressed, —
O, then, and then only, the boast may be thine,
    That the stripes and stars wave o'er a land of the blest.

---

[1] *Lexington*: On 19 April 1775, Lexington, Massachusetts, was the site of the first battle of the American Revolution.

[2] *Prate*: To babble or talk pointlessly.

[3] *Penn*: William Penn (1644–1718) was an English Quaker and the founder of Pennsylvania. The Quakers were strongly opposed to the institution of slavery.

From Letter to *Frederick Douglass' Paper*

A regular contributor to *Frederick Douglass' Paper* during the 1850s, James McCune Smith (1813–1865) was one of the most prominent black intellectuals and abolitionists of the period. The son of former slaves, Smith, who was born and educated in New York City, enrolled in Glasgow University in 1832 after he was denied entry to American colleges. By 1837 he had received three degrees, including a doctorate of medicine, whereupon he returned to New York City and established a successful medical and pharmacy practice. Committed to political abolitionism, he edited and contributed to a number of black newspapers and magazines, published several important pamphlets, including *The Destiny of the People of Color* (1843), wrote the introduction to Douglass's *My Bondage and My Freedom* (1855), and participated in black conventions and a number of other abolitionist and antiracist initiatives. Like Douglass in the 1850s, Smith regarded the Constitution as an antislavery document, and thus he was particularly troubled by the contradictions he perceived at the heart of Jefferson's writings and social practices. Published under the pseudonym "Communipaw," Smith's Letter, from which these passages on Jefferson and slavery are drawn, appeared in the 25 March 1852 issue of *Frederick Douglass' Paper.*

. . . [I]t is well known that Jefferson contradicted his philosophy of negro hate, by seeking the dalliance of black women as often as he could, and by leaving so many descendants of mixed blood, that they are to be found as widely scattered as his own writings throughout the world. One at least, a grand daughter, is a shouting Methodist, in Liberia.[1] I have heard, from an eye witness, that on more than one occasion, when the sage of Monticello left that retreat, for the Presidential abode, at Washington, there would be on the top of the same coach, a yellow boy of his own begetting, "running away." And when told that one of his slaves was going off without leave, Jefferson said, well! let

---

[1] *Liberia:* At the time a colony in West Africa governed in large part by agents and representatives of the American Colonization Society, whose goal was to ship free African Americans to Africa.

him go, his right is as good as his father's! And, somehow, *that* boy would get a doceur[2] before the "parting of the ways."

Ah me! The pride of old Virginia! I might exclaim of it as Black Dan[3] did of our Republic, *Epese, Epese.* "Thou hast fallen, thou hast fallen!" These crocus colored products of unphilosophical lust, are now reared, and penned up, and branded, and sold, by slaveholding fathers in Old Dominion,[4] who go to Presbyterian and Methodist churches, and to the altars of Episcopacy, and drink the "blood which Christ shed for all;" and thank God that they are not heathen Circassians[5] who sell their daughters as prostitutes to *Mahommedan*[6] [*sic*], not *Christian*, lust!

[2] *doceur*: A gratuity or small amount of money.
[3] *Black Dan*: A reference to Daniel Webster; see *Clotel*, p. 173, note 18.
[4] *Old Dominion*: Virginia.
[5] *Circassians*: Natives of Circassia, a region in Europe bordering the Black Sea.
[6] *Mahommedan*: Usually *Mahammadan*; a reference to the Islamic followers of Muhammed (570–632).

MADISON HEMINGS

From *Life among the Lowly*

James Madison Hemings (1805–1877) was in all likelihood Thomas Jefferson and Sally Hemings's sixth child. His life story, as told to a reporter in 1873, was published in the 13 March 1873 issue of Ohio's *Pike County Republican*, the source of the excerpt below. Much of what Hemings recounts in his narrative suggests the complicated genealogical entanglements of slavery in eighteenth-century Virginia. Jefferson met his wife, Martha Wayles Jefferson (1748–1782), at the nearby slave plantation owned by her father, John Wayles (1715–1773), who was also the father of the slave Sally Hemings. Upon Wayles's death, Jefferson inherited Sally Hemings and her mother, the slave Elizabeth Hemings (1735–1807). Jefferson and Martha had two children who survived into adulthood, Martha (1772–1836) and Maria (1778–1804). Several years after his wife's death at the age of thirty-four, Jefferson became U.S. minister to France; and in 1787, he summoned Maria to join him in Paris. Sally Hemings, who was only fourteen at the time, accompanied her on the transatlantic voyage from Virginia to England, and then onward to Paris. As Madison Hemings suggests, after Sally Hemings and Jefferson became sexually involved, it was Sally herself who set the conditions for her return to Virginia.

Thos. Jefferson was a visitor at the "great house" of John Wales [*sic*], who had children about his own age. He formed the acquaintance of his daughter Martha (I believe that was her name, though I am not positively sure,) and an intimacy sprang up between them which ripened into love, and they were married. They afterwards went to live at his country seat, Monticello, and in course of time had born to them a daughter, whom they named Martha. About the time she was born my mother, the second daughter of John Wales and Elizabeth Hemings was born. On the death of John Wales, my grandmother, his concubine, and her children by him fell to Martha, Thomas Jefferson's wife, and consequently became the property of Thomas Jefferson, who in the course of time became famous, and was appointed minister to France during our revolutionary troubles, or soon after independence was gained. About the time of the appointment and before he was ready to leave the country his wife died, and as soon after her interment as he could attend to and arrange his domestic affairs in accordance with the changed circumstances of his family in consequence of this misfortune (I think not more than three weeks thereafter) he left for France, taking his eldest daughter with him. He had had sons born to him, but they died in early infancy,[1] so he then had but two children—Martha and Maria. The latter was left at home, but was afterwards ordered to follow him to France. She was three years or so younger than Martha. My mother accompanied her as her body servant. When Mr. Jefferson went to France Martha was a young woman grown, my mother was about her age, and Maria was just budding into womanhood. Their stay (my mother and Maria's) was about eighteen months. But during that time my mother became Mr. Jefferson's concubine, and when he was called home she was *enceinte*[2] by him. He desired to bring my mother back to Virginia with him but she demurred. She was just beginning to understand the French language well, and in France she was free, while if she returned to Virginia she would be re-enslaved. So she refused to return with him. To induce her to do so he promised her extraordinary privileges, and made a solemn pledge that her children should be freed at the age of twenty-one years.[3] In consequence of his promise, on which she implicitly relied,

---

[1] *died in early infancy*: Four of Thomas and Martha Jefferson's children died in infancy: Jane (1774–1775), an unnamed son who was born and died in 1777, Lucy Elizabeth (1780–1781), and a second Lucy Elizabeth (1782–1784).

[2] *enceinte*: pregnant (French).

[3] *should be freed at the age of twenty-one years*: Jefferson either freed at his death or allowed to escape all of the children he had with Sally Hemings.

she returned with him to Virginia. Soon after their arrival, she gave birth to a child, of whom Thomas Jefferson was the father.[4] It lived but a short time. She gave birth to four others, and Jefferson was the father of all of them. Their names were Beverly, Harriet, Madison (myself), and Eston—three sons and one daughter.[5] We all became free agreeably to the treaty entered into by our parents before we were born. We all married and have raised families.

. . . I was named Madison by the wife of James Madison,[6] who was afterwards President of the United States. Mrs. Madison happened to be at Monticello at the time of my birth, and begged the privilege of naming me, promising my mother a fine present for the honor. She consented, and Mrs. Madison dubbed me by the name I now acknowledge, but like many promises of white folks to the slaves she never gave my mother anything. I was born at my father's seat of Monticello, in Albermarle county, Va., near Charlottesville, on the 19th day of January, 1805. My very earliest recollections are of my grandmother Elizabeth Hemings. That was when I was about three years old. She was sick and upon her death bed. I was eating a piece of bread and asked her if she would have some. She replied: "No, granny don't want bread any more." She shortly afterwards breathed her last. I have only a faint recollection of her.

Of my father, Thomas Jefferson, I knew more of his domestic than his public life during his life time. It is only since his death that I have learned much of the latter, except that he was considered as a foremost man in the land, and held many important trusts, including that of President. I learned to read by inducing the white children to teach me the letters and something more; what else I know of books I have picked up here and there till now I can read and write. I was almost 21½ years of age when my father died, on 4th of July, 1826. About his own home he was the quietest of men. He was hardly ever known to get angry, though sometimes he was irritated when matters went wrong, but even then he hardly ever allowed himself to be made unhappy any

---

[4] *of whom Thomas Jefferson was the father*: The unnamed child was born and died in 1790.

[5] *three sons and one daughter*: William Beverly Hemings (1798–?), Harriet Hemings (1801–?), and Thomas Eston Hemings (1808–1856). William Beverly and Harriet both left Monticello in 1822 and disappeared from the historical record. The evidence suggests that Jefferson and Hemings had seven children, three of whom died in infancy.

[6] *James Madison*: Jefferson's Virginian friend James Madison (1751–1836) was the fourth president of the United States (1808–1817). He was married to Dolley Madison (1768–1849).

great length of time. Unlike Washington he had but little taste or care for agricultural pursuits. He left matters pertaining to his plantations mostly with his stewards and overseers. He always had mechanics at work for him, such as carpenters, blacksmiths, shoemakers, coopers, &c. It was his mechanics he seemed mostly to direct, and in their operations he took great interest. Almost every day of his latter years he might have been seen among them. He occupied much of the time in his office engaged in correspondence and reading and writing. His general temperament was smooth and even; he was very undemonstrative. He was uniformly kind to all about him. He was not in the habit of showing partiality or fatherly affection to us children. We were the only children of his by a slave woman. He was affectionate toward his white grandchildren, of whom he had fourteen, twelve of whom lived to manhood and womanhood.

"All These Combined Have Made Up My Story"
Source Texts about Slavery and Race

What is a "source" of a literary text? The answer can initially seem fairly straightforward. To take the example of a novel published two years before *Clotel*: one might initially respond that the source of Herman Melville's *Moby-Dick* (1851), an account of the pursuit of a mythically powerful white whale, is J. N. Reynolds's "Mocha Dick," an account of the pursuit of a mythically powerful white whale that Melville read in the May 1839 issue of the *Knickerbocker* magazine. But not only are there numerous other accounts of whale pursuits that Melville may have read and borrowed from, there are also numerous aspects of Melville's complex text that owe nothing to whaling stories. The portrayal of Captain Ahab raging in the stormy seas, finding solace only in the company of the black cabin boy Pip, owes much to Shakespeare's portrayal of King Lear raging in a storm, finding solace only in the company of the Fool. Melville's conception of the blasphemous Ahab also clearly draws on Milton's conception of the blasphemous Satan in *Paradise Lost*; the numerous comic descriptions of human and whale bodies owe much to the bawdy writings of François Rabelais and Jonathan Swift; and one could go on and on tracing Melville's indebtedness to such key literary sources as Dante's *Inferno*, Hawthorne's short fiction, Dickens's novels, and the Bible. Critics have also identified a different set of sources for Melville's great novel: contemporaneous discourses that have traditionally been viewed as non- or extraliterary, such as debates on race, gender, religion, economics, politics, and sexuality printed in books, magazines, and newspapers. The presentation of the developing friendship between Ishmael and the tattooed South Sea islander Queequeg, for example, draws heavily on debates of the 1840s and early 1850s on colonialism, sexuality, race, and religion. Moreover, the white whale itself would appear to be conceived not only in relation to folk accounts of mighty whales but also in relation to images of a white United States championed in very different ways by John C. Calhoun and Daniel Webster. And literary and "nonliterary" printed materials do not completely cover the range of Melville's sources, for Melville himself went to sea and spent some time on a whaler; surely his life experiences, and those of the sailors he talked to, are also important sources for *Moby-Dick*. Ultimately, when the question of textual origins and sources is pushed to its limits, one might quickly come to the semiparanoiac conclusion of Edgar Allan Poe, who became convinced of the impossibility, or near impossibility, of writing an "original" text, and consequently became obsessed with the problem of plagiarism, accusing Henry Wadsworth Longfellow, Nathaniel Hawthorne, and many others of lifting from his own and other works.

But with the exception of those unhappy instances when a writer attempts to pass off another's work as his or her own, authors do not simply "lift" texts; they work revisionary transformations, making something new from their sources. Appropriation and revision are part of an author's ongoing dialogue with the present and the past; arguably, these practices are central aspects of what could be termed authorial power. For instance, Melville does not simply draw on Shakespeare's *King Lear*; he aggressively revises this canonical text by encouraging his readers to see royalty and grandeur both in the strivings of an American sea captain and in the existential despair of a black cabin boy. From a somewhat different perspective, Melville's sympathetic portrayals of the black Pip, the Native American Tashtego, and the South Sea islander Queequeg, which drew on his reading of contemporaneous writings on race, ultimately pose a subtle though aggressive challenge to the white supremacist ideologies that inform much of the racial writing of the period.

Though William Wells Brown similarly poses an aggressive challenge to racist ideologies, when he discusses his use of sources in the "Conclusion" to *Clotel*, he presents himself as simply a collector of texts and testimonials. Like Harriet Beecher Stowe in her 1853 *Key to Uncle Tom's Cabin*, he wants to underscore the fact that his antislavery novel is based on truth: the terrible dehumanizing practices of slavery that he hopes his novel will help to abolish. Because of the urgent political purposes of his novel, and because he feels a strong sense of community with other antislavery writers, he chooses to celebrate, rather than to be embarrassed by, his indebtedness to a range of sources, particularly those that attack slavery. He acknowledges autobiographical sources ("I have personally participated in many of those scenes"), sources in the oral testimonies of "those who, like myself, have run away from the land of bondage," and sources in printed texts that, in some cases, he lifted verbatim from "American Abolitionist journals." He expresses his particular indebtedness to Lydia Maria Child "for part of a short story," "The Quadroons," which by twentieth-century standards he could be accused of having plagiarized. Referring to the wide range of antislavery source materials that helped him to create *Clotel*, Brown states: "All these combined have made up my story" (p. 226 in this volume).

On the basis of Brown's own discussion of his relation to his source materials, we might initially think of him as a kind of documentary historian who combines fact and fiction to reveal the evils of slavery. In this sense there would seem to be a crucial difference in the ways Melville and Brown use their sources. Melville revises his source materials by reconceiving them; Brown presents his source materials pretty much as he found them.

Or does he? For Brown "found" his materials in a white supremacist culture in which slavery was the law of the land; he "combined" those materials in a black-authored novel whose primary purpose is simultaneously to contest and provide a fuller historical understanding of that racist culture. Central to Brown's revisionary relation to his sources, then, is a massive, complex, often brilliant effort to recontextualize his source materials, using techniques of pastiche (a typically ironic rearticulation of cultural discourses) and bricolage (a reassembling of "found" documents) to raise questions about how meanings are produced in a white racist culture, and ultimately to suggest new ways of reading that culture.

In his "Conclusion," it should be emphasized, Brown mentions only a few of the sources that he "combined" in *Clotel*. In addition to drawing on antislavery writings, he also made considerable use of proslavery texts and other contemporaneous materials—speeches on slavery by Northern and Southern politicians, sermons by proslavery ministers, reports about slavery from Southern newspapers, writings on race by "scientific" racialists, tracts by temperance advocates and other reformers, proslavery and antislavery fictions, slave narratives, and numerous other writings ranging from the Declaration of Independence to Andrew Jackson's proclamations to the free people of color. Brown's use of all these sources prompts one to ask a key interpretive question: What is the difference, say, between reading a proslavery sermon as it initially appeared in a book of sermons for masters to read to their slaves, and then reading it again, with only minor variations, as spoken by a fictional character in an antislavery novel? Nothing much has changed in the sermon, but then again, everything has changed. Or what happens to the iconic image of Thomas Jefferson when rumors of his consortings with at least one of his slave women, allegations that were pretty much dismissed in white culture, are transported into a black-authored novel where the truth of these assertions is presented as a given? What happens to the author of the Declaration of Independence when he is viewed, however obliquely, in the light of a legacy of slavery and miscegenation? And perhaps most important, what happens to the Declaration of Independence when it is regularly alluded to in a novel that traces the careers of Jefferson's enslaved "black" children?

Clearly, Brown's every act of textual appropriation becomes an act of cultural revisioning. He does not simply "combine" sources; he creates something new, and in the process of unsettling established truths and hierarchies he encourages his readers, then and now, to participate in a complex process of ideological critique. In this respect it is worth emphasizing another important difference between Melville's and Brown's conception of their relationship to their sources. In revising the works of such authors as Shakespeare and Milton, for example, Melville revises a literary and cultural tradition that he regards relatively unproblematically as his own. Brown, as an African American author, necessarily has a very different relation to the sources he draws on, as most of those sources come from a culture and a tradition that regard him as an outsider. Working with the texts that constitute the culture that had enslaved him, Brown, particularly in his allusions to Jefferson, produces what was referred to in the general Introduction as a genealogical fiction (p. 14), an historical novel that investigates and ultimately attempts to desacralize the political, cultural, and ideological origins of the United States.

In his own way, then, Brown, like Melville, assumes a highly aggressive relation to his sources, wresting them from their place in white supremacist culture and repositioning them in a genealogical fiction that works to demonumentalize the Founding Fathers and ultimately to raise large questions about the nation's putative commitment to liberty and freedom for all. As will become apparent by looking at some of Brown's acknowledged source materials in relation to his actual use of them, when Brown appropriates textual sources, he really does appropriate them, at times making use of much of the language of the original text. Rather than portraying himself as the creator of a discrete, transcendent work, however, Brown makes it clear in *Clotel*'s final chapter that he sees himself as in dialogue with a range of texts and sources. Unlike Poe, who strives for authorial originality, he conceives of revision (and in a sense plagiary) as fundamental to authorship itself.

Breaking down the perceived dichotomy between literary text and source, *Clotel* suggests the slipperiness of the very concepts of "sources" and "revisions." Notwithstanding the title of this chapter, virtually every text in this Cultural Edition of *Clotel* can be regarded as a source, particularly given Brown's genealogical understanding of how texts permeate other texts and undergird a history of social practices and beliefs. Moreover, given Brown's broad sense of what constitutes a source (cultural practices, discourses, oral traditions, literary texts, personal experiences and testimony, and so on), the texts in this edition cover only a fraction of the sources that inform Brown's novel. Writing from a minority position as a black and former slave, Brown assumes that there are intimate connections between his novel's sources and the sources of the nation, which is hardly surprising in a novel that repeatedly invokes the Declaration. By revising his textual and cultural sources, through appropriation (theft) and recontextualization, Brown hoped to inspire larger efforts to revise the nation.

The eleven selections in this chapter, beginning with the excerpts from Thomas Bacon's proslavery sermons (reprinted in 1813) and concluding with Martin Delany's 1852 reprinting of the Compromise of 1850's Fugitive Slave Law, provide a record of some of the texts that Brown "kidnapped" into his novel, and thus allow us to better understand how his recontexutalizing techniques of bricolage and pastiche transformed these source materials. Included among the selections are Andrew Jackson's two 1814 proclamations to the black troops participating in the Battle of New Orleans (the second of which Brown puts into the mouth of the white character Georgiana Peck), excerpts from the 1831 *The Confessions of Nat Turner* (which informs Brown's portrayal of the black rebel Picquilo), proslavery documents collected in Theodore Weld's 1839 *American Slavery As It Is* (an important source for discussions at the Peck plantation), excerpts from Harriet Martineau's 1837 *Society in America* (which Brown drew on for his presentation of mixed-race blacks), a speech by Frederick Douglass (a source text for a key scene of the novel), and three literary texts (a short story, a chapter from a novel, and a poem).

Two of the literary texts, Lydia Maria Child's "The Quadroons" and Grace Greenwood's "The Leap from the Long Bridge," are reproduced nearly word for word in *Clotel*, and yet many readers will find the experience of reading them outside of this context to be quite different from reading them as part of Brown's novel. In *Clotel*, the story and poem lose their identity as autonomous works with a clear beginning, middle, and end, and necessarily exist in conversation with other appropriated texts and Brown's own writing. This is particularly true of the Child story, which Brown divides into three sections that are strategically placed at key points in the novel. The chapter from Stowe's *Uncle Tom's Cabin*, which is a more suggestive, lightly borrowed source, helps us to consider ongoing processes of revision in the culture, for the story of Cassy, who ultimately escapes from slavery and is reunited with her daughter, can itself be read as a revisionary account of the story of Rosalie in "The Quadroons." Brown's own revisions of Child may well have been inspired by Stowe's. Both the Child and Stowe selections, moreover, point to the centrality of the figure of the tragic mulatta in antislavery writing. Concerned about the vulnerability of slave women, Brown, like Child and Stowe, sought to engage white readers' sympathies by focusing on the situation of slave women who looked white to the eye. As mentioned in the general Introduction, there are risks to such a rhetorical strategy, specifically, that white readers will continue to be concerned only about the fate of the nation's "whites." Stowe took different sorts of risks in idealizing the Christ-like character of the black Uncle Tom. Brown's depiction of the rebellious black militant Picquilo suggests that he is working with and against not just Stowe's characterization of the tragic mulatta but also her celebration of the heroic black martyr.

The chapter concludes with writings by Daniel Webster and Martin Delany on the Compromise of 1850 (there is an amusing story about Webster in *Clotel* [p. 173]). The Fugitive Slave provision of the Compromise of 1850 was vilified by antislavery writers, who regarded a law forcing Northerners to return escaped blacks to their "masters" as an unconscionable extension of slavery into the free states. Stowe claimed that her anger at the Fugitive Slave Law was one factor that led her to write *Uncle Tom's Cabin*. Brown, like a number of escaped blacks, was concerned about being returned to his owner under the provisions of the law, and he remained in England until a British reformer purchased his freedom. In *Clotel*, the Fugitive Slave Law stands behind all of the representations of blacks attempting to escape from slavery. Delany argued that the Fugitive Slave revealed that the United States would always be a white supremacist nation, and he began to champion black emigration. Several years after the publication of *Clotel*, Brown, perhaps inspired by Delany, developed his own interest in black emigration, which led him to revise some of his thinking about race and nation.

THOMAS BACON

From *Sermons Addressed to Masters and Servants*

Proslavery religious writers regularly turned to the Bible to defend the master-slave relationship as a "natural," divinely ordained relationship that placed a spiritual burden on the master and slave alike. According to these writers, masters were responsible for caring for their slaves' bodies and souls, while the slaves were responsible for pursuing their salvation by remaining true to their worldly "duty" of serving their masters. In his influential *Christian Directory* (1673), the Anglican Richard Baxter (1615–1691) argued that slavery offered masters and slaves myriad opportunities for spiritual growth and redemption. Maryland's Reverend Thomas Bacon (1700–1768) took up Baxter's arguments and published a number of sermons on the mutual obligations of masters and slaves. Several of those sermons were reprinted by Bishop William Meade (1789–1862) of the Episcopal Diocese of Virginia in an edited collection, *Sermons Addressed to Masters and Servants, and Published in the Year 1743, by the Rev. Thomas Bacon, Minister of the Protestant Episcopal Church in Maryland. Now Republished with other Tracts and Dialogues on the Same Subject, and Recommended to all Masters and Mistresses to be Used in Their Families. By the Rev. William Meade* (Winchester, Virginia: John Heiskell, 1813), from which the selection below is drawn. The arguments of Baxter, Bacon, Meade, and other divines were adduced by antebellum proslavery writers to defend the social and racial hierarchies central to slavery. Antislavery writers countered that slaveholders blasphemously usurped God's place as the "master" of humankind. In *Clotel*, Brown lifts liberally from Bacon's sermons to the slaves, putting his words into the mouth of the cynical Northern proslavery "missionary" Hontz Snyder.

And now, *my dear* BLACK *brethren and sisters,* I beg that you will listen seriously to what I shall say—You all know what love and affection I have for you, and I do believe that most of you have the like love for me, as you have always found me ready to serve you, when you wanted my help.—I doubt not therefore, that you will readily hearken to the good advice I shall now give you, (as you know me to be your friend and wellwisher) and hope you will remember it hereafter, and think upon it at home, and talk of it to your fellow-servants that are not here, that they may receive advantage by it, as well as you, that hear it from my own mouth. [*Here masters may begin to read to their servants.*] . . .

That you may easier understand, and better carry away in your memory what you shall hear, I shall endeavour, by GOD's help, to lay before you, in the plainest words,

I. Why you ought to serve GOD.

II. What service, or what good things GOD expects from you.

III. What kind of reward you may expect to receive from him.

I. And the first reason why you ought to serve GOD, is,—BECAUSE THAT GOD MADE YOU;—and he *made* you, and all men, to *serve* him.—You know that when you were born, you did not come into the world by any power or help of your own:—Nay, you were so far from knowing any thing about it, or how you came here;—whether you were found in the woods, or grew out of the ground,—that it was some years before you could help yourselves, or had so much sense as to know your right hand from your left.—It was Almighty GOD, therefore, who made you, and all the world, that sent you here, as he had sent your fathers and mothers, your masters and mistresses before you, to take care of you, and provide for you, while you could take no care of, or help, or provide for yourselves.—And can you think that Almighty GOD, who is so wise and good himself, would send you into the world for any bad purposes?—Can you be so silly as to fancy, that he, who made every thing so good and useful in its kind, sent you here to be idle, to be wicked, or to make a bad use of any thing he hath made?—No, my brethren, the most ignorant among you has more sense than to think any such thing:—And there is none of you but knows that you ought to be good;—and whosoever is good, let him be ever so poor and mean, is serving GOD.—For this whole world is but one large family, of which Almighty GOD is the head and master:—. . .

II. Having thus shown you the chief duties you owe to your great master in heaven, I now come to lay before you the duties you owe to your *masters* and *mistresses* here upon earth.

And for this, you have one general rule that you ought always to carry in your minds;—and that is,—*to do all service for them, as if you did it for* God *himself.*—Poor creatures! you little consider, when you are idle and neglectful of your master's business,—when you *steal* and *waste*, and *hurt* any of their substance,—when you are *saucy* and *impudent*,—when you are telling them *lies*, and deceiving them,—or when you prove *stubborn* or *sullen*, and will not do the work you are set about without stripes and vexation;—you do not consider, I say, that what faults you are guilty of towards your masters and mistresses are faults done against God himself, who hath set your masters and mistresses over you, in his own stead, and expects that you will do for them, just as you would do for him.—And pray, do not think that I want to deceive you, when I tell you, that your *masters* and *mistresses* are God's *overseers*,—and that if you are faulty towards them, God himself will punish you severely for it in the next world, unless you repent of it, and strive to make amends, by your *faithfulness* and *diligence*, for the time to come;—for God himself hath declared the same. And you have at the same time this comfort, that if any of your *owners* should prove *wicked overseers*, and use you, who are his under servants here, as they ought not to do;—though you must submit to it, and can have no remedy in this world, yet, when God calls you and them together face to face before him in the next world, and examines into these matters, he will do you strict justice, and punish those that have been bad stewards and overseers over you with the greater severity, as they had more of this world entrusted to their care:—and that whatever you have suffered *unjustly* here, God will make you amends for it in heaven. . . .

You are *not* to be *eye-servants.*—Now *eye-servants* are such as will *work hard*, and seem mighty diligent, while they think that any body is taking notice of them, but when their masters and mistresses backs are turned, they are idle, and neglect their business.

—I am afraid that there are a great many such *eye servants* among you,—and that you do not consider how great a sin it is to be so, and how severely God will punish you for it.—You may easily deceive your owners, and make them have an opinion of you that you do not deserve, and get the praise of men by it. But remember, that you cannot deceive Almighty God, who sees your wickedness and deceit, and will punish you accordingly. For the rule is, that you must *obey your masters in all things*, & do the work they set you about *with fear and trembling, in singleness of heart, as unto Christ, not with eye-service, as men pleasers, but as the servants of Christ, doing the will of God from the heart: With good will doing service, as to the Lord, and not as to men.* — If then, you would but think, and say within yourselves, — "My master hath set me about this work, and his back is turned, so that I may loiter and idle if I please, for he does not see me. — But there is my great *master* in heaven, whose overseer my other master is — and his eyes are always upon me, and taking notice of me, and I cannot get any where out of his sight, not be idle without his knowing it, and what will become of me if I loose his good will, and make him angry with me." — If, I say, you would once get the way of thinking and saying thus, upon all occasions, you then would do what GOD commands you, and serve your masters with singleness of heart, — that is, with honesty and sincerity; you would do the work you are set about *with fear and trembling*, not for fear of your masters and mistresses upon earth (for you may easily cheat them, and make them believe you are doing their business when you do not) — but with *fear and trembling*, lest GOD, your heavenly master, whom you cannot deceive, should call you to account, and punish you in the next world, for your *deceitfulnes*, and *eye-service* in this.

3. You are to be *faithful and honest to your masters and mistresses — not purloining* (or wasting their goods or substance) *but showing all good fidelity in all things....*

Thus I have endeavoured to show you, why you ought to serve GOD, and what duty in particular you owe to him: — I have also shown you, that while you are serving your masters and mistresses, or doing any thing that GOD hath commanded, you are at the same time *serving* him; and have endeavoured to show you what duty or service you owe to your owners, in obedience to GOD, and that in so plain a manner, as I hope the greatest part of you did well understand. — The other parts of your duty and the rewards which GOD hath promised to you (if you will honestly set about doing it) I shall endeavour to lay before you at our next meeting here for that purpose. — In the mean time, consider well what hath been said. — Think upon it, and talk about it one with another, and strive to fix it on your memories. — And may GOD of his infinite mercy grant, that it may sink deep into your hearts, and, taking root there, may bring forth in you the fruit of good living, to the honour and praise of his holy name, the spreading abroad of his gospel, and the eternal salvation of your precious souls, through our Lord and Saviour JESUS CHRIST, to whom, with the father, and the holy spirit, be all honor and glory, world without end. — *Amen.*

ANDREW JACKSON

Two Proclamations

Andrew Jackson (1767–1845), the seventh president of the United States, was celebrated as the champion of the common man. During the 1830s he led a popular fight against what he portrayed as the elitist, oligarchical Bank of the United States, and in 1833 he faced down a Southern bloc led by John C. Calhoun that was attempting to nullify a federal tariff. Informing Jackson's egalitarianism and unionism, however, was an even larger commitment to white supremacy, for he was a slaveholder who also supported, indeed spearheaded, the Indian removal policies of the 1820s and 1830s. Nevertheless, Jackson was celebrated by many free blacks for having issued two proclamations during the War of 1812: a proclamation calling on blacks to join the white troops in defending New Orleans against the British army, and a proclamation praising the black troops for their heroic conduct under fire. Issued in 1814 when Jackson was serving as major general, the proclamations asserted African Americans' rights to citizenship, and came to assume a sort of sacred status within the free black community. In 1851, two years before the publication of *Clotel*, the proclamations were reprinted in W. C. Nell's influential *Services of Colored Americans*.

Born in Boston, William Cooper Nell (1816–1874) devoted his life to the causes of antislavery and black civil rights. He founded one of the first African American antislavery societies, the Massachusetts Colored Association; he campaigned to integrate Boston's public schools; and he worked closely with both William Lloyd Garrison and Frederick Douglass, contributing essays and letters to Garrison's *Liberator* and helping Douglass to publish *The North Star*. Though he remained committed to Garrison's principles of nonviolence and moral suasion, he actively opposed the Fugitive Slave Law during the 1850s. He also wrote two books celebrating black military service to the United States, *Services of Colored Americans in the Wars of 1776 and 1812* (Boston: Prentiss & Sawyer, 1851), from which this selection is taken, and an expanded volume, *Colored Patriots of the American Revolution* (1855). Nell's main argument in both volumes is that blacks' participation in the American Revolution and the War of 1812, along with their overall contributions to the development of the nation, should have earned them rights to citizenship. Drawing on Nell's account in *Services*, Brown makes a similar point in *Clotel* when Georgiana Peck, in the course of freeing her slaves, quotes from General Andrew Jackson's proclamation on the black soldiers' heroic defense of New Orleans.

In 1814, when New Orleans was in danger, and the proud and criminal distinctions of caste were again demolished by one of those emergencies in which nature puts to silence for the moment the base partialities of art, the free Colored people were called into the field in common with the whites; and the importance of their services was thus acknowledged by General Jackson:—

"HEAD QUARTERS, SEVENTH MILITARY DISTRICT, MOBILE, SEPTEMBER 21, 1814.

"*To the Free Colored Inhabitants of Louisiana*:

"Through a mistaken policy, you have heretofore been deprived of a participation in the glorious struggle for national rights, in which *our* country is engaged. This no longer shall exist.

"As Sons of Freedom, you are now called upon to defend our most inestimable blessings. *As Americans*, your country looks with confidence to her adopted children, for a valorous support, as a faithful return for the advantages enjoyed under her mild and equitable government. As fathers, husbands, and brothers, you are summoned to rally round the standard of the Eagle, to defend all which is dear in existence.

"*Your country*, although calling for your exertions, does not wish you to engage in her cause, without remunerating you for the services rendered. Your intelligent minds are not to be led away by false representations—your love of honor would cause you to despise the man who should attempt to deceive you. In the sincerity of a soldier, and the language of truth, I address you.

"To every noble hearted free man of Color, volunteering to serve during the present contest with Great Britain, and no longer, there will be paid the same bounty in money and lands, now received by the white soldiers of the United States, namely, one hundred and twenty-four dollars in money, and one hundred and sixty acres of land. The non-commissioned officers and privates will also be entitled to the same monthly pay and daily rations, and clothes furnished to any American soldier.

"On enrolling yourselves in companies, the Major General commanding will select officers for your government, from your white fellow citizens. Your non-commissioned officers will be appointed from among yourselves.

"Due regard will be paid to the feelings of freemen and soldiers. You will not, by being associated with white men in the same corps be exposed to improper comparisons, or unjust sarcasm. As a distinct, independent battalion or regiment, pursuing the path of glory, you will, undivided, receive the applause and gratitude of your countrymen.

"To assure you of the sincerity of my intentions, and my anxiety to engage your invaluable services to our country, I have communicated my wishes to the Governor of Louisiana, who is fully informed as to the manner of enrolments, and will give you every necessary information on the subject of this address.

ANDREW JACKSON,
Major General Commanding."

The second proclamation is one of the highest compliments ever paid by a military chief to his soldiers.

On December 18, 1814, General Jackson issued, in the French language, the following address to the free people of Color:—

"SOLDIERS! When on the banks of the Mobile I called you to take up arms, inviting you to partake the perils and glory of your *white fellow citizens, I expected much from you*: for I was not ignorant that you possessed qualities most formidable to an invading enemy. I knew with what fortitude you could endure hunger and thirst, and all the fatigues of a campaign. *I knew well how you loved your native country*, and that you, as well as ourselves, had to defend what *man* holds most dear—his parents, wife, children, and property. *You have done more than I expected.* In addition to the previous qualities I before knew you to possess, I found among you a noble enthusiasm, which leads to the performance of great things.

"Soldiers! The President of the United States shall hear how praiseworthy was your conduct in the hour of danger, and the representatives of the American people will give you the praise your exploits entitle you to. Your General anticipates them in applauding your noble ardor."

"The enemy approaches; his vessels cover our lakes; our brave citizens are united, and all contention has ceased among them. Their only dispute is who shall win the prize of valor, or who the most glory, its noblest reward.

By Order,
THOMAS BUTLER,[1] Aid-de Camp."

---

[1] *THOMAS BUTLER*: A lawyer from Louisiana, Thomas Butler (1787–1847) fought in the Mississippi territory in the early 1800s and eventually served as a judge and congressman.

THOMAS R. GRAY

From *The Confessions of Nat Turner*

In the early morning of 22 August 1831, the slave preacher Nat Turner (1800–1831) and approximately fifty fellow slaves initiated a bloody rebellion in Southampton County, Virginia, that left over two hundred dead, including at least fifty-five whites. The militia quickly captured or killed most of the rebels; Turner managed to hide out in the swamps until October 30 and was subsequently tried and executed within two weeks of his capture. While incarcerated, Turner was interviewed by a local lawyer, Thomas R. Gray, who was convinced that Turner was insane. Hoping to make money from an interview with the leader of the bloodiest slave revolt in the nation's history, Gray published the *Confessions* later that year and sold approximately fifty thousand copies. While most U.S. whites were unnerved (or horrified) by the Nat Turner rebellion, Brown and other abolitionists found Turner to be an inspiring figure. In addition to making Turner's insurrection an important part of *Clotel*, Brown devoted a chapter to Turner in *The Black Man, His Antecedents, His Genius, and His Achievements* (1863). The following is the complete text of *The Confessions of Nat Turner* (Baltimore: Thomas R. Gray, 1831), with the exception of the affidavits accompanying the Clerk's and Court's seal, the list of people killed, and the list of slaves who testified at the trial.

TO THE PUBLIC

The late insurrection in Southampton has greatly excited the public mind, and led to a thousand idle, exaggerated and mischievous reports. It is the first instance in our history of an open rebellion of the slaves, and attended with such atrocious circumstances of cruelty and destruction, as could not fail to leave a deep impression, not only upon the minds of the community where this fearful tragedy was wrought, but throughout every portion of our country, in which this population is to be found. . . .

It will thus appear, that whilst every thing upon the surface of society wore a calm and peaceful aspect; whilst not one note of preparation was heard to warn the devoted inhabitants of woe and death, a gloomy fanatic was revolving in the recesses of his own dark, bewildered, and overwrought mind, schemes of indiscriminate massacre to the whites. Schemes too fearfully executed as far as his fiendish band proceeded in their desolating march. No cry for mercy penetrated their flinty bosoms. No acts of remembered kindness made the least impression upon these remorseless murderers. Men, women and children, from hoary age to helpless infancy were involved in the same cruel fate. Never did a band of savages do their work of death more unsparingly. . . . Nat has survived all his followers, and the gallows will speedily close his career. His own account of the conspiracy is submitted to the public, without comment. It reads an awful, and it is hoped, a useful lesson, as to the operations of a mind like his, endeavoring to grapple with things beyond its reach. How it first became bewildered and confounded, and finally corrupted and led to the conception and perpetration of the most atrocious and heart-rending deeds. It is calculated also to demonstrate the policy of our laws in restraint of this class of our population, and to induce all those entrusted with their execution, as well as our citizens generally, to see that they are strictly and rigidly enforced. Each particular community should look to its own safety, whilst the general guardians of the laws, keep a watchful eye over all. If Nat's statements can be relied on, the insurrection in this county was entirely local, and his designs confided but to a few, and these in his immediate vicinity. It was not instigated by motives of revenge or sudden anger, but the results of long deliberation, and a settled purpose of mind. The offspring of gloomy fanaticism, acting upon materials but too well prepared for such impressions. It will be long remembered in the annals of our country, and many a mother as she presses her infant darling to her bosom, will shudder at the recollection of Nat Turner, and his band of ferocious miscreants.

Believing the following narrative, by removing doubts and conjectures from the public mind which otherwise must have remained, would give general satisfaction, it is respectfully submitted to the public by their ob't serv't,

T. R. GRAY.

CONFESSION

Agreeable to his own appointment, on the evening he was committed to prison, with permission of the jailer, I visited NAT on Tuesday the 1st November, when, without being questioned at all, he commenced his narrative in the following words:—

SIR,—You have asked me to give a history of the motives which induced me to undertake the late insurrection, as you call it—To do so I must go back to the days of my infancy, and even before I was born. I was thirty-one years of age the 2d of October last, and born the property of Benj. Turner, of this county. In my childhood a circumstance occurred which made an indelible impression on my mind, and laid the ground work of that enthusiasm, which has terminated so fatally to many, both white and black, and for which I am about to atone at the gallows. It is here necessary to relate this circumstance—trifling as it may seem, it was the commencement of that belief which has grown with time, and even now, sir, in this dungeon, helpless and forsaken as I am, I cannot divest myself of. Being at play with other children, when three or four years old, I was telling them something, which my mother overhearing, said it had happened before I was born—I stuck to my story, however, and related somethings which went, in her opinion, to confirm it—others being called on were greatly astonished, knowing that these things had happened, and caused them to say in my hearing, I surely would be a prophet, as the Lord had shewn me things that had happened before my birth. And my father and mother strengthened me in this my first impression, saying in my presence, I was intended for some great purpose, which they had always thought from certain marks on my head and breast—[a parcel of excrescences[1] which I believe are not at all uncommon, particularly among negroes, as I have seen several with the same. In this case he has either cut them off or they have nearly disappeared]—My grandmother, who was very religious, and to whom I was much attached—my master, who belonged to the church, and other religious persons who visited the house, and whom I often saw at prayers, noticing the singularity of my manners, I suppose, and my uncommon intelligence for a child, remarked I had too much sense to be raised, and if I was, I would never be of any service to any one as a slave—To a mind like mine, restless, inquisitive and observant of every thing that was passing, it is easy to suppose that religion was the subject to which it would be directed, and although this subject principally occupied my thoughts—there was nothing that I saw or heard of to which my attention was not directed—The manner in which I learned to read and write, not only had great influence on my own mind, as I acquired it with the most

---

[1] *excrescences*: Abnormal growths. This remark on Turner's skin is supplied by Thomas Gray, who several times interrupts Turner's narrative, using brackets or parentheses, to add information or to editorialize.

perfect ease, so much so, that I have no recollection whatever of learning the alphabet—but to the astonishment of the family, one day,
when a book was shewn me to keep me from crying, I began spelling
the names of different objects—this was a source of wonder to all in
the neighborhood, particularly the blacks. . . . Knowing the influence I
had obtained over the minds of my fellow servants, (not by the means
of conjuring and such like tricks—for to them I always spoke of such
things with contempt) but by the communion of the Spirit whose revelations I often communicated to them, and they believed and said my
wisdom came from God. I now began to prepare them for my purpose,
by telling them something was about to happen that would terminate
in fulfilling the great promise that had been made to me—About this
time I was placed under an overseer, from whom I ran away—and
after remaining in the woods thirty days, I returned, to the astonishment of the negroes on the plantation, who thought I had made my
escape to some other part of the country, as my father had done before.
But the reason of my return was, that the Spirit appeared to me and
said I had my wishes directed to the things of this world, and not to
the kingdom of Heaven, and that I should return to the service of my
earthly master—"For he who knoweth his Master's will, and doeth
it not, shall be beaten with many stripes, and thus have I chastened
you."[2] And the negroes found fault, and murmured against me, saying that if they had my sense they would not serve any master in the
world. And about this time I had a vision—and I saw white spirits and
black spirits engaged in battle, and the sun was darkened—the thunder rolled in the Heavens, and blood flowed in streams—and I heard a
voice saying, "Such is your luck, such you are, called to see, and let it
come rough or smooth, you must surely bear it." I now withdrew
myself as much as my situation would permit, from the intercourse of
my fellow servants, for the avowed purpose of serving the Spirit more
fully—and it appeared to me, and reminded me of the things it had
already shown me, and that it would then reveal to me the knowledge
of the elements, the revolution of the planets, the operation of tides,
and changes of the seasons. After this revelation in the year 1825, and
the knowledge of the elements being made known to me, I sought
more than ever to obtain true holiness before the great day of judgment should appear, and then I began to receive the true knowledge of
faith. And from the first steps of righteousness until the last, was I

[2] *"For he . . . chastened you"*: Luke 12.47.

made perfect; and the Holy Ghost was with me, and said, "Behold me as I stand in the Heavens"—and I looked and saw the forms of men in different attitudes—and there were lights in the sky to which the children of darkness gave other names than what they really were—for they were the lights of the Saviour's hands, stretched forth from east to west, even as they were extended on the cross on Calvary[3] the redemption of sinners. And I wondered greatly at these miracles, and prayed to be informed of a certainty of the meaning thereof—and shortly afterwards, while laboring in the field, I discovered drops of blood on the corn as though it were dew from heaven—and I communicated it to many, both white and black, in the neighborhood—and I then found on the leaves in the woods hieroglyphic characters, and numbers, with the forms of men in different attitudes, portrayed in blood, and representing the figures I had seen before in the heavens. And now the Holy Ghost had revealed itself to me, and made plain the miracles it had shown me—For as the blood of Christ had been shed on this earth, and had ascended to heaven for the salvation of sinners, and was now returning to earth again in the form of dew—and as the leaves on the trees bore the impression of the figures I had seen in the heavens, it was plain to me that the Saviour was about to lay down the yoke he had borne for the sins of men, and the great day of judgment was at hand. . . . *Ques.* Do you not find yourself mistaken now? *Ans.* Was not Christ crucified? And by signs in the heavens that it would make known to me when I should commence the great work—and until the first sign appeared, I should conceal it from the knowledge of men—And on the appearance of the sign, (the eclipse of the sun last February) I should arise and prepare myself, and slay my enemies with their own weapons. And immediately on the sign appearing in the heavens, the seal was removed from my lips, and I communicated the great work laid out for me to do, to four in whom I had the greatest confidence. (Henry, Hark, Nelson, and Sam)—It was intended by us to have begun the work of death on the 4th July last—Many were the plans formed and rejected by us, and it affected my mind to such a degree, that I fell sick, and the time passed without our coming to any determination how to commence—Still forming new schemes and rejecting them, when the sign appeared again, which determined me not to wait longer.

Since the commencement of 1830, I had been living with Mr. Joseph Travis, who was to me a kind master, and placed the greatest confi-

---

[3] *Calvary:* The place where Christ was crucified; see Luke 23.

dence in me; in fact, I had no cause to complain of his treatment to me. On Saturday evening, the 20th of August, it was agreed between Henry, Hark and myself, to prepare a dinner the next day for the men we expected, and then to concert a plan, as we had not yet determined on any. Hark, on the following morning, brought a pig, and Henry brandy, and being joined by Sam, Nelson, Will and Jack, they prepared in the woods a dinner, where, about three o clock, I joined them.

Q. Why were you so backward in joining them.

A. The same reason that had caused me not to mix with them for years before.

I saluted them on coming up, and asked Will how came he there, he answered, his life was worth no more than others, and his liberty as dear to him. I asked him if he thought to obtain it? He said he would, or lose his life. This was enough to put him in full confidence. Jack, I knew, was only a tool in the hands of Hark, it was quickly agreed we should commence at home (Mr. J. Travis') on that night, and until we had armed and equipped ourselves, and gathered sufficient force, neither age nor sex was to be spared, (which was invariably adhered to.) We remained at the feast, until about two hours in the night, when we went to the house and found Austin; they all went to the cider press and drank, except myself. On returning to the house, Hark went to the door with an axe, for the purpose of breaking it open, as we knew we were strong enough to murder the family, if they were awaked by the noise; but reflecting that it might create an alarm in the neighborhood, we determined to enter the house secretly, and murder them whilst sleeping. Hark got a ladder and set it against the chimney, on which I ascended, and hoisting a window, entered and came down stairs, unbarred the door, and removed the guns from their places. It was then observed that I must spill the first blood. On which, armed with a hatchet, and accompanied by Will, I entered my master's chamber, it being dark, I could not give a death blow, the hatchet glanced from his head, he sprang from the bed and called his wife, it was his last word, Will laid him dead, with a blow of his axe, and Mrs. Travis shared the same fate, as she lay in bed. The murder of this family, five in number, was the work of a moment, not one of them awoke; there was a little infant sleeping in a cradle, that was forgotten, until we had left the house and gone some distance, when Henry and Will returned and killed it; we got here, four guns that would shoot, and several old muskets, with a pound or two of powder. We remained some time at the barn, where we paraded; I formed them in a line as soldiers, and after carrying them through all the manœuvres I was master of, marched them off to Mr. Salathul Francis', about six hundred yards distant. Sam and Will went to the door and knocked. Mr. Francis asked who was there, Sam replied it was him, and he had a letter for him, on which he got up and came to the door; they immediately seized him, and dragging him out a little from the door, he was dispatched by repeated blows on the head; there was no other white person in the family. . . . I do not know what became of them, as I never saw them afterwards. Pursuing our course back and coming in sight of Captain Harris', where we had been the day before, we discovered a party of white men at the house, on which all deserted me but two, (Jacob and Nat,) we concealed ourselves in the woods until near night, when I sent them in search of Henry, Sam, Nelson, and Hark, and directed them to rally all they could, at the place we had had our dinner the Sunday before, where they would find me, and I accordingly returned there as soon as it was dark and remained until Wednesday evening, when discovering white men riding around the place as though they were looking for some one, and none of my men joining me, I concluded Jacob and Nat had been taken, and compelled to betray me. On this I gave up all hope for the present; and on Thursday night after having supplied myself with provisions from Mr. Travis's, I scratched a hole under a pile of fence rails in a field, where I concealed myself for six weeks, never leaving my hiding place but for a few minutes in the dead of night to get water which was very near; thinking by this time I could venture out, I began to go about in the night and eaves drop the houses in the neighborhood; pursuing this course for about a fortnight and gathering little or no intelligence, afraid of speaking to any human being, and returning every morning to my cave before the dawn of day, I know not how long I might have led this life, if accident had not betrayed me, a dog in the neighborhood passing by my hiding place one night while I was out, was attracted by some meat I had in my cave, and crawled in and stole it, and was coming out just as I returned. A few nights after, two negroes having started to go hunting with the same dog, and passed that way, the dog came again to the place, and having just gone out to walk about, discovered me and barked, on which thinking myself discovered, I spoke to them to beg concealment. On making myself known they fled from me. Knowing then they would betray me, I immediately left my hiding place, and was pursued almost incessantly until I was taken a fortnight afterwards by Mr. Benjamin Phipps, in a little hole I had dug out with my sword, for the purpose of concealment, under the top of a fallen tree. On Mr. Phipps' discovering the place of my concealment, he cocked his gun and aimed at me. I requested him not to shoot and I would give up, upon which he demanded my sword. I delivered it to him, and he brought me to prison. During the time I was pursued, I had many hair breadth escapes, which your time will not permit you to relate. I am here loaded with chains, and willing to suffer the fate that awaits me.

I[4] here proceeded to make some inquiries of him, after assuring him of the certain death that awaited him, and that concealment would only bring destruction on the innocent as well as guilty, of his own color, if he knew of any extensive or concerted plan. His answer was, I do not. When I questioned him as to the insurrection in North Carolina[5] happening about the same time, he denied any knowledge of it; and when I looked him in the face as though I would search his inmost thoughts, he replied, "I see sir, you doubt my word; but can you not think the same ideas, and strange appearances about this time in the heaven's might prompt others, as well as myself, to this undertaking." I now had much conversation with and asked him many questions, having forborne to do so previously, except in the cases noted in parenthesis; but during his statement, I had, unnoticed by him, taken notes as to some particular circumstances, and having the advantage of his statement before me in writing, on the evening of the third day that I had been with him, I began a cross examination, and found his statement corroborated by every circumstance coming within my own knowledge or the confessions of others whom had been either killed or executed, and whom he had not seen nor had any knowledge since 22d of August last, he expressed himself fully satisfied as to the impracticability of his attempt. It has been said he was ignorant and cowardly, and that his object was to murder and rob for the purpose of obtaining money to make his escape. It is notorious, that he was never known to have a dollar in his life; to swear an oath, or drink a drop of spirits. As to his ignorance, he certainly never had the advantages of education, but he can read and write, (it was taught him by his parents,) and for natural intelligence and quickness of apprehension, is surpassed by few men I have ever seen. As to his being a coward, his reason as given for not resisting Mr. Phipps, shews the decision of his character. When he saw Mr. Phipps present his gun, he said he knew it

---

[4] At this point Thomas R. Gray resumes his narration.

[5] *the insurrection in North Carolina*: During September 1831 there were rumors of slave revolts in Fayetteville and several other North Carolina towns. Though there may have been a few isolated small slave uprisings, for the most part these rumors were used by some whites to justify "retributive" violence against North Carolina's free and enslaved blacks.

was impossible for him to escape as the woods were full of men; he therefore thought it was better to surrender, and trust to fortune for his escape. He is a complete fanatic, or plays his part most admirably. On other subjects he possesses an uncommon share of intelligence, with a mind capable of attaining any thing; but warped and perverted by the influence of early impressions. He is below the ordinary stature, though strong and active, having the true negro face, every feature of which is strongly marked. I shall not attempt to describe the effect of his narrative, as told and commented on by himself, in the condemned hole of the prison. The calm, deliberate composure with which he spoke of his late deeds and intentions, the expression of his fiend-like face when excited by enthusiasm, still bearing the stains of the blood of helpless innocence about him; clothed with rags and covered with chains; yet daring to raise his manacled hands to heaven, with a spirit soaring above the attributes of man; I looked on him and my blood curdled in my veins.

THEODORE DWIGHT WELD

From *American Slavery As It Is*

A massive compendium of testimony about the horrors of slavery, Weld's *American Slavery As It Is,* published in 1839, was one of the most influential antislavery books of the time, serving as a kind of source book for Brown, Stowe, and many other antislavery writers. Born in Connecticut, Theodore Dwight Weld (1803–1895) converted to Presbyterianism in 1825, and in 1832 enrolled at the Lane Theological Seminary in Cincinnati, Ohio. Convinced that slavery was a crime against God, he emerged as the leader of the "Lane Rebels," a group of students who decided to leave the seminary after the faculty, trustees, and president Lyman Beecher (Harriet Beecher Stowe's father) attempted to suppress students' antislavery activities. Thereafter, Weld became an important lecturer and organizer in the American Anti-Slavery Society, taking on the major responsibility of training its traveling agents. In 1838 he married the notorious South Carolina abolitionist Angelina E. Grimké. He continued his antislavery efforts into the 1840s, and in 1854 established a racially integrated school in Eagelswood, New Jersey. The selections below, taken from *American Slavery As It Is: Testimony of a Thousand Witnesses* (New York: American Anti-Slavery Society, 1839), provided Brown with sources for the important advertisements in chapters I and XI of *Clotel.*

As slaveholders and their apologists are volunteer witnesses in their own cause, and are flooding the world with testimony that their slaves are kindly treated; that they are well fed, well clothed, well housed, well lodged, moderately worked, and bountifully provided with all things needful for their comfort, we propose—first, to disprove their assertions by the testimony of a multitude of impartial witnesses, and then to put slaveholders themselves through a course of cross-questioning which shall draw their condemnation out of their own mouths. We will prove that the slaves in the United States are treated with barbarous inhumanity; that they are overworked, underfed, wretchedly clad and lodged, and have insufficient sleep; that they are often made to wear round their necks iron collars armed with prongs, to drag heavy chains and weights at their feet while working in the field, and to wear yokes, and bells, and iron horns; that they are often kept confined in the stocks day and night for weeks together, made to wear gags in their mouths for hours or days, have some of their front teeth torn out or broken off, that they may be easily detected when they run away; that they are frequently flogged with terrible severity, have red pepper rubbed into their lacerated flesh, and hot brine, spirits of turpentine, &c., poured over the gashes to increase the torture; that they are often stripped naked, their backs and limbs cut with knives, bruised and mangled by scores and hundreds of blows with the paddle, and terribly torn by the claws of cats, drawn over them by their tormentors; that they are often hunted with blood hounds and shot down like beasts, or torn in pieces by dogs; that they are often suspended by the arms and whipped and beaten till they faint, and when revived by restoratives, beaten again till they faint, and sometimes till they die; that their ears are often cut off, their eyes knocked out, their bones broken, their flesh branded with red hot irons; that they are maimed, mutilated and burned to death over slow fires. All these things, and more, and worse, we shall *prove*. Reader, we know whereof we affirm, we have weighed it well; *more and worse* WE WILL PROVE. Mark these words, and read on; we will establish all these facts by the testimony of scores and hundreds of eye witnesses, by the testimony of *slaveholders* in all parts of the slave states, by slaveholding members of Congress and of state legislatures, by ambassadors to foreign courts, by judges, by doctors of divinity, and clergy men of all denominations, by merchants, mechanics, lawyers and physicians, by presidents and professors in colleges and *professional* seminaries, by planters, overseers and drivers. We shall show, not merely that such deeds are committed, but that they are frequent; not done in corners, but before the sun; not in one of the slave states, but in all of them; not perpetrated

by brutal overseers and drivers merely, but by magistrates, by legislators, by professors of religion, by preachers of the gospel, by governors
of states, by "gentlemen of property and standing," and by delicate
females moving in the "highest circles of society." . . .

A late PROSPECTUS of the South Carolina Medical College, located
in Charleston, contains the following passage:—

"Some advantages of a *peculiar* character are connected with this
Institution, which it may be proper to point out. No place in the United
States offers as great opportunities for the acquisition of anatomical
knowledge, SUBJECTS BEING OBTAINED FROM AMONG THE COLORED
POPULATION IN SUFFICIENT NUMBER FOR EVERY PURPOSE, AND PROPER
DISSECTIONS CARRIED ON WITHOUT OFFENDING ANY INDIVIDUALS IN
THE COMMUNITY!!"

Without offending any individuals in the community! More than
half the population of Charleston, we believe, is 'colored;' *their* graves
may be ravaged, their dead may be dug up, dragged into the dissecting
room, exposed to the gaze, heartless gibes, and experimenting knives,
of a crowd of inexperienced operators, who are given to understand
in the prospectus, that, if they do not acquire manual dexterity in
dissection, it will be wholly their own fault, in neglecting to improve
the unrivalled advantages afforded by the institution—since each can
have as many human bodies as he pleases to experiment upon—and
as to the fathers, mothers, husbands, wives, brothers, and sisters, of
those whom they cut to pieces from day to day, why, they are not 'individuals in the community,' but 'property,' and however *their* feelings
may be tortured, the 'public opinion' of slaveholders is entirely too
'chivalrous' to degrade itself by caring for them! . . .

In the "Charleston (South Carolina) Mercury" of October 12,
1838, we find an advertisement of half a column, by a Dr. T. Stillman,
setting forth the merits of another 'Medical Infirmary,' under his own
special supervision, at No. 110 Church street, Charleston. The doctor,
after inveighing loudly against 'men totally ignorant of medical science,' who flood the country with quack nostrums backed up by 'fab-
ricated proofs of miraculous cures,' proceeds to enumerate the diseases
to which his 'Infirmary' is open, and to which his practice will be
mainly confined. Appreciating the importance of 'interesting cases,' as
a stock in trade, on which to commence his experiments, he copies the
example of the medical professors, and advertises for them. But, either
from a keener sense of justice, or more generosity, or greater confidence in his skill, or for some other reason, he proposes to *buy up* an
assortment of *damaged* negroes, given over, as incurable, by others,

and to make such his 'interesting cases,' instead of experimenting on those who are the 'property' of others.

Dr. Stillman closes his advertisement with the following notice:—

"To PLANTERS AND OTHERS.—Wanted *fifty negroes.* Any person having sick negroes, considered incurable by their respective physicians, and wishing to dispose of them, Dr. S. will pay cash for negroes affected with scrofula or king's evil, confirmed hypocondriasm, apoplexy, diseases of the liver, kidneys, spleen, stomach and intestines, bladder and its appendages, diarrhea, dysentery, &c. The highest cash price will be paid on application as above."

The absolute barbarism of a 'public opinion' which not only tolerates, but *produces* such advertisements as this, was outdone by nothing in the dark ages. If the reader has a heart of flesh, he can feel it without help, and if he has not, comment will not create it. The total indifference of slaveholders to such a cold blooded proposition, their utter unconsciousness of the paralysis of heart, and death of sympathy, and every feeling of common humanity for the slave, which it reveals, is enough, of itself, to show that the tendency of the spirit of slaveholding is, to kill in the soul whatever it touches. It has no eyes to see, nor ears to hear, nor mind to understand, nor heart to feel for its victims as *human beings.* To show that the above indication of the savage state is not an index of individual feeling, but of 'public opinion,' it is sufficient to say, that it appears to be a standing advertisement in the Charleston Mercury, the leading political paper of South Carolina, the organ of the Honorables John C. Calhoun, Robert Barnwell Rhett,[1] Hugh S. Legare,[2] and others regarded as the elite of her statesmen and literati. Besides, candidates for popular favor, like the doctor who advertises for the fifty 'incurables,' take special care to conciliate, rather than outrage, 'public opinion.' Is the doctor so ignorant of 'public opinion' in his own city, that he has unwittingly committed violence upon it in his advertisement? We trow not. The same 'public opinion' which gave birth to the advertisement of doctor Stillman, and to those of the professors in both the medical institutions, founded the Charleston 'Work House'—a soft name for a Moloch temple[3] dedicated to

---

[1] *Robert Barnwell Rhett*: An ardent supporter of Southern states' rights, the South Carolina politician Robert B. Rhett (1800–1876) emerged as a leading secessionist by the 1850s.

[2] *Hugh S. Legare*: A prominent South Carolina politician, Hugh Swinton Legare (1797–1843) rejected nullification in favor of unionism.

[3] *Moloch temple*: A temple dedicated to the Canaanite god of fire, Moloch. In the Bible, the Jewish prophets strongly objected to such worship.

torture, and reeking with blood, in the midst of the city; to which masters and mistresses send their slaves of both sexes to be stripped, tied up, and cut with the lash till the blood and mangled flesh flow to their feet, or to be beaten and bruised with the terrible paddle, or forced to climb the tread-mill till nature sinks, or to experience other nameless torments. . . .

That the 'public opinion' of *the highest class of society* in South Carolina, regards slaves as mere *cattle*, is shown by the following advertisement, which we copy from the "Charleston (S.C.) Mercury" of May 16:

"NEGROES FOR SALE.—A GIRL about twenty years of age, (raised in Virginia,) and her two female children, one four and the other two years old—is remarkably strong and healthy—never having had a day's sickness, with the exception of the small pox, in her life. The children are fine and healthy. She is VERY PROLIFIC IN HER GENERATING QUALITIES, *and affords a rare opportunity to any person who wishes to raise a family of strong and healthy servants for their own use.*

"Any person wishing to purchase, will please leave their address at the Mercury office."

The Charleston Mercury, in which this advertisement appears, is the *leading political paper in South Carolina*, and is well known to be the political organ of Messrs. Calhoun, Rhett, Pickens,[4] and others of the most prominent politicians in the state. Its editor, John Stewart, Esq., is a lawyer of Charleston, and of a highly respectable family. He is a brother-in-law of Hon. Robert Barnwell Rhett, the late Attorney-General, now a Member of Congress, and Hon. James Rhett, a leading member of the Senate of South Carolina; his wife is a niece of the late Governor Smith, of North Carolina, and of the late Hon. Peter Smith, Intendant (Mayor) of the city of Charleston; and a cousin of the late Hon. Thomas S. Grimké.[5]

The circulation of the 'Mercury' among the wealthy, the literary, and the fashionable, is probably much larger than that of any other paper in the state.

These facts in connection with the preceding advertisement, are a sufficient exposition of the 'public opinion' towards slaves, prevalent in these classes of society.

---

[4] *Pickens*: Francis Wilkinson Pickens (1805–1869) supported Southern states' rights and was governor of South Carolina when the state seceded from the Union.

[5] *Thomas S. Grimké*: A peace reformer from South Carolina, Thomas Grimké (1786–1834) was the brother of Angelina E. Grimké.

HARRIET MARTINEAU

From *Society in America*

Regarded as one of the founders of modern sociology, the popular English author and journalist Harriet Martineau (1802–1876) secured her reputation with the publication of the nine-volume *Illustrations of Political Economy* (1832–1834). She subsequently traveled to the United States in late 1834 and became an outspoken opponent of slavery, publishing *Society in America* in 1837. Part travel narrative and part social analysis, *Society in America* was widely read in the United States and Great Britain. Martineau's discussion of the "Quadroons" of New Orleans influenced Lydia Maria Child's representation of Virginia's similar color politics in "The Quadroons," one of the most important sources of *Clotel*. Brown read extensively in British antislavery writings, particularly after traveling to England in 1849, and greatly admired Martineau. The excerpt below is taken from volume two of Martineau's three-volume *Society in America* (London: Saunders and Otley, 1837).

MORALS OF SLAVERY

This title is not written down in a spirit of mockery; though there appears to be a mockery somewhere, when we contrast slavery with the principles and the rule which are the test of all American institutions: — the principles that all men are born free and equal; that rulers derive their just powers from the consent of the governed; and the rule of reciprocal justice. This discrepancy between principles and practice needs no more words. But the institution of slavery exists; and what we have to see is what the morals are of the society which is subject to it. . . .

It is a common boast in the south that there is less vice in their cities than in those of the north. This can never, as a matter of fact, have been ascertained; as the proceedings of slave households are, or may be, a secret: and in the north, what licentiousness there is may be detected. But such comparisons are bad. Let any one look at the positive licentiousness of the south, and declare if, in such a state of society, there can be any security for domestic purity and peace. The Quadroon connexions in New Orleans are all but universal, as I was assured on the spot by ladies who cannot be mistaken. The history of such connexions is a melancholy one: but it ought to be made known while there are any who boast of the superior morals of New Orleans, on account of the decent quietness of the streets and theatres.

The Quadroon girls of New Orleans are brought up by their mothers to be what they have been; the mistresses of white gentlemen. The boys are some of them sent to France; some placed on land in the back of the State; and some are sold in the slave-market. They marry women of a somewhat darker colour than their own; the women of their own colour objecting to them, "ils sont si dégoutants!"[1] The girls are highly educated, externally, and are, probably, as beautiful and accomplished a set of women as can be found. Every young man early selects one, and establishes her in one of those pretty and peculiar houses, whole rows of which may be seen in the Remparts.[2] The connexion now and then lasts for life: usually for several years. In the latter case, when the time comes for the gentleman to take a white wife, the dreadful news reaches his Quadroon partner, either by a letter entitling her to call the house and furniture her own, or by the newspaper which announces his marriage. The Quadroon ladies are rarely or ever known to form a second connexion. Many commit suicide: more die broken-hearted. Some men continue the connexion after marriage. Every Quadroon woman believes that her partner will prove an exception to the rule of desertion. Every white lady believes that her husband has been an exception to the rule of seduction.

What security for domestic purity and peace there can be where every man has had two connexions, one of which must be concealed; and two families, whose existence must not be known to each other; where the conjugal relation begins in treachery, and must be carried on with a heavy secret in the husband's breast, no words are needed to explain. If this is the system which is boasted of as a purer than ordinary state of morals, what is to be thought of the ordinary state? It can only be hoped that the boast is an empty one.

There is no occasion to explain the management of the female slaves on estates where the object is to rear as many as possible, like stock, for the southern market: nor to point out the boundless licentiousness caused by the practice: a practice which wrung from the wife of a planter, in the bitterness of her heart, the declaration that a planter's wife was only "the chief slave of the harem." Mr. Madison[3] avowed

---

[1] *ils sont si dégoutants*: They are disgusting (French).

[2] *Remparts*: A neighborhood by a main avenue in New Orleans.

[3] *Mr. Madison*: The Virginian James Madison (1751–1836) served as the fourth president of the United States (1809–1817).

that the licentiousness of Virginian plantations stopped just short of destruction; and that it was understood that the female slaves were to become mothers at fifteen.

LYDIA MARIA CHILD

The Quadroons

The Massachusetts-born fiction writer, abolitionist, educator, editor, domestic theorist, feminist, and Indian rights advocate Lydia Maria Child (1802–1880), née Lydia Francis, was one of the great literary activists of nineteenth-century America. Her well-received first book, the novel *Hobomok, A Tale of Early Times*, which favorably represented an interracial marriage between a white woman and an Indian man, appeared in 1824, when she was twenty-two years old. Soon after, she published another highly regarded novel, *The Rebels* (1825), and founded the children's magazine *Juvenile Miscellany*. In 1828 she married David Child and began writing advice manuals for women. *The Frugal Housewife* (1829) went through over thirty editions and established her as one of America's most popular domestic writers. However, she became ostracized from genteel Boston culture in 1833 when she published *An Appeal in Favor of that Class of Americans Called Africans*, which advocated immediate emancipation. Child remained passionately committed to antiracist reforms for the rest of her long, prolific career. Among her important books are *Letters from New York* (1843), *Correspondence between Lydia Maria Child and Gov. Wise and Mrs. Mason* (1860), *A Romance of the Republic* (1867), and *An Appeal for the Indians* (1868). In 1860 she edited Harriet Jacobs's *Incidents of the Life of a Slave Girl* (1861).

One of the major literary sources of *Clotel*, "The Quadroons" first appeared in the antislavery miscellany *The Liberty Bell* (Boston: Massachusetts Anti-Slavery Fair, 1842), the source of the text below. It was reprinted in Child's *Fact and Fiction: A Collection of Stories* (1846). Though Brown changed the names and the settings of Child's story, he lifted large swatches of text verbatim for his novel. Surely an important motivation for his appropriation of Child's story was his admiration for her brave antislavery writings. But it is important to note that, in his reworking of "The Quadroons," Brown strategically broke the story into three different sections and, through his use of pastiche and bricolage, put Child's sentimental discourse, plotting, and motifs into dialogue with discourses, plottings, and motifs that granted greater agency to rebellious blacks. Unlike Child's Rosalie and Xarifa, Brown's Clotel and Mary do not die of despair. With his portrayal of Mary and George at the end of *Clotel* (and, later, Clotelle and Jerome at the end of the two versions of *Clotelle*), Brown moved beyond the somewhat truncated, melodramatic ending of Child's story.

> "I promised thee a sister tale,
> Of man's perfidious cruelty;
> Come then and hear what cruel wrong
> Befell the dark ladie."[1]
>
> —COLERIDGE.

Not far from Augusta, Georgia, there is a pleasant place called Sand-Hills, appropriated almost exclusively to summer residences for the wealthy inhabitants of the neighbouring city. Among the beautiful cottages that adorn it was one far retired from the public roads, and almost hidden among the trees. It was a perfect model of rural beauty. The piazzas that surrounded it were wreathed with Clematis and Passion Flower. Magnificent Magnolias, and the superb Pride of India, threw shadows around it, and filled the air with fragrance. Flowers peeped out from every nook, and nodded to you in bye-places, with a most unexpected welcome. The tasteful hand of Art had not learned to *imitate* the lavish beauty and harmonious disorder of Nature, but they lived together in loving unity, and spoke in according tones. The gateway rose in a Gothic arch, with graceful tracery in iron-work, surmounted by a Cross, around which fluttered and played the Mountain Fringe, that lightest and most fragile of vines.

The inhabitants of this cottage remained in it all the year round, and peculiarly enjoyed the season that left them without neighbours. To one of the parties, indeed, the fashionable summer residents, that came and went with the butterflies, were merely neighbours-in-law. The edicts of society had built up a wall of separation between her and them; for she was a quadroon. Conventional laws could not be reversed in her favour, though she was the daughter of a wealthy merchant, was highly cultivated in mind and manners, graceful as an antelope, and beautiful as the evening star. She had early attracted the attention of a handsome and wealthy young Georgian; and as their acquaintance

---

[1] *"I promised . . . dark ladie"*: See *Clotel*, p. 149, note 1.

increased, the purity and bright intelligence of her mind, inspired him with far deeper interest than is ever excited by mere passion. It was genuine love; that mysterious union of soul and sense, in which the lowliest dew-drop reflects the image of the highest star.

The tenderness of Rosalie's conscience required an outward form of marriage; though she well knew that a union with her proscribed race was unrecognised by law, and therefore the ceremony gave her no legal hold on Edward's constancy. But her high poetic nature regarded the reality, rather than the semblance of things; and when he playfully asked how she could keep him if he wished to run away, she replied, "Let the church that my mother loved sanction our union, and my own soul will be satisfied, without the protection of the state. If your affections fall from me, I would not, if I could, hold you by a legal fetter."

It was a marriage sanctioned by Heaven, though unrecognised on earth. The picturesque cottage at Sand-Hills was built for the young bride under her own direction; and there they passed ten as happy years as ever blessed the heart of mortals. It was Edward's fancy to name their eldest child Xarifa; in commemoration of a quaint old Spanish ballad, which had first conveyed to his ears the sweet tones of her mother's voice. Her flexile form and nimble motions were in harmony with the breezy sound of the name; and its Moorish[2] origin was most appropriate to one so emphatically "a child of the sun." Her complexion, of a still lighter brown than Rosalie's, was rich and glowing as an autumnal leaf. The iris of her large, dark eye had the melting, mezzotinto outline, which remains the last vestige of African ancestry, and gives that plaintive expression, so often observed, and so appropriate to that docile and injured race.

Xarifa learned no lessons of humility or shame, within her own happy home; for she grew up in the warm atmosphere of father's and mother's love, like a flower open to the sunshine, and sheltered from the winds. But in summer walks with her beautiful mother, her young cheek often mantled at the rude gaze of the young men, and her dark eye flashed fire, when some contemptuous epithet met her ear, as white ladies passed them by, in scornful pride and ill-concealed envy.

Happy as Rosalie was in Edward's love, and surrounded by an outward environment of beauty, so well adapted to her poetic spirit, she felt these incidents with inexpressible pain. For herself, she cared but

---

[2] *Moorish*: In the style of the Moors—Arab-African Muslims of Northwest Africa celebrated for their art and architecture.

little; for she had found a sheltered home in Edward's heart, which the world might ridicule, but had no power to profane. But when she looked at her beloved Xarifa, and reflected upon the unavoidable and dangerous position which the tyranny of society had awarded her, her soul was filled with anguish. The rare loveliness of the child increased daily, and was evidently ripening into most marvellous beauty. The father rejoiced in it with unmingled pride; but in the deep tenderness of the mother's eye there was an in-dwelling sadness, that spoke of anxious thoughts and fearful forebodings.

When Xarifa entered her ninth year, these uneasy feelings found utterance in earnest solicitations that Edward would remove to France, or England. This request excited but little opposition, and was so attractive to his imagination, that he might have overcome all intervening obstacles, had not "a change come o'er the spirit of his dream."[3] He still loved Rosalie, but he was now twenty-eight years old, and, unconsciously to himself, ambition had for some time been slowly gaining an ascendency over his other feelings. The contagion of example had led him into the arena where so much American strength is wasted; he had thrown himself into political excitement, with all the honest fervour of youthful feeling. His motives had been unmixed with selfishness, nor could he ever define to himself when or how sincere patriotism took the form of personal ambition. But so it was, that at twenty-eight years old, he found himself an ambitious man, involved in movements which his frank nature would have once abhorred, and watching the doubtful game of mutual cunning with all the fierce excitement of a gambler.

Among those on whom his political success most depended, was a very popular and wealthy man, who had an only daughter. His visits to the house were at first of a purely political nature; but the young lady was pleasing, and he fancied he discovered in her a sort of timid preference for himself. This excited his vanity, and awakened thoughts of the great worldly advantages connected with a union. Reminiscences of his first love kept these vague ideas in check for several months; but Rosalie's image at last became an unwelcome intruder; for with it was associated the idea of restraint. Moreover Charlotte, though inferior in beauty, was yet a pretty contrast to her rival. Her light hair fell in silken profusion, her blue eyes were gentle, though inexpressive, and her delicate cheeks were like blush-rose-buds.

[3] "*a change . . . dream*": See *Clotel*, p. 101, note 3.

He had already become accustomed to the dangerous experiment of resisting his own inward convictions; and this new impulse to ambition, combined with the strong temptation of variety in love, met the ardent young man weakened in moral principle, and unfettered by laws of the land. The change wrought upon him was soon noticed by Rosalie.

> "In many ways does the full heart reveal
> The presence of the love it would conceal;
> But in far more the estranged heart lets know
> The absence of the love, which yet it fain would show."[4]

At length the news of his approaching marriage met her ear. Her head grew dizzy, and her heart fainted within her; but, with a strong effort at composure, she inquired all the particulars; and her pure mind at once took its resolution. Edward came that evening, and though she would have fain met him as usual, her heart was too full not to throw a deep sadness over her looks and tones. She had never complained of his decreasing tenderness, or of her own lonely hours; but he felt that the mute appeal of her heart-broken looks was more terrible than words. He kissed the hand she offered, and with a countenance almost as sad as her own, led her to a window in the recess, shadowed by a luxuriant Passion Flower. It was the same seat where they had spent the first evening in this beautiful cottage, consecrated to their youthful loves. The same calm, clear moonlight looked in through the trellis. The vine then planted had now a luxuriant growth; and many a time had Edward fondly twined its sacred blossoms with the glossy ringlets of her raven hair. The rush of memory almost overpowered poor Rosalie; and Edward felt too much oppressed and ashamed to break the long, deep silence. At length, in words scarcely audible, Rosalie said, "Tell me, dear Edward, are you to be married next week?" He dropped her hand, as if a rifle-ball had struck him; and it was not until after long hesitation, that he began to make some reply about the necessity of circumstances. Mildly, but earnestly, the poor girl begged him to spare apologies. It was enough that he no longer loved her, and that they must bid farewell. Trusting to the yielding tenderness of her character, he ventured, in the most soothing accents, to suggest that as he still loved her better than all the world, she would ever be his real wife, and they might see each other frequently. He was not prepared for the storm of indignant emotion his words excited. Hers was a passion too

---

[4] "*In many . . . would show*": See *Clotel*, p. 120, note 1.

absorbing to admit of partnership; and her spirit was too pure and kind to enter into a selfish league against the happiness of the innocent young bride.

At length this painful interview came to an end. They stood together by the Gothic gate, where they had so often met and parted in the moonlight. Old remembrances melted their souls. "Farewell, dearest Edward," said Rosalie. "Give me a parting kiss." Her voice was choked for utterance, and the tears flowed freely, as she bent her lips toward him. He folded her convulsively in his arms, and imprinted a long, impassioned kiss on that mouth, which had never spoken to him but in love and blessing.

With effort like a death-pang, she at length raised her head from his heaving bosom, and turning from him with bitter sobs, she said, "It is our *last*. God bless you. I would not have you so miserable as I am. Farewell. A *last* farewell." "The *last!*" exclaimed he, with a wild shriek. "Oh, Rosalie, do not say that!" and covering his face with his hands, he wept like a child.

Recovering from his emotion, he found himself alone. The moon looked down upon him mild, but very sorrowful; as the Madonna seems to gaze on her worshipping children, bowed down with consciousness of sin. At that moment he would have given worlds to have disengaged himself from Charlotte; but he had gone so far, that blame, disgrace, and duels with angry relatives, would now attend any effort to obtain his freedom. Oh, how the moonlight oppressed him with its friendly sadness! It was like the plaintive eye of his forsaken one; like the music of sorrow echoed from an unseen world.

Long and earnestly he gazed at that dwelling, where he had so long known earth's purest foretaste of heavenly bliss. Slowly he walked away; then turned again to look on that charmed spot, the nestling-place of his young affections. He caught a glimpse of Rosalie, weeping beside a magnolia, which commanded a long view of the path leading to the public road. He would have sprung toward her, but she darted from him, and entered the cottage. That graceful figure, weeping in the moonlight, haunted him for years. It stood before his closing eyes, and greeted him with the morning dawn.

Poor Charlotte! had she known all, what a dreary lot would hers have been; but fortunately, she could not miss the impassioned tenderness she had never experienced; and Edward was the more careful in his kindness, because he was deficient in love. Once or twice she heard him murmur, "dear Rosalie," in his sleep; but the playful charge she brought was playfully answered, and the incident gave her no real uneasiness. The summer after their marriage, she proposed a residence at Sand-Hills; little aware what a whirlwind of emotion she excited in her husband's heart. The reasons he gave for rejecting the proposition appeared satisfactory; but she could not quite understand why he was never willing that their afternoon drives should be in the direction of those pleasant rural residences, which she had heard him praise so much. One day, as their barouche rolled along a winding road that skirted Sand-Hills, her attention was suddenly attracted by two figures among the trees by the way-side; and touching Edward's arm, she exclaimed, "Do look at that beautiful child!" He turned, and saw Rosalie and Xarifa. His lips quivered, and his face became deadly pale. His young wife looked at him intently, but said nothing. There were points of resemblance in the child, that seemed to account for his sudden emotion. Suspicion was awakened, and she soon learned that the mother of that lovely girl bore the name of Rosalie; with this information came recollections of the "dear Rosalie," murmured in uneasy slumbers. From gossiping tongues she soon learned more than she wished to know. She wept, but not as poor Rosalie had done; for she never had loved, and been beloved, like her, and her nature was more proud. Henceforth a change came over her feelings and her manners; and Edward had no further occasion to assume a tenderness in return for hers. Changed as he was by ambition, he felt the wintry chill of her polite propriety, and sometimes in agony of heart, compared it with the gushing love of her who was indeed his wife.

But these, and all his emotions, were a sealed book to Rosalie, of which she could only guess the contents. With remittances for her and her child's support, there sometimes came earnest pleadings that she would consent to see him again; but these she never answered, though her heart yearned to do so. She pitied his fair young bride, and would not be tempted to bring sorrow into their household by any fault of hers. Her earnest prayer was that she might never know of her existence. She had not looked on Edward since she watched him under the shadow of the magnolia, until his barouche passed her in her rambles some months after. She saw the deadly paleness of his countenance, and had he dared to look back, he would have seen her tottering with faintness. Xarifa brought water from a little rivulet, and sprinkled her face. When she revived, she clasped the beloved child to her heart with a vehemence that made her scream. Soothingly she kissed away her fears, and gazed into her beautiful eyes with a deep, deep sadness of expression, which Xarifa never forgot. Wild were the thoughts that pressed around her aching heart, and almost maddened her poor brain; thoughts which had almost driven her to suicide the night of that last farewell. For her child's sake she conquered the fierce temptation then;

and for her sake, she struggled with it now. But the gloomy atmosphere of their once happy home overclouded the morning of Xarifa's life.

> "She from her mother learnt the trick of grief,
> And sighed among her playthings."[5]

Rosalie perceived this; and it gave her gentle heart unutterable pain. At last, the conflicts of her spirit proved too strong for the beautiful frame in which it dwelt. About a year after Edward's marriage, she was found dead in her bed, one bright autumnal morning. She had often expressed to her daughter a wish to be buried under a spreading oak, that shaded a rustic garden-chair, in which she and Edward had spent many happy evenings. And there she was buried; with a small white cross at her head, twined with the cypress vine. Edward came to the funeral, and wept long, very long, at the grave. Hours after midnight, he sat in the recess-window, with Xarifa folded to his heart. The poor child sobbed herself to sleep on his bosom; and the convicted murderer had small reason to envy that wretched man, as he gazed on the lovely countenance, which so strongly reminded him of his early and his only love.

From that time, Xarifa was the central point of all his warmest affections. He hired an excellent old negress to take charge of the cottage, from which he promised his darling child that she should never be removed. He employed a music master, and dancing master, to attend upon her; and a week never passed without a visit from him, and a present of books, pictures, or flowers. To hear her play upon the harp, or repeat some favourite poem in her mother's earnest accents and melodious tones, or to see her pliant figure float in the garland-dance, seemed to be the highest enjoyment of his life. Yet was the pleasure mixed with bitter thoughts. What would be the destiny of this fascinating young creature, so radiant with life and beauty? She belonged to a proscribed race; and though the brown colour on her soft cheek was scarcely deeper than the sunny side of a golden pear, yet was it sufficient to exclude her from virtuous society. He thought of Rosalie's wish to carry her to France: and he would have fulfilled it, had he been unmarried. As it was, he inwardly resolved to make some arrangement to effect it in a few years, even if it involved separation from his darling child.

But alas for the calculations of man! From the time of Rosalie's death, Edward had sought relief for his wretched feelings in the free

---

[5] *"She . . . sighed among her playthings"*: From William Wordsworth, *The Excursion* (1814), Book First.

use of wine. Xarifa was scarcely fifteen, when her father was found dead by the road-side; having fallen from his horse, on his way to visit her. He left no will; but his wife, with kindness of heart worthy of a happier domestic fate, expressed a decided reluctance to change any of the plans he had made for the beautiful child at Sand-Hills.

Xarifa mourned her indulgent father; but not as one utterly desolute. True, she had lived "like a flower deep hid in rocky cleft;"[6] but the sunshine of love had already peeped in upon her. Her teacher on the harp was a handsome and agreeable young man of twenty, the only son of an English widow. Perhaps Edward had not been altogether unmindful of the result, when he first invited him to the flowery cottage. Certain it is, he had more than once thought what a pleasant thing it would be, if English freedom from prejudice should lead him to offer legal protection to his graceful and winning child. Being thus encouraged, rather than checked, in his admiration, George Elliot could not be otherwise than strongly attracted toward his beautiful pupil. The lonely and unprotected state in which her father's death left her, deepened this feeling into tenderness. And lucky was it for her enthusiastic and affectionate nature; for she could not live without an atmosphere of love. In her innocence, she knew nothing of the dangers in her path; and she trusted George with an undoubting simplicity, that rendered her sacred to his noble and generous soul. It seemed as if that flower-embosomed nest was consecrated by the Fates to Love. The French have well named it *La Belle Passion*; for without it life were "a year without spring, or a spring without roses." Except the loveliness of infancy, what does earth offer so much like Heaven, as the happiness of two young, pure, and beautiful beings, living in each other's hearts?

Xarifa inherited her mother's poetic and impassioned temperament; and to her, above others, the first consciousness of these sweet emotions was like a golden sunrise on the sleeping flowers.

> "Thus stood she at the threshold of the scene
> Of busy life. * * * *
> How fair it lay in solemn shade and sheen!
> And he beside her, like some angel, posted
> To lead her out of childhood's fairy land,
> On to life's glancing summit, hand in hand."[7]

---

[6] *"like a flower . . . cleft"*: From "A Poem on the Death of Charlotte Princess of Wales," by English poet Rann Kennedy (1759–1805).

[7] *Thus stood . . . hand in hand"*: From *The Death of Wallenstein* (1799), a play by the German author Friedrich Schiller (1759–1805).

Alas, the tempest was brooding over their young heads. Rosalie, though she knew it not, had been the daughter of a slave, whose wealthy master, though he remained attached to her to the end of her days, yet carelessly omitted to have papers of manumission recorded. His heirs had lately failed, under circumstances which greatly exasperated their creditors; and in an unlucky hour, they discovered their claim on Angelique's grand-child.

The gentle girl, happy as the birds in spring-time accustomed to the fondest indulgence, surrounded by all the refinements of life, timid as a fawn, and with a soul full of romance, was ruthlessly seized by a sheriff, and placed on the public auction-stand in Savannah. There she stood, trembling, blushing, and weeping; compelled to listen to the grossest language, and shrinking from the rude hands that examined the graceful proportions of her beautiful frame. "Stop that!" exclaimed a stern voice. "I bid two thousand dollars for her, without asking any of their d—d questions." The speaker was probably about forty years of age, with handsome features, but a fierce and proud expression. An older man, who stood behind him, bid two thousand five hundred. The first bid higher; then a third, a dashing young man, bid three thousand; and thus they went on, with the keen excitement of gamblers, until the first speaker obtained the prize, for the moderate sum of five thousand dollars.

And where was George, during this dreadful scene? He was absent on a visit to his mother, at Mobile. But, had he been at Sand-Hills, he could not have saved his beloved from the wealthy profligate, who was determined to obtain her at any price. A letter of agonized entreaty from her brought him home on the wings of the wind. But what could he do? How could he ever obtain a sight of her, locked up as she was in the princely mansion of her master? At last, by bribing one of the slaves, he conveyed a letter to her, and received one in return. As yet, her purchaser treated her with respectful gentleness, and sought to win her favour, by flattery and presents; but she dreaded every moment, lest the scene should change, and trembled at the sound of every footfall. A plan was laid for escape. The slave agreed to drug his master's wine; a ladder of ropes was prepared, and a swift boat was in readiness. But the slave, to obtain a double reward, was treacherous. Xarifa had scarcely given an answering signal to the low cautious whistle of her lover, when the sharp sound of a rifle was followed by a deep groan, and a heavy fall on the pavement of the court-yard. With frenzied eagerness she swung herself down by the ladder of ropes, and, by the glancing light of lanthorns, saw George, bleeding and lifeless at her feet. One wild shriek, that pierced the brains of those who heard it, and she fell senseless by his side.

For many days she had a confused consciousness of some great agony, but knew not where she was, or by whom she was surrounded. The slow recovery of her reason settled into the most intense melancholy, which moved the compassion even of her cruel purchaser. The beautiful eyes, always pensive in expression, were now so heart-piercing in their sadness, that he could not endure to look upon them. For some months, he sought to win her smiles by lavish presents, and delicate attentions. He bought glittering chains of gold, and costly bands of pearl. His victim scarcely glanced at them, and her attendant slave laid them away, unheeded and forgotten. He purchased the furniture of the Cottage at Sand-Hills, and one morning Xarifa found her harp at the bedside, and the room filled with her own books, pictures, and flowers. She gazed upon them with a pang unutterable, and burst into an agony of tears; but she gave her master no thanks, and her gloom deepened.

At last his patience was exhausted. He grew weary of her obstinacy, as he was pleased to term it; and threats took the place of persuasion.

*   *   *   *   *   *   *

In a few months more, poor Xarifa was a raving maniac. That pure temple was desecrated; that loving heart was broken; and that beautiful head fractured against the wall in the frenzy of despair. Her master cursed the useless expense she had cost him; the slaves buried her; and no one wept at the grave of her who had been so carefully cherished, and so tenderly beloved.

Reader, do you complain that I have written fiction? Believe me, scenes like these are of no unfrequent occurrence at the South. The world does not afford such materials for tragic romance, as the history of the Quadroons.

HARRIET BEECHER STOWE

The Quadroon's Story

With the publication of *Uncle Tom's Cabin* in 1852, the heretofore little-known New England regionalist writer Harriet Beecher Stowe (1811–1896), author of *The Mayflower; or, Sketches of Scenes and Characters Among the Descendants of the Puritans* (1843), became famous. But fame had always gone hand in hand with the Beecher family. Her father, Lyman

Beecher, was a prominent Congregationalist clergyman who in 1832 became president of the soon-to-be embattled Lane Theological Seminary; her sister Catharine Beecher was a pioneer in women's education and the best-known domestic writer of the time; and her brother Henry Ward Beecher was a celebrated New York preacher. (Her husband, Calvin Ellis Stowe, a professor of biblical literature at Lane when she married him in 1836, was rather more retiring.) Harriet Beecher Stowe became interested in the debate on slavery in the mid-1830s, when Theodore Dwight Weld and the other "Lane Rebels" challenged her father's authority, and in 1845 Stowe wrote her first antislavery sketch, "Immediate Emancipation." *Uncle Tom's Cabin*, serialized in the *National Era* between 1851 and 1852, was inspired in large part by her angry response to the Fugitive Slave Law, though her haunting depictions of slave mothers separated from their children may have been inspired by her grief at the death of her young son Samuel in 1849. The novel was widely read in the United States and abroad, selling approximately 350,000 copies during its first year in print, and around one million copies by the end of the decade. African Americans had a mixed but mostly positive response to the novel. Frederick Douglass, for example, thought the book a godsend that would help to inspire worldwide sympathy for the plight of the American slave; Martin Delany, however, found the novel to be racist and overly sympathetic to the colonizationists' agenda of shipping African Americans to Africa. In a letter to William Lloyd Garrison printed in the 3 June 1853 issue of the *Liberator*, Brown praised Stowe, declaring that her novel "has come down upon the dark abodes of slavery like a morning's sunlight, unfolding to view its enormities in a manner which has fastened all eyes upon the 'peculiar institution,' and awakening sympathy in hearts that never before felt for the slave" (pp. 377–78). Whatever their views on Stowe, it was difficult for African Americans writing in the wake of *Uncle Tom's Cabin* to ignore its images, rhetorical strategies, and ideas. In 1856 Stowe published a second antislavery novel, *Dred; A Tale of the Great Dismal Swamp*.

Like Lydia Maria Child's "The Quadroons," Stowe's chapter "The Quadroon's Story," which comes late in *Uncle Tom's Cabin*, works with the figure of the "tragic mulatta." Tom has been purchased by the satanic slave master Simon Legree, who has also purchased and brought to his Louisiana plantation the young slave woman Emmeline, whom he intends to make into his concubine. At the plantation is the older slave woman Cassy, Legree's former forced concubine, who regards the slaves' situation with an apparently hopeless despair. The prideful and embittered Cassy, who wields a certain power over Legree, tells Tom her life history after he has been viciously flogged by Legree's overseers. Though by reputation a passive, Christlike hero, Tom has been flogged for actively refusing Legree's command to flog an infirm slave woman. The selection is from *Uncle Tom's Cabin; Or, Life Among the Lowly* (Boston: John P. Jewett and Company, 1852), 198–212.

And behold the tears of such as are oppressed; and on the side of their oppressors there was power. Wherefore I praised the dead that are already dead more than the living that are yet alive.

—Eccl. 4 : 1.

It was late at night, and Tom lay groaning and bleeding alone, in an old forsaken room of the gin-house, among pieces of broken machinery, piles of damaged cotton, and other rubbish which had there accumulated.

The night was damp and close, and the thick air swarmed with myriads of mosquitos, which increased the restless torture of his wounds; whilst a burning thirst—a torture beyond all others—filled up the uttermost measure of physical anguish.

"O, good Lord! *Do* look down,—give me the victory!—give me the victory over all!" prayed poor Tom, in his anguish.

A footstep entered the room, behind him, and the light of a lantern flashed on his eyes.

"Who 's there? O, for the Lord's massy, please give me some water!"

The woman Cassy—for it was she—set down her lantern, and, pouring water from a bottle, raised his head, and gave him drink. Another and another cup were drained, with feverish eagerness.

"Drink all ye want," she said; "I knew how it would be. It is n't the first time I 've been out in the night, carrying water to such as you."

"Thank you, Missis," said Tom, when he had done drinking.

"Don't call me Missis! I 'm a miserable slave, like yourself,—a lower one than you can ever be!" said she, bitterly; "but now," said she, going to the door, and dragging in a small pallaise,[1] over which she had spread linen cloths wet with cold water, "try, my poor fellow, to roll yourself on to this."

Stiff with wounds and bruises, Tom was a long time in accomplishing this movement; but, when done, he felt a sensible relief from the cooling application to his wounds.

[1] *pallaise*: A mattress filled with sawdust or straw; from the French *paillasse*, and in English usually *palliasse*.

The woman, whom long practice with the victims of brutality had made familiar with many healing arts, went on to make many applications to Tom's wounds, by means of which he was soon somewhat relieved.

"Now," said the woman, when she had raised his head on a roll of damaged cotton, which served for a pillow, "there 's the best I can do for you."

Tom thanked her; and the woman, sitting down on the floor, drew up her knees, and embracing them with her arms, looked fixedly before her, with a bitter and painful expression of countenance. Her bonnet fell back, and long wavy streams of black hair fell around her singular and melancholy face.

"It 's no use, my poor fellow!" she broke out, at last, "it 's of no use, this you 've been trying to do. You were a brave fellow, — you had the right on your side; but it 's all in vain, and out of the question, for you to struggle. You are in the devil's hands; — he is the strongest, and you must give up!"

Give up! and, had not human weakness and physical agony whispered that, before? Tom started; for the bitter woman, with her wild eyes and melancholy voice, seemed to him an embodiment of the temptation with which he had been wrestling.

"O Lord! O Lord!" he groaned, "how can I give up?"

"There 's no use calling on the Lord, — he never hears," said the woman, steadily; "there is n't any God, I believe; or, if there is, he 's taken sides against us. All goes against us, heaven and earth. Everything is pushing us into hell. Why should n't we go?"

Tom closed his eyes, and shuddered at the dark, atheistic words.

"You see," said the woman, "*you* don't know anything about it; — I do. I 've been on this place five years, body and soul, under this man's foot; and I hate him as I do the devil! Here you are, on a lone plantation, ten miles from any other, in the swamps; not a white person here, who could testify, if you were burned alive, — if you were scalded, cut into inch-pieces, set up for the dogs to tear, or hung up and whipped to death. There 's no law here, of God or man, that can do you, or any one of us, the least good; and, this man! there 's no earthly thing that he 's too good to do. I could make any one's hair rise, and their teeth chatter, if I should only tell what I 've seen and been knowing to, here, — and it 's no use resisting! Did I *want* to live with him? Was n't I a woman delicately bred; and he — God in heaven! what was he, and is he? And yet, I 've lived with him, these five years, and cursed every moment of my life, — night and day! And now, he 's got a new one, —

a young thing, only fifteen, and she brought up, she says, piously. Her good mistress taught her to read the Bible; and she 's brought her Bible here—to hell with her!"—and the woman laughed a wild and doleful laugh, that rung, with a strange, supernatural sound, through the old ruined shed.

Tom folded his hands; all was darkness and horror.

"O Jesus! Lord Jesus! have you quite forgot us poor critturs?" burst forth, at last;—"help, Lord, I perish!"

The woman sternly continued:

"And what are these miserable low dogs you work with, that you should suffer on their account? Every one of them would turn against you, the first time they got a chance. They are all of 'em as low and cruel to each other as they can be; there 's no use in your suffering to keep from hurting them."

"Poor critturs!" said Tom,—"what made 'em cruel?—and, if I give out, I shall get used to 't, and grow, little by little, just like 'em! No, no, Missis! I 've lost everything,—wife, and children, and home, and a kind Mas'r,—and he would have set me free, if he 'd only lived a week longer;—I 've lost everything in *this* world, and it 's clean gone, forever,—and now I *can't* lose Heaven, too; no, I can't get to be wicked, besides all!"

"But it can't be that the Lord will lay sin to our account," said the woman; "he won't charge it to us, when we 're forced to it; he 'll charge it to them that drove us to it."

"Yes," said Tom; "but that won't keep us from growing wicked. If I get to be as hard-hearted as that ar' Sambo,[2] and as wicked, it won't make much odds to me how I come so; it 's the *bein' so*,—that ar 's what I 'm a dreadin'."

The woman fixed a wild and startled look on Tom, as if a new thought had struck her; and then, heavily groaning, said,

"O God a' mercy! you speak the truth! O—O—O!"—and, with groans, she fell on the floor, like one crushed and writhing under the extremity of mental anguish.

There was a silence, a while, in which the breathing of both parties could be heard, when Tom faintly said, "O, please, Missis!"

The woman suddenly rose up, with her face composed to its usual stern, melancholy expression.

"Please, Missis, I saw 'em throw my coat in that ar' corner, and in my coat-pocket is my Bible;—if Missis would please get it for me."

---

[2] *Sambo*: The name given to this particular slave overseer on Simon Legree's plantation; usually a derogatory term for the supposedly loyal and happy black slave.

Cassy went and got it. Tom opened, at once, to a heavily marked passage, much worn, of the last scenes in the life of Him by whose stripes we are healed.

"If Missis would only be so good as read that ar', — it 's better than water."

Cassy took the book, with a dry, proud air, and looked over the passage. She then read aloud, in a soft voice, and with a beauty of intonation that was peculiar, that touching account of anguish and of glory. Often, as she read, her voice faltered, and sometimes failed her altogether, when she would stop, with an air of frigid composure, till she had mastered herself. When she came to the touching words, "Father forgive them, for they know not what they do,"[3] she threw down the book, and, burying her face in the heavy masses of her hair, she sobbed aloud, with a convulsive violence.

Tom was weeping, also, and occasionally uttering a smothered ejaculation.

"If we only could keep up to that ar'!" said Tom; —"it seemed to come so natural to him, and we have to fight so hard for 't! O Lord, help us! O blessed Lord Jesus, do help us!"

"Missis," said Tom, after a while, "I can see that, some how, you 're quite 'bove me in everything; but there 's one thing Missis might learn even from poor Tom. Ye said the Lord took sides against us, because he lets us be 'bused and knocked round; but ye see what come on his own Son, — the blessed Lord of Glory, — wan't he allays poor? and have we, any on us, yet come so low as he come? The Lord han't forgot us, — I 'm sartin' o' that ar'. If we suffer with him, we shall also reign, Scripture says; but, if we deny Him, he also will deny us. Did n't they all suffer? — the Lord and all his? It tells how they was stoned and sawn asunder, and wandered about in sheep-skins and goat-skins, and was destitute, afflicted, tormented. Sufferin' an't no reason to make us think the Lord 's turned again us; but jest the contrary, if only we hold on to him, and does n't give up to sin."

"But why does he put us where we can't help but sin?" said the woman.

"I think we *can* help it," said Tom.

"You 'll see," said Cassy; "what 'll you do? To-morrow they 'll be at you again. I know 'em; I 've seen all their doings; I can't bear to think of all they 'll bring you to; — and they 'll make you give out, at last!"

[3] *"Father forgive . . . do"*: Christ's words on the Cross; see Luke 23.34.

"Lord Jesus!" said Tom, "you *will* take care of my soul? O Lord, do!—don't let me give out!"

"O dear!" said Cassy; "I 've heard all this crying and praying before; and yet, they 've been broken down, and brought under. There 's Emmeline, she 's trying to hold on, and you 're trying,—but what use? You must give up, or be killed by inches."

"Well, then, I *will* die!" said Tom. "Spin it out as long as they can, they can't help my dying, some time!—and, after that, they can't do no more. I 'm clar, I 'm set! I *know* the Lord 'll help me, and bring me through."

The woman did not answer; she sat with her black eyes intently fixed on the floor.

"May be it 's the way," she murmured to herself; "but those that *have* given up, there 's no hope for them!—none! We live in filth, and grow loathsome, till we loathe ourselves! And we long to die, and we don't dare to kill ourselves!—No hope! no hope! no hope!—this girl now,—just as old as I was!

"You see me now," she said, speaking to Tom very rapidly; "see what I am! Well, I was brought up in luxury; the first I remember is, playing about, when I was a child, in splendid parlors;—when I was kept dressed up like a doll, and company and visitors used to praise me. There was a garden opening from the saloon windows; and there I used to play hide-and-go-seek, under the orange-trees, with my brothers and sisters. I went to a convent, and there I learned music, French and embroidery, and what not; and when I was fourteen, I came out to my father's funeral. He died very suddenly, and when the property came to be settled, they found that there was scarcely enough to cover the debts; and when the creditors took an inventory of the property, I was set down on it. My mother was a slave woman, and my father had always meant to set me free; but he had not done it, and so I was set down in the list. I 'd always known who I was, but never thought much about it. Nobody ever expects that a strong, healthy man is a going to die. My father was a well man only four hours before he died;—it was one of the first cholera cases in New Orleans. The day after the funeral, my father's wife took her children, and went up to her father's plantation. I thought they treated me strangely, but did n't know. There was a young lawyer who they left to settle the business; and he came every day, and was about the house, and spoke very politely to me. He brought with him, one day, a young man, whom I thought the handsomest I had ever seen. I shall never forget that evening. I walked with him in the garden. I was lonesome and full of sorrow, and he was so kind and gentle to me; and he told me that he had seen me before I went to the convent, and that he had loved me a great while, and that he would be my friend and protector;—in short, though he did n't tell me, he had paid two thousand dollars for me, and I was his property,—I became his willingly, for I loved him. Loved!" said the woman, stopping. "O, how I *did* love that man! How I love him now,—and always shall, while I breathe! He was so beautiful, so high, so noble! He put me into a beautiful house, with servants, horses, and carriages, and furniture, and dresses. Everything that money could buy, he gave me; but I did n't set any value on all that,—I only cared for him. I loved him better than my God and my own soul; and, if I tried, I could n't do any other way from what he wanted me to.

"I wanted only one thing—I did want him to *marry* me. I thought, if he loved me as he said he did, and if I was what he seemed to think I was, he would be willing to marry me and set me free. But he convinced me that it would be impossible; and he told me that, if we were only faithful to each other, it was marriage before God. If that is true, was n't I that man's wife? Was n't I faithful? For seven years, did n't I study every look and motion, and only live and breathe to please him? He had the yellow fever, and for twenty days and nights I watched with him. I alone,—and gave him all his medicine, and did everything for him; and then he called me his good angel, and said I 'd saved his life. We had two beautiful children. The first was a boy, and we called him Henry. He was the image of his father,—he had such beautiful eyes, such a forehead, and his hair hung all in curls around it; and he had all his father's spirit, and his talent, too. Little Elise, he said, looked like me. He used to tell me that I was the most beautiful woman in Louisiana, he was so proud of me and the children. He used to love to have me dress them up, and take them and me about in an open carriage, and hear the remarks that people would make on us; and he used to fill my ears constantly with the fine things that were said in praise of me and the children. O, those were happy days! I thought I was as happy as any one could be; but then there came evil times. He had a cousin come to New Orleans, who was his particular friend,— he thought all the world of him;—but, from the first time I saw him, I could n't tell why, I dreaded him; for I felt sure he was going to bring misery on us. He got Henry to going out with him, and often he would not come home nights till two or three o'clock. I did not dare say a word; for Henry was so high-spirited, I was afraid to. He got him to the gaming-houses; and he was one of the sort that, when he once got a going there, there was no holding back. And then he introduced him to another lady, and I saw soon that his heart was gone from me. He never told me, but I saw it,—I knew it, day after day,—I felt my heart breaking, but I could not say a word! At this, the wretch offered to buy me and the children of Henry, to clear off his gambling debts, which stood in the way of his marrying as he wished;—and *he sold us.* He told me, one day, that he had business in the country, and should be gone two or three weeks. He spoke kinder than usual, and said he should come back; but it did n't deceive me. I knew that the time had come; I was just like one turned into stone; I could n't speak, nor shed a tear. He kissed me and kissed the children, a good many times, and went out. I saw him get on his horse, and I watched him till he was quite out of sight; and then I fell down, and fainted.

"Then *he* came, the cursed wretch! he came to take possession. He told me that he had bought me and my children; and showed me the papers. I cursed him before God, and told him I 'd die sooner than live with him.

" 'Just as you please,' he said; 'but, if you don't behave reasonably, I'll sell both the children, where you shall never see them again.' He told me that he always had meant to have me, from the first time he saw me; and that he had drawn Henry on, and got him in debt, on purpose to make him willing to sell me. That he got him in love with another woman; and that I might know, after all that, that he should not give up for a few airs and tears, and things of that sort.

"I gave up, for my hands were tied. He had my children;—whenever I resisted his will anywhere, he would talk about selling them, and he made me as submissive as he desired. O, what a life it was! to live with my heart breaking, every day,—to keep on, on, on, loving, when it was only misery; and to be bound, body and soul, to one I hated. I used to love to read to Henry, to play to him, to waltz with him, and sing to him; but everything I did for this one was a perfect drag,—yet I was afraid to refuse anything. He was very imperious, and harsh to the children. Elise was a timid little thing; but Henry was bold and high-spirited, like his father, and he had never been brought under, in the least, by any one. He was always finding fault, and quarrelling with him; and I used to live in daily fear and dread. I tried to make the child respectful;—I tried to keep them apart, for I held on to those children like death; but it did no good. *He sold both those children.* He took me to ride, one day, and when I came home, they were nowhere to be found! He told me he had sold them; he showed me the money, the price of their blood. Then it seemed as if all good forsook me. I raved and cursed,—cursed God and man; and, for a while, I believe, he really was afraid of me. But he did n't give up so. He told me that my children were sold, but whether I ever saw their faces again, depended on him; and that, if I was n't quiet, they should smart for it. Well, you can do anything with a woman, when you 've got her children. He made me submit; he made me be peaceable; he flattered me with hopes that, perhaps, he would buy them back; and so things went on, a week or two. One day, I was out walking, and passed by the calaboose;[4] I saw a crowd about the gate, and heard a child's voice,— and suddenly my Henry broke away from two or three men who were holding him, and ran, screaming, and caught my dress. They came up to him, swearing dreadfully; and one man, whose face I shall never forget, told him that he would n't get away so; that he was going with him into the calaboose, and he 'd get a lesson there he 'd never forget. I tried to beg and plead,—they only laughed; the poor boy screamed and looked into my face, and held on to me, until, in tearing him off, they tore the skirt of my dress half away; and they carried him in, screaming 'Mother! mother! mother!' There was one man stood there seemed to pity me. I offered him all the money I had, if he 'd only inter- fere. He shook his head, and said that the boy had been impudent and disobedient, ever since he bought him; that he was going to break him in, once for all. I turned and ran; and every step of the way, I thought that I heard him scream. I got into the house; ran, all out of breath, to the parlor, where I found Butler. I told him, and begged him to go and interfere. He only laughed, and told me the boy had got his deserts. He 'd got to be broken in,—the sooner the better; 'what did I expect?' he asked.

"It seemed to me something in my head snapped, at that moment. I felt dizzy and furious. I remember seeing a great sharp bowie-knife on the table; I remember something about catching it, and flying upon him; and then all grew dark, and I did n't know any more—not for days and days.

"When I came to myself, I was in a nice room,—but not mine. An old black woman tended me; and a doctor came to see me, and there was a great deal of care taken of me. After a while, I found that he had gone away, and left me at this house to be sold; and that 's why they took such pains with me.

"I did n't mean to get well, and hoped I should n't; but, in spite of me, the fever went off, and I grew healthy, and finally got up. Then, they made me dress up, every day; and gentlemen used to come in and

[4] *calaboose*: Building used as a jail, prison, or, in this instance, slave pen.

stand and smoke their cigars, and look at me, and ask questions, and debate my price. I was so gloomy and silent, that none of them wanted me. They threatened to whip me, if I was n't gayer, and did n't take some pains to make myself agreeable. At length, one day, came a gentleman named Stuart. He seemed to have some feeling for me; he saw that something dreadful was on my heart, and he came to see me alone, a great many times, and finally persuaded me to tell him. He bought me, at last, and promised to do all he could to find and buy back my children. He went to the hotel where my Henry was; they told him he had been sold to a planter up on Pearl river;[5] that was the last that I ever heard. Then he found where my daughter was; an old woman was keeping her. He offered an immense sum for her, but they would not sell her. Butler found out that it was for me he wanted her; and he sent me word that I should never have her. Captain Stuart was very kind to me; he had a splendid plantation, and took me to it. In the course of a year, I had a son born. O, that child! — how I loved it! How just like my poor Henry the little thing looked! But I had made up my mind, — yes, I had. I would never again let a child live to grow up! I took the little fellow in my arms, when he was two weeks old, and kissed him, and cried over him; and then I gave him laudanum,[6] and held him close to my bosom, while he slept to death. How I mourned and cried over it! and who ever dreamed that it was anything but a mistake, that had made me give it the laudanum? but it 's one of the few things that I 'm glad of, now. I am not sorry, to this day; he, at least, is out of pain. What better than death could I give him, poor child! After a while, the cholera came, and Captain Stuart died; everybody died that wanted to live, — and I, — I, though I went down to death's door, — *I lived!* Then I was sold, and passed from hand to hand, till I grew faded and wrinkled, and I had a fever; and then this wretch bought me, and brought me here, — and here I am!"

The woman stopped. She had hurried on through her story, with a wild, passionate utterance; sometimes seeming to address it to Tom, and sometimes speaking as in a soliloquy. So vehement and overpowering was the force with which she spoke, that, for a season, Tom was beguiled even from the pain of his wounds, and, raising himself on one elbow, watched her as she paced restlessly up and down, her long black hair swaying heavily about her, as she moved.

---

[5] *Pearl river:* River in central Mississippi.
[6] *laudanum:* A solution of alcohol and opium.

"You tell me," she said, after a pause, "that there is a God,—a God that looks down and sees all these things. May be it's so. The sisters in the convent used to tell me of a day of judgment, when everything is coming to light;—won't there be vengeance, then!

"They think it's nothing, what we suffer,—nothing, what our children suffer! It's all a small matter; yet I've walked the streets when it seemed as if I had misery enough in my one heart to sink the city. I've wished the houses would fall on me, or the stones sink under me. Yes! and, in the judgment day, I will stand up before God, a witness against those that have ruined me and my children, body and soul!

"When I was a girl, I thought I was religious; I used to love God and prayer. Now, I'm a lost soul, pursued by devils that torment me day and night; they keep pushing me on and on—and I'll do it, too, some of these days!" she said, clenching her hand, while an insane light glanced in her heavy black eyes. "I'll send him where he belongs,—a short way, too,—one of these nights, if they burn me alive for it!" A wild, long laugh, rang through the deserted room, and ended in a hysteric sob; she threw herself on the floor, in convulsive sobbings and struggles.

In a few moments, the frenzy fit seemed to pass off; she rose slowly, and seemed to collect herself.

"Can I do anything more for you, my poor fellow?" she said, approaching where Tom lay; "shall I give you some more water?"

There was a graceful and compassionate sweetness in her voice and manner, as she said this, that formed a strange contrast with the former wildness.

Tom drank the water, and looked earnestly and pitifully into her face.

"O, Missis, I wish you'd go to him that can give you living waters!"

"Go to him! Where is he? Who is he?" said Cassy.

"Him that you read of to me,—the Lord."

"I used to see the picture of him; over the altar, when I was a girl," said Cassy, her dark eyes fixing themselves in an expression of mournful reverie; "but, *he isn't here*! there's nothing here, but sin and long, long, long despair! O!" She laid her hand on her breast and drew in her breath, as if to lift a heavy weight.

Tom looked as if he would speak again; but she cut him short, with a decided gesture.

"Don't talk, my poor fellow. Try to sleep, if you can." And, placing water in his reach, and making whatever little arrangements for his comfort she could, Cassy left the shed.

FREDERICK DOUGLASS

From *Reception Speech at Finsbury Chapel*

In May 1846, Douglass, who was still legally a slave in the United States, gave an antislavery speech before approximately 3,000 people at London's Finsbury Chapel. Near the end of the speech, which he titled "Reception Speech at Finsbury Chapel, Moorfields, England, May 12, 1846," he described an incident that would appear to have inspired Grace Greenwood's poem "The Leap from the Long Bridge" and a key chapter of *Clotel*. The speech was reprinted in antislavery newspapers in Great Britain and the United States. The text is taken from Douglass's own later reprinting in *My Bondage and My Freedom* (New York and Auburn: Miller, Orton, and Mulligan, 1855).

Some two years since, the Hon. Seth M. Gates,[1] an anti-slavery gentleman of the state of New York, a representative in the congress of the United States, told me he saw with his own eyes the following circumstance. In the national District of Columbia, over which the star-spangled emblem is constantly waving, where orators are holding forth on the subject of American liberty, American democracy, American republicanism, there are two slave prisons. When going across a bridge, leading to one of these prisons, he saw a young woman run out, barefooted and bare-headed, and with very little clothing on. She was running with all speed to the bridge he was approaching. His eye was fixed upon her, and he stopped to see what was the matter. He had not paused long before he saw three men run out after her. He now knew what the nature of the case was; a slave escaping from her chains — a young woman, a sister — escaping from the bondage in which she had been held. She made her way to the bridge, but had not reached it, ere from the Virginia side there came two slaveholders. As soon as they saw them, her pursuers called out, "Stop her!" True to their Virginian instincts, they came to the rescue of their brother kidnappers, across the bridge. The poor girl now saw that there was no chance for her. It was a trying time. She knew if she went back, she must be a

---

[1] *Seth M. Gates:* A New York lawyer, Seth Merrill Gates (1800–1877) served two terms in Congress (1839–43) as an antislavery Whig. His house in Warsaw, New York, became an important stop on the Underground Railroad for runaway slaves fleeing to Canada.

slave forever—she must be dragged down to the scenes of pollution
which the slaveholders continually provide for most of the poor, sink-
ing, wretched young women, whom they call their property. She
formed her resolution; and just as those who were about to take her,
were going to put hands upon her, to drag her back, she leaped over
the balustrades of the bridge, and down she went to rise no more. She
chose death, rather than to go back into the hands of those christian
slaveholders from whom she had escaped.

GRACE GREENWOOD

The Leap from the Long Bridge.
An Incident at Washington.

Born Sara Jane Clarke, Grace Greenwood (1823–1904), the popular
journalist, children's writer, and poet, adopted her pen name at the age of
nineteen after moving from New York to Pennsylvania and beginning her
career as a journalist. She wrote for *Godey's Lady's Book*, the antislavery
National Era, and other magazines and journals. Among her best-known
books are *Greenwood Leaves* (1850), a collection of her periodical sketches,
and *Haps and Mishaps of a Tour in Europe* (1854). She regularly lectured
on social reform, and during the Civil War earned President Lincoln's praise
as "Grace Greenwood, the Patriot" for her many visits to Union hospitals
and camps. An important source for a key scene in *Clotel*, and perhaps
influenced by the account in Douglass's "Reception Speech," "The Leap
from the Long Bridge" appeared in Grace Greenwood, *Poems* (Boston:
Ticknor, Reed, and Fields, 1851), 73–75, from which this text is taken.
In *Clotel*, Brown also "takes" the text, reprinting it with several minor
changes and one major change—a new final stanza.

A woman once made her escape from the slave-prison, which stands mid-
way between the Capitol and the President's house, and ran for the Long
Bridge, crossing the Potomac to the extensive grounds and woodlands of
Arlington Place.

> Now rest for the wretched. The long day is past,
> And night on yon prison descendeth at last.
> Now lock up and bolt.—Ha, jailer! look there!

The Long Bridge, circa 1862. Courtesy of the Library of Congress.

Who flies like a wild bird escaped from the snare?
   A woman,—a slave! Up! out in pursuit,
     While linger some gleams of the day!
   Ho! rally thy hunters, with halloo and shout,
     To chase down the game,—and away!

A bold race for freedom!—On, fugitive, on!
Heaven help but the right, and thy freedom is won.
How eager she drinks the free air of the plains!
Every limb, every nerve, every fibre, she strains;
   From Columbia's glorious Capitol
     Columbia's daughter flees
   To the sanctuary God hath given,
     The sheltering forest-trees.

Now she treads the Long Bridge,—joy lighteth her eye,—
Beyond her the dense wood and darkening sky;
Wild hopes thrill her breast as she neareth the shore,—
O despair!—there are *men* fast advancing before!
   Shame, shame on their manhood!—they hear, they heed,
     The cry her flight to stay,
   And, like demon-forms, with their outstretched arms
     They wait to seize their prey!

She pauses, she turns,—ah! will she flee back?
Like wolves her pursuers howl loud on her track;
She lifteth to Heaven one look of despair,
Her anguish breaks forth in one hurried prayer.
   Hark, her jailer's yell!—like a bloodhound's bay
     On the low night-wind it sweeps!
   Now death, or the chain!—to the stream she turns,
     And she leaps, O God, she leaps!

The dark and the cold, yet merciful wave
Receives to its bosom the form of the slave.
She rises,—earth's scenes on her dim vision gleam,
But she struggleth not with the strong, rushing stream,
   And low are the death-cries her woman's heart gives
     As she floats adown the river;
   Faint and more faint grows her drowning voice,
     And her cries have ceased for ever!

Now back, jailer, back to thy dungeons again,
To swing the red lash and rivet the chain!
The form thou wouldst fetter a valueless clod,
The soul thou wouldst barter returned to her God!
   She lifts in His light her unmanacled hands;
      She flees through the darkness no more;
   To freedom she leaped through drowning and death,
      And her sorrow and bondage are o'er.

DANIEL WEBSTER

From *The Constitution and the Union*

On 7 March 1850, Daniel Webster (1782–1852) addressed the Senate on the importance of supporting the Compromise of 1850. By reputation America's greatest orator, and at the time a Whig senator from Massachusetts, Webster was known for his absolute, almost mystical commitment to the idea of Union, and had made his political reputation by attacking the nullification arguments of John C. Calhoun and other Southern politicians. Concerned that abolitionism was pushing the Southern states toward secession, Webster saw the Compromise of 1850 as the best possible hope for preserving the Union, a goal that he regarded as far more desirable than fighting for an immediate end to slavery. Webster, who previously as congressman, presidential candidate, secretary of state, and senator had voiced his opposition to slavery, remained hopeful that slavery in the United States would eventually come to an end. But given what he regarded as the exigencies of the time, he called on his colleagues and constituents to support a bill that, among other things, would make it the legal obligation of all U.S. citizens to return fugitive slaves to their supposed masters. Webster's support for the Compromise of 1850, the passage of which only further heightened sectional tensions, diminished his reputation as a champion of liberty and made him a particular object of wrath among antislavery reformers. In *Clotel*, Brown takes a jab at Webster by noting that the dark-complected senator was sometimes regarded as a black (with the implication that Webster, too, could become a victim of the Fugitive Slave Law). The text of Webster's speech on the compromise, "The Constitution and the Union: A Speech Delivered in the Senate of the United States, on the 7th of March, 1850," is taken from *The Great Speeches and Orations of Daniel Webster, With an Essay on Daniel Webster as a Master of English Style*, ed. Edwin P. Whipple (Boston: Little, 1879), 616–18.

Mr. President, in the excited times in which we live, there is found to exist a state of crimination and recrimination between the North and South. There are lists of grievances produced by each; and those grievances, real or supposed, alienate the minds of one portion of the country from the other, exasperate the feelings, and subdue the sense of fraternal affection, patriotic love, and mutual regard. I shall bestow a little attention, Sir, upon these various grievances existing on the one side and on the other. I begin with complaints of the South. I will not answer, further than I have, the general statements of the honorable Senator from South Carolina,[1] that the North has prospered at the expense of the South in consequence of the manner of administering this government, in the collecting of its revenues, and so forth. These are disputed topics, and I have no inclination to enter into them. But I will allude to other complaints of the South, and especially to one which has in my opinion just foundation; and that is, that there has been found at the North, among individuals and among legislators, a disinclination to perform fully their constitutional duties in regard to the return of persons bound to service who have escaped into the free States. In that respect, the South, in my judgment, is right, and the North is wrong. Every member of every Northern legislature is bound by oath, like every other officer in the country, to support the Constitution of the United States; and the article of the Constitution[2] which says to these States that they shall deliver up fugitives from service is as binding in honor and conscience as any other article. No man fulfils his duty in any legislature who sets himself to find excuses, evasions, escapes from this constitutional obligation. I have always thought that the Constitution addressed itself to the legislatures of the States or to the States themselves. It says that those persons escaping to other States "shall be delivered up," and I confess I have always been of the opinion that it was an injunction upon the State themselves. When it is said that a person escaping into another State, and coming therefore within the jurisdiction of that State, shall be delivered up, it seems to me the import of the clause is, that the State itself, in obedience to the Constitution, shall cause him to be delivered up. That is my judgment. I have always entertained that opinion, and I entertain it now. But when the subject, some years ago, was before the Supreme Court of the United States, the majority of the judges held that the power to cause fugitives from service to be delivered up was a power to be exer-

[1] *Senator from South Carolina*: John C. Calhoun; see p. 168, note 8.
[2] *article of the Constitution*: Article IV, section 2.

cised under the authority of this government. I do not know, on the whole, that it may not have been a fortunate decision.[3] My habit is to respect the result of judicial deliberations and the solemnity of judicial decisions. As it now stands, the business of seeing that these fugitives are delivered up resides in the power of Congress and the national judicature, and my friend at the head of the Judiciary Committee[4] has a bill on the subject now before the Senate, which, with some amendments to it, I propose to support, with all its provisions, to the fullest extent. And I desire to call the attention of all sober-minded men at the North, of all conscientious men, of all men who are not carried away by some fanatical idea or some false impression, to their constitutional obligations. I put it to all the sober and sound minds at the North as a question of morals and a question of conscience. What right have they, in their legislative capacity or any other capacity, to endeavor to get round this Constitution, or to embarrass the free exercise of the rights secured by the Constitution to the persons whose slaves escape from them? None at all; none at all. Neither in the forum of conscience, nor before the face of the Constitution, are they, in my opinion, justified in such an attempt. Of course it is a matter for their consideration. They probably, in the excitement of the times, have not stopped to consider of this. They have followed what seemed to be the current of thought and of motives, as the occasion arose, and they have neglected to investigate fully the real question, and to consider their constitutional obligations; which, I am sure, if they did consider, they would fulfil with alacrity. I repeat, therefore, Sir, that here is a well-founded ground of complaint against the North, which ought to be removed, which it is now in the power of the different departments of this government to remove; which calls for the enactment of proper laws authorizing the judicature of this government, in the several States, to do all that is necessary for the recapture of fugitive slaves and for their restoration to those who claim them. Wherever I go, and whenever I speak on the subject, and when I speak here I desire to speak to the whole North, I say that the South has been injured in this respect, and has a right to complain; and the North has been too careless of what I think the Constitution peremptorily and emphatically enjoins upon her as a duty.

---

[3] *fortunate decision*: In *Prigg* v. *Pennsylvania* (1842), the Supreme Court upheld Congress's Fugitive Slave Law of 1793, denying states the right to develop their own legislation on fugitive slaves.

[4] *my friend . . . Committee*: James Murray Mason (1798–1871), U.S. senator from Virginia. Mason drafted the Fugitive Slave Act of 1850.

MARTIN R. DELANY

From *The Condition, Elevation, Emigration and Destiny of the Colored People of the United States*

Born in what is now West Virginia, Martin Robison Delany (1812–1885) was the son of a free black seamstress and a plantation slave. In the early 1820s he moved to western Pennsylvania, and by the late 1830s he had emerged as an important black leader in Pittsburgh. During the 1840s he edited one of the first black newspapers, *The Mystery*, and in 1847 he became the coeditor of Frederick Douglass's *North Star*, championing moral reform and black elevation in the United States. Delany resigned from the *North Star* in 1849, and two key events during the fall of 1850 contributed to his increasing disillusionment with what he came to regard as Douglass's accommodationism. First, after having been admitted to Harvard Medical School during the summer of 1850, Delany was abruptly asked to leave in the fall by the dean, Oliver Wendell Holmes, who caved in to students' demands that Harvard remain an all-white institution. At around the same time, Congress passed the Compromise of 1850, with its infamous Fugitive Slave Law. Convinced that blacks would forever remain second-class noncitizens in the United States, Delany subsequently began to explore the possibility of black emigration to Central and South America. Delany's emigrationism influenced the Haitian emigration movement of the late 1850s and early 1860s, which Brown initially championed. However, during the Civil War both Delany and Brown eventually decided to support the Union's cause and to abandon their emigration plans.

Delany published *The Condition, Elevation, Emigration and Destiny of the Colored People of the United States* in 1852, a time when he was angry about the Compromise of 1850. In the selection printed below, Delany quotes from the text of the Compromise itself. As he makes clear, the Fugitive Slave provision of the Compromise, in addition to making it difficult for slaves to escape from their masters, created new dangers for the free blacks, who could be falsely identified as slaves and taken against their will to the South. The Compromise of 1850, with its Fugitive Slave Law, was an important "source" for *Clotel*, which has several scenes involving fugitive slaves. Delany's extensive quotation from the dry legalese of the legislative provision powerfully shows how legal language can be used to cloak human suffering and racism. The excerpt is taken from Martin R. Delany, *The Condition, Elevation, Emigration and Destiny of the Colored People of the United States* (Philadelphia: published by the author, 1852).

CHAPTER XVI.
NATIONAL DISFRANCHISEMENT OF COLORED PEOPLE

WE give below the Act of Congress, known as the "Fugitive Slave Law," for the benefit of the reader, as there are thousands of the American people of all classes, who have never read the provisions of this enactment; and consequently, have no conception of its enormity. We had originally intended, also, to have inserted here, the Act of Congress of 1793,[1] but since this Bill includes all the provisions of that Act, in fact, although called a "supplement," is a substitute, *de facto*,[2] it would be superfluous; therefore, we insert the Bill alone, with explanations following:—

AN ACT
TO AMEND, AND SUPPLEMENTARY TO THE ACT, ENTITLED, "AN ACT RESPECTING FUGITIVES FROM JUSTICE, AND PERSONS ESCAPING FROM THE SERVICE OF THEIR MASTERS," APPROVED FEBRUARY 12, 1793.

Be it enacted by the Senate and House of Representatives of the United States of America in Congress assembled, That the persons who have been, or may hereafter be, appointed commissioners, in virtue of any act of Congress, by the circuit courts of the United States, and who, in consequence of such appointment, are authorized to exercise the powers that any justice of the peace or other magistrate of any of the United States may exercise in respect to offenders for any crime or offence against the United States, by arresting, imprisoning, or bailing the same under and by virtue of the thirty-third section of the act of the twenty-fourth of September, seventeen hundred and eighty-nine, entitled, "An act to establish the judicial courts of the United States," shall be, and are hereby authorized and required to exercise and discharge all the powers and duties conferred by this act. . . .

SEC. 6. *And be it further enacted,* That when a person held to service or labor in any State or Territory of the United States has heretofore or shall hereafter escape into another State or Territory of the United

---

[1] *Act of Congress of 1793*: Congress had passed a Fugitive Slave law in 1793, which became the basis of the revamped Fugitive Slave Law of 1850.
[2] *de facto*: "by the fact" (Latin). In legal terms, in practice, but not necessarily mandated by law.

States, the person or persons to whom such service or labor may be
due, or his, her, or their agent or attorney, duly authorized, by power
of attorney, in writing, acknowledged and certified under the seal of
some legal office or court of the State or Territory in which the same
may be executed, may pursue and reclaim such fugitive person, either
by procuring a warrant from some one of the courts, judges, or commissioners aforesaid, of the proper circuit, district or county, for the
apprehension of such fugitive from service or labor, or by seizing and
arresting such fugitive, where the same can be done without process,
and by taking and causing such person to be taken forthwith before
such court, judge or commissioner, whose duty it shall be to hear and
determine the case of such claimant in a summary manner; and upon
satisfactory proof being made, by deposition or affidavit, in writing, to
be taken and certified by such court, judge, or commissioner, or by
other satisfactory testimony, duly taken and certified by some court,
magistrate, justice of the peace, or other legal officer authorized to
administer an oath, and take depositions under the laws of the State or
Territory from which such person owing service or labor may have
escaped, with a certificate of such magistracy or other authority, as
aforesaid, with the seal of the proper court or officer thereto attached,
which seal shall be sufficient to establish the competency of the proof,
and with proof, also by affidavit, of the identity of the person whose
service or labor is claimed to be due as aforesaid, that the person so
arrested does in fact owe service or labor to the person or persons
claiming him or her, in the State of Territory from which such fugitive
may have escaped as aforesaid, and that said person escaped, to make
out and deliver to such claimant, his or her agent or attorney, a certificate setting forth the substantial facts as to the service or labor due
from such fugitive to the claimant, and of his or her escape from the
State or Territory in which such service or labor was due to the State
or Territory in which he or she was arrested, with authority to such
claimant, or his or her agent or attorney to use such reasonable force
and restraint as may be necessary under the circumstances of the case,
to take and remove such fugitive person back to the State or Territory
from whence he or she may have escaped as aforesaid. In no trial or
hearing under this act shall the testimony of such alleged fugitive be
admitted in evidence; and the certificates in this and the first section
mentioned shall be conclusive of the right of the person or persons in
whose favor granted to remove such fugitive to the State or Territory
from which he escaped, and shall prevent all molestation of said per-

son or persons by any process issued by any court, judge, magistrate, or other person whomsoever. . . .

HOWELL COBB,
Speaker of the House of Representatives.
William R. King,
President of the Senate, pro tempore.
Approved September 18, 1850.

MILLARD FILLMORE[3]

The most prominent provisions of the Constitution of the United States, and those which form the fundamental basis of personal security, are they which provide, that every person shall be secure in their person and property: that no person may be deprived of liberty without due process of law, and that for crime or misdemeanor; that there may be no process of law that shall work corruption of blood. By corruption of blood is meant, that process, by which a person is *degraded* and deprived of rights common to the enfranchised citizen—of the rights of an elector, and of eligibility to the office of a representative of the people; in a word, that no person nor their posterity, may ever be debased beneath the level of the recognised basis of American citizenship. This debasement and degradation is "corruption of blood;" politically understood—a legal acknowledgement of inferiority at birth.

Heretofore, it ever has been denied, that the United States recognised or knew any difference between the people—that the Constitution makes no distinction, but includes in its provisions, all the people alike. This is not true, and certainly is blind absurdity in us at least, who have suffered the dread consequences of this delusion, not now to see it.

By the provisions of this bill, the colored people of the United States are positively degraded beneath the level of the whites—are made liable at any time, in any place, and under all circumstances, to be arrested—and upon the claim of any white person, without the privilege, even of making a defence, sent into endless bondage. Let no visionary nonsense about *habeas corpus*, or a *fair trial*, deceive us;

---

[3] *Howell Cobb . . . Millard Fillmore:* Howell Cobb (1815–1868) was a Democratic congressman from Georgia who favored the Whig position on compromise; William R. King (1786–1853) was a Democratic senator from Alabama; and Millard Fillmore (1800–1874), the thirteenth president of the United States (1850–1853), was a Whig from New York.

there are no such rights granted in this bill, and except where the commissioner is too ignorant to understand when reading it, or too stupid to enforce it when he does understand, there is no earthly chance — no hope under heaven for the colored person who is brought before one of these officers of the law. Any leniency that may be expected, must proceed from the whims or caprice of the magistrate — in fact, it is optional with them; and our rights and liberty entirely at their disposal.

We are slaves in the midst of freedom, waiting patiently, and unconcernedly — indifferently, and stupidly, for masters to come and lay claim to us, trusting to their generosity, whether or not they will own us and carry us into endless bondage.

The slave is more secure than we; he knows who holds the heel upon his bosom — we know not the wretch who may grasp us by the throat. His master may be a man of some conscientious scruples; ours may be unmerciful. Good or bad, mild or harsh, easy or hard, lenient or severe, saint or satan — whenever that master demands any one of us — even our affectionate wives and darling little children, *we must go into slavery* — there is *no alternative.* The *will* of the man who sits in judgment on our liberty, is the law. To him is given *all power* to say, whether or not we have a right to enjoy freedom. This is the power over the slave in the South — this is now extended to the North. The will of the man who sits in judgment over us is the law; because it is explicitly provided that the *decision* of the commissioner shall be final, from which there can be no appeal.

The freed man of the South is even more secure than the freeborn of the North; because such persons usually have their records in the slave states, bringing their "papers" with them; and the slaveholders will be faithful to their own acts. The Northern freeman knows no records; he despises the "papers."

Depend upon no promised protection of citizens in any quarter. Their own property and liberty are jeopardised, and they will not sacrifice them for us. This we may not expect them to do.

Besides, there are no people who ever lived, love their country and obey their laws as the Americans.

Their country is their Heaven — their Laws their Scriptures — and the decrees of their Magistrates obeyed as the fiat of God. It is the most consummate delusion and misdirected confidence to depend upon them for protection; and for a moment suppose even our children safe while walking in the streets among them.

A people capable of originating and sustaining such a law as this, are not the people to whom we are willing to entrust our liberty at discretion.

What can we do?—What shall we do? This is the great and important question:—Shall we submit to be dragged like brutes before heartless men, and sent into degradation and bondage?—Shall we fly, or shall we resist? Ponder well and reflect.

4

Writing and Revising *Clotel*

Throughout his authorial career, Brown regularly revised his writings, regarding his published work as a perpetual source for writings to come. He published multiple versions of his autobiography, sometimes with vastly different accounts of similar incidents, and he published three revised versions of *Clotel*. A restless and inventive writer, Brown always had something new to report or a different way of telling the same story. Just as his use of cultural materials challenged the notion of the finished, discrete text, so his acts of authorial revision, which often involved reconceptualization and recontextualization, worked against the idea of the published work as a finished, immutable artifact. Sharing Melville's suspicion of totalized systems of meaning, Brown would no doubt have offered his assent to Ishmael's paean to the revisionary process in *Moby-Dick*: "God keep me from ever completing anything" (Melville 145).

This chapter presents a number of selections that highlight Brown's act of writing and revising *Clotel*, a process that extended from the mid-1840s to 1867. In addition to drawing on the cultural materials collected in Chapter 3, Brown drew on his own published writings about slavery and race, as well as his autobiographical accounts of his experience as a slave. Brown emphasized the close connection between his life and fiction by prefacing *Clotel* with a third-person autobiographical narrative, which revised aspects of his first-person 1847 *Narrative*. He then revised aspects of this preface in later autobiographical accounts. Given the centrality of revision to Brown's career as a writer, we might regard as part of his life history everything that he wrote up to the moment of the publication of *Clotel*. So in addition to drawing on his autobiographies, he worked with and revised a number of his earlier writings about slavery in the United States. His short piece on the Liberty Party, published in 1846, provided him with a source for Reverend Peck, and his writings on William and Ellen Craft were revised, reconceived, and recontextualized for his account of the escapes of William, George, and Clotel in *Clotel*. Brown reworked a section from his 1850 *Original Panoramic Views* for his portrayal of Althesa and Morton; and his 1847 lecture to the Female Anti-Slavery Society of Salem and his 1852 "A True Story of Slave Life" can be seen retrospectively as rehearsals for his powerful presentation of gender and sexuality in *Clotel*.

Brown sailed to England in 1849, toured the British Isles, became involved with the transatlantic antislavery movement, and wrote *Clotel* and other works, including a travel narrative, while residing in London. Some of the selections in this chapter help to illuminate the British context of Brown's writing. "A True Story of Slave Life," for instance, is clearly calculated for a British audience, stretching the truth about such U.S. figures as James Forten and Robert Purvis in order to underscore some of the ironies about the slave trade and race in the United States. Brown was in London when *Uncle Tom's Cabin* was published, and his novel responds in part to the Anglo-American excitement over Stowe's novel. The two letters included in this chapter show Brown at work on *Clotel* while engaging in discussions of *Uncle Tom's Cabin* and other aspects of the transatlantic antislavery movement; and the reviews included here, most of which were first published in England, show that British readers were surprisingly responsive to *Clotel*, although hesitant about some aspects of its plotting. Brown's subsequent revisions of *Clotel*, which turned to a more conventional narration, may have been influenced by the response he got from British readers.

Brown returned to the United States in 1854, where he confronted such developments as the passage of the Kansas-Nebraska Act, which opened new territories for slavery, and the Supreme Court's 1857 *Dred Scott* ruling, which asserted that blacks could never become U.S. citizens and "had no rights which the white man was bound to respect" (qtd. Foner 292-3). The increasingly dire situation in the United States encouraged a number of African Americans to circulate calls for black emigration. In the late 1850s, Henry Highland Garnet and Martin

Delany championed emigration to Africa, while James Holly and Brown urged African Americans to emigrate to Haiti and thereby remain in the Americas. In his 1855 lecture on the revolutions in San Domingo, which anticipates his support for black emigration to Haiti, Brown presents the revolutionary leader Toussaint L'Ouverture as a black "American" patriot. Brown's celebration of blackness would appear to have had a significant impact on his revisions of *Clotel*, for in his first revision, the serialized *Miralda; or the Beautiful Quadroon* (1860–61), he changed the complexion of the George figure in *Clotel* from light to black and kept that change in the 1864 and 1867 revisions. Both the 1855 lecture and the celebration of George's blackness reveal a more diasporic Brown, but by 1863 he had embraced the Civil War as a war against slavery and recommitted himself to African American uplift and citizenship in the United States. In his 1867 *The Negro in the American Rebellion*, Brown extols the bravery and patriotism of the black troops who defended Milliken's Bend. Nevertheless, in the revised versions of *Clotel* published in 1864 and 1867, he portrays the persistence of whites' antiblack racism, which (he particularly emphasizes in the 1867 revision) suggests that blacks' heroic participation in the Civil War may have been in vain. The 1867 *Clotelle* provides a stark picture of *Clotel*'s George (now named Jerome) fruitlessly sacrificing his life as a soldier in the Union army.

In the final selection of Chapter 4, which jumps forward to 1880, Brown in *My Southern Home* conveys his disgust and dismay at the failure of Reconstruction. At the same time, he clings to the possibility that racial harmony can emerge in the United States through interracial marriages and the development of black pride. He concludes his last published book with the image of an impending reconciliatory handshake between white and black. It was Brown's hope that such a handshake would begin the process of redeeming a legacy of violation and betrayal that had its origins in Jefferson's contradictory "fathering" of slavery, slaves, and freedom.

WILLIAM WELLS BROWN

From *Narrative of William W. Brown*

Inspired by the success of Frederick Douglass's *Narrative*, Brown wrote a narrative of his bondage and eventual escape from slavery, which was published in 1847 by the Anti-Slavery Society of Boston. Brown's *Narrative* proved to be highly popular, selling approximately ten thousand copies and helping to make him one of the most prominent black abolitionists of the time. After publishing the *Narrative*, Brown would retell his life history as a slave in a number of other writings, including the third-person "Narrative of the Life and Escape of William Wells Brown" prefacing *Clotel.* In the selection that follows from *Narrative of William W. Brown, A Fugitive Slave. Written By Himself* (Boston: Anti-Slavery Society, 1847), Brown, in a complex and troubling moment, shows how he used his wits to save himself from a flogging ordered by his master, Mr. Walker, but only at the expense of a fellow slave. When he described the scene again in his 1880 *My Southern Home*, Brown, perhaps out of a sense of guilt, displaced the same action onto a slave named "Pompey." The depiction of Pompey (and Sam) in *Clotel* may have similarly complicated autobiographical sources in Brown's firsthand knowledge of the ways in which slavery, as he puts it, "makes its victims lying and mean."

Mr. Walker, though not a good master, had not flogged a slave since I had been with him, though he had threatened me. The slaves were kept in the pen, and he always put up at the best hotel, and kept his wines in his room, for the accommodation of those who called to negotiate with him for the purchase of slaves. One day while we were at Vicksburg,[1] several gentlemen came to see him for this purpose, and as usual the wine was called for. I took the tray and started around with it, and having accidentally filled some of the glasses too full, the gentlemen spilled the wine on their clothes as they went to drink. Mr. Walker apologized to them for my carelessness, but looked at me as though he would see me again on this subject.

After the gentlemen had left the room, he asked me what I meant by my carelessness, and said that he would attend to me. The next morning, he gave me a note to carry to the jailer, and a dollar in money to

---

[1] *Vicksburg*: A city in western Mississippi, on the Mississippi River.

give him. I suspected that all was not right, so I went down near the landing where I met with a sailor, and walking up to him, asked him if he would be so kind as to read the note for me. He read it over, and then looked at me. I asked him to tell me what was in it. Said he,

"They are going to give you hell."

"Why?" said I.

He said, "This is a note to have you whipped, and says that you have a dollar to pay for it."

He handed me back the note, and off I started. I knew not what to do, but was determined not to be whipped. I went up to the jail—took a look at it, and walked off again. As Mr. Walker was acquainted with the jailer, I feared that I should be found out if I did not go, and be treated in consequence of it still worse.

While I was meditating on the subject, I saw a colored man about my size walk up, and the thought struck me in a moment to send him with my note. I walked up to him, and asked him who he belonged to. He said he was a free man, and had been in the city but a short time. I told him I had a note to go into the jail, and get a trunk to carry to one of the steamboats; but was so busily engaged that I could not do it, although I had a dollar to pay for it. He asked me if I would not give him the job. I handed him the note and the dollar, and off he started for the jail.

I watched to see that he went in, and as soon as I saw the door close behind him, I walked around the corner, and took my station, intending to see how my friend looked when he came out. I had been there but a short time, when a colored man came around the corner, and said to another colored man with whom he was acquainted—

"They are giving a nigger scissors in the jail."

"What for?" said the other. The man continued,

"A nigger came into the jail, and asked for the jailer. The jailer came out, and he handed him a note, and said he wanted to get a trunk. The jailer told him to go with him, and he would give him the trunk. So he took him into the room, and told the nigger to give up the dollar. He said a man had given him the dollar to pay for getting the trunk. But that lie would not answer. So they made him strip himself, and then they tied him down, and are now whipping him."

I stood by all the while listening to their talk, and soon found out that the person alluded to was my customer. I went into the street opposite the jail, and concealed myself in such a manner that I could not be seen by any one coming out. I had been there but a short time, when the young man made his appearance, and looked around for me.

I, unobserved, came forth from my hiding-place, behind a pile of brick, and he pretty soon saw me and came up to me complaining bitterly, saying that I had played a trick upon him. I denied any knowledge of what the note contained, and asked him what they had done to him. He told me in substance what I heard the man tell who had come out of the jail.

"Yes," said he, "they whipped me and took my dollar, and gave me this note."

He showed me the note which the jailer had given him, telling him to give it to his master. I told him I would give him fifty cents for it, — that being all the money I had. He gave it to me, and took his money. He had received twenty lashes on his bare back, with the negro-whip.

I took the note and started for the hotel where I had left Mr. Walker. Upon reaching the hotel, I handed it to a stranger whom I had not seen before, and requested him to read it to me. As near as I can recollect, it was as follows: —

"DEAR SIR: — By your direction, I have given your boy twenty lashes. He is a very saucy boy, and tried to make me believe that he did not belong to you, and I put it on to him well for lying to me.

I remain,
Your obedient servant."

It is true that in most of the slave-holding cities, when a gentleman wishes his servants whipped, he can send him to the jail and have it done. Before I went in where Mr. Walker was, I wet my cheeks a little, as though I had been crying. He looked at me, and inquired what was the matter. I told him that I had never had such a whipping in my life, and handed him the note. He looked at it and laughed; — "and so you told him that you did not belong to me." "Yes, sir," said I. "I did not know that there was any harm in that." He told me I must behave myself, if I did not want to be whipped again.

This incident shows how it is that slavery makes its victims lying and mean; for which vices it afterwards reproaches them, and uses them as arguments to prove that they deserve no better fate. I have often, since my escape, deeply regretted the deception I practised upon this poor fellow; and I heartily desire that it may be, at some time or other, in my power to make him amends for his vicarious sufferings in my behalf.

JOSEPHINE BROWN

From *Biography of an American Bondman*

Not much is known about Josephine Brown, the second daughter of William Wells Brown and Elizabeth Schooner Brown. Born in Buffalo in 1839, she was educated at a school in New Bedford following the separation of her parents in 1847. In 1851 Brown summoned to London both Josephine and her older sister, Clarissa (b. 1836), and subsequently placed them in a seminary in Calais, France. They completed their education at the Home and Colonial School in London, where they received their teaching certificates in 1854. Soon after, they both found teaching jobs in England—the fifteen-year-old Josephine at the East Plumstead School in Woolwich. Returning to the United States in 1855, Josephine accompanied her father on his antislavery speaking engagements, and in 1856 published a biography of him. That same year she returned to England to take up a teaching position, and vanished from the historical record.

In chapter XIX of *Clotel*, the fictional character William challenges Jim Crow practices on Northern railways. The account in Josephine Brown's biography of her father's own challenge to Jim Crow practices suggests that his life history was a source of the railway scene in *Clotel*. Yet the possibility remains that Josephine Brown's account was shaped by her reading of *Clotel*. The text of the selection is taken from *Biography of An American Bondman, by His Daughter* (Boston: R. F. Wallcut, 1856).

If there is one thing at the North which seems more cruel and hateful than another, connected with American slavery, it is the way in which colored persons are treated by the whites. The withering influence which this hatred exerts against the elevation of the free colored people, can scarcely be imagined. Wherever the black man makes his appearance in the United States, he meets this hatred. In some sections of the country it is worse than in others. As you advance nearer to the slave States, you feel this prejudice the more. Twenty years ago, if colored persons travelled by steamboat, they were put on the deck; if by coach, on the outside; if by railway, in the *Jim Crow car*. Even the respectable eating saloons have been closed against colored persons. In New York and Philadelphia, the despised race are still excluded from most places of refreshment. To the everlasting shame of the Church, she still holds on to this unchristian practice of separating

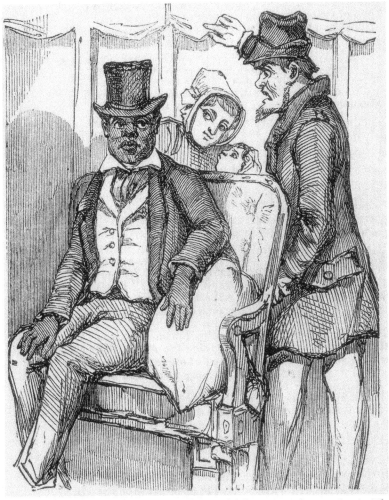

"Negro Expulsion from Railway Car, Philadelphia." Wood engraving in *The Illustrated London News*, 27 September 1856. Courtesy of the Photographs and Prints Division, Schomburg Center for Research in Black Culture, The New York Public Library, Astor, Lennox and Tilden Foundations.

persons on account of their complexion. In the refined city of Boston, there was a church, as late as 1847, deeded its pews upon condition that no colored person should ever be permitted to enter them! Most of these churches have a place set off in the gallery, where the negro may go if he pleases. A New York D.D.,[1] while on a visit to England, some years since, was charged by a London divine with putting his colored members in the furthest part of the gallery. The American clergyman, with a long face and upturned eyes, exclaimed, "Ah! my dear brother, I think more of my colored members than I do of the whites, and therefore I place them in the top of the house, so as to get them nearer to heaven." CHARLES LENOX REMOND,[2] during the many years that he has labored in the Anti-Slavery cause, has, in all probability, experienced greater insults and more hardships than any other person of color. To hear him relate what he has undergone, while travelling to and from the places of his meetings, makes one's blood chill.

This pretended fastidiousness on the part of the whites has produced some of the most ridiculous scenes. WILLIAM WELLS BROWN, while travelling through Ohio in 1844, went from Sandusky to Republic, on the Mad River and Lake Erie Railroad. On arriving at Sandusky, he learned that colored people were not allowed to take seats in the cars with whites, and that, as there was no *Jim Crow car* on that road, blacks were generally made to ride in the baggage-car. Mr. Brown, however, went into one of the best passenger cars, seated himself, crossed his legs, and looked as unconcerned as if the car had been made for his sole use. At length, one of the railway officials entered the car, and asked him what he was doing there. "I am going to Republic," said Mr. Brown. "You can 't ride here," said the conductor. "Yes I can," returned the colored man. "No you can 't," rejoined the railway man. "Why?" inquired Mr. Brown. "Because we don 't allow *niggers* to ride with white people," replied the conductor. "Well, I shall remain here," said Mr. Brown. "You will see, pretty soon, whether you will or not," retorted the railway man, as he turned to leave the car. By this time, the passengers were filling up the seats, and every thing being made ready to start. After an absence of a few minutes, the conductor again entered the car, accompanied by two stout men, and took Mr. Brown by the collar and pulled him out. Pressing business demanded

---

[1] *D.D.*: Doctor of Divinity.

[2] *CHARLES LENOX REMOND*: A pioneering African American abolitionist, Charles Remond (1810–1873) of Salem, Massachusetts, was best known for his work as a lecturing agent for William Lloyd Garrison's Massachusetts Anti-Slavery Society.

that Mr. Brown should go, and by that train; he therefore got into the freight car, just as the train was moving off. Seating himself on a flour barrel, he took from his pocket the last number of the *Liberator*, and began reading it. On went the train, making its usual stops, until within four or five miles of Republic, when the conductor, (who, by-the-by, was the same man who had moved Mr. Brown from the passenger car) demanded his ticket. "I have no ticket," returned he. "Then I will take your fare," said the conductor. "How much is it?" inquired Mr. Brown. "One dollar and a quarter," was the answer. "How much do you charge those who ride in the passenger cars?" inquired the colored man. "The same," said the conductor. "Do you suppose that I will pay the same price for riding up here in the freight car, that those do who are in the passenger car?" asked Mr. Brown. "Certainly," replied the conductor. "Well, you are very much mistaken, if you think any such thing," said the passenger. "Come, black man, out with your money, and none of your nonsense with me," said the conductor. "I won 't pay you the price you demand, and that 's the end of it," said Mr. Brown. "Don 't you intend paying your fare?" inquired the conductor. "Yes," replied the colored man; "but I won 't pay you a dollar and a quarter." "What do you intend to pay, then?" demanded the official. "I will pay what 's right, but I don 't intend to give you all that sum." "Well, then," said the conductor, "as you have had to ride in the freight car, give me one dollar and you may go." "I won 't do any such thing," returned Mr. Brown. "Why won 't you?" inquired the railway man. "If I had come in the passenger car, I would have paid as much as others do; but I won 't ride up here on a flour barrel, and pay you a dollar." "You think yourself as good as white people, I suppose?" said the conductor; and his eyes flashed as if he meant what he said. "Well, being you seem to feel so bad because you had to ride in the freight car, give me seventy-five cents, and I 'll say no more about it," continued he. "No, I won 't. If I had been permitted to ride with the other passengers, I would pay what you first demanded; but I won 't pay seventy-five cents for riding up here, astride a flour barrel, in the hot sun." "Don 't you intend paying any thing at all?" asked the conductor. "Yes, I will pay what is right." "Give me half a dollar, and I will say no more about it." "No, I won 't," returned the other; "I shall not pay fifty cents for riding in a freight car." "What will you pay, then?" demanded the conductor. "What do you charge per hundred on this road?" asked Mr. Brown. "Twenty-five cents," answered the conductor. "Then I will pay you thirty-seven and a half cents," said the passenger, "for I weigh just one hundred and fifty pounds." "Do you expect to get off by paying that trifling sum?" "I have come as freight, and I will pay for freight, and nothing more," said Mr. Brown. The conductor took the thirty-seven and a half cents, declaring, as he left the car, that that was the most impudent negro that ever travelled on that road.

WILLIAM WELLS BROWN

From *The New Liberty Party*

Founded in 1840 under the leadership of the abolitionists Gerrit Smith (1797–1874) and James Birney (1792–1857), the Liberty Party was committed to fighting a broadly conceived "Slave Power" but was somewhat vague about its specific programs for eradicating slavery. A number of abolitionists, including William Wells Brown and Frederick Douglass, were suspicious of the Liberty Party's constituency and political goals, and thus continued to support the moral suasion abolitionism of William Lloyd Garrison. In a letter to Sydney Howard Gay (1814–1888), editor of the *National Anti-Slavery Standard*, Brown reported skeptically on the New York State Liberty Party's 1846 convention in Farmington, New York. The letter appeared under the title "The New Liberty Party, or Re-organization" in the 25 June 1846 issue of the *Standard*, the source of this selection. Of particular interest in the letter is Brown's account of a remark on Jefferson by one Reverend Peck of Rochester, clearly a source for *Clotel*'s Reverend John Peck of Connecticut.

The Liberty party of this State, or at least, the wire-pullers of that party, have just closed the last session of a two days' Convention, called for the purpose of finding out where the Liberty party is. The Convention was well attended. . . . I saw among the speakers five clergymen, with whom I was acquainted; how many more there were present, I cannot say. One of them, (Mr. Peck, of Rochester,) said, "Mr. President, it has been said in this Convention, 'that all men had inalienable rights;' now I deny that. I know that Jefferson wrote that sentiment, but it is false! It is utterly untrue. The doctrine that all men are created equal, and with inalienable rights, is a humbug. Let that doctrine be carried out, and in a short time every gallows will be cut down, every prison will be empty, and over their doors will be written in red, — for it should be in blood, — 'All men are born free and equal, and have inalienable rights.'" This clergyman was a Liberty party man.

WILLIAM WELLS BROWN

From *A Lecture Delivered before the Female Anti-Slavery Society of Salem*

In 1847, Brown began lecturing as an agent of William Lloyd Garrison's Massachusetts Anti-Slavery Society. His *A Lecture Delivered before the Female Anti-Slavery Society of Salem,* which he gave in Salem, Massachusetts, to the first antislavery society organized exclusively by women, addresses issues that would become central to *Clotel:* the horrors of the slave trade, the hypocrisy of a slaveholding nation supposedly dedicated to liberty for all, the hypocrisy of proslavery "Christians," and the sufferings specific to female slaves. The speech concludes with an ironic description of the sale of a religious female slave, which he would revise for the ending of *Clotel's* first chapter. The excerpt is taken from Brown's *A Lecture Delivered before the Female Anti-Slavery Society of Salem, at Lyceum Hall, Nov. 14, 1847* (Boston: Massachusetts Anti-Slavery Society, 1847).

I ask, what is the influence that Slavery has had upon the character of the American people? But for the blighting influence of Slavery, the United States of America would have a character, would have a reputation, that should outshine the reputation of any other government that is to be found upon God's green earth.

Look at the struggle of the fathers of this country for liberty. What did they struggle for? What did they go upon the battle-field for, in 1776? They went there, it is said, for the purpose of obtaining liberty; for the purpose of instituting a democratic, republican government. What is Democracy? Solon,[1] upon one occasion, while speaking to the Athenians said, "A democratic government is a government where an injury done to the least of its citizens is regarded as an insult and an

---

[1] *Solon:* Famous Athenian lawgiver and statesman (c.639 B.C.–559 B.C.), known for his commitment to democratic practices and principles.

injury to the whole commonwealth." That was the opinion of an old law-maker and statesman upon the subject of Democracy. But what says an American statesman? A South Carolina governor says that Slavery is the corner-stone of our Republic. Another eminent American statesman says that two hundred years have sanctioned and sanctified American Slavery, and that is property which the law declares to be property. Which shall we believe? One that is reared in republican America, or one that is brought up in the lap of aristocracy? Every one must admit that democracy is nothing more or less than genuine freedom and liberty, protecting every individual in the community.

I might carry the audience back to the time when your fathers were struggling for liberty in 1776. When they went forth upon the battle-field and laid down their bones, and moistened the soil with their blood, that their children might enjoy liberty. What was it for? Because a three-penny tax upon tea, a tax upon paper, or something else had been imposed upon them. We are not talking against such taxes upon the Slave. The Slave has no tea; he has no paper; he has not even himself; he has nothing at all.

When we examine the influence of Slavery upon the character of the American people, we are led to believe that if the American Government ever had a character, she has lost it. I know that upon the 4th of July, our 4th of July orators talk of Liberty, Democracy, and Republicanism. They talk of liberty, while three millions of their own countrymen are groaning in abject Slavery. This is called the "land of the free, and the home of the brave;" it is called the "Asylum of the oppressed;" and some have been foolish enough to call it the "Cradle of Liberty." If it is the "cradle of liberty," they have rocked the child to death. It is dead long since, and yet we talk about democracy and republicanism, while one-sixth of our countrymen are clanking their chains upon the very soil which our fathers moistened with their blood. They have such scenes even upon the holy Sabbath, and the American people are perfectly dead upon the subject. The cries, and shrieks, and groans of the Slave do not wake them. . . .

Go to the capital of our country, the city of Washington; the capital of the freest government upon the face of the world. Only a few days since, an American mother and her daughter were sold upon the auction-block in that city,[2] and the money was put into the Treasury of

---

[2] *sold . . . in that city*: The slave trade was abolished in Washington, D.C., in 1850, though slavery remained legal there until 1862.

the United States of America. Go there and you can scarcely stand an hour but you will see caufles[3] of Slaves driven past the Capitol, and likely as not you will see the foremost one with the stars and stripes in his hand; and yet the American Legislators, the people of the North and of the South, the "assembled wisdom" of the nation, look on and see such things and hold their peace; they say not a single word against such oppression, or in favor of liberty.

In conclusion let me say, that the character of the American people and the influence of Slavery upon that character have been blighting and withering the efforts of all those that favor liberty, reform, and progression. But it has not quite accomplished it. There are those who are willing to stand by the Slave. I look upon the great Anti-Slavery platform as one upon which those who stand, occupy the same position,—I would say, a higher position, than those who put forth their Declaration in 1776, in behalf of American liberty. Yes, the American Abolitionists now occupy a higher and holier position than those who carried on the American Revolution. They do not want that the husband should be any longer sold from his wife. They want that the husband should have a right to protect his wife; that the brother should have a right to protect his sister. They are tired and sick at heart in seeing human beings placed upon the auction-block and sold to the highest bidder. They want that man should be protected. They want that a stop should be put to this system of iniquity and bloodshed; and they are laboring for its overthrow.

· I would that every one here could go into the Slave-States, could go where I have been, and see the workings of Slavery upon the Slave. When I get to talking upon the subject I am carried back to the day when I saw a dear mother chained and carried off in a Southern steamboat to supply the cotton, sugar, or rice plantations of the South. I am carried back to the day when a dear sister was sold and carried off in my presence. I stood and looked at her. I could not protect her. I could not offer to protect her. I was a Slave, and the only testimony that I could give her that I sympathised with her, was to allow the tears to flow freely down my cheeks; and the tears flowing freely down her cheeks told me that my affection was reciprocated. I am carried back to the day when I saw three dear brothers sold, and carried off.

---

[3] *caufles*: coffles—groups of slaves, typically chained together when traveling to places of labor or to a slave market.

When I speak of Slavery, I am carried back to the time when I saw, day after day, my own fellow-countrymen placed upon the auction-stand; when I saw the bodies, and sinews, and hearts, and the souls of men sold to the highest bidder. I have with me an account of a Slave recently sold upon the auction-stand. The auctioneer could only get a bid of $400, but as he was about to knock her off, the owner of the Slave made his way through those that surrounded him and whispered to the auctioneer. As soon as the owner left, the auctioneer said, "I have failed to tell you all the good qualities of this Slave. I have told you that she was strong, healthy, and hearty, and now I have the pleasure to announce to you that she is very pious. She has got religion." And although, before that, he could only get $400, as soon as they found that she had got religion they commenced bidding upon her, and the bidding went up to $700. The writer says that her body and mind were sold for $400, and her religion was sold for $300.

WILLIAM WELLS BROWN

Singular Escape

In a letter of 4 January 1849 to William Lloyd Garrison, printed in the 12 January 1849 *Liberator* under the title "Singular Escape," William Wells Brown became the first person to report on the amazing escape from slavery of William Craft (1824–1900) and Ellen Craft (1826–1900). Slaves on a Georgia plantation, the Crafts, whose marriage had no legal basis in Southern culture, escaped in December 1848 by having the light-complected Ellen masquerade as a Southern gentleman accompanied by "his" servant William. Brown's letter on the Crafts in the *Liberator*, the source of the selection below, described some of the other creative tactics contributing to their escape. During 1849, the Crafts regularly spoke with Brown at antislavery meetings. In 1850, under threat from fugitive slave hunters, the Crafts sailed to England, and in 1851 they joined Brown for a tour on the British antislavery lecture circuit. The Crafts' story of their escape through gender and racial cross-dressing was an important source for Brown's representations of some of the slaves' stratagems in *Clotel*. In 1860 William Craft published his own account of the couple's ingenious escape, *Running a Thousand Miles for Freedom; or, The Escape of William and Ellen Craft from Slavery*.

"Ellen Craft, A Fugitive Slave." Wood engraving in *The Illustrated London News*, 19 April 1851. Courtesy of the Photographs and Prints Division, Schomburg Center for Research in Black Culture, The New York Public Library, Astor, Lennox and Tilden Foundations.

PINEVILLE, (Pa.) Jan. 4, 1849.

DEAR FRIEND GARRISON:

One of the most interesting cases of the escape of fugitives from American slavery that have ever come before the American people, has just occurred, under the following circumstances:—William and Ellen Craft, man and wife, lived with different masters in the State of Georgia. Ellen is so near white, that she can pass without suspicion for a white woman. Her husband is much darker. He is a mechanic, and by working nights and Sundays, he laid up money enough to bring himself and his wife out of slavery. Their plan was without precedent; and though novel, was the means of getting them their freedom. Ellen dressed in man's clothing, and passed as the *master*, while her husband passed as the *servant*. In this way they travelled from Georgia to Philadelphia. They are now out of the reach of the blood-hounds of the South. On their journey, they put up at the best hotels where they stopped. Neither of them can read or write. And Ellen, knowing that she would be called upon to write her name at the hotels, &c., tied her right hand up as though it was lame, which proved of some service to her, as she was called upon several times at hotels to 'register' her name. In Charleston, S.C., they put up at the hotel which Gov. M'Duffie and John C. Calhoun generally make their home, yet these distinguished advocates of the 'peculiar institution' say that the slaves cannot take care of themselves. They arrived in Philadelphia, in four days from the time they started. Their history, especially that of their escape, is replete with interest. They will be at the meeting of the Massachusetts Anti-Slavery Society, in Boston, in the latter part of this month, where I know the history of their escape will be listened to with great interest. They are very intelligent. They are young, Ellen 22, and Wm. 24 years of age. Ellen is truly a heroine.

Yours, truly,
WM. W. BROWN.

P.S. They are now hid away within 25 miles of Philadelphia, where they will remain until the 6th, when they will leave with me for New England. Will you please say in the Liberator that I will lecture, in connexion with them, as follows:—

At Norwich, Ct., Thursday evening, Jan. 18
" Worcester,   Mass., Friday evening, 19.
" Pawtucket,   "   Saturday evening, 20.
" New Bedford,   "   Sunday afternoon and evening, 28.

WILLIAM WELLS BROWN

From *Original Panoramic Views*

During his 1850 tour of Great Britain, Brown commissioned several artists to paint a twenty-four-scene canvas depicting slavery in the United States. He used the canvas to dramatic effect during some of his antislavery lectures. To accompany the canvas, which he first displayed in October of 1850, he authored a pamphlet offering short descriptions of each scene, titled *A Description of William Wells Brown's Original Panoramic Views of the Scenes in the Life of An American Slave, from His Birth in Slavery to His Death or His Escape to His First Home of Freedom on British Soil* (London: Charles Gilpin, 1850), the source of this selection. "View Eighth" contains the germ of *Clotel*'s story of Henry and Althesa Morton.

VIEW EIGHTH.

The New Orleans Calaboose—Sale of Slaves— Mode of Punishment.

One of the oldest and most celebrated public buildings in New Orleans, is the Calaboose. This building is built mainly of stone and iron, and is very large and strong. Some parts of the building are let out to Slave-traders, who use it as a depository for their slaves; although the building is the public property of the city.

You here see the mode of punishing slaves. If an owner wishes his slaves whipped, he can have it done to "order," by sending them to the Calaboose, and paying a fee of one dollar. I was once sent to be whipped in this way (see "Narrative of W. W. BROWN"), but escaped the infliction.

The sale before us is a sale of Slaves, although that woman on the auction-stand who is now being sold, together with the other who is standing among the bystanders, is perfectly white. Unfortunately for these poor girls, their mother was a Slave; and therefore they are also Slaves by the Slave-laws of all the American Slave States.

These are the facts as regards the two white girls now before us. A young physician from one of the Free States went to New Orleans, to commence the practice of his profession. On arriving in the city, he took lodgings at a house, where he observed occasionally waiting on the mistress, a young woman apparently white; and knowing that white persons seldom or never acted as servants in the Slave States, he was induced to make some inquiries respecting her. He was much astonished to learn that she was a Slave. Not being accustomed to see persons in a state of Slavery, he felt very much interested in her behalf. This feeling eventually warmed into love; and he determined to purchase the Slave and to make her his wife. He saw the owner, and ascertained that he was actually the father of the girl, and on this account professed some feelings of paternal affection. When he found the purpose for which the young physician wanted her, he sold her, as an especial favour (!) under the circumstances, for 800 dollars, which he gladly paid, and they were united in marriage. They resided in the city of New Orleans, and spent many years in the happy enjoyment of each other's company, in wealth and affluence. At length they both died, and the physician's brother came down to see to his estate, on behalf of two beautiful and handsome daughters whom they had left behind them. He found that his brother's estate was heavily involved in debt; and the case coming before the Courts, the barristers discovered, amongst his papers, the document of the purchase of his wife for 800 dollars. He had failed to manumit his wife from slavery, to save the fact of her having been a slave from becoming known to his friends, and thus causing them probably to look upon her with less kindly and friendly feelings than they otherwise did. The laws of the United States provide, that, if a Slave should be sold out of Slavery, and live for many years a life of freedom, notwithstanding the fact of her becoming married and living in perfect freedom, yet, if the documents of manumission are not taken out, she is still a Slave in the eye of the law, and all the children are Slaves also. Well, the consequence was, that the schedule of the property was handed back to the brother, with an information that he had not given a correct return of his brother's property, and requiring him to amend it, under the penalties of the law. On inquiring where the incorrectness of the return lay, he was told he had not entered his brother's Slaves; and on his replying that he had none, he was coolly referred to these two girls. "Why," said he, "they are my brother's daughters." Nevertheless, they were, he was told, his brother's Slaves. The document was handed to him; and for the first time the painful fact of their mother having been a Slave was made known to her beautiful daughters, accompanied with the still more painful reality that they were, in the eye of the law, Slaves also. The brother was compelled to enter the girls in the schedule as property, with a heavy amount to each as their value; and there not being assets sufficient to cover the debts, the brother tried hard to raise the purchase-money to release them from their unhappy position. But the sale was hurried on before he could do so; and these handsome but unfortunate girls were placed on the auction-stand, and sold; one for 1,500 dollars and the other for 2,000 dollars. For what purpose such high sums were given all those who were acquainted with the iniquities of American Slavery will readily suspect.

The following advertisements, taken from the *New Orleans Picayune*, will give some idea of the American internal Slave-trade, now in active operation: —

[From the *New Orleans Picayune*.]

Slaves for Sale. — HOPE H. SLATTER, who has retired from the trade, has sold to me his establishment in Baltimore, and leased for a number of years his old stand at the corner of Esplanade and Moreau streets, at which place I shall keep up a large and general assortment of *Slaves* for sale, imported direct from Maryland and Virginia.

WALTER L. CAMPBELL,
Successor to Hope H. Slater.

Negroes — Negroes. — Just received, and for sale at No. 7, Moreau-street, Third Municipality, a large and likely lot of *Negroes*, consisting of field hands, house servants, and mechanics. Will be receiving new lots regularly from Virginia during the season.

WM. F. TALBOTT.

Negroes for Sale on Time. — Nine valuable and well trained Negroes, consisting of men, women, and boys, for sale on a credit of four to six months.

PEGRAM & BRYAN.

WILLIAM WELLS BROWN

A True Story of Slave Life

Brown published "A True Story of Slave Life," an intriguing mix of fact and fiction, in the December 1852 issue of London's *Anti-Slavery Advocate* (the source of the text below). He then drew on the tale for the opening of *Clotel* and for the reconciliation scene between the slave owner and his black daughter in the 1860s revisions of *Clotel*. Although Brown presents the story as "true," there is no documentation to support such a claim. Brown visited Philadelphia in 1848, at which time he may have met members of the prominent free black Forten and Purvis families. James Forten (1766–1842) was an antislavery activist who established his own sailmaking company; his second wife, Charlotte Vandine Forten (1786–1886), was an antislavery activist and educator; and Robert Purvis (1810–1898) was a Garrisonian abolitionist who married the Fortens' daughter Harriet in 1832. In the story, Brown presents the Fortens and Purvises as a harmonious extended family, but the fact is that shortly after the death of James Forten, Robert Purvis sued James Forten, Jr., in order to gain access to some of his father-in-law's funds. That lawsuit would have been working its way through the courts around the time of the events described in "A True Story of Slave Life." Ultimately, the "truth" of the story centers on Brown's belief in blacks' capacities for uplift and his outrage at the dehumanizing force of slavery.

In October of 1844, amongst a number of slaves who were exposed for sale at a slave auction in Richmond, Virginia, was a woman of middle size, slim, and delicately built. Her skin was lighter than many a northern brunette's, and her features were oval, with thin lips; indeed, many thought no African blood coursed through her veins. The day was as fine as one could wish to behold. The auctioneer's flag hung listless by the pole, and not a breeze had leave to stir.

The white slave girl, with tears in her eyes, ascended the auction block, and the auctioneer, hammer in hand, began with, "Who bids for this nice young woman? How much, gentlemen? Real albino, fit for a fancy girl for any one. She enjoys good health, and is an excellent house servant. How much do you say?" "Five hundred dollars." "Only five hundred for such a girl as this? Gentlemen, she is worth double that sum. I am sure if you knew the superior qualities of the girl, you would give more. Here, gentlemen, I hold in my hand a paper certifying that she has a good moral character—" "Seven hundred." "Ah, gentlemen, that is something like. This paper also states that she is very intelligent." "Eight hundred." "She is a devoted Christian and perfectly trustworthy." "Nine hundred," "Nine-fifty," exclaimed a second, "Ten hundred," said a third, and the woman was struck off to the last bidder for one thousand dollars. This was a southern auction, at which the bones, muscles, sinews, blood, and nerves of a young lady of twenty-eight years of age sold for five hundred dollars; her moral character for two hundred dollars; her improved intellect for another hundred; and her Christianity—the person of Christ in his follower—for two hundred more. The woman had scarcely descended from the auction-block, when a little girl, ten years of age, took her place, and the auctioneer announced her for sale. The child was perfectly white, and all seemed surprised at the announcement that she was a slave. Among the crowd of spectators was a gentlemanly looking man, apparently about fifty years of age, remarkable for his snow white hair and red face. Upon this man the eyes of the slave woman were fixed, and even the child watched him so attentively that it was remarked by many. He was the owner of the mother and the father of the child. The good qualities of the little girl were vividly pourtrayed by the auctioneer, but as no one bid for her, the sale closed, and she followed her master home again. The mother, who had been sold to a negro speculator, was placed in prison until his gang was ready to depart for the cotton, sugar, and rice districts.

The next day was the sabbath, and the bells called to mass and prayer-meeting. Methodists sang, Baptists immersed, and Presbyterians sprinkled, while the poor slave mother lay on the scanty straw of her dungeon, uncared for even by those who professed the same faith and belonged to the same church as herself. This woman had been housekeeper to her owner, and he had formed a matrimonial alliance with a lady in the neighbourhood, one of the conditions of which was that the housekeeper and her child should be sent off before the arrival of the bride. The child not being sold, her unfeeling father resolved to send her off with a family who were on the eve of a journey to the northern states; and a few days after, the little slave girl was left in Lombard-street, Philadelphia, a district in which the coloured people reside. No provision was made for her maintenance, and she was left without a change of clothing. In this forlorn condition she was met by Robert Purvis, Esq., a philanthropist distinguished for his goodness of heart, and certainly the most accomplished coloured gentleman in the United States. Mr. Purvis took the little girl into his own family, where she remained about four years, receiving the same attention and education as his own children; and in 1848, he placed her in the family of his father-in-law, the late venerable James Forten. Mrs. Forten became much attached to her, and learning the address of her father, she resolved to write to him and to attempt to awaken in his breast a feeling for his child; she accordingly wrote, but received no reply. However, she continued to write, until at last answer came that Mr. Carter would pass through Philadelphia in the course of a few weeks, on his way to the springs of Saratoga,[1] and would call upon her.

It was on a fine day in the latter part of July, when the street-bell summoned the servant to the door, and a gentleman presented himself, who inquired for Mrs. Forten. His tall stature, white hair, and ruddy complexion announced him at once as Mr. Carter. Being shown into the drawing-room, he was received by Mrs. Forten, who said, "I presume, sir, you are anxious to see your daughter?" "I have no daughter here," replied the slaveholder; "but having learned from your letters that there is a girl here who was raised on my farm, I have called to see her." He seated himself on the sofa, and awaited the entrance of the girl. He had pictured in his mind's eye the little slave girl of ten years old, with short hair, dressed in the homespun attire in which he last saw her on his tobacco plantation in Virginia. A few moments elapsed when the door opened and Miss Carter entered. She was tall, with prominent features, dark hair, hazel eyes, Grecian nose, mouth rather large, a fine set of teeth as white as snow, a turned and well-rounded chin—in short, her whole countenance had an appearance of beauty seldom seen in any except the quadroon girls of America. Yet she was so white that no one would suppose for a moment that a drop of negro blood flowed through her veins. As she had resided for six years in the refined and educated families of the Forten's and Purvis's, she had lost the uncouthness of the Southern slave life, and her manners were easy, graceful, and pleasing. Such was the appearance of Elizabeth Carter when she entered the room, to behold for the first time after a lapse of six years, the man who, though her own father, had thrown her upon the bosom of a cold and unfeeling world. Her appearance contrasted so strangely with what she was when he last saw her, that Mr. Carter, though remaining seated on the sofa with an apparent determination not to stir from his seat, or even give his daughter a nod of recognition on her entrance, arose, bowed, and seemed bewildered at the appearance of the young lady. Miss Carter seated herself near Mrs. Forten, as if to say, "The protection you denied me I have found amongst strangers." Silence followed the entrance of the young lady, so that for some moments not a word was spoken; at last Mrs. Forten turned, and was in the act of speaking to Mr. Carter, when she saw that he was weeping. The sweet smile, the innocent look and girlish beauty of the discarded child had touched the finer feelings of the father; the hard heart melted to tears, and the *man* took the place of the *slaveholder*. Mrs. Forten rose from her seat and said, "I will leave you with your daugh-

---

[1] *Saratoga*: A resort area in upstate New York.

ter." Miss Carter was asked by her father to take a seat on the sofa beside him, and an hour after Mrs. Forten was called in, and the father said to his child, "Lizzy, hereafter you may call me father." The expense of the girl's maintenance up to that time was paid, and her future support and education were amply provided for.

During the summer of 1848, while on a visit to Philadelphia, I met with and was introduced to Miss Carter; and when informed that she had been a slave, I could scarcely believe that a lady endowed with such rare accomplishments had ever been a victim to the inhuman institution from which I had myself escaped only a few years earlier.

WILLIAM WELLS BROWN

Letters from London

Brown traveled to England in 1849 and remained there until 1854, when he was purchased from slavery by a British reformer. He regularly wrote letters to antislavery newspapers about his experiences abroad, extolling England for its antislavery policies and sympathies. In the two letters below, which appeared in William Lloyd Garrison's *Liberator*, Brown conveys the excitement of participating in the transatlantic antislavery movement while working on *Clotel*. The movement had been newly energized by the 1852 publication of Stowe's *Uncle Tom's Cabin*, which probably inspired Brown to write his own novel. Brown's letters to Garrison and Samuel May Jr. appeared in issues of the *Liberator* of 3 June 1853 and 4 November 1853, respectively, which are the sources of the texts below. The letter to Garrison was reprinted in the 10 June 1853 issue of *Frederick Douglass' Paper*.

LETTER FROM WILLIAM W. BROWN

DEAR MR. GARRISON:

I forward to you, by this day's mail, the papers containing accounts of the great meeting held in Exeter Hall[1] last night. No meeting during this anniversary has caused so much talk and excitement as this gathering. No time could possibly have been more appropriate for such a meeting than the present. Uncle Tom's Cabin has come down upon the

[1] *Exeter Hall:* In London. See p. 63, note 18.

dark abodes of slavery like a morning's sunlight, unfolding to view its enormities in a manner which has fastened all eyes upon the 'peculiar institution,' and awakening sympathy in hearts that never before felt for the slave. Had Exeter Hall been capable of holding fifty thousand instead of five thousand, it would no doubt have been filled to its utmost capacity. For more than a week before the meeting came off, the tickets were all disposed of, and it was understood that hundreds were applying every day. With those who may be classed as Mrs. Stowe's converts, that lady was the centre of attraction for them; while the elder abolitionists came for the sake of the cause. I entered the great Hall an hour before the time, and found the building filled, there scarcely being standing room, except on the platform, which was in charge of the officials, to keep places for those who had tickets to that part of the house. At half-past six, the Earl of Shaftesbury[2] appeared upon the platform, followed by the Committee and speakers, amid the most deafening applause. The Noble Earl, who has many more nobler qualities than that of a mere nobleman, made the opening speech, and, as you will see, a good one. While his lordship was speaking, Her Grace, the Duchess of Sutherland,[3] came in, and took her seat in the balcony on the right of the platform, and an half hour after, a greater lady (the authoress of Uncle Tom) made her appearance, and took her seat by the side of the Duchess. At this stage of the meeting, there was a degree of excitement in the room that can better be imagined than described. The waving of hats and handkerchiefs, the clapping of hands, the stamping of feet, and the screaming and fainting of ladies, went on as if it had been in the programme, while the thieves were at work helping themselves out of the abundance of the pockets of those who were most crowded. A few arrests by the police soon taught the latter that there was no room there for pickpockets. Order was once more restored, and the speaking went on. Many good things were said by the different speakers, who were mostly residents of the metropolis. Professor Stowe,[4] as you might expect, was looked upon as the lion of

[2] *Earl of Shaftesbury*: Anthony Ashley Cooper, the 7th earl of Shaftesbury (1801–1885) was a prominent social reformer, committed to antislavery and improving the conditions of factory workers.

[3] *Duchess of Sutherland*: Harriet Elizabeth Georgiana Sutherland-Leveson-Gower, Duchess of Sutherland (1806–1868). Like the Earl of Shaftesbury, she was known for her commitment to social reform.

[4] *Professor Stowe*: Calvin Stowe (1802–1886), the husband of Harriet Beecher Stowe and a professor of religion at Andover Theological Seminary. Harriet would have thought it improper for a woman to speak before a "promiscuous" mixed audience of men and women.

the speakers; but his speech disappointed all, except those of us who knew enough of American divines not to anticipate much from them on the subject of slavery. For my own part, I was not disappointed, for I have long since despaired of anything being done by clergymen; and the Professor's speech at Glasgow, and subsequent addresses, had prepared me to look for but little from him. He evidently wishes for no agitation on the subject, and said it would do no good as long as England purchased America's cotton. I look upon this cotton question as nothing more than to divert the public from the main subject itself. Mr. Stowe is not very young, yet he is only a child in the anti-slavery movement. He is now lisping his A, B, C, and if his wife succeeds in making him a good scholar, she will find it no easy thing.

The best speech of the evening was made by our countryman, Samuel R. Ward.[5] Mr. Ward did himself great credit, and exposed the hypocrisy of the American pro-slavery churches in a way that caused Professor Stowe to turn more than once upon his seat. I have but little faith in the American clergy—either colored or white; but I believe Ward to be not only one of the most honest, but an uncompromising and faithful advocate of his countrymen. He is certainly the best colored minister that has yet visited this country.

I recognized in the audience several of our American friends. Among them was Mrs. Follen, Miss Cabot, J. Miller M'Kim, Miss Pugh, Professor Wm. G. Allen and lady, and Wm. and Ellen Craft.[6] Upon the whole, the anti-slavery cause is in a more healthy state than it ever was before, and from all appearance much good will be done by the present excitement. The fact that no American clergyman has dared to appear at any of the anniversary meetings without professing anti-slavery principles, and that one at least (Rev. Mr. Prime[7]) was denied a

---

[5] *Samuel R. Ward*: Born a slave, Samuel Ringgold Ward (1817–1866) escaped from slavery with his parents in 1820. He became a prominent abolitionist and minister in New York City, before traveling to Canada and England and eventually settling in Jamaica. He is best known for his narrative, *Autobiography of a Fugitive Slave: His Anti-Slavery Labours in the United States, Canada, and England* (1855).

[6] *Mrs. Follen . . . Ellen Craft*: Various white and black abolitionists: Eliza Lee (Cabot) Follen (1787–1860) of Boston; Follen's sister Susan Copley Cabot (1794–1861); James Miller McKim (1810–1874), editor of the antislavery newspaper the *Pennsylvania Freeman*; Sarah Pugh (1800–1884), a Quaker from Philadelphia; William G. Allen (1820–?), a black abolitionist based in New York whose marriage to the white Mary King in March 1853 caused such a scandal that they sailed to London, never returning to the United States. On the Crafts, see the headnote to Brown's "Singular Escape" (p. 368 in this volume).

[7] *Rev. Mr. Prime*: A clergyman and editor of the New York *Observer*, Samuel Irenæus Prime (1812–1885) was suspicious of what he regarded as the radicalism of abolitionists, though he ultimately was not a champion of slavery.

seat as a delegate at one of these meetings, shows the feeling already created in Great Britain; and I hope it will soon be understood in America, that no man will be welcomed here, unless he is an out-and-out abolitionist; and then the days of the slave's deliverance will be close at hand.

Yours, very sincerely,

WM. WELLS BROWN.

22 Cecil Street, Strand, London, May 17th, 1853.

EXTRACT OF A LETTER
FROM WILLIAM WELLS BROWN

☞ Our friend Brown, we hope, will forgive this publication of a portion of his friendly private letter. There are very many here who remember him with great regard, and often inquire about him, to whom these few lines will be pleasant tidings: —

22 CECIL STREET, STRAND,
LONDON, OCT. 3, 1853.

MY DEAR FRIEND[8]—I cannot think of letting Miss C.[9] leave England without sending you a few lines, to acknowledge the receipt of your kind note sent over in the last anti-slavery box. I must also confess my negligence in not writing to you oftener. You and our mutual friend, Wendell Phillips,[10] are the only persons who give me information of the doings of my American friends. Miss Estlin,[11] no doubt, acquainted you long since of the severe illness of her father; and you will regret to learn from Miss C. that he is still in a feeble state. * * * *

My daughters are still at school here, the youngest[12] of whom acts as my amanuensis in conveying these few sentences to you. Does n't

---

[8] *MY DEAR FRIEND*: The letter is to Samuel May Jr. (1810–1899), a prominent Garrisonian abolitionist who served as general agent of the Massachusetts Anti-Slavery Society from 1847 to 1865.

[9] *Miss C.*: Probably Susan Copley Cabot, who was a friend of Garrison's and May's and a contributor to the *Liberator*.

[10] *Wendell Phillips*: An influential Boston abolitionist, Phillips (1811–1884) worked closely with Garrison.

[11] *Miss Estlin*: Mary Anne Estlin (1820–1902), a British abolitionist who also fought for women's rights. Her father was the Unitarian minister John Bishop Estlin (1785–1855), who supported Garrison's cause in England.

[12] *youngest*: Josephine Brown (b. 1839), who would publish a biography of her father in 1855. See the selection from *Biography of an American Bondman* (pp. 360–65).

she write a good hand? Is n't she a good girl? I think I have told you before that they are being trained for teachers. They will soon have finished their eighteen months in the Training School, and will leave at Christmas. Craft[13] called today to see me, and wished to be kindly remembered to you. He thinks of setting up a lodging-house in London. Ellen does not enjoy very good health. I am still going the rounds, giving lectures on American slavery, and sometimes on other subjects, to mechanics and literary institutions. I am now looking over the proof-sheet of 'Clotel, or the President's Daughter,' a new work of mine now going through the press. I watch with interest the doings of my old coadjutors, and never take up a *Liberator* or a *Standard*,[14] containing accounts of meetings or conventions, without feeling like taking the next boat for Boston. I am not tired of old England, yet I want to be back in America. Please remember me most kindly to Parker Pillsbury, Lucy Stone, the Fosters,[15] and those immediately around you in the Anti-Slavery Office, and believe me to be

Yours, very truly,
W. WELLS BROWN.

Rev. S. MAY, JR.

[13] *Craft*: William Craft, the escaped slave; the subsequent reference is to his wife, Ellen.

[14] *Standard*: The antislavery newspaper *National Anti-Slavery Standard*, based in New York City.

[15] *Parker Pillsbury . . . Fosters*: Born in Hamilton, Massachusetts, Parker Pillsbury (1809–1898) was a reformer committed to antislavery and women's rights; the Massachusetts reformer Lucy Stone (1818–1893) shared his interests in both reform causes. Married in 1845, Abigail Kelley Foster (1810–1877) and Stephen Symonds Foster (1809–1881) were prominent Garrisonian abolitionists and supporters of women's rights.

SELECTED REVIEWS OF *CLOTEL*

Published in England, *Clotel* received more attention from English than U.S. reviewers, though a number of the English reviews were reprinted in U.S. journals. Like many antislavery novels published in the wake of Stowe's *Uncle Tom's Cabin*, *Clotel* was regarded somewhat condescendingly as "Uncle Tom" literature. Nevertheless, reviews on both sides of the Atlantic were appreciative, with commentators taking note of the novel's sharp critique of slavery and its indictment of Thomas Jefferson. English reviewers in particular took pride in the fact that their country had abolished slavery. As the reviewer for the *British Mothers' Magazine* put it, English readers of *Clotel* "will be enlisted in the cause of the oppressed, and their love of Old England rendered more ardent than ever." Reviewers failed to appreciate, or simply failed to discuss, Brown's fictional techniques, such as his appropriations and reworkings of previously published texts, and his sometimes jarring (but highly revealing) narrative leaps back and forth in chronological time. Perhaps in an effort to engage more readers, Brown in his 1860s revisions of *Clotel* chose to work with a more conventional narrative that more closely followed the unfolding of plot.

From the *Hereford*[1] *Times*, 17 December 1853

'Clotel' is a tale, made up (as we learn from the preface) chiefly from incidents in which Mr. Brown was either an actor or an eye-witness. It records the life of a daughter of the late President Jefferson, who, upon her father's death, suffered all the horrors of a system which he so eloquently denounced, yet from which he left his own child unguarded. In that case, the greater part of the crime must be put down to the account of the executors of the President, who, of course, knew or cared nothing about his child, except as she was a marketable chattel; but the traffic is often dyed in an infinitely deeper guilt than theirs. In the case of Mr. Brown himself, his uncle was the 'master' who sold him, his sisters, and his mother; while every hour, American fathers pollute that sacred title by selling their own children like cattle. The profligacy which this infernal system produces among the slaveholders themselves, is appalling: the female slave may be sister or daughter to her master; the law knows no such relationship in a slave, but requires implicit obedience from her, on pain of death, if her tyrant chooses to sacrifice her market value by killing her. These 'peculiar' features of the 'peculiar institution of the South,' are working out its punishment. The large infusion of Anglo-Saxon blood among the slaves, has made them all the more difficult to keep down. As Mr. Brown remarks, it is that element which has produced the insurrectionary movements of late years; and we do not doubt that a half-breed Tell[2] will some day avenge the wrongs of his maternal ancestors upon their corruptors and

---

[1] *Hereford*: A cathedral city and agricultural trading center approximately 140 miles west of London. The review was republished in the 20 January 1854 issue of the *Liberator*, which is the source of this text.

[2] *Tell*: William Tell, the legendary and perhaps apocryphal Swiss national hero of the late thirteenth and early fourteenth centuries, who defied Austrian authority in the cause of political and individual freedom.

oppressors. If the 'chivalry' of the South continue deaf to the calls of both justice and mercy, it would be but prudent for them to get rid of slavery as a measure of personal safety.

In 'Clotel,' the writer has touched lightly upon his dreadful subject, yet, writing upon a matter of which he has had such painful experience, he could hardly fail to be interesting. His portraitures of character, especially the slaveholding parson, his excellent daughter, and Carleton, disgusted with religion because it is perverted by hypocrites to sanction slavery, are each graphically drawn. Some of his sketches are drily humorous. Witness the stage-coach discussion between the Massachusetts clergyman and his Louisianan friend.

From the *Eastern Star*,[3] December 1853

The book before us appears to have been written for the purpose of proving—if any additional proof were needed—that the incidents which the authoress of "Uncle Tom's Cabin" has related in that admirable work are no mere inventions of fancy, but actual occurrences, the counterparts of which are to be met with in the daily scenes of slave life. The author has imagined, perhaps, and we think with justice, a book written by one who has himself tasted of the horrors he describes, by one who has taken part in the ghastly scenes which he delineates, would be more convincing than any vindication, any appeal to facts, any arguments put forth by those who are necessarily compelled to receive their information from others. Accordingly, "Clotel" is a reproduction of many of the events in the author's life, bound together by the lightest possible thread of fiction, more for the purpose of giving a connected form to the narrative than of investing it with the interest of imaginative incident. Those, therefore, who expect to find in its pages the thrilling power, the easy humour, or the graphic description of Mrs. Stowe, will be disappointed. But to all who may still entertain doubts as to the truthfulness of the pictures of slave life which that authoress has drawn; to all who may wish to accumulate evidence of the capacity of the human mind, even under the worst circumstances, to elevate itself above the influences which tend to darken and debase it; to all who wish freedom to the captive negro, and who hail with delight any fresh evidence of his power to appreciate and to obtain it, "Clotel" will be welcomed as a remarkable and an interest-

---

[3] *Eastern Star*: Published in London. The review was reprinted in the (New York) *National Anti-Slavery Standard*, 31 December 1853, which is the source of this text.

ing book. Mr. Brown writes with ease and fluency; he does not pretend to possess those finished graces of style which belong to the writers of fiction; but he expresses himself in a clear, intelligible, manly manner, oftentimes writing with considerable force, when more than ordinarily aroused by the recollection of his wrongs and the wrongs of his race. There is a dash, too, of humour in many parts of the work which we could scarcely have expected from one who has suffered so much, and which relieves the more painful portions of the narrative. The following extracts[4] afford fair evidence of the author's style and powers. We cordially recommend "Clotel" to all our readers.

From the *Pennsylvania Freeman*, 29 December 1853

CLOTEL, OR THE PRESIDENT'S DAUGHTER—We find, in our English exchanges, warmly commendatory notices of a narrative of slave life in the United States, just published in London, with the above title. It is from the pen of Wm. W. Brown, and though presented in the garb of fiction, it is largely composed of facts which have come within the range of his personal experience, or under his observation, or which he learned directly from other fugitives from the Patriarchal Paradise of Slavery, during several years service on the under-ground railroad.

The heroine of the tale is a daughter of President Jefferson, doomed to slavery, like so many other children of proud Virginian fathers, by her maternity.

Her history, through a changeful and eventful life, to a tragic death, is traced with a skill and tact that interweaves with it many thrilling and important incidents of slave life. The London *Morning Advertiser* styles it a "tale of deep and lasting interest, calculated to impress the most heedless, and give renewed vigor to the sacred cause of universal freedom," and adds of it:

> "What the genius of Mrs. Stowe has accomplished by *Uncle Tom*, that of William Wells Brown, though marked by different qualities and incidents, will accomplish most certainly by the tale of *Clotel*, which, like the other, is only too true."

We trust that we shall soon see it on this side of the ocean. Mr. Brown has many friends here who will welcome it cordially, and the public mind has not been so sated with "Uncle Tom" literature, that it will refuse more.

---

[4] *The following extracts*: At the end of the review, the writer quotes from the steamboat gambling scene in chapter II and from the account of the slave burnt at the stake in chapter III.

From the *British Mothers' Magazine*, 1 January 1854

Thomas Jefferson was, we believe, the second president of the United States. He wrote eloquently in defence of freedom; he declaimed earnestly against slavery. But Thomas Jefferson was a slaveholder, and many of his slaves were his own children.—Clotel, with two sisters, were his descendants, literally his grand-daughters. Although, as quadroons, these young ladies were nearly white in complexion, they were, nevertheless, sold as slaves, and their sufferings and their wrongs are most vividly related by Mr. Brown. The statements contained in this volume, are, as we understand, statements of facts; and in point of interest do not yield even to that wonderful book "Uncle Tom's Cabin." Great principles are advocated in connexion with the thrilling incidents which this powerful writer has so impressively recorded. The lovers of "light-reading" need not resort to fiction if they require excitement as their mental food. In this volume they will find more than enough to excite, whilst their sympathies will be enlisted in the cause of the oppressed, and their love of Old England rendered more ardent than ever.

From the *Liberator*,[5] 3 February 1854

A fugitive slave successfully turning author—giving spirited sketches of men and things in the old world, as well as of the hideous system of tyranny from which he has made his escape, so as to excite the interest and extort the admiration of highly cultivated minds—is a surprising event even in this age of wonders. 'That a man,' says the London *Weekly News and Chronicle*, referring to Mr. Brown's 'Three Years in Europe,'[6] 'who was a slave for the first twenty years of his life, and who has never had a day's schooling, should produce such a book as this, cannot but astonish those who speak disparagingly of the African race.' Of the present work, 'Clotel,' the English journals speak in terms of the warmest commendation. For a copy of it, we are greatly obliged to the author; and, having read it, we wish it might be reprinted in this country, believing it would find many readers. While the Declaration of Independence is preserved, the memory of Thomas Jefferson, its author, will be cherished, for the clear recognition it makes of the natural equality of mankind, and the inalienable right of every human

---

[5] *Liberator*: The influential antislavery newspaper published in Boston by William Lloyd Garrison. In all likelihood, Garrison is the author of this review.

[6] *Three Years in Europe*: A reference to Brown's travel narrative *Three Years in Europe; or, Places I Have Seen and People I Have Met* (1852).

being to freedom and the pursuit of happiness. But it will also be to his eternal disgrace that he lived and died a slave-holder, emancipating none of his slaves at his death,[7] and, it is well understood, leaving some of his own children to be sold to the slave speculators, and thus to drag out a miserable life of servitude. Of the last, 'Clotel' was one— beautiful, intelligent, captivating. 'Her appearance on the auction block created a deep sensation amongst the crowd. Here she stood, with a complexion as white as most of those who were waiting with a wish to become her purchasers; her features as finely defined as any of her sex of pure Anglo-Saxon; her long, black, wavy hair done up in the neatest manner; her form tall and graceful, and her whole appearance indicating one superior to her position.' The auctioneer eloquently expatiated upon her beauty and many good qualities, and the bids rapidly increased as he proceeded, so that she was struck off for fifteen hundred dollars—'her bones, muscles, sinews, blood and nerves were sold for five hundred dollars; her moral character for two hundred; her improved intellect for two hundred; her Christianity for three hundred; and her chastity and virtue for four hundred dollars more. And this, too, in a city thronged with churches, whose tall spires look like so many signals pointing to heaven, and whose ministers preach that slavery is a God-ordained institution!'

'Clotel' is sold into various hands, and experiences the painful vicissitudes to which one in her condition is ever liable, till at length, about to be transported to New Orleans, as her prison in Washington was being closed for the night, she suddenly darted past her keeper, and ran for her life towards the famous 'Long Bridge,' which spans the Potomac from the lower part of the city; but, being hemmed in by her pursuers, and seeing escape impossible, she vaulted over the railings of the bridge, and sunk forever beneath the waters of the Potomac.

Mr. Brown has skillfully embodied in his affecting tale numerous well-authenticated occurrences, which have transpired at the South within a comparatively short period—all calculated to intensify the moral indignation of the world against American slavery.

---

[7] *emancipating none of his slaves at his death*: In fact, Jefferson's will emancipated the children he had had with Sally Hemings.

WILLIAM WELLS BROWN

From *St. Domingo: Its Revolutions and Its Patriots*

Sparked by the French Revolution and the refusal of Haitian planters to permit mulatto participation in the French National Assembly, the San Domingo insurrection, which resulted in the deaths of tens of thousands of blacks and whites between 1791 and 1804, ultimately led to the emergence of Haiti as an independent black nation in the Americas. Like many African Americans of the period, Brown was inspired by the heroic leadership of Toussaint L'Ouverture (c.1744–1803), a self-educated former slave who helped to guide the rebellion, eventually becoming the governor of San Domingo in 1801. In 1802 Napoleon sent troops to the region in a last-gasp effort to regain control over the blacks. Toussaint L'Ouverture was arrested and deported to France, where he died in prison a martyr to the principles of liberty in an age of revolution. Brown, who would promote black emigration to Haiti during 1861 and 1862, lectured on San Domingo in London and Philadelphia in 1854. Drawing on John R. Beard's *The Life of Toussaint L'Ouverture* (1853), a source for chapter XXIV of *Clotel*, he presented Toussaint as a true "American" revolutionary—a rebel who, unlike Jefferson himself, embodied the very principles of the Declaration of Independence. The selection is taken from Brown, *St. Domingo: Its Revolutions and Its Patriots. A Lecture* (Boston: Bela Marsh, 1855).

Toussaint's career as a Christian, a statesman, and a general, will lose nothing by a comparison with that of Washington. Each was the leader of an oppressed and outraged people, each had a powerful enemy to contend with, and each succeeded in founding a government in the New World. Toussaint's government made liberty its watchword, incorporated it in its constitution, abolished the slave-trade, and made freedom universal amongst the people. Washington's government incorporated slavery and the slave-trade, and enacted laws by which claims were fastened upon the limbs of millions of people. Toussaint liberated his countrymen; Washington enslaved a portion of his, and aided in giving strength and vitality to an institution that will one day rend asunder the UNION that he helped to form. Already the slave in his chains, in the rice swamps of Carolina and the cotton fields of Mississippi, burns for revenge.

In contemplating the fact that the slave would rise and vindicate his right to freedom by physical force, Jefferson said:—

> "Indeed, I tremble for my country when I reflect that God is just; that his justice cannot sleep forever; that, considering numbers, nature, and natural means only, a revolution of the wheel of fortune, an exchange of situation, is among possible events; that it may become probable by supernatural interference! The Almighty has no attribute which can take side with us in such a contest.
>
> "What an incomprehensible machine is man! who can endure toil, famine, stripes, imprisonment, and death itself, in vindication of his own liberty, and the next moment be deaf to all those motives whose power supported him through his trial, and inflict on his fellow-men a bondage, one hour of which is fraught with more misery than ages of that which he rose in rebellion to oppose."[1]

And, should such a contest take place, the God of Justice will be on the side of the oppressed blacks. The exasperated genius of Africa would rise from the depths of the ocean, and show its threatening form; and war against the tyrants would be the rallying cry. The indignation of the slaves of the south would kindle a fire so hot that it would melt their chains, drop by drop, until not a single link would remain; and the revolution that was commenced in 1776 would then be finished, and the glorious sentiments of the Declaration of Independence, "That all men are created equal, and endowed by their Creator with certain inalienable rights, among which are life, liberty, and the pursuit of happiness," would be realized, and our government would no longer be the scorn and contempt of the friends of freedom in other lands, but would really be the LAND OF THE FREE AND HOME OF THE BRAVE.

---

[1] *"Indeed . . . oppose"*: From Jefferson's *Notes on the State of Virginia* and "Observations"; see *Clotel*, p. 157, note 2.

WILLIAM WELLS BROWN

From *Clotelle: A Tale of the Southern States*

In late 1860, during a time when he was considering the possibility of emigrating to Haiti, Brown dramatically reconceived *Clotel* for serial publication in the *Weekly Anglo-African*, a New York newspaper whose principal audience was the city's free black population. The new narrative, titled *Miralda; or, The Beautiful Quadroon. A Romance of American Slavery, Founded on Fact*, appeared in the issues of 1 December 1860 to 16 March 1861. To highlight just some of the significant changes from *Clotel* to *Miralda*: Brown renamed most of the characters, jettisoned his collage narrative technique for a more traditional narrative storytelling, extended the tale past the European reunion and marriage that concludes *Clotel*, and included just one passing reference to Jefferson. In late 1863, at a time when Brown had come to embrace the Civil War as a war of emancipation, he revised *Miralda* for James Redpath's "Books for the Camp Fires" series—cheaply produced books for Union soldiers and sympathizers. It was published as *Clotelle: A Tale of the Southern States* (Boston: James Redpath Publishers, 1864), the source of the selection below. Indicative of Brown's commitment to what he came to regard as the antislavery politics of the Declaration of Independence and the Constitution, he cuts *all* references to Jefferson in this revised version.

This selection presents in full the final two chapters of the 1864 *Clotelle*. Jerome and Clotelle (George and Mary in *Clotel*) are on their wedding journey in a small town outside of Geneva. They are surprised to meet Clotelle's father, Henry Linwood, who tells the story of one Mrs. Miller, the mother of his wife, Gertrude. While Mrs. Miller in both versions of *Clotelle* goes out of her way to inflict suffering on the slaves, Gertrude is presented as considerably kinder than Horatio Green's wife, also named Gertrude, in *Clotel*. Significantly, Jerome, unlike his white-skinned predecessor George in *Clotel*, is presented as black to the eye. Racial reconciliation, black pride, and hopes for emancipation are addressed at the end of *Clotelle* in ways very different from the ending of *Clotel*.

CHAPTER XXXIV.
CLOTELLE MEETS HER FATHER.

The clouds that had skirted the sky during the day broke at last, and the rain fell in torrents, as Jerome and Clotelle retired for the night, in the little town of Ferney, on the borders of Lake Leman.[1] The peals of thunder, and flashes of vivid lightening, which seemed to leap from mountain to mountain and from crag to crag, reverberating among the surrounding hills, foretold a heavy storm.

---

[1] *Ferney, on the borders of Lake Leman*: On the French-Swiss frontier, near Geneva.

"I would we were back at Geneva," said Clotelle, as she heard groans issuing from an adjoining room. The sounds, at first faint, grew louder and louder, plainly indicating that some person was suffering extreme pain.

"I did not like this hotel, much, when we came in," said Jerome, relighting the lamp, which had been accidentally extinguished.

"Nor I," returned Clotelle.

The shrieks increased, and an occasional "She's dead!" "I killed her!" "No, she is not dead!" and such-like expressions, would be heard from the person, who seemed to be deranged.

The thunder grew louder, and the flashes of lightening more vivid, while the noise from the sick-room seemed to increase.

As Jerome opened the door, to learn, if possible, the cause of the cries and groans, he could distinguish the words, "She's dead! yes, she's dead! but I did not kill her. She was my child! my own daughter. I loved her, and yet I did not protect her."

"Whoever he is," said Jerome, "he's crack-brained; some robber, probably, from the mountains."

The storm continued to rage, and the loud peals of thunder and sharp flashes of lightening, together with the shrieks and moans of the maniac in the adjoining room, made the night a fearful one. The long hours wore slowly away, but neither Jerome nor his wife could sleep, and they arose at an early hour in the morning, ordered breakfast, and resolved to return to Geneva.

"I am sorry, sir, that you were so much disturbed by the sick man last night," said the landlord, as he handed Jerome his bill. "I should be glad if he would get able to go away, or die, for he's a deal of trouble to me. Several persons have left my house on his account."

"Where is he from?" inquired Jerome.

"He's from the United States, and has been here a week to-day, and has been crazy ever since."

"Has he no friends with him?" asked the guest.

"No, he is alone," was the reply.

Jerome related to his wife what he had learned from the landlord, respecting the sick man, and the intelligence impressed her so strongly, that she requested him to make further inquiries concerning the stranger.

He therefore consulted the book in which guests usually register their names, and, to his great surprise, found that the American's name was Henry Linwood, and that he was from Richmond, Va.

It was with feelings of trepidation that Clotelle heard these particulars from the lips of her husband.

"We must see this poor man, whoever he is," said she, as Jerome finished the sentence.

The landlord was glad to hear that his guests felt some interest in the sick man, and promised that the invalid's room should be got ready for their reception.

The clock in the hall was just striking ten, as Jerome passed through and entered the sick man's chamber. Stretched upon a mattress, with both hands tightly bound to the bedstead, the friendless stranger was indeed a pitiful sight. His dark, dishevelled hair prematurely gray, his long, unshaven beard, and the wildness of the eyes which glanced upon them as they opened the door and entered, caused the faint hope which had so suddenly risen in Clotelle's heart, to sink, and she felt that this man could claim no kindred with her. Certainly, he bore no resemblance to the man whom she had called her father, and who had fondly dandled her on his knee in those happy days of childhood.

"Help!" cried the poor man, as Jerome and his wife walked into the room. His eyes glared, and shriek after shriek broke forth from his parched and fevered lips.

"No, I did not kill my daughter!—I did not! she is not dead! Yes, she is dead! but I did not kill her—poor girl! Look! that is she! No, it cannot be! she cannot come here! it cannot be my poor Clotelle."

At the sound of her own name, coming from the maniac's lips, Clotelle gasped for breath, and her husband saw that she had grown deadly pale. It seemed evident to him that the man was either guilty of some terrible act, or imagined himself to be. His eyeballs rolled in their sockets, and his features showed that he was undergoing "the tortures of that inward hell,"[2] which seemed to set his whole brain on fire.

After recovering her self-possession and strength, Clotelle approached the bedside, and laid her soft hand upon the stranger's hot and fevered brow.

One long, loud shriek rang out on the air, and a piercing cry, "It is she!—Yes, it is she! I see, I see! Ah! no, it is not my daughter! She would not come to me if she could!" broke forth from him.

"I am your daughter," said Clotelle, as she pressed her handkerchief to her face, and sobbed aloud.

Like balls of fire, the poor man's eyes rolled and glared upon the company, while large drops of perspiration ran down his pale and emaciated face. Strange as the scene appeared, all present saw that it

---

[2] *"tortures ... hell"*: From Lord Byron, *The Giaour: A Fragment of a Turkish Tale* (1813).

was indeed a meeting between a father and his long-lost daughter. Jerome now ordered all present to leave the room, except the nurse, and every effort was at once made to quiet the sufferer. When calm, a joyous smile would illuminate the sick man's face, and a strange light beam in his eyes, as he seemed to realize that she who stood before him was indeed his child.

For two long days and nights did Clotelle watch at the bedside of her father before he could speak to her intelligently. Sometimes, in his insane fits, he would rave in the most frightful manner, and then, in a few moments, would be as easily governed as a child. At last, however, after a long and apparently refreshing sleep, he awoke suddenly to a full consciousness that it was indeed his daughter who was watching so patiently by his side.

The presence of his long absent child had a soothing effect upon Mr. Linwood, and he now recovered rapidly from the sad and almost hopeless condition in which she had found him. When able to converse, without danger of a relapse, he told Clotelle of his fruitless efforts to obtain a clew to her whereabouts after old Mrs. Miller had sold her to the slave-trader. In answer to his daughter's inquiries about his family affairs up to the time that he left America, he said, —

"I blamed my wife for your being sold and sent away, for I thought she and her mother were acting in collusion; but I afterwards found that I had blamed her wrongfully. Poor woman! she knew that I loved your mother, and feeling herself forsaken, she grew melancholy and died in a decline three years ago."

Here both father and daughter wept at the thought of other days. When they had recovered their composure, Mr. Linwood went on again:

"Old Mrs. Miller," said he, "after the death of Gertrude, aware that she had contributed much toward her unhappiness, took to the free use of intoxicating drinks, and became the most brutal creature that ever lived. She whipped her slaves without the slightest provocation, and seemed to take delight in inventing new tortures with which to punish them. One night last winter, after having flogged one of her slaves nearly to death, she returned to her room, and by some means the bedding took fire, and the house was in flames before any one was awakened. There was no one in the building at the time but the old woman and the slaves, and although the latter might have saved their mistress, they made no attempt to do so. Thus, after a frightful career of many years, this hard-hearted woman died a most miserable death, unlamented by a single person."

Clotelle wiped the tears from her eyes, as her father finished this story, for, although Mrs. Miller had been her greatest enemy, she regretted to learn that her end had been such a sad one.

"My peace of mind destroyed," resumed the father, "and broke down in health, my physician advised me to travel, with the hope of recruiting myself, and I sailed from New York two months ago."

Being brought up in America, and having all the prejudice against color which characterizes his white fellow-countrymen, Mr. Linwood very much regretted that his daughter, although herself tinctured with African blood, should have married a black man, and he did not fail to express to her his dislike of her husband's complexion.

"I married him," said Clotelle, "because I loved him. Why should the white man be esteemed as better than the black? I find no difference in men on account of their complexion. One of the cardinal principles of Christianity and freedom is the equality and brotherhood of man."

Every day Mr. Linwood became more and more familiar with Jerome, and eventually they were on the most intimate terms.

Fifteen days from the time that Clotelle was introduced into her father's room, they left Ferney for Geneva. Many were the excursions Clotelle made under the shadows of Mont Blanc,[3] and with her husband and father for companions; she was now in the enjoyment of pleasures hitherto unknown.

CHAPTER XXXV.
THE FATHER'S RESOLVE.

Aware that her father was still a slave-owner, Clotelle determined to use all her persuasive power to induce him to set them free, and in this effort she found a substantial supporter in her husband.

"I have always treated my slaves well," said Mr. Linwood to Jerome, as the latter expressed his abhorrence of the system; "and my neighbors, too, are generally good men; for slavery in Virginia is not like slavery in the other States," continued the proud son of the Old Dominion.

"Their right to be free, Mr. Linwood," said Jerome, "is taken from them, and they have no security for their comfort, but the humanity and generosity of men, who have been trained to regard them not as brethren, but as mere property. Humanity and generosity are, at best,

---

[3] *Mont Blanc:* Alpine mountain range southeast of Geneva; one of its highest peaks is also called Mont Blanc.

but poor guaranties for the protection of those who cannot assert their rights, and over whom law throws no protection."

It was with pleasure that Clotelle obtained from her father a promise that he would liberate all his slaves on his return to Richmond. In a beautiful little villa, situated in a pleasant spot, fringed with hoary rocks and thick dark woods, within sight of the deep blue waters of Lake Leman, Mr. Linwood, his daughter, and her husband, took up their residence for a short time. For more than three weeks, this little party spent their time in visiting the birth-place of Rousseau, and the former abodes of Byron, Gibbon, Voltaire, De Stael, Shelley,[4] and other literary characters.

We can scarcely contemplate a visit to a more historic and interesting place than Geneva and its vicinity. Here, Calvin,[5] that great luminary in the Church, lived and ruled for years; here, Voltaire, the mighty genius, who laid the foundation of the French Revolution, and who boasted, "When I shake my wig, I powder the whole republic," governed in the higher walks of life.

Fame is generally the recompense, not of the living, but of the dead, — not always do they reap and gather in the harvest who sow the seed; the flame of its altar is too often kindled from the ashes of the great. A distinguished critic has beautifully said, "The sound which the stream of high thought, carried down to future ages, makes, as it flows — deep, distant, murmuring ever more, like the waters of the mighty ocean." No reputation can be called great that will not endure this test. The distinguished men who had lived in Geneva transfused their spirit, by their writings, into the spirit of other lovers of literature and everything that treated of great authors. Jerome and Clotelle lingered long in and about the haunts of Geneva and Lake Leman.

An autumn sun sent down her bright rays, and bathed every object in her glorious light, as Clotelle, accompanied by her husband and father set out one fine morning on her return home to France. Throughout the whole route, Mr. Linwood saw by the deference paid to Jerome, whose black complexion excited astonishment in those who met him, that there was no hatred to the man in Europe, on account of his color;

---

[4] *Byron . . . De Stael, Shelley*: References to the British Romantic poets Lord Bryon (1788–1824) and Percy Shelley (1792–1822), or to Byron and the novelist Mary Shelley (1797–1851), and to the English historian Edward Gibbon (1737–1794), the French philosopher François Voltaire (1694–1778), and the French-Swiss woman of letters Germaine de Staël (1766–1817).

[5] *Calvin*: The French Protestant theologian John Calvin (1509–1564) was one of the leaders of the Protestant Reformation.

that what is called prejudice against color is the offspring of the institution of slavery; and he felt ashamed of his own countrymen, when he thought of the complexion as distinctions, made in the United States, and resolved to dedicate the remainder of his life to the eradication of this unrepublican and unchristian feeling from the land of his birth, on his return home.

After a stay of four weeks at Dunkirk, the home of the Fletchers,[6] Mr. Linwood set out for America, with the full determination of freeing his slaves, and settling them in one of the Northern States, and then to return to France to end his days in the society of his beloved daughter.

THE END.

NOTE.—The author of the foregoing tale was formerly a Kentucky slave. If it serves to relieve the monotony of camp-life to the soldiers of the Union, and therefore of Liberty, and at the same time kindles their zeal in the cause of universal emancipation, the object both of its author and publisher will be gained.   J.R.[7]

---

[6] *Fletchers*: Jerome and Clotelle.

[7] *J.R.*: James Redpath (1833–1891). A Scottish-born American journalist, publisher, and abolitionist, Redpath ran the Haytian Bureau of Emigration in Boston during the early 1860s before embracing the cause of the Civil War.

WILLIAM WELLS BROWN

From *Clotelle; or, The Colored Heroine*

Following the Civil War, Brown published a revised and expanded version of *Clotelle: A Tale of the Southern States*. He made several small changes in the prefatory matter, added four chapters on the Civil War and its aftermath, and supplied a new title, *Clotelle; or, The Colored Heroine. A Tale of the Southern States* (Boston: Lee & Shepard, 1867). The selection below presents in full the final four chapters of the 1867 edition. Like Frances Harper in *Iola Leroy* (1892), a novel influenced by *Clotel* and the two *Clotelle*s, Brown portrays black patriotism and sacrifice during the Civil War in order to develop black pride, assert claims for black citizenship, and mobilize white support for Reconstruction. Harper and other African American women writers of the Reconstruction period were also influenced, indeed inspired, by Brown's implicit critique of patriarchal marriage and, perhaps more important, by his portrayal of "the colored heroine" as an "Angel of Mercy" for her selfless community-building work. Brown's concluding vignette of Jim and Dinah, however, raises questions about the depth of his commitment to an antipatriarchal politics.

CHAPTER XXXVI.

THE RETURN HOME

The first gun fired at the American Flag, on the 12th of April, 1861, at Fort Sumter,[1] reverberated all over Europe, and was hailed with joy by the crowned heads of the Old World, who hated republican institutions, and who thought they saw, in this act of treason, the downfall of the great American experiment. Most citizens, however, of the United States, who were then sojourning abroad, hastened home to take part in the struggle,—some to side with the rebels, others to take their stand with the friends of liberty. Among the latter, none came with swifter steps or more zeal than Jerome and Clotelle Fletcher. They arrived in New Orleans a week after the capture of that city by the expedition under the command of Major-Gen. B. F. Butler.[2] But how changed was society since Clotelle had last set feet in the Crescent City! Twenty-two years had passed; her own chequered life had been through many shifting scenes, her old acquaintances in New Orleans had all disappeared; and with the exception of the black faces which she beheld at every turn, and which in her younger days were her associates, she felt herself in the midst of strangers; and these were arrayed against each other in mortal combat. Possessed with ample means, Mr. and Mrs. Fletcher set about the work of assisting those whom the rebellion had placed in a state of starvation and sickness.

With a heart overflowing with the milk of human kindness, and a tear for every sufferer, no matter of what color or sect, Clotelle was soon known as the "Angel of Mercy."

The "General Order No. 63," issued on the 22d of August, 1862, by Gen. Butler, recognizing, and calling into the service of the Federal Government, the battalion of colored men known as the "Native

---

[1] *Fort Sumter*: The Confederate troops' attack on the federally controlled Fort Sumter, in the harbor of Charleston, South Carolina, helped to inaugurate the Civil War.

[2] *Major-Gen. B. F. Butler*: The Union military leader Benjamin Franklin Butler (1818–1893) acted as the military governor of New Orleans from May 1862 to December 1862.

Guard," at once gave full scope to Jerome's military enthusiasm; and he made haste to enlist in the organization.

The "Native Guard" did good service in New Orleans and vicinity, till ordered to take part in the seige of Port Hudson,[3] where they appeared under the name of the "First Louisiana," and under the immediate command of Lieut.-Col. Bassett. The heroic attack of this regiment, made on the 27th of May, 1863, its unsurpassed "charge," its great loss, and its severe endurance on the field of battle, are incidents which have passed into history. The noble daring of the First Louisiana gained for the black soldiers in our army the praise of all Americans who value Republican institutions.

There was, however, one scene, the closing one in the first day's attack on Port Hudson, which, while it reflects undying credit upon the bravery of the negro, pays but a sorry tribute to the humanity of the white general who brought the scene into existence. The field was strewn with the dead, the dying, and the wounded; and as the jaded regiments were leaving the ground, after their unsuccessful attack, it was found that Capt. Payne, of the Third Louisiana, had been killed; and his body, which was easily distinguished by the uniform, was still on the battle-field. The colonel of the regiment, pointing to where the body lay, asked "Are there four men here who will fetch the body of Capt. Payne from the field?" Four men stepped out, and at once started. But, as the body lay directly under the range of the rebel batteries, they were all swept down by the grape, canister, and shell which were let loose by the enemy. The question was again repeated, "Are there four men who will go for the body?" The required number came forth, and started upon a run; but, ere they could reach the spot, they were cut down. "Are there four more men who will try?" The third call was answered in the affirmative, and the men started upon the double-quick. They, however, fell before getting as far as the preceding four. Twelve men had been killed in the effort to obtain the body of the brave Payne, but to no purpose. Humanity forbade another trial, and yet it was made. "Are there four more men in the regiment who will volunteer to go for Capt. Payne's body?" shouted the officer. Four men sprang forward, as if fearful that they would miss the opportunity of these last: one was Jerome Fletcher, the hero of our story. They started

[3] *the seige of Port Hudson*: After taking Vicksburg, Mississippi, in July 1863, Union troops stormed the Confederate garrision of Port Hudson, approximately 250 miles south of Vicksburg. Two Union regiments of Louisiana blacks played a heroic role in this successful assault.

upon the run; and, strange to tell, all of them reached the body, and had nearly borne it from the field, when two of the number were cut down. Of these, one was Jerome. His head was entirely torn off by a shell. The body of the deceased officer having been rescued, an end was put to the human sacrifice.

CHAPTER XXXVII.
THE ANGEL OF MERCY.

The sad intelligence of Jerome's death was brought to Clotelle while she was giving her personal attention to the sick and wounded that filled the hospitals of New Orleans. For a time she withdrew from the gaze of mankind, and gave herself up to grief. Few unions had been productive of more harmonious feelings than hers. And this blow, so unexpected and at a time when she was experiencing such a degree of excitement caused by the rebellion, made her, indeed, feel the affliction severely.

But the newspaper accounts of the intense suffering of Union prisoners in the rebel States aroused her, and caused her to leave her retirement. In the month of October, 1863, Clotelle resolved to visit Andersonville, Ga., for the purpose of alleviating the hardships of our sick and imprisoned soldiers,[4] and at once put her resolution into effect by going immediately to that place. After crossing the lines, she passed as a rebel lady, to enable her the more successfully to carry out her object. On her arrival at Andersonville, Clotelle took up her abode with a private family, of Union proclivities, and commenced her work of mercy. She first visited the hospitals, the buildings of which were merest excuses for hospitals.

It was the beginning of November; and, even in that southern latitude, the cold made these miserable abodes uncomfortable nights and mornings. The dirty, unventilated rooms, with nothing but straw upon the cold, damp floor, for beds, upon which lay the ragged, emaciated Union prisoners, worn down to skin and bone with disease and starvation, with their sunken eyes and wild looks, made them appear hideous in the extreme. The repulsive scenes, that showed the suffering, neglect, and cruelty which these poor creatures had experienced, made her heart sink within her.

[4] *Andersonville . . . soldiers:* Located in southwest Georgia, the Confederates' prison in the villlage of Andersonville confined tens of thousands of Union soldiers under brutal conditions.

Having paid considerable attention to hospital life in Europe, and so recently from amongst the sick at New Orleans, Clotelle's experience, suggestions, and liberal expenditure of money, would have added greatly to the comfort of these helpless men, if the rebel authorities had been so disposed. But their hatred to Union prisoners was so apparent, that the interest which this angel of humanity took in the condition of the rebel sick could not shield her from the indignation of the secession officials for her good feeling for Union men. However, with a determination to do all in her power for the needy, she labored in season and out.

The brutal treatment and daily murders committed upon our soldiers in the Andersonville prisons caused Clotelle to secretly aid prisoners in their escape. In the latter work, she brought to her assistance the services of a negro man named Pete. This individual was employed about the prison, and, having the entire confidence of the commandant, was in a position to do much good without being suspected. Pete was an original character, of a jovial nature, and, when intending some serious adventure, would appear very solemn, and usually singing a doleful ditty, often the following, which was a favorite with him:—

"Come listen, all you darkies, come listen to my song:
It am about ole Massa, who use me bery wrong.
In de cole, frosty mornin', it an't so bery nice,
Wid de water to de middle, to hoe among de rice;

When I neber hab forgotten
How I used to hoe de cotton,
How I used to hoe de cotton,
On de ole Virginny shore;
But I'll neber hoe de cotton,
Oh! neber hoe de cotton,
Any more.

"If I feel de drefful hunger, he tink it am a vice,
And he gib me for my dinner a little broken rice,—
A little broken rice and a bery little fat,
And he grumble like de debbil if I eat too much of dat;

When I neber hab forgotten, etc.

"He tore me from my Dinah; I tought my heart would burst:
He made me lub anoder when my lub was wid de first;
He sole my picanninnies becase he got dar price,
And shut me in de marsh-field to hoe among de rice;

When I neber hab forgotten, etc.

"And all de day I hoe dar, in all de heat and rain;
And, as I hoe away dar, my heart go back again,—
Back to de little cabin dat stood among de corn,
And to de ole plantation where she and I war born!

   Oh! I wish I had forgotten, etc.

"Den Dinah am beside me, de chil'ren on my knee,
And dough I am a slave dar, it 'pears to me I'm free,
Till I wake up from my dreaming, and wife and chil'ren gone,
I hoe away and weep dar, and weep dar all alone!

   Oh! I wish I had forgotten, etc.

"But soon a day am comin', a day I long to see,
When dis darky in de cole ground, foreber will be free,
When wife and chil'ren wid me, I'll sing in Paradise,
How He, de blessed Jesus, hab bought me wid a price;

   How de Lord hab not forgotten
   How well I hoed de cotton,
    On de ole Virginny shore;
   Dar I'll neber hoe de cotton,
   Oh! I'll neber hoe de cotton
    Any more."

When away from the whites, and among his own class, Pete could often be heard in the following strains:—

   "A storm am brewin' in de Souf,
    A storm am brewin' now.
   Oh! hearken den, and shut your mouf,
    And I will tell you how:
   And I will tell you how, ole boy,
    De storm of fire will pour,
   And make de darkies dance for joy,
    As dey neber danced afore;
   So shut your mouf as close as deafh,
   And all you niggas hole your breafh,
    And I will tell you how.

   "De darkies at de Norf am ris,
    And dey am comin' down—
   Am comin'down, I know dey is,
    To do de white folks brown!
   Dey'll turn ole Massa out to grass,
    And set de niggas free,
   And when dat day am come to pass
    We'll all be dar to see!

So shut your mouf as close as deafh,
And all you niggas hole your breafh,
  And do de white folks brown!

"Den all de week will be as gay
  As am de Chris'mas time;
We'll dance all night and all de day,
  And make de banjo chime—
And made de banjo chime, I tink,
  And pass de time away,
Wid 'nuf to eat and nuf to drink,
  And not a bit to pay!
So shut your mouf as close as deafh,
And all you niggas hole your breafh,
  And make de banjo chime."

How to escape from prison was ever the thoughts by day and dreams by night of the incarcerated. Plans were concocted, partly put into execution, and then proved failures. Some of these caused increased suffering to the prisoners after their discovery; for, where the real parties could not be found, the whole were ill-treated as a punishment to the guilty. Tunnelling was generally the mode for escape; and tunnelling became the order of the day, or, rather, the work for the night. In the latter part of November, 1863, the unusual gaiety of the prisoners showed that some plan of exit from the prison was soon to be exhibited.

CHAPTER XXXVIII.
THE GREAT TUNNEL AND THE MISTAKE.

For several weeks, some ten or fifteen of the most able-bodied of the prisoners had been nightly at work; and the great tunnel, the *largest* ever projected by men for their escape from prison, was thought to be finished, with the exception of the tapping outside of the prison wall. The digging of a tunnel is not an easy job, and, consequently, is of slow progress. The Andersonville prisoners had to dig ten feet down into the earth, after cutting through the floor, and then went a distance of fifty feet to get beyond the wall. The digging was done in the following way: As soon as the operator was below the surface, and had a place large enough to admit the body, he laid down upon his face, at full length, and with his knife, spoon, piece of earthenware, or old iron, dug away with all his energies, throwing the dirt behind him, which was gathered up by a confederate, carried off, and hid. This mode of operating was carried on night after night, and the flooring replaced during the day, to prevent suspicion. The want of fresh air in the tunnel, as it progressed to completion, often drove the men from their work, and caused a delay, which proved fatal to their successful escape.

The long-looked for day arrived. More than three hundred had prepared to leave this hated abode, by the tunnel. All they waited for was the tapping and the signal. The time came, the place of egress was tapped, and the leader had scarcely put his head out of the hole, ere he was fired upon by the sentinels, which soon alarmed and drew the entire guard to the spot. Great was the commotion throughout the prison, and all who were caught in the tunnel were severely punished.

This failure seemed to depress the spirits of the men more than any previous attempt. Heavy irons were placed upon the limbs of many of the prisoners, and their lot was made otherwise harder by the keepers. Clotelle, though often permitted to see the prisoners and contribute to their wants, and, though knowing much of their designs, knew nothing of the intended escape, and therefore was more bold in her intercessions in their behalf when failure came upon them.

The cruelty which followed this mishap, induced Clotelle to interest herself in another mode of escape for the men thus so heavily ironed.

Pete, the man of all work, whose sympathies were with the Union prisoners, was easily gained over to a promise of securing the keys of the prison and letting the men escape, especially when Clotelle offered him money to enable him to make good his own way to the North.

The night of the exodus came. It was favored with darkness; and it so happened that the officials were on a spree, owing to the arrival of Confederate officers with news of a rebel victory.

Before getting the keys, Pete supplied the sentinels on duty with enough whiskey, which he had stolen from the keepers' store-room, to make them all drunk. At the chosen moment, the keys were obtained by Pete, the doors and gates were opened, and ninety-three prisoners, including the tunnel workers, whose irons were taken off, made their escape, allowing the faithful negro to accompany them. Nothing was known of the exit of the men till breakfast hour on the next morning. On examination of the store-room, it was found, that, in addition to the whiskey Pete had taken a large supply of stores for the accommodation of the party. Added to this, a good number of arms with ammunition had been furnished the men by the African.

The rebels were not prepared to successfully pursue the fleeing prisoners, although armed men were sent in different directions. Nothing, however, was heard of them till they reached the Union lines. Long suspected of too freely aiding Union prisoners, Clotelle was now openly charged with a knowledge of the escape of these men, and was compelled to leave Andersonville.

CHAPTER XXXIX.
CONCLUSION.

The fiendish and heartless conduct of a large number of the people of the South towards Union men during the war, and especially the unlady-like demeanor of rebel women at New Orleans and other points, is a matter that has passed into history. In few places were the women more abusive to those of Union proclivities than the female portion of the inhabitants of Greenville, Alabama. While passing through this town, on her return from Andersonville to New Orleans, Clotelle had to encounter the fierce ill-treatment of these chivalrous daughters of the South. There were, during the rebellion, many brave and generous women, who, in the mountains and lowlands of Alabama, gave aid to Federals,—soldiers and civilians,—in their wanderings and escape from the cruelties of the traitors. One of these patriotic women was arrested while on a visit to Greenville for the purpose of procuring medicine and other necessaries for sick Union men then hid away in the woods. This large-hearted woman—Eunice Hastings—had her horse taken from her, robbed of the goods she had purchased, and, after experiencing almost death at the hands of the rebel women, was released and turned out penniless, and without the means of reaching her home in the country; when Clotelle, who had just arrived at the dilapidated and poorly kept hotel, met her, and, learning the particulars of her case, offered assistance to the injured woman, which brought down upon her own head the condemnation of the secesh[5] population of the place. However, Clotelle purchased a fine horse from the landlord, gave it to Miss Hastings, who, after securing some articles for which she had come to Greenville, left town under cover of night, and escaped further molestation. This act of kindness to a helpless sister at once stirred up the vilest feelings of the people.

"The worst of slaves is he whom passion rules."[6]

---

[5] *secesh*: Secessionist.
[6] *"The worst . . . rules"*: From Thomas Francklin (1721–1784), *The Earl of Warwick* (1766), I.iii.109.

As has already been said, there was nothing in the appearance of Clotelle to indicate that a drop of African blood coursed through her veins, except, perhaps, the slight wave in the hair, and the scarcely perceptible brunettish tinge upon the countenance. She passed as a rebel lady; yet the inhabitants of Greenville could not permit sympathy with, and aid to, a Union woman to pass unnoticed, and therefore resolved on revenge.

> "Revenge, at first though sweet,
> Bitter ere long, back on itself recoils."[7]

Clotelle's person, trunks, and letters were all searched with the hope and expectation of finding evidences of a spy. Nothing of the kind being found, she was then rigorously interrogated as to her sympathies with the two contending armies. With no wish whatever to conceal her opinions, she openly avowed that she was a Union woman. This was enough. After being persecuted during the day, she was put in charge of a committee of rebel women for the night, with a promise of more violent treatment on the morrow. The loyalty of the negroes of the South, during the severest hours of the rebellion, reflects the greatest possible credit on the race. Through their assistance, hundreds of Union men were enabled to make their escape from prisons, and thousands kept from starvation when on their way to the Federal lines, or while keeping out of the way of rebel recruiting gangs. They seldom, if ever, hesitated to do the white Unionists a service, at the risk even of life, and, under the most trying circumstances, revealed a devotion and a spirit of self-sacrifice that were heroic. No one ever made an appeal to them they did not answer. They were degraded and ignorant, which was attributable to the cruel laws and equally unchristian practices of the people of the South; but their hearts were always open, and the slightest demand upon their sympathies brought forth their tears. They never shunned a man or woman who sought food or shelter on their way to freedom. The goodness of heart and the guileless spirit of the blacks was not better understood by any one than Clotelle; and she felt a secret joy at seeing all the servants in the Greenville hotel negroes. She saw from their very looks that she had their undivided sympathies. One of the servants overheard the rebels in a conversation, in which it was determined to send Clotelle to the county town, for safe keeping in the jail, the following day; and this fact was communicated to the

---

[7] *"Revenge . . . recoils"*: From John Milton (1608–1674), *Paradise Lost* (1667), book IX.

unfortunate woman. The slave woman who gave the information told her that she could escape if she desired.

Having already been robbed of every thing except the apparel upon her person and some money she had concealed about her, she at once signified to the black woman her wish to get out of the reach of her persecutors. The old worn-out clock in the narrow dining hall had struck one; a cold rain was patting upon the roof, and the women watchers, one after another, had fallen asleep; and even the snuff-dippers, whose dirty practice creates a nervousness that keeps them awake longer than any other class, had yielded to the demands of Morpheus,[8] when Aggy, the colored servant, stealthily entered the room, beckoned to Clotelle, and both left in silence.

Cautiously and softly the black woman led the way, followed by the "Angel of Mercy," till, after passing down through the cellar with the water covering the floor, they emerged into the back yard. Two horses had been provided. Clotelle mounted one, and a black man the other; the latter leading the way. Both dashed off at a rapid pace, through a drenching storm, with such a pall-like darkness that they could not see each other. After an hour's ride the negro halted, and informed Clotelle that he must leave her, and return with the horses, but that she was with friends. He then gave a whistle, and for a moment held his breath. Just as the faithful black was about to repeat the signal, he heard the response; and in a moment the lady alighted, and with dripping garments, limbs chilled to numbness, followed her new guide to a place of concealment, near the village of Taitsville.

"You is jes as wet as a drownded rat," said the mulatto woman, who met Clotelle as she entered the negro's cabin.

"Yes," replied the latter, "this is a stormy night for one to be out."

"Yes mam, dese is hard times for eberybody dat 'bleves in de Union. I 'spose deys cotched your husband, an' put him in de army, ain't dey?"

"No: my husband died at Port Hudson, fighting for the Union," said Clotelle.

"Oh, mam, dats de place whar de black people fight de rebels so, wasn't it?" remarked Dinah, for such was her name.

"Yes, that was the place," replied the former. "I see that your husband has lost one of his hands: did he lose it in the war?"

"Oh no, missus," said Dinah. "When dey was taken all de men, black an white, to put in de army, dey cotched my ole man too, and

---

[8] *Morpheus*: Greek and Roman god of dreams.

took him long wid 'em. So you see, he said he'd die afore he'd shoot at de Yanks. So you see, missus, Jimmy jes took and lay his left han' on a log, and chop it off wid de hatchet. Den, you see, dey let him go, an' he come home. You see, missus, my Jimmy is a free man: he was born free, an' he bought me, an' pay fifteen hundred dollars for me."

It was true that Jim had purchased his wife; nor had he forgotten the fact, as was shown a day or two after, while in conversation with her. The woman, like many of her sex, was an inveterate scold, and Jim had but one way to govern her tongue. "Shet your mouf, madam, an' hole your tongue," said Jim, after his wife had scolded and sputtered away for some minutes. "Shet your mouf dis minit, I say: you shan't stan' dar, an' talk ter me in dat way. I bought you, an' paid my money fer you, an' I ain't a gwine ter let you sase me in dat way. Shet your mouf dis minit: ef you don't I'll sell you; 'fore God I will. Shet up, I say, or I'll sell you." This had the desired effect, and settled Dinah for the day.

After a week spent in this place of concealment, Jim conveyed Clotelle to Leaksville, Mississippi, through the Federal lines, and from thence she proceeded to New Orleans.

The Rebellion was now drawing to a close. The valley of the Mississippi was in full possession of the Federal government. Sherman was on his raid, and Grant was hemming in Lee.[9] Everywhere the condition of the freedmen attracted the attention of the friends of humanity, and no one felt more keenly their wants than Clotelle; and to their education and welfare she resolved to devote the remainder of her life, and for this purpose went to the State of Mississippi, and opened a school for the freedmen; hired teachers, paying them out of her own purse. In the summer of 1866, the Poplar Farm, on which she had once lived as a slave, was confiscated and sold by Government authority, and was purchased by Clotelle, upon which she established a Freedmen's School, and where at this writing,—now June, 1867,—resides the "Angel of Mercy."

---

[9] *Sherman . . . Lee*: The Union general William T. Sherman (1820–1891) led the Atlanta Campaign (May–September 1864), and presided over the burning of Atlanta on 15 November 1864 and the subsequent devastation of Savannah, Georgia. Ulysses S. Grant (1822–1885), commander in chief of the Union Army, led Union forces against Robert E. Lee (1807–1870), general in chief of the Confederate Army, whose surrender at Virginia's Appomattox Courthouse on 9 April 1865 ended the Civil War.

WILLIAM WELLS BROWN

Battle of Milliken's Bend

In a key Civil War battle of June 1863, Confederate troops attacked a Union garrison near Vicksburg, Mississippi, at Milliken's Bend on the Mississippi River, and were repulsed by the black soldiers defending the supply line. This was one of the first battles involving black troops, and their courage and skills were widely praised in the North. Brown described the battle in a chapter of *The Negro in the American Rebellion: His Heroism and His Fidelity* (Boston: Lee & Shepard, 1867), the source of this selection. A historical overview of blacks' participation in the American Revolution, the War of 1812, and the Civil War, the book was written with the express purpose of developing black pride, confuting white racists' notions of black inferiority, and making the case for African American citizenship. It appeared several months before the 1867 publication of *Clotelle*, Brown's final revision of his novel, which in a similar spirit portrayed the heroic contributions of blacks to the war effort.

On the 7th of June, 1863, the first regular battle was fought between the blacks and whites in the valley of the Mississippi. The planters had boasted, that, should they meet their former slaves, a single look from them would cause the negroes to throw down their weapons and run. Many Northern men, especially copperheads,[1] professed to believe that such would be the case. Therefore, all eyes were turned to the far off South, the cotton, sugar, and rice-growing States, to see how the blacks would behave on the field of battle; for it is well known that the most ignorant of the slave population belonged in that section.

The following account of the fight is from an eye witness: —

"My informant states that a force of about five hundred negroes, and two hundred men of the Twenty-third Iowa, belonging to the second brigade, Carr's division (the Twenty-third Iowa had been up the river with prisoners, and was on its way back to this place), was surprised in camp by a rebel force of about two thousand men. The first intimation that the commanding officer received was from one of the black men, who went into the colonel's tent, and said, 'Massa, the secesh are in camp.' The colonel ordered him to have the men load

---

[1] *copperheads*: Northerners who sympathized with the South during the Civil War.

their guns at once. He instantly replied, 'We have done did dat now, massa.' Before the colonel was ready, the men were in line, ready for action. As before stated, the rebels drove our force towards the gunboats, taking colored men prisoners and murdering them. This so enraged them that they rallied, and charged the enemy more heroically and desperately than has been recorded during the war. It was a genuine bayonet-charge, a hand-to-hand fight, that has never occurred to any extent during this prolonged conflict. Upon both sides men were killed with the butts of muskets. White and black men were lying side by side, pierced by bayonets, and in some instances transfixed to the earth. In one instance, two men—one white and the other black—were found dead, side by side, each having the other's bayonet through his body. If facts prove to be what they are now represented, this engagement of Sunday morning will be recorded as the most desperate of this war. Broken limbs, broken heads, the mangling of bodies, all prove that it was a contest between enraged men: on the one side, from hatred to a race; and, on the other, desire for self-preservation, revenge for past grievances, and the inhuman murder of their comrades. One brave man took his former master prisoner, and brought him into camp with great gusto. A rebel prisoner made a particular request, that *his own* negroes should not be placed over him as a guard."

Capt. M. M. Miller, of Galena, Ill., who commanded a company in the Ninth Louisiana (colored) Regiment, in a letter, gives the following account of the battle:—

"We were attacked here on June 7, about three o'clock in the morning, by a brigade of Texas troops, about two thousand five hundred in number. We had about six hundred men to withstand them, five hundred of them negroes. I commanded Company I, Ninth Louisiana. We went into the fight with thirty-three men. I had sixteen killed, eleven badly wounded, and four slightly. I was wounded slightly on the head, near the right eye, with a bayonet, and had a bayonet run through my right hand, near the forefinger; that will account for this miserable style of penmanship.

"Our regiment had about three hundred men in the fight. We had one colonel wounded, four captains wounded, two first and two second lieutenants killed, five lieutenants wounded, and three white orderlies killed, and one wounded in the hand, and two fingers taken off. The list of killed and wounded officers comprised nearly all the officers present with the regiment, a majority of the rest being absent recruiting.

"We had about fifty men killed in the regiment and eighty wounded; so you can judge of what part of the fight my company sustained. I never felt more grieved and sick at heart, than when I saw how my brave soldiers had been slaughtered,—one with six wounds, all the rest with two or three, none less than two wounds. Two of my colored sergeants were killed; both brave, noble men, always prompt, vigilant, and ready for the fray. I never more wish to hear the expression, 'The niggers won't fight.' Come with me, a hundred yards from where I sit, and I can show you the wounds that cover the bodies of sixteen as brave, loyal, and patriotic soldiers as ever drew bead on a rebel.

"The enemy charged us so close that we fought with our bayonets, hand to hand. I have six broken bayonets to show how bravely my men fought. The Twenty-third Iowa joined my company on the right; and I declare truthfully that they had all fled before our regiment fell back, as we were all compelled to do.

"Under command of Col. Page, I led the Ninth and Eleventh Louisiana when the rifle-pits were retaken and held by our troops, our two regiments doing the work.

"I narrowly escaped death once. A rebel took deliberate aim at me with both barrels of his gun; and the bullets passed so close to me that the powder that remained on them burnt my cheek. Three of my men, who saw him aim and fire, thought that he wounded me each fire. One of them was killed by my side, and he fell on me, covering my clothes with his blood; and, before the rebel could fire again, I blew his brains out with my gun.

"It was a horrible fight, the worst I was ever engaged in,—not even excepting Shiloh.[2] The enemy cried, 'No quarter!' but some of them were very glad to take it when made prisoners.

"Col. Allen, of the Sixteenth Texas, was killed in front of our regiment, and Brig.-Gen. Walker was wounded. We killed about one hundred and eighty of the enemy. The gunboat 'Choctaw' did good service shelling them. I stood on the breastworks[3] after we took them, and gave the elevations and direction for the gunboat by pointing my sword; and they sent a shell right into their midst, which sent them in all directions. Three shells fell there, and sixty-two rebels lay there when the fight was over.

"My wound is not serious but troublesome. What few men I have left seem to think much of me, because I stood up with them in the

---

[2] *Shiloh*: One of the bloodiest battles of the Civil War, the battle of Shiloh (6–7 April 1862), which took place near the Shiloh Church in Tennessee, resulted in the deaths of over ten thousand men on each side and has usually been regarded as a Union victory.

[3] *breastworks*: Hastily constructed defensive barriers generally standing breast high.

fight. I can say for them that I never saw a braver company of men in my life.

"Not one of them offered to leave his place until ordered to fall back. I went down to the hospital, three miles, to-day to see the wounded. Nine of them were there, two having died of their wounds. A boy I had cooking for me came and begged a gun when the rebels were advancing, and took his place with the company; and, when we retook the breastworks, I found him badly wounded, with one gunshot and two bayonet wounds. A new recruit I had issued a gun to the day before the fight was found dead, with a firm grasp on his gun, the bayonet of which was broken in three pieces. So they fought and died, defending the cause that we revere. They met death coolly, bravely: not rashly did they expose themselves, but all were steady and obedient to orders."

This battle satisfied the slave-masters of the South that their charm was gone; and that the negro, as a slave, was lost forever. Yet there was one fact connected with the battle of Milliken's Bend which will descend to posterity, as testimony against the humanity of slave-holders; and that is, that no negro was ever found alive that was taken a prisoner by the rebels in this fight.

WILLIAM WELLS BROWN

From *My Southern Home*

After touring several Southern states in the winter of 1879–80, Brown published *My Southern Home* in May 1880. More than half the book consists of Brown's autobiographical reflections on slave life, as he retells—often with significant variations—some of the stories that make up his *Narrative*, his several memoirs, and *Clotel*. He also devotes at least a third of the book to excoriating the Southern states for abandoning the goals of Reconstruction. Angered by the persistence of antiblack racism and discrimination, he encourages blacks to consider moving North, hoping that a black exodus may encourage Southerners to realize just how crucial blacks are to the Southern economy. In addition to blaming the plight of the South's African Americans on white racists, he criticizes blacks themselves for allegedly failing to take full responsibility for their uplift by adopting temperance and industry. In the book's final chapter, which is printed in its entirety below, Brown, like Frederick Douglass during this time, encourages "amalgamation" between whites and blacks as a way of ending racial strife. In the context of *Clotel*, Brown's appeal for marriages between blacks and whites, along with the book's accompanying image of a cross-racial handshake, encourages us to reimagine the relationship between Thomas Jefferson and Sally Hemings as a kind of rehearsal for a deracialized, progressive, reformative union between blacks and whites that promises to redeem the United States. But even as Brown encourages amalgamation, he strongly asserts the importance of developing black pride. The selection is from Brown, *My Southern Home: Or, The South and Its People* (Boston: A. G. Brown & Co., 1880).

In America, the negro stands alone as a race. He is without mate or fellow in the great family of man. Whatever progress he makes, it must be mainly by his own efforts. This is an unfortunate fact, and for which there seems to be no remedy.

All history demonstrates the truth that amalgamation is the great civilizer of the races of men. Wherever a race, clan, or community have kept themselves together, prohibiting by law, usage, or common consent, inter-marriage with others, they have made little or no progress. The Jews, a distinct and isolated people, are good only at driving a bargain and getting rich. The Gipsies commence and stop with trading horses. The Irish, in their own country, are dull. The Coptic race[1] form but a handful of what they were—those builders, unequalled in ancient or modern times. What has become of them? Where are the Romans? What races have they destroyed? What races have they supplanted? For fourteen centuries they lorded it over the semi-civilized world; and now they are of no more note than the ancient Scythians, or Mongols, Copts, or Tartars.[2] An un-amalgamated, inactive people will decline. Thus it was with the Mexicans, when Cortes[3] marched on Mexico, and the Peruvians, when Pizarro[4] marched on Peru.

---

[1] *Coptic race*: Ancient Egyptians.

[2] *Scythians, or Mongols, Copts, or Tartars*: References to ancient peoples who possessed what Brown regards as distinct racial or ethnic identities: the Scythians resided in southeast Europe and Asia; the Mongols in Asia; and the Tartars in Asia and eastern Europe.

[3] *Cortes*: The Spanish explorer Hernán Cortés (1485–1547) conquered Mexico in 1520.

[4] *Pizarro*: During the 1530s, the Spanish explorer Francisco Pizarro (1476–1541) invaded and conquered Peru.

The Britons were a dull, lethargic people before their country was invaded, and the hot, romantic blood of Julius Caesar and William of Normandy coursed through their veins.

Caractacus,[5] king of the Britons, was captured and sent to Rome in chains. Still later, Hengist and Horsa,[6] the Saxon generals, imposed the most humiliating conditions upon the Britons, to which they were compelled to submit. Then came William of Normandy, defeated Harold at Hastings,[7] and the blood of the most renowned land-pirates and sea-robbers that ever disgraced humanity, mixed with the Briton and Saxon, and gave to the world the Anglo-Saxon race, with its physical ability, strong mind, brave and enterprising spirit. And, yet, all that this race is, it owes to its mixed blood. Civilization, or the social condition of man, is the result and test of the qualities of every race. The benefit of this blood mixture, the negro is never to enjoy on this continent. In the South where he is raised, in the North, East, or West, it is all the same, no new blood is to be infused into his sluggish veins.

His only hope is education, professions, trades, and copying the best examples, no matter from what source they come.

This antipathy to amalgamation with the negro, has shown itself in all of the States. Most of the Northern and Eastern State Legislatures have passed upon this question years ago. Since the coming in of the present year, Rhode Island's Senate refused to repeal the old law forbidding the intermarriage of whites and blacks. Thus the colored man is left to "paddle his own canoe" alone. Where there is no law against the mixture of the two races, there is a public sentiment which is often stronger than law itself. Even the wild blood of the red Indian refuses to mingle with the sluggish blood of the negro. This is no light matter, for race hate, prejudice and common malice all die away before the melting power of amalgamation. The beauty of the half-breeds of the South, the result of the crime of slavery, have long claimed the attention of writers, and why not a lawful mixture? And then this might help in

"Making a race far more lovely and fair,
    Darker a little than white people are:

---

[5] *Caractacus*: British chieftan who opposed the Romans, circa A.D. 50.

[6] *Hengist and Horsa*: Brothers who led the Teutonic (Germanic) invasion of Britain circa A.D. 440.

[7] *William of Normandy, defeated Harold at Hastings*: A reference to the Norman Conquest of 1066, in which England's King Harold (c.1022–1066) was defeated by William, Duke of Normandy (c.1027–1087), who became William I, King of England.

> Stronger, and nobler, and better in form,
> Hearts more voluptuous, kinder, and warm;
> Bosoms of beauty, that heave with a pride
> Nature had ever to white folks denied."

Emigration to other States, where the blacks will come in contact with educated and enterprising whites, will do them much good. This benefit by commercial intercourse is seen in the four thousand colored people who have come to Boston, where most of them are employed as servants. They are sought after as the best domestics in the city. Some of these people, who were in slavery before the war, are now engaged in mercantile pursuits, doing good business, and showing what contact will do. Many of them rank with the ablest whites in the same trades. Indeed, the various callings are well represented by Southern men, showing plainly the need of emigration. Although the colored man has been sadly at fault in not vindicating his right to liberty, he has, it is true, shown ability in other fields. Benjamin Banneker,[8] a negro of Maryland, who lived a hundred years ago, exhibited splendid natural qualities. He had a quickness of apprehension, and a vivacity of understanding, which easily took in and surmounted the most subtile and knotty parts of mathematics and metaphysics. He possessed in a large degree that genius which constitutes a man of letters; that quality without which judgment is cold, and knowledge is inert; that energy which collects, combines, amplifies, and animates.

The rapid progress made in acquiring education and homesteads by the colored people of the South, in the face of adverse circumstances, commends the highest admiration from all classes.

The product of their native genius and industry, as exhibited at county and State Agricultural Fairs, speak well for the race.

At the National Fair, held at Raleigh, N.C., in the autumn of 1879, the exhibition did great credit to the colored citizens of the South, who had the matter in charge. Such manifestations of intellectual and mechanical enterprise will do much to stimulate the people to further development of their powers, and higher facilities.

The colored people of the United States are sadly in need of a National Scientific Association, to which may be brought yearly reports of such investigations as may be achieved in science, philosophy, art, philology, ethnology, jurisprudence, metaphysics, and whatever may

---

[8] *Benjamin Banneker*: See Banneker's letter exchange with Thomas Jefferson on pp. 251–55 in this volume.

tend to *unite* the race in their moral, social, intellectual and physical improvement.

We have negro artists of a high order, both in painting and sculpture; also, discoverers who hold patents, and yet the world knows little or nothing about them. The time for the negro to work out his destiny has arrived. Now let him show himself equal to the hour.

In this work I frequently used the word "Negro," and shall, no doubt, hear from it when the negro critics get a sight of the book. And why should I not use it? Is it not honorable? What is there in the word that does not sound as well as "English," "Irish," "German," "Italian," "French?"

"Don't call me a negro; I'm an American," said a black to me a few days since.

"Why not?" I asked.

"Well, sir, I was born in this country, and I don't want to be called out of my name."

Just then, an Irish-American came up, and shook hands with me. He had been a neighbor of mine in Cambridge. When the young man was gone, I inquired of the black man what countryman he thought the man was.

"Oh!" replied he, "he's an Irishman."

"What makes you think so?" I inquired.

"Why, his brogue is enough to tell it."

"Then," I said, "why is not your color enough to tell that you're a negro?"

"Arh!" said he, "that's a horse of another color," and left me with a "Ha, ha, ha!"

Black men, don't be ashamed to show your colors, and to own them.

Selected Bibliography

This bibliography is divided into two sections, "Works Cited" and "Suggestions for Further Reading." All books and articles quoted in the general introduction, chapter introductions, and headnotes are listed in "Works Cited." The "Suggestions for Further Reading" provides a primary bibliography of Brown's works and a secondary bibliography in Brown studies. "Critical Studies on Brown" lists works devoted exclusively to Brown, but many of the works listed in "Literary and Historical Studies" also have chapters or sections on Brown. Some of the books and articles that appear in "Works Cited" are not listed again in "Suggestions for Further Reading." A recommended starting point for further reading on Brown is William Edward Farrison's excellent biography, *William Wells Brown: Author and Reformer.*

WORKS CITED

Andrews, William L. "The 1850s: The First Afro-American Literary Renaissance." *Literary Romanticism in America*. Ed. Andrews. Baton Rouge: Louisiana State UP, 1981. 38–60. Print.

Berlin, Ira. *Many Thousands Gone: The First Two Centuries of Slavery in North America*. Cambridge: Harvard UP, 1998. Print.

Brown, Josephine. *Biography of an American Bondman, by His Daughter*. Boston: R. F. Wallcut, 1856. Print.

Brown, William Wells. *The Black Man, His Antecedents, His Genius, and His Achievements.* 1863. Miami: Mnemosyne, 1969. Print.

———. *Three Years in Europe; or, Places I Have Seen and People I Have Met.* London: Charles Gilpin, 1852. Print.

Callender, James. [Untitled.] *Richmond Recorder* 1 Sept. 1802: 2. Print.

———. [untitled] *Richmond Recorder* 22 Sept. 1802:2. Print.

Castronovo, Russ. *Fathering the Nation: American Genealogies of Slavery and Freedom.* Berkeley: U of California P, 1995. Print.

Chaney, Michael A. *Fugitive Vision: Slave Image and Black Identity in Antebellum Narrative.* Bloomington: Indiana UP, 2008. Print.

Davis, David Brion. "American Slavery and the Revolution." *Slavery and Freedom in the Age of the American Revolution.* 1983. Ed. Ira Berlin and Ronald Hoffman. Urbana: U of Illinois P, 1986. 262–80. Print.

Douglass, Frederick. *My Bondage and My Freedom.* 1855. Ed. William L. Andrews. Urbana: U of Illinois P, 1987. Print.

duCille, Ann. *The Coupling Convention: Sex, Text, and Tradition in Black Women's Fiction.* New York: Oxford UP, 1993. Print.

Ellis, Joseph J. *American Sphinx: The Character of Thomas Jefferson.* New York: Knopf, 1997. Print.

———, and Eric S. Lander. "Founding Father." *Nature* 5 Nov. 1998: 68–9. Print.

Ernest, John. *Resistance and Reformation in Nineteenth-Century African-American Literature.* Jackson: UP of Mississippi, 1995. Print.

Finkelman, Paul. "Jefferson and Slavery: 'Treason Against the Hopes of the World.'" *Jeffersonian Legacies.* Ed. Peter S. Onuf. Charlottesville: U of Virginia P, 1993. 181–221. Print.

Foner, Eric. *Free Soil, Free Labor, Free Man: The Ideology of the Republican Party before the Civil War.* New York: Oxford UP, 1970. Print.

Foster, Eugene A., et al. "Jefferson Fathers Slave's Last Child." *Nature* 5 Nov. 1998: 27–28. Print.

Fredrickson, George M. *The Black Image in the White Mind: The Debate on African-American Character and Destiny, 1817–1914.* New York: Harper, 1972. Print.

Garrison, William Lloyd. "The Insurrection." *Liberator* 3 Sept. 1831: 143. Print.

Gilmore, Paul. *The Genuine Article: Race, Mass Culture, and American Literary Manhood.* Durham: Duke UP, 2001. Print.

Gordon-Reed, Annette. *The Hemingses of Monticello: An American Family.* New York: Norton, 2008. Print.

———. *Thomas Jefferson and Sally Hemings: An American Controversy.* Charlottesville: UP of Virginia, 1997. Print.

Hawthorne, Nathaniel. *The House of the Seven Gables.* 1851. New York: Penguin, 1981. Print.

Jefferson, Thomas. *The Works of Thomas Jefferson.* Vol. 6. Ed. Paul Leicester Ford. New York: Putnam's, 1904. Print.

———. *Writings.* Ed. Merrill Peterson. New York: Library of America, 1984. Print.

Jordan, Winthrop D. *White over Black: American Attitudes toward the Negro, 1550–1812.* Chapel Hill: U of North Carolina P, 1968. Print.

Levine, Robert S. *Dislocating Race and Nation: Episodes in Nineteenth-Century American Literary Nationalism.* Chapel Hill: U of North Carolina P, 2008. Print.

Loughran, Trish. *The Republic in Print: Print Culture in the Age of U.S. Nation Building, 1770–1870.* New York: Columbia UP, 2007. Print.

Marryat, Frederick. *A Diary in America: With Remarks on Its Institutions.* 1839. Ed. Sydney Jackman. New York: Knopf, 1962. Print.

Melville, Herman. *Moby-Dick; or, The Whale.* 1851. Ed. Harrison Hayford, Hershel Parker, and G. Thomas Tanselle. Evanston: Northwestern UP; Chicago: Newberry Library, 1988. Print.

Nelson, Dana D. *National Manhood: Capitalist Citizenship and the Imagined Fraternity of White Men.* Durham: Duke UP, 1998. Print.

Quinby, Lee, ed. *Genealogy and Literature.* Minneapolis: U of Minnesota P, 1995. Print.

Rachman, Stephen. " 'Es lässt sich nicht schreiben': Plagiarism and 'The Man of the Crowd.' " *The American Face of Edgar Allan Poe.* Ed. Shawn Rosenheim and Stephen Rachman. Baltimore: Johns Hopkins UP, 1995. 49–87. Print.

Ripley, C. Peter, et al., eds. *The Black Abolitionist Papers.* 5 vols. Chapel Hill: U of North Carolina P, 1985–92. Print.

Stowe, Harriet Beecher. *Uncle Tom's Cabin.* 1852. Ed. Elizabeth Ammons. New York: Norton, 1994. Print.

Weinauer, Ellen. "Plagiarism and the Proprietary Self: Policing the Boundaries of Authorship in Herman Melville's 'Hawthorne and His Mosses.' " *American Literature* 69 (1997): 697–717. Print.

SUGGESTIONS FOR FURTHER READING

Works by Brown

Narrative of William W. Brown, A Fugitive Slave. Written by Himself. Boston: American Anti-Slavery Society, 1847. Print.

A Lecture Delivered before the Female Anti-Slavery Society of Salem, at Lyceum Hall, Nov. 14, 1847. Boston: Massachusetts Anti-Slavery Society, 1847. Print.

Ed. *The Anti-Slavery Harp: A Collection of Songs for Anti-Slavery Meetings Compiled by William W. Brown, A Fugitive Slave.* Boston: Bela Marsh, 1848. Print.

A Description of William Wells Brown's Original Panoramic Views of the Scenes in the Life of an American Slave, from His Birth in Slavery to His Death or His Escape to His First Home of Freedom on British Soil. London: Charles Gilpin, 1850. Print.

Three Years in Europe; or, Places I Have Seen and People I Have Met. London: Charles Gilpin, 1852. Print.

Clotel; or, The President's Daughter: A Narrative of Slave Life in the United States. London: Partridge & Oakey, 1853. Print.

The American Fugitive in Europe: Sketches of Places and People Abroad. Boston: John P. Jewett, 1855. Print.

St. Domingo: Its Revolutions and Its Patriots. A Lecture. Boston: Bela Marsh, 1855. Print.

The Escape; or, A Leap for Freedom. A Drama in Five Acts. Boston: R. F. Walcutt, 1858. Print.

Memoir of William Wells Brown, an American Bondman, Written by Himself. Boston: Boston Anti-Slavery Office, 1859. Print.

Miralda; or, The Beautiful Quadroon. A Romance of American Slavery, Founded on Fact. In *Weekly Anglo-African*, 1 December 1860–16 March 1861. Print.

The Black Man, His Antecedents, His Genius, and His Achievements. New York: Thomas Hamilton, 1863. Print.

Clotelle: A Tale of the Southern States. Boston: James Redpath, 1864. Print.

Clotelle; or, The Colored Heroine. A Tale of the Southern States. Boston: Lee & Shephard, 1867. Print.

The Negro in the American Rebellion: His Heroism and His Fidelity. Boston: Lee & Shephard, 1867. Print.

The Rising Son; or, The Antecedents and Advancement of the Colored Race. Boston: A. G. Brown, 1874. Print.

My Southern Home: or, The South and Its People. Boston: A. G. Brown, 1880. Print.

Biographies

Brown, Josephine. *Biography of an American Bondman, by His Daughter.* Boston: R. F. Wallcut, 1856. Print.

Farrison, William Edward. *William Wells Brown: Author and Reformer.* Chicago: U of Chicago P, 1969. Print.

Brown Readers and Electronic Edition

Garrett, Paula, and Hollis Robbins, eds. *Using His "Strong, Manly Voice": The Works of William Wells Brown.* New York: Oxford UP, 2006. Print.

Greenspan, Ezra, ed. *William Wells Brown: A Reader.* Athens: U of Georgia P, 2008. Print.

Mulvey, Christopher, ed. *Clotel by William Wells Brown: An Electronic Scholarly Edition.* Charlottesville: U of Virginia P, 2006.

For a generous sampling of speeches and letters by Brown, see *The Black Abolitionist Papers.* Ed. C. Peter Ripley et al. 5 vols. Chapel Hill: U of North Carolina P, 1985–92. Print.

Critical Studies on Brown

Adéèkó, Adélékè. "Signatures of Blood in William Wells Brown's *Clotel.*" *Nineteenth-Century Contexts* 21 (1999): 115–34. Print.

Andrews, William L. "Mark Twain, William Wells Brown, and the Problem of Authority in New South Writing." *Southern Literature and Literary Theory.* Ed. Jefferson Humphries. Athens: U of Georgia P, 1990. 1–21. Print.

Dorsey, Peter A. "De-authorizing Slavery: Realism in Stowe's *Uncle Tom's Cabin* and Brown's *Clotel.*" *ESQ* 41 (1995): 257–88. Print.

duCille, Ann. "Where in the World Is William Wells Brown? Thomas Jefferson, Sally Hemings, and the DNA of African-American Literary History." *American Literary History* 12 (2000): 443–62. Print.

Ellis, R. J. "Body Politics and the Body Politic in William Wells Brown's *Clotel* and Harriet Wilson's *Our Nig.*" *Soft Canons: American Women Writers and Masculine Tradition.* Ed. Karen L. Kilcup. Iowa City: U of Iowa P, 1999. 99–122. Print.

Ernest, John. "The Reconstruction of Whiteness: William Wells Brown's *The Escape; or, A Leap for Freedom.*" *PMLA* 113 (1998): 1108–21. Print.

———. "William Wells Brown Maps the South in *My Southern Home: Or, the South and Its People.*" *Southern Quarterly* 45 (2008): 88–107. Print.

Fabi, M. Giulia. "Introduction." *Clotel; or, The President's Daughter.*
    By William Wells Brown. New York: Penguin, 2004. vii–xxviii.
    Print.

————. "The 'Unguarded Expressions of the Feelings of the Negroes':
    Gender, Slave Resistance, and William Wells Brown's Revisions
    of *Clotel.*" *African American Review* 27 (1993): 639–54. Print.

Fagan, Ben. "Reclaiming Revolution: William Wells Brown's Irreduc-
    ible Haitian Heroes." *Comparative American Studies* 5 (2007):
    367–83. Print.

Farrison, William Edward. "Clotel, Thomas Jefferson, and Sally
    Hemings." *CLA Journal* 17 (1973): 147–74. Print.

Gilmore, Paul. " 'De Genewine Artekil': William Wells Brown, Black-
    face Minstrelsy, and Abolitionism." *American Literature* 69
    (1997): 743–80. Print.

Heermance, J. Noel. *William Wells Brown and Clotelle: A Portrait
    of the Artist in the First Negro Novel.* Hamden: Archon, 1969.
    Print.

Levine, Robert S. " 'Whiskey, Blacking, and All': Temperance and
    Race in William Wells Brown's *Clotel.*" *The Serpent in the Cup:
    Temperance in American Literature.* Ed. David S. Reynolds and
    Debra J. Rosenthal. Amherst: U of Massachusetts P, 1997.
    93–114. Print.

Lewis, Richard O. "Literary Conventions in the Novels of William
    Wells Brown." *CLA Journal* 29 (1985): 129–56. Print.

Mitchell, Angelyn. "Her Side of His Story: A Feminist Analysis of
    Two Nineteenth-Century Antebellum Novels—Williams Wells
    Brown's *Clotel* and Harriet E. Wilson's *Our Nig.*" *American
    Literary Realism* 24 (1992): 7–21. Print.

Mulvey, Christopher. "The Fugitive Self and the New World of the
    North: William Wells Brown's Discovery of America." *The Black
    Columbiad: Defining Moments in African American Literature
    and Culture.* Ed. Werner Sollors and Maria Diedrich. Cambridge:
    Harvard UP, 1994. 99–111. Print.

Nabers, Deak. "The Problem of Revolution in the Age of Slavery:
    Clotel, Fiction, and the Government of Man." *Representations*
    91 (2005): 84–108. Print.

Schell, Jennifer. " 'This Life Is a Stage': Performing the South in
    William Wells Brown's *Clotel; or, The President's Daughter.*"
    Southern Quarterly 45 (2008): 48–69. Print.

Schweninger, Lee. "*Clotel* and the Historicity of the Anecdote."
    MELUS 24 (1999): 21–36. Print.

Wisecup, Kelly. " 'The Progress of the Heat Within': The West Indies,
    Yellow Fever, and Citizenship in William Wells Brown's *Clotel.*"
    Southern Literary Journal 41 (2008): 1–19. Print.

Literary and Historical Studies

Andrews, William L. "The Novelization of Voice in Early African American Narrative." *PMLA* 105 (1990): 23–34. Print.

———. *To Tell a Free Story: The First Century of Afro-American Autobiography, 1760–1865.* Urbana: U of Illinois P, 1986. Print.

Bell, Bernard W. *The Afro-American Novel and Its Tradition.* Amherst: U of Massachusetts P, 1987. Print.

Bentley, Nancy. "White Slaves: The Mulatto Hero in Antebellum Fiction." *American Literature* 65 (1993): 501–22. Print.

Berzon, Judith R. *Neither White Nor Black: The Mulatto Character in American Fiction.* New York: New York UP, 1978. Print.

Blackett, R. J. M. *Building an Antislavery Wall: Black Americans in the Atlantic Abolitionist Movement, 1830–1860.* Baton Rouge: Louisiana State UP, 1983. Print.

Boulton, Alexander O. "The American Paradox: Jeffersonian Equality and Racial Science." *American Quarterly* 47 (1995): 467–93. Print.

Carpio, Glenda. *Laughing Fit to Kill: Black Humor in the Fictions of Slavery.* New York: Oxford UP, 2008. Print.

Cassuto, Leonard. *The Inhuman Race: The Racial Grotesque in American Literature and Culture.* New York: Columbia UP, 1997. Print.

Castronovo, Russ. *Fathering the Nation: American Genealogies of Slavery and Freedom.* Berkeley: U of California P, 1995. Print.

Chaney, Michael A. *Fugitive Vision: Slave Image and Black Identity in Antebellum Narrative.* Bloomington: U of Indiana P, 2008. Print.

Cooper, Frederick. "Elevating the Race: The Social Thought of Black Leaders, 1827–1850." *American Quarterly* 24 (1972): 604–25. Print.

Drexler, Michael J., and Ed White, eds. *Beyond Douglass: New Perspectives on Early African-American Literature.* Lewisburg: Bucknell UP, 2008. Print.

duCille, Ann. *The Coupling Convention: Sex, Text, and Tradition in Black Women's Fiction.* New York: Oxford UP, 1993. Print.

Ernest, John. *Liberation Historiography: African American Writers and the Challenge of History, 1794–1861.* Chapel Hill: U of North Carolina P, 2004. Print.

———. *Resistance and Reformation in Nineteenth-Century African-American Literature.* Jackson: UP of Mississippi, 1995. Print.

Fabi, M. Giulia. *Passing and the Rise of the African American Novel.* Urbana: U of Illinois P, 2001. Print.

Finkelman, Paul. *Slavery and the Founders: Race and Liberty in the Age of Jefferson.* New York: Sharpe, 1996. Print.

Foster, Frances Smith. *Witnessing Slavery: The Development of Antebellum Slave Narratives.* Westport: Greenwood, 1979. Print.

Fredrickson, George M. *The Black Image in the White Mind: The Debate on African-American Character and Destiny, 1817–1914.* New York: Harper, 1972. Print.

French, Scott, and Edward L. Ayers. "The Strange Career of Thomas Jefferson: Race and Slavery in American Memory, 1943–1993." *Jeffersonian Legacies.* Ed. Peter S. Onuf. Charlottesville: U of Virginia P, 1993. 418–56. Print.

Gardner, Eric. *Unexpected Places: Relocating Nineteenth-Century African American Literature.* Jackson: U of Mississippi P, 2009. Print.

Gilmore, Paul. *The Genuine Article: Race, Mass Culture, and American Literary Manhood.* Durham: Duke UP, 2001. Print.

Ginsberg, Elaine K., ed. *Passing and the Fictions of Identity.* Durham: Duke UP, 1996. Print.

Gordon-Reed, Annette. *The Hemingses of Monticello: An American Family.* New York: Norton, 2008. Print.

———. *Thomas Jefferson and Sally Hemings: An American Controversy.* Charlottesville: UP of Virginia, 1997. Print.

Gossett, Thomas F. *Race: The History of an Idea in America.* 1963. New York: Oxford UP, 1997. Print.

———. *Uncle Tom's Cabin and American Culture.* Dallas: Southern Methodist UP, 1985. Print.

Hinks, Peter P. *To Awaken My Afflicted Brethren: David Walker and the Problem of Antebellum Slave Resistance.* University Park: Pennsylvania State UP, 1997. Print.

Horsman, Reginald. *Race and Manifest Destiny: The Origins of American Racial Anglo-Saxonism.* Cambridge: Harvard UP, 1981. Print.

Jackson, Blyden. *A History of Afro-American Literature.* Vol I. Baton Rouge: Louisiana State UP, 1989. Print.

James, Jennifer C. *A Freedom Bought with Blood: African American War Literature from the Civil War to World War II.* Chapel Hill: U of North Carolina P, 2007. Print.

Karcher, Carolyn L. *The First Woman in the Republic: A Cultural Biography of Lydia Maria Child.* Durham: Duke UP, 1994. Print.

Kraditor, Aileen S. *Means and Ends in American Abolitionism: Garrison and His Critics in Strategy and Tactics, 1834–1850.* New York: Vintage, 1970. Print.

Levine, Robert S. *Martin Delany, Frederick Douglass, and the Politics of Representative Identity.* Chapel Hill: U of North Carolina P, 1997. Print.

Lewis, Jan Ellen, and Peter S. Onuf, eds. *Sally Hemings and Thomas Jefferson: History, Memory, and Civic Culture.* Charlottesville: U of Virginia P, 1999. Print.

Lewis, Leslie W. *Telling Narratives: Secrets in African American Literature*. Urbana: U of Illinois P, 2007. Print.

Loggins, Vernon. *The Negro Author: His Development in America to 1900*. 1931. Port Washington, NY: Kennikat, 1959. Print.

Lott, Eric. *Love and Theft: Blackface Minstrelsy and the American Working Class*. New York: Oxford UP, 1993. Print.

Loughran, Trish. *The Republic in Print: Print Culture in the Age of U.S. Nation Building, 1770–1870*. New York: Columbia UP, 2007. Print.

Martin, Charles D. *The White African American Body: A Cultural and Literary Exploration*. New Brunswick: Rutgers UP, 2002. Print.

Miller, Floyd J. *The Search for a Black Nationality: Black Emigration and Colonization, 1787–1863*. Urbana: U of Illinois P, 1975. Print.

Mills, Bruce. *Lydia Maria Child and the Literature of Reform*. Athens: U of Georgia P, 1994. Print.

Morgan, Edmund. *American Slavery, American Freedom: The Ordeal of Colonial Virginia*. New York: Norton, 1975. Print.

Moses, Wilson Jeremiah. *Black Messiahs and Uncle Toms: Social and Literary Manipulations of a Religious Myth*. University Park: Pennsylvania State UP, 1993. Print.

———. *The Golden Age of Black Nationalism, 1850–1925*. New York: Oxford UP, 1978. Print.

Nelson, Dana D. *National Manhood: Capitalist Citizenship and the Imagined Fraternity of White Men*. Durham: Duke UP 1998. Print.

———. *The Word in Black and White: Reading "Race" in American Literature, 1638–1867*. New York: Oxford UP, 1992. Print.

Nyong'o, Tavia. *The Amalgamation Waltz: Race, Performance, and the Ruses of Memory*. Minneapolis: U of Minnesota P, 2009. Print.

Pease, Jane H., and William H. Pease. *They Who Would Be Free: Blacks' Search for Freedom, 1830–1861*. 1974. Urbana: U of Illinois P, 1990. Print.

Quarles, Benjamin. *Black Abolitionists*. New York: Oxford UP, 1969. Print.

———. *The Negro in the American Revolution*. 1961. Chapel Hill: U of North Carolina P, 1996. Print.

Raimon, Eve Allegra. *The "Tragic Mulatta" Revisited: Race and Nationalism in Nineteenth-Century Antislavery Fiction*. New Brunswick: Rutgers UP, 2004. Print.

Reid-Pharr, Robert F. *Conjugal Union: The Body, the House, and the Black American*. New York: Oxford UP, 1999. Print.

Roediger, David. *The Wages of Whiteness: Race and the Making of the American Working Class*. New York: Verso, 1991. Print.

Sánchez-Eppler, Karen. "Bodily Bonds: The Intersecting Rhetorics of
    Feminism and Abolition." *Representations* 24 (1988): 28–59.
    Print.
Smith, Valerie. *Self-Discovery and Authority in Afro-American Nar-
    rative.* Cambridge: Harvard UP, 1987. Print.
Sollors, Werner. "National Identity and Ethnic Diversity: 'Of Ply-
    mouth Rock and Jamestown and Ellis Island'; or, Ethnic Litera-
    ture and Some Redefinitions of America." *History and Memory
    in African-American Culture.* Ed. Geneviève Fabre and Robert
    O'Meally. New York: Oxford UP, 1994. 92–121. Print.
———. *Neither Black Nor White Yet Both: Thematic Explorations
    of Interracial Literature.* New York: Oxford UP, 1997. Print.
Stadler, Gustavas. *Troubling Minds: The Cultural Politics of Genius
    in the United States, 1840–1890.* Minneapolis: U of Minnesota P,
    2006. Print.
Stepto, Robert B. *From Behind the Veil: A Study of Afro-American
    Narrative.* Urbana: U of Illinois P, 1979. Print.
Stuckey, Sterling. *Going Through the Storm: The Influence of African
    American Art in History.* New York: Oxford UP, 1994. Print.
———. *Slave Culture: Nationalist Theory and the Foundations of
    Black America.* New York: Oxford UP, 1987. Print.
Sundquist, Eric J. *To Wake the Nations: Race in the Making of Amer-
    ican Literature.* Cambridge: Harvard UP, 1993. Print.
Takaki, Ronald T., ed. *Violence in the Black Imagination: Essays and
    Documents.* New York: Oxford UP, 1993. Print.
Tamarkin, Elisa. *Anglophilia: Deference, Devotion, and Antebellum
    America.* Chicago: U of Chicago P, 2008. Print.
Walker, Clarence. *Mongrel Nation: The America Begotten by Thomas
    Jefferson and Sally Hemings.* Charlottesville: U of Virginia P,
    2009. Print.
Weinauer, Ellen M. "'A Most Respectable Looking Gentleman':
    Passing, Possession, and Transgression in *Running a Thousand
    Miles for Freedom.*" *Passing and the Fictions of Identity.* Ed.
    Elaine K. Ginsberg. Durham: Duke UP, 1996. 37–56. Print.
Wiegman, Robyn. *American Anatomies: Theorizing Race and Gen-
    der.* Durham: Duke UP, 1995. Print.
Wonham, Henry B., ed. *Criticism and the Color Line: Desegregating
    American Literary Studies.* New Brunswick: Rutgers UP, 1996.
    Print.
Yellin, Jean Fagan. *The Intricate Knot: Black Figures in American
    Literature, 1776–1863.* New York: New York UP, 1972. Print.
Zafar, Rafia. *We Wear the Mask: African Americans Write American
    Literature, 1760–1870.* New York: Columbia UP, 1997. Print.
Zanger, Jules. "The 'Tragic Octoroon' in Pre-Civil War Fiction."
    American Quarterly 18 (1966): 63–70. Print.